AMERICAN ODYSSEY
LETTERS AND JOURNALS
1940–1947

WILHELM REICH

AMERICAN ODYSSEY

LETTERS AND JOURNALS
1940–1947

EDITED BY MARY BOYD HIGGINS

WITH TRANSLATIONS BY
DEREK AND INGE JORDAN AND PHILIP SCHMITZ

FARRAR, STRAUS AND GIROUX
NEW YORK

Farrar, Straus and Giroux
19 Union Square West, New York 10003

Library of Congress Cataloging-in-Publication Data
Reich, Wilhelm, 1897–1957.
  [Selections. English. 1999]
  American odyssey : letters and journals, 1940–1947 / Wilhelm
Reich. — 1st ed.
    p.   cm.
  Direct continuation of the author's Beyond psychology.
  Includes index.
  ISBN 0-374-10436-0 (alk. paper)
  1. Reich, Wilhelm, 1897–1957 — Diaries. 2. Reich, Wilhelm,
1897–1957 — Correspondence. 3. Psychoanalysts — Austria — Diaries.
4. Psychoanalysts — Austria — Correspondence. I. Reich, Wilhelm,
1897–1957. Beyond psychology. II. Title.
RC339.52.R44A3   1999
150.19'5'092 — dc21
[B]   98-48372

Love, work, and knowledge are the wellsprings of our life.
They should also govern it.

WILHELM REICH

Created from Reich's journals and correspondence, this book is a direct continuation of *Beyond Psychology*.* Its narrative begins in January 1940. Reich has been living in the United States for four months, teaching at the New School for Social Research in New York City, reestablishing his laboratory and cancer research, becoming acquainted again with his daughters, Eva and Lore, and involved in a new personal relationship with a German-born woman, Ilse Ollendorff.

Beyond Psychology (New York: Farrar, Straus and Giroux, 1994).

AMERICAN ODYSSEY
LETTERS AND JOURNALS
1940–1947

1940

"I am faced with the task of having to introduce something new; I have to adapt myself to the American mentality; I am struggling with my children, who up until recently were firmly convinced that I was mad; I am financially still not out of the hole; etc. The worst thing is the bitter feeling of being intellectually alone."

6 January 1940

Ilse tells everyone that I go this way ⟶ and the world goes that way ⟵⊃ . How long shall I be able to keep on?

My state of mind is so burdened that I am really beginning to be concerned:

1. The children come as guests—are influenced by that narrow-minded woman.*

2. I always understand people but am not supposed to react with normal anger.

3. The war.

4. Insight into man's incapability of being free.

5. Have lost Elsa† but still love her.

6. To be basically so right, but still see obstacles that are as insurmountable as Mount Everest.

7. Fenichel‡ is off on a tangent—says I'm insane.

When I listen to good music, resignation seems unthinkable. Then I feel I must carry on the struggle, bear it—somehow. I don't care about leading a quiet, orderly, bourgeois life. I have discovered the principle of life and must confirm it completely.

I am much too far advanced—must not lose touch!

Someday, when I die a lonely death, I shall know that I did not live in isolation, that I understood the world around me—or at least honestly tried to do so.

There is a certain logic in the human mind, even in the insane mind.

---

*Reich's first wife, Annie, the mother of his two daughters. Annie and Reich were divorced in 1934 and she had tried to alienate the children from him.
†Elsa Lindenberg, with whom Reich lived from 1932 to 1939. He considered her his second wife.
‡Otto Fenichel, Austrian psychoanalyst. Once a friend, he had become bitterly hostile toward Reich.

There is sense in all this nonsense. The world of mankind is causing its own downfall by selling itself into dependency.

It is my contention that a last remnant of the knowledge of life
dwells within every individual. That is why life will triumph. It runs
its course, the holy, truly holy course of meaningful productivity. And
were a thousand Hitlers to corrupt it—to try, rashly and crudely, to
solve the existential questions through anti-Semitic agitation—life
would still triumph—would *give* of itself!—give without expecting a
return—the *capacity* to give is the key.

I must not make stupid mistakes, or allow myself to be ensnared
by fear—that perfectly simple, understandable, *animal fear of being
alone*, deserted, slandered.

If God exists in the form of nature, then may God help me! Love,
truth, integrity and a sense of life will win out, not people like
Fenichel.

The following people are despicable—ought to be shot: business-
men, diplomats, sycophants, party big shots, tormentors of children,
fake scientists.

January 1940

Science, *real, honest* science, should be the only dominant power
in the world, securing life, guiding the course of human effort, protecting the newcomers to the human race from damage by false education and lack of knowledge!

Let us fight for this holy aim. There is no other meaning in human
struggle!

❖* *13 January 1940*

Briehl and Wolfe† regard me as a poor political refugee, whereas
I had pointed out, in letters and conversation, that I would not come
to New York if I am not needed and wanted.

---

*Indicates that the following was written in English.
†Walter Briehl, M.D., and Theodore P. Wolfe, M.D., American psychiatrists who had
been in treatment with Reich in Europe.

❖ *15 January 1940*

On my advice Wolfe stopped today. He is no fighter, is afraid of standing for sex economy—from his inner feeling and because of the danger from the scientific world. His rational fear was connected with irrational denial of sex. I gave him four weeks to decide further steps.

15 January 1940

This war is getting wilder all the time. But what has that to do with me? I didn't start it, did my best to prevent it. The human race has simply gone mad. Things are going to go completely berserk.

This American democracy is all idle talk. One is not allowed to champion the truth about life after all! And no one gets very far with the "Christian attitude."

The war will change everything—everything! How to hold out? Ilse is a welcome relief! Poor Elsa! She made a very stupid mistake.

I do not have the courage to admit that I have found the solution to the great mystery of life. Am too afraid of paranoia, of rumors, to do that—don't feel vain enough either. Nevertheless, I am completely aware of what I have accomplished and what I have grasped.

The joy of life will prevail, sooner or later, more likely later. For the moment it is destroying itself because it is not allowed to live. People are bursting for want of an outlet. *This abused life will take bitter revenge*—at first it may even destroy itself—but then it will break forth, in splendor, like a Beethoven symphony.

I must get hold of myself again, the person I once was, self-confident, trusting in truth. For a while I almost lost everything, was on the verge of losing my self-esteem.

Someone once said: As long as you trust in yourself and know what you want, things will go well with you. True indeed.

I lost myself in Elsa, in my colleagues, in my pupils. *I must be completely alone again.*

With only a loving woman who knows what I want—that's my one real weakness.

Once I am able to take risks again, there will be progress!

The issue is clear: *be destroyed* or be *proven correct*. There is no other alternative. Under no circumstances can I, at age forty-three, after twenty-two years of the most intensive work, yield to a person like Wolfe or Briehl.

That would be a disgrace!! I'd feel like a coward.

17 January 1940

I am much quieter. Things aren't so bad. Only the war is bad. It is ghastly to know that people are fiery patriots only because they no longer *feel life*, because they have died a living death. Ghastly to know that and be unable to improve the situation.

❖ 24 January 1940

Yesterday I took heart blood from a cancer mouse, put it into bouillon + KCl, added dried serum, and autoclaved half an hour. Immediately afterward there were *only T-bacilli** and gram cells to be seen!

Why this time no bions,† but T-bacilli? (a) Cancer blood more apt to disintegrate into T than into blue bions? (b) Was it the serum that made it?

What significance does this experiment have?

❖ 25 January 1940

Today we autoclaved:

One 10 cc + serum

One 10 cc without serum to find out whether the T-bacilli were result of autoclaving (a) cancer blood or of the (b) serum added to blood. If (a), then very important to find out further.

❖ 31 January 1940

I don't understand New York. People promise much but don't keep the promise. They seem to show tremendous interest in new matters, but they don't do anything about it. As everywhere, not take and give,

---

*T-bacilli (Tod = death) were first found by Reich in a culture of sarcoma tissue. They are lancet-shaped, gram-negative, and exhibit a zigzag motion. They originate from degeneration and putrid disintegration of living and nonliving matter.
†Energy vesicles representing transitional stages between nonliving and living substance. They form in nature by a process of disintegration of inorganic and organic matter, a process that can be repeated experimentally. Charged with orgone energy, they may develop into protozoa and bacteria. See *The Bion Experiments* (New York: Farrar, Straus and Giroux, 1979).

but take where you get, and give where it is demanded, seems to rule. They talk so much about psychosomatic research. I believed in its seriousness. But when it comes, they don't seem to grasp it.

TO FRITZ BRUPBACHER *
5 February 1940

Dear Dr. Brupbacher,

It was very nice to receive another letter from you. Despite the massive misfortune which has affected all our hopes, a nucleus of thought and manner of living which might prove valuable in the future has been preserved here and there. You are certainly right in saying that the disappointment in all kinds of parties and leaders is far too great for any rational action to be conceivable along traditional lines. Nevertheless, I personally remain optimistic. What you refer to as new individualism I believe I have, for my part, simply formulated under the concept of "work democracy."† However, since I do not have the slightest ambition to be regarded as a political leader, it is sufficient for me to use this concept merely to preserve some remnant of clarity within my working sphere and to distance myself from the general madness.

Please send me any new material which you publish. As for my own work, all I have to report is that, more by luck than by understanding, I am making some very fruitful progress in the field of cancer research. I wish I had the chance to have a really good chat with you again about everything.

Warmest greetings to you and your wife.

---

*Swiss sexologist and author of 40 Jahre Ketzer (Forty Years a Heretic).
†Reich's concept of work democracy was "directed exclusively to the fulfillment of the biological life functions of love, work, and knowledge." Intrinsic to it was the capacity of each individual to assume responsibility for his own existence and social function. See The Mass Psychology of Fascism (New York: Farrar, Straus and Giroux, 1970).

6 *February 1940*

1 a.m. Have had another very great success, a big hit! Held my first lecture, attended by ten psychiatrists from Columbia, students of psychoanalysis. I spoke English well—good contact—good questions from the students. They understood me completely. I've made a breakthrough.

The first complete happiness in a long time, enormous success— made contact—no isolation.

Perhaps, perhaps I will not die a lonely death. Careful, Willi, don't get carried away. *However, biogenesis has been established!*

❖ *14 February 1940*

Today Wolfe told me what Dr. Tauber had told him about my first lecture: nine-tenths was not worth listening to. They (Tauber and McGraw) were not interested in protozoa. That had nothing to do with the subject.

❖ *15 February 1940*

I am confused again:

It seems as if the body would mobilize its blood to destroy the ca tissue, succeeding partially. But in doing so, the ca disintegrates into T, *which kill the body in the process of cure.*

The tissue from the untreated ca mouse shows holes similar to those in treated ca. But the piece which showed masses of T-bacilli on the skin, but no ca cells in the living state shows, when stained, *ca cells organizing out of T-bacilli mass.*

Thus, it seems that:

1. Disintegrating tissue.
2. T-bacilli from it.
3. Ca cells organizing out of T-bacilli.
4. Red cells entering to nourish and *to fight* against them.
5. Destruction of both the ca and the red cells into T-bacilli.
6. These destructive T-bacilli masses are killing the body by intoxication.
7. Killed ca T-bacilli attract other ca to die.

The fight of blood versus ca goes on normally without treatment.

Ca death seems intoxication death.

Therefore inoculation with autoclaved—not living—1 gram ca and red cells may kill the tissue and the T-bacilli.

❖ *16 February 1940*

My suspicion that not the tumor but its destruction kills the body (except where the tumor penetrates important organs) seemed supported by one untreated Herrlein mouse today. She had about *12*(!) pea- to bean-size tumors all over the body (subskin, abdomen, lungs) and seemed, when alive, very healthy, only a bit heavy as if pregnant.

How was it possible, so many tumors and not really ill?

The answer is the following:

1. The tumors were white, hard, not destructed.
2. Few T-bacilli in blood.
3. Yet the blood shows ⟟⟡⟟.
4. No tumors filled with bloody holes.

Following possibilities:

1. Tumors don't kill.
2. Destruction of tumors kills.
3. Destruction by red cells.
4. Lack of supply of red cells.
5. T-bacilli degenerates into ca cells ⟶ T-bacilli.

The ca therapy has to take account of the danger of quick destruction and has to fight against the living T-bacilli.

NEAR!

19 February 1940

This world is becoming more dismal all the time. The war will decide so much! Dare not voice the opinion, but logic demands it of me:

1. The "democracies" are lost.
2. The dictatorships are leading the masses, those millions of people who, as they become aware, feel socialism but do not know what it is.
3. Hitler and Stalin are the "best" that revolutionary sentiments in the masses were able to produce. Disgusting, these human hordes, frightful, and they alone will decide.

I am astonished by the feeling that this war has nothing to do with me. I'm not responsible for it—my task is only to protect a fragment of the truth and guard it from the war. I am confronted with the question of whether I should start an endeavor such as I had before. In which direction? This would mean:

1. The chore of publishing.
2. Raising funds for this purpose.
3. And in addition having to face the explosions.

The work on cancer is making good progress. I am surrounded by difficulties, but every few days or weeks it surges ahead. Am presently concerned with finding out whether autoclaved blood taken from cancer mice is capable of destroying ca.

Still suffering about Elsa—poor girl! But she would not be able to stand it here. How dearly I love her! How cruel life is! If I could have her with me for just one evening—but we are forced to be power politicians!

The situation with my children seems unalterable! Eva is sick and Lore is sweet but helpless, overpowered by old women.

3 March 1940

A possible letter to Elsa:

My Elsa: Your short letter was shattering. You wrote that I had ruined your happiness. No, not I, but *it* ruined your happiness. I still feel as though blocked, cannot find my old path or regain my previous temperament. Did I lose it—along with you? I don't know. True, I do my work each day, but in the past I actually lived outside of the daily routine. Now I do nothing! I would like to publish, but don't. I no longer have confidence in my future. It is as if something very important had crumbled in the forty-third year of my life. However, those sudden ideas still come to me in my work. They are so good and productive because they intuitively strike the mark as if they had been shot from a cannon. It happened just recently when I suddenly had the impulse to grow a tumor in a cancer mouse. Lo and behold, it contained blood from which I derived a serum, and this serum, in turn, is effective against cancer. Nevertheless, something has snapped. I began to fear new attacks by my enemies and wanted to hide. Am no longer the lighthearted man I once was! Deep in my heart I am convinced that you would not be able to stand it here, that I would no longer be enough for you and that it would cause unhappiness. I would, of necessity, have to be your home, your shelter, while at the same time I have become extremely needful of shelter myself. I no longer believe in people. My ability to give, simply give, without fear of disappointment, has left me. Will it return? I don't know. You would no longer be happy with me. In addition to this, I am still convinced as to the nature of your secret. Don't be sad, darling! Your unhappiness is not my fault, and I would like you to be happy again. Should fate someday grant us another meeting, we shall be dear friends, like children who love each other.

I am very lonely, fighting a hard fight against myself, against aging or losing the zest of life too soon. I do not believe in America, nor do I believe in contemporary mankind. It is totally corrupt. I can no longer enter into this life and have but *one* task to do as well as I am able—namely, to dispel as much as possible of the darkness which overlays life's basic principles. In this respect I can still accomplish a great deal, but to do this I must shun today's conventions and views. I do not believe that I will hold out very much longer unless I receive material help or help of some other kind. This cannot and must not be expected of my pupils. They have their own troubles. As much as I trust in the future of mankind, I trust very little in my own personal future.

Ilse will not be lost here when I am no longer able to carry on. She has relatives and connections in America whereas you do not. You yourself wrote that you would be destroyed if I were suddenly to leave you. However, *I* would not do that, but *it* would. And therefore it cannot be. Elschen, please keep on loving me just a little. I have so few friends and I would like you to be one of them.

3 March 1940

12 p.m. Draft for my last will and testament:

In the event of my natural or violent death, I request the following stipulations of my will to be carried out:

1. At present I possess very little cash. Should there be more cash available at the time of my death it is to be used to pay for a modest funeral. The remainder is to be divided in equal parts among

my wife, Ilse Ollendorff, and

my two daughters, Eva and Lore.

2. My possessions further include my scientific library, my laboratory, my scientific archives, containing unpublished manuscripts, daily journals, personal diaries, my scientific documentary, films on the results of bion research, photographs and reproductions; the furnishings of my study.

If it is at all possible, the equipment constituting my laboratory is to remain intact as a complete unit. I request my pupils in Scandinavia and North America to see to it that the laboratory as a whole continues to be used for practical and theoretical research. At present I know of no one who could replace me in bion and cancer research work. My findings from cancer research have been compiled in a manuscript entitled "The Cancer Biopathy"*—to the extent they have been validated. In the event that I should not succeed in preparing a drug against cancer, I request my followers in bion research to devote all attention to the T-bacilli, as *they contain the secret.*

My assistant, Gertrud Gaasland, is very well informed on all details. My thanks to her for her devoted help over more than five years.

3. Work with my instruments shall be bound to the condition that handling of the question of sex will not be altered in any way and will be continued along the lines I have set forth.

4. My physical remains are to be cremated. I do not wish to have a religious ceremony, because I believe in God only in the form of a law of nature which created living beings from lifeless matter. I request that during the burial Schubert's "Unfinished Symphony" be played, even if it is only a recording. I should like to recall to my friends' minds the Beethoven "Moonlight Sonata," and how, on warm summer evenings, in quiet conversations far from the politics of the day, it allowed us a glimpse of a better future for mankind. To have made a small contribution toward securing that future was a comfort to me in my most difficult periods. I shall list my most important discoveries and views, in abbreviated form:

The electrical nature of sexuality

The tension-charge formula

Orgone radiation

Bion development from cooked, prepared matter

The Cancer Biopathy (New York: Farrar, Straus and Giroux, 1973).

The self-decomposition of the human organism due to poor breathing, which serves to repress instincts

The T-bacilli as a product of self-decomposition and incipient cancer biopathy

The radiating SAPA bions

Vegetotherapy

The sociology of sex

In concluding, I ask that the following be noted: During my entire lifetime, I never consciously wished to hurt anyone. Whenever this occurred, it was because I was *constrained* to follow my path, to separate from a person I loved but who threatened to rock my convictions.*

(signed) Wilhelm Reich

❖ *6 March 1940*

Today I talked with Dr. Malcolm from Lederle, Inc., in Pearl River—a serum factory—about making serum.

TO DR. MALCOLM
❖ *8 March 1940*

Dear Dr. Malcolm,

Referring to our discussion of 6 March, I met some difficulties to start new experiments on T-bacilli serum at your laboratories at once.

---

*At this time it is also appropriate to consider a personal accusation raised by friends who are turning antagonistic. Professional rifts are usually blamed on difficulties in getting along with me. Supposedly, working with me is strenuous. I must reject this reproach. No one has yet proven that he is better equipped than I to captain such a scientifically laden ship on an everlasting voyage. Every rupture, whether of a personal or professional nature, has invariably revealed that the individual involved was not capable of walking the straight road which the cause required and which I felt impelled to follow for better or worse. In every instance to date, an attempt has been made to disguise this incapacity by claiming that I was difficult or impossible to deal with. It is correct that I was unyielding when people told me that the exclusion of sex sociology or the orgasm theory from my teachings would net me more friends and fewer enemies; unyielding when they said that "sex economy" is a concept which "provokes people unnecessarily." Yes indeed, I was unyielding in my refusal to follow the path of no responsibility; in that respect I was certainly "difficult." [W.R.]

To find out whether the colloid mentioned in our discussion would transfer its influence on cancer tissue to the blood, I would have to watch the process closely, I suppose every day, and that would be impossible at this distance. So I had to decide to try it out first on a small scale in my own laboratory. But I hope very much that our agreement will still be valid on a later date, when those complicated first steps in transferring the influence upon the blood will be made.

8 March 1940

The body undoubtedly exerts "action at a distance," with orgone effect—i.e., specific excitation. For example, if the palms of the hands are brought together *slowly* from a distance of about 20 cm, an "air cushion sensation"—i.e., slight resistance—is felt at a distance of 1–10 cm, but at the same time a *magnetic* attraction is also present and this is particularly noticeable when the palms of the hands are moved apart. (They should not come into contact with each other!)

The palms of my hands exhibit this reaction when they are still about 15 cm apart. The magnetic effect is obviously linked with the iron in the hemoglobin. The orgone is transported in the body by the red blood corpuscles to the organs and cells by which it is taken up.

The orgone capacity of the body must be greater during a person's youth than in old age. Death occurs when the cells lose their orgone. Cancer is the result of either excess orgone (proliferation) or a loss of orgone (T-bacilli). (Red blood corpuscles lose their radiation.)

❖ 9 March 1940

Anti-ca serum kills T-bacilli, protozoa, hence ca cells as well. Reduces size of tumors in mice. At last!

Wonder when I'll heal the first ca patient? I am happy.

Just wrote a letter to Elsa. Either she responds or it is simply over. I will not give in. How difficult it is to face the truth.

❖ 15 March 1940

I don't seem to like the idea, but I dare not fight against it any longer:

The T-bacilli are nothing else than degenerative products of quite simple rot bacteria like this:

That fits with the idea that cancer is a result of rotting tissue, and the cancer tissue degenerates quickly into rot bacteria, further T-bacilli, finally destroying the body. The cancer therapy would have simply to find a serum against rot bacteria and their product— T-bacilli.

Simple—stupid—but so it seems to be.

It is just as in rotting moss:

a. Swelling

b. Protozoa and bacteria

c. Complete degeneration of everything into bacteria.

❖ *16 March 1940*

The orgone rays must be a magnetic power, and one opposite to usual magnetism:

a. A magnet does not attract the leaf of the electroscope; the charged rubber does.

b. If the Nordlicht is magnetic ray from the universe, attracted by the N pole, then those rays must be opposite to N magnetism, and yet no S magnetism, but something quite different.

c. The orgone diminishes the magnet power of the N pole.

18 March 1940

I have now found a method for measuring orgone energy in amps or volts. The new problem is to make it usable—i.e., either to convert it into electricity or to find orgone-specific means for utilizing it.

21 March 1940

3 *a.m.* Can't sleep. It occurred to me that, before moving to New York, I was just about to plunge into a deep abyss. It was a time when I thought I could (or should) obliterate the past and make a new,

proper start. The debacle in Oslo hit me harder than I realized, especially in my academic vanity. I wanted fast, large-scale recognition from bourgeois academicians instead of simply bowling them over, conquering them along with their bosses. I was on the verge of becoming unfaithful to the cause which had guided me so faithfully. In other words, I was being a bastard. I was close to becoming an unsocialistic reactionary. The objective reason for this was my isolation in Norway, to which I yielded by "keeping quiet." Keeping quiet doesn't pay. The canaille in man scents the danger of truth no matter where it is hidden. It's no use. Fight, come what may—that is the only right thing to do.

I tried to preserve my bit of comfortable life and was about to forfeit my backbone in the process. In my depths I felt guilt, thought it was sinful to fight for sexual order.

❖ *23 March 1940*

All tumor mice treated. One or two with anti-ca Lorin* serum from rabbits had the tumors diminished. T-bacilli mice were saved. Well! Go on!

24 March 1940

A lonely birthday. Ilse is touching, but I hunger for Elsa. It is tremendously difficult to know that this entire civilization, including myself, will fall, and why, and not be able to improve matters quickly despite my knowledge of how things could be. The least I can do is try to put into words the attitudes and errors of which one must be aware if one wishes matters to be different someday.

❖ *26 March 1940*

Of two French Presbyterian mice, the one that was untreated died, the other, which was treated, lives. And now, after finding out which combination of serum will work best (serum + KCl; serum + blood + KCl; blood + KCl), the next step: *influence human blood—or blood which would not harm human beings—with Lorin, and inject into human being.*

---

*A type of bion named for Reich's daughter Lore.

29 *March 1940*

Yesterday a letter came from Elsa calling for help. She is on the verge of a breakdown. The situation is serious. I cabled: Ready to help, wire how. But it's perfectly obvious what kind of help she wants.

Inwardly I am furious about my cowardice. Here I sit, acting modest—I am not modest—playing the role of a "pure scientist"—I am not a "pure scientist"—inventing so many ways of proving that "people must find their own way!" I am simply evading the responsibility and unpleasantness of coming out into the open.

6 *April 1940*

Elschen dearest! I need to talk with you—just have a chat across the five thousand miles between America and Europe, after all the letters back and forth. I ask myself repeatedly why I am capable of all this, and it brings my spirits down. The world has become so mean and stupid, it's disgusting. That is why I often flee to the memories of those wonderful hours we spent in the Vienna woods, in the forests of Denmark, and on the beaches of Sweden. I am enclosing a short letter which I wrote in a small restaurant when I went into the city last night and drove around until 3 a.m. in sheer desperation. Viewed superficially, things have never been better for me, and yet I take no pleasure in all this. As long as rich, productive, crucial work lies neglected, as long as diplomats and clergymen hold sway, as long as lies are triumphant, I cannot find happiness.

TO ELSA LINDENBERG
5 *April 1940*

Darling! Elschen!

You write that I should decide between you and Ilse! I do not have to "decide" anything, with regard to either you or Ilse. In times of deepest distress, I have always been left to sort out my problems *by myself* and so I do not feel obligated to anybody at all. I am genuinely well disposed toward whatever is actually there—whether it is my work, a friend, or a woman! My first wife wanted to make me "socially acceptable." Just take a look at her, how she sits there with a man who suits her taste. My second wife found life so exciting "outside the home"—now she has it. My third wife will probably want to present me to her family as a famous husband. Nobody has yet grasped the fact that I am prevented from playing any of the usual roles in life. I am not God, nor am I a father figure, nor am I an important and respected scholar of whom one need not be ashamed. I try, as long as possible, to stay the person that I am and I yearn for a companion who will share my dangers and my joys with me. I do not have any "disciples" or "collaborators," I am not a political leader, nor do I point the way to the future. I have merely—so far—managed to remain intellectually honest. I wish that many other people could be that too. I am neither happy nor unhappy. I can be both; happy, for example, when, as yesterday, I made biological energy flash in a small box;* unhappy, when my dearest Elsa does not understand me. If I do not decide "for you" now, this does not mean that I have decided "for Ilse." I am merely waiting for the next quarrel to erupt and I watch with some amusement as my colleagues here develop the same attributes with which I was familiar over there [in Europe]: They want to learn but they don't want to take any risks; secretly they are ashamed of me; they want me here, but then they want me to go away again. And all I can do is carry on—and think often of my Somali girl.

Your
Willi

6 April 1940

3 a.m. This is the way things stand:

1. Ilse wants to show off with me—is a little girl who thinks she's found her daddy—insists on being called "Mrs. Reich."

2. Wolfe is afraid of embarrassing himself with a "sexual swine."

---

*Reich refers to an orgone energy accumulator, the mechanism by which atmospheric orgone energy can be concentrated. It consists of a casing or outer layer of organic or non-metallic material, which absorbs the energy and releases it slowly, and an inner layer of metallic material, which also attracts the energy but reflects it immediately. This arrangement gives a direction to the orgone energy with a potential directed more strongly to the inside.

3. Not a single coworker is doing anything correctly.

4. The publishing has not been paid since September.

5. The "free human beings" do not trust their own freedom and mistrust anyone who takes it seriously.

6. The entire academic world views sexuality as something dirty.

I don't know how, what, wherefore, or where to.

The situation is utterly hopeless!

9 April 1940

This morning Norway and Denmark were occupied by the Nazis. This means

1. Philipson, Leunbach, Elsa, Sigurd, Oeverland,* and others will die. Possibly this has already happened.

2. I can do nothing to help them.

3. The entire professional organization is lost.

4. Elsa is definitely lost.

5. A complete vacuum. What now?

    a. Academic research appears to be senseless.

    b. Take up political-psychological work again as I did in Scandinavia?

11 April 1940

Today I spent a happy day. Eva invited three of her sixteen-year-old girlfriends to go for a drive in the car. Lore came along. I felt very young in their company, they were completely at ease with me. This youth is good. And I am proud that I have not grown old. Lore flirted with every boy that went by. One of the girls immediately had contact with me. She was very smart. I have regained my courage. Forward!

Basic problem: How to get orgone-sun energy into the body. The SAPA† or safe means for doing this. This gives rise to the problem that the T-bacilli are nothing more than matter which has lost its sun energy. How can orgone energy be introduced into the body without

*Scandinavian students and friends of Reich.

†SAnd PAcket bions derived from cultures of ocean sand.

the material substrate, the T-bacilli, also getting in or forming in the body. One possibility is offered by the fact that the Lorin bions dissolve in undiluted serum—i.e., they simply give off their orgone energy to the serum protein and break down into T-bacilli. Large amounts of Lorin would have to be introduced into undiluted serum until the orgone is resorbed. Afterward the serum would be filtered. Or the serum could be exposed to the effect of orgone energy, either directly from the sun or in the orgone box.

Today I started to inject mice intravenously.

25 April 1940

An idea!

Earth humus is the most natural substance in nature, crystal well heated to incandescence, completely broken down into bions. I shall mix human blood with autoclaved earth. The blood will take up large amounts of orgone and kill ca.

Totally logical.

I am an idiot not to have thought of this before.

T O   A .   S .   N E I L L *

❖ 28 April 1940

My dear Neill:

Your letter arrived yesterday together with the offer of Mr. Read. I shall send a copy of the Jugendbuch,† but I doubt whether it would be wise to have it published first in England. Dr. Theodore Wolfe from the Columbia, whom you remember, is now translating another book of mine, which has not been published yet.‡ It deals with the fundamental problems of sex economy, presenting them according to their development within the International Psychoanalytic Association, beginning 1919, up to date. It is much more simply written than my other books, and I think it would best suit the purpose of intro-

---

*Founder of the Summerhill School in Leiston, England.
†*Der sexuelle kampf der Jugend.* Revised and retitled by Reich as *The Sexual Rights of Youth.* Included in *Children of the Future* (New York: Farrar, Straus and Giroux, 1983).
‡Published in 1942 as *The Function of the Orgasm.*

ducing my work into English countries. It contains in the first part the controversy with Freud, and in the second the autonomous development of my clinical work. If you get clear whether Kegan would be interested in this book first, I shall send you a copy as soon as it is available. After this the Jugendbuch will be accepted much easier.

I was glad to hear from you. We had terrible days when Norway was invaded, and are still worried in spite of a telegram from Raknes* saying that "friends here [Norway] all well." I try hard to find out how I could manage to get Elsa and some others out and over here. I fear the worst. It is dreadful.

Somehow this war will be over as the first was, and life and work will continue. Question is: Who will survive?

11 May 1940

Orgone radiation is not an electrical but a magnetic property.

1. It can be collected.
2. It passes through a wire.
3. It causes fluorescent material to fluoresce.
4. It magnetizes iron.
5. It contains three types of radiation.
6. It passes through anything which is organic in origin.
7. It is without doubt stronger than electrical energy.
8. It fills outer space.

I must finally abandon the idea that it has anything to do with electrical energy and I must concentrate on the peculiarities of magnetism.

12 May 1940

I have just noticed:

a. In the dark, after it has been in the accumulator, a shimmering blue light is visible between the N and S poles of the magnet.

b. Luminous substance kept in the dark inside tubes does not luminesce. When it is stroked with magnets it begins to glow, very weakly.

*Ola Raknes, Norwegian psychoanalyst and student of Reich.

Magnetism is the expression of an energy which emanates from metal and is taken up by insulators.

21 May 1940

Spent the evening in New York with my pupils. Last evening of classes—applause. Everything can be done, but when will other people start fighting the way I do? When will they begin to take risks instead of only talking?

I am running around with just as much loneliness and longing inside me as ever! A woman—Ilse is a dear, but she's weak. She helps me, but I want excitement. The blond—

TO DR. ALBERT LEPRINCE *
24 May 1940

Dear colleague,

I confirm receipt, with many thanks, of your two books on the electromagnetism of the human body. I found them extremely interesting, even if I could not follow your argument in every detail.

You are probably aware that for some time I have been successfully experimenting on the phenomena of electricity in the human body, which is fundamentally different from inorganic electricity. Not long ago, using a specially constructed apparatus, I was able to make this energy visible with the aid of certain luminous substances. This energy, without doubt, determines the functioning of the human body. At present I am engaged in summarizing my observations and the theoretical consequences.

*Professor, Institut International de Hautes Etudes de Nice.

26 May 1940

ASSUMPTIONS ABOUT BIOLOGICAL ENERGY,
BASED ON OBSERVATIONS TO DATE

Life comes from solar energy which radiates through space. It is necessary to assume that millions of other planetary systems have life on them, just like our Earth.

Life is orgone-charged matter. If orgone energy escapes from a physical system, that system is "dead." This organic body cannot be restored after death because life is bound to a functional system unit which breaks down after the loss of orgone energy and no longer constitutes a functioning unit.

It is not possible to talk of rebirth after death because the orgone energy escaping from the body disperses so rapidly and diffusely in space that it can no longer be conceived of as a unit. And a living organism represents a concentrated quantum of energy which communicates with the energy of space through membranes (surface of the skin).

The organic system of the body consists predominantly of orgone energy bound to water. Matter plays only a small role, chiefly in forming the boundaries of orgone-charged vesicles. Expansion and contraction, which characterize life, are physical functions which take place in the orgone body, thus supplying the needs of respiration and metabolism.

Orgone energy is particularly strong and concentrated in the gametes. The fertilization of the egg essentially involves the supply of energy via the sperm cells.

Growth is in all probability an expansion of the orgone system by excess orgone, which lasts until the limit is reached—i.e., the system reaches equilibrium with the environment, probably as a function of the tension of the membranes and the available matter.

The sex act is based on the equalization of excess orgone energy, concentrated in the genitals, by friction between the genital insulators. In the sex act, both bodies form a single orgonotic system. In those cases where this does not happen (no fusion), orgastic impotence and a lack of gratification are the result.

Organisms depend orgonotically on the cosmic energy.

❖ *19 June 1940*

Today a three-hour afternoon demonstration of treated and untreated cancer mice, cancer film, and slides. Dr. Hegersen from
Columbia's Pathology Department was here. A complete idiot!

1. I showed him the bloody holes in treated mice. "That I know
from normal cancer." I: I support a process in mice which is taking
place automatically, blood destroying ca tissue but being destroyed
itself—it has to be helped.

2. Cancer diagnosed in T-mice testes, heated to incandescence.
"But that is spontaneous cancer." I explain how I found the inflammation at the site of injection of the tissue. He repeats "spontaneous
cancer."

3. The film does not mean anything to him. The moving cancer
cells are "from contamination," their similarity to the ca cells in vag-
inal secretion does not mean anything. The spindle forms are epi-
thelial cells on the *edges*. I explain that the living cells he saw were
from the same tissue he diagnosed as cancerous when stained.

4. The respiration theory does not mean anything.

5. He had never seen above 600×.

Nothing means anything to him. A complete idiot!

T O   H E R B E R T   J .   H A M I L T O N *
❖ *19 June 1940*

Dear Sir:

I received your letter of 18 June, and may point out that I never
applied for admission to the medical test, but for endorsement of my
Viennese medical doctor degree in the State of New York, according
to my letter of 14 March 1940, to the Commissioner of Education.
Mr. Conroe of the Division of Higher Education informed me in his
letter of May 22 that it will be necessary for me to pass the examination in English for foreigners. I, therefore, shall apply for this examination to Mr. Field. I have no intention of taking the medical
test.

*Chief, New York State Bureau of Professional Examinations.

24 June 1940

France has fallen, because of internal machinations. This world is going to become a very different place. I do not understand why my optimism has not failed me despite all the fascist victories. I cannot even lay claim to scientific security because the biology of the organism itself demonstrates that mankind has only begun to grasp its life energy. And as long as this energy is not functional in a practical sense, not a single sociological problem will be solved. The fact that men are killing one another is related to mighty rhythms of the universe. Hitler's proclamations are ludicrous in the light of such issues. After all, what does it mean to the world that he had a railroad car brought from Compiègne to Berlin? Ridiculous and stupid! I have deep confidence in man's life energy and in his feeling for life itself.

Yesterday I explained to Eva the struggle of life forces in our contemporary world:

The bourgeoisie thrives on moral ideas, demands, and concepts which it has formed as protection against secondary drives.* In Hitlerism, the secondary drives erupt and overrun the forces of morality. Freud discovered the secondary drives, but there exists a third kingdom of life which lies behind them, and this kingdom will conquer everything—the morality as well as the Hitlerism.

❖ *27 June 1940*

I am very tired!! It's too much struggle and fighting. I am right, but am incapable of making something out of myself.

---

*The continual frustration of primary natural needs leads to chronic contraction of the biosystem (muscular armor, sympatheticotonia, etc.). The conflict between inhibited primary drives and the armor gives rise to secondary, antisocial drives i.e., in the process of breaking through the armor, primary biological impulses are transformed into destructive sadistic impulses. [W.R., 1945]

T O   L O R E   R E I C H
❖ *30 June 1940*

Mein liebes Lorchen!
My dear Lore!

I hope that you were not too sad not to have accepted our gifts for
your birthday. We were not offended at all, because we fully understood your troubles. I wish only to let you know that you are *not*
alone, that we love you, that you can come at any time, to find a
home with us. You only feel alone and spoken badly of because you
behave in a way which is not yours but derives from the poison which
your mother has put into you. She made you believe that I am crazy,
a worthless human being. She is merely afraid to lose you. Please, be
sure that I am there as your father, and nobody else. As your father
I do not wish that Mr. Rubinstein* should be the one who would
have any right to bring you up. Your mother has behaved so dishon-
estly and miserably, has told you so many lies about your father and
has omitted to let you have so many important things, that I have to
take back all the rights of education. I cannot and do not wish to
force you to leave that bad, unpleasant, poisonous home. But I know
you will realize sooner or later that you are unhappy there. I advise
you to follow your own feelings, as you told me so often about. You
know we shall always be glad to have you here and to secure everything you may need. No child has to sacrifice itself and its future to
its mother. I am going to fight against your mother until I am sure
that you are safe.

2 July 1940
11.30 p.m. Today there is a great deal of confusion. In order to
check the orgonoscope† and the question whether solar energy is
responsible, I ventilated the cellar for two days, using fans; I took

---

*Thomas Rubinstein, Annie's second husband.
†A simple optical device designed by Reich to study orgone radiation. The fact that it
can magnify the wave-like flickering in the atmosphere is a specific refutation of the idea
that this phenomena is merely a subjective ocular impression or due to diffusion of light.

apart the accumulator boxes, placed the metal plates in water (water takes away the charge), opened up the Faraday cage.

I wanted to know whether the orgone sparks can still be seen. *They could be seen!*

After a half hour the same phenomena could be seen in the room. Stripes, blue-gray, violet—

Where do the rays come from?

SAPA, no doubt about it. They could be seen on the ceiling. From the sun, no doubt about it. Rubber exhibits an electroscopic effect. But they are also present when neither SAPA nor the sun are present. *They must come from the earth or quite simply they are everywhere* and are just a little less concentrated here and there.

Both laboratories (Oslo and New York) were situated in cellars = ground level.

Courage! I may have discovered and made visible the universal radiation of all living matter. *I am frightened at the consequences.*

8 July 1940

Assistant Secretary of State Berle inquired of Dr. Dunbar* as to whether I was a "fifth columnist." They also received another anonymous telephone call from someone who wanted to know whether I was "practicing medicine." Somewhere, a denunciation must have occurred. In the midst of this war hysteria much could happen to ruin even the best-laid plans.

My intimate contact with people on a daily basis makes my task very difficult. I always did my best, most lucid work when I was alone. Then I can think in terms of centuries. When you're together with other people you can't see any farther than your own nose. I lack courage and optimism. What does it matter? So many people are perishing today. But to perish without reason is foolish and I do not want to be a fool!

I am certain that my theory will be borne out. While I am not modest enough to forget myself and my friends entirely, I am too skeptical toward myself to revel in scientific triumph. The gap between today and tomorrow is too great. One lives in the former, not in the latter. It is today that man's abysmal maliciousness demon-

---

*H. Flanders Dunbar, American psychosomaticist and first wife of T. P. Wolfe.

strates itself. Tomorrow the practices of today will appear as mere banalities—and the day after a new maliciousness will be directed against these same banalities.

Business reverses the vital stream connecting yesterday with tomorrow. One of the elements involved here is the recognition of the fact that mankind is sick in the ordinary sense of the word "sick." Putting this into words means risking the suspicion that you consider yourself the only healthy person. I am willing to risk that suspicion. The health which I sense and live for and am trying to preserve dwells in all men. The fact that they fear it, and hide it, is the very cornerstone of Hitlerism.

❖ *10 July 1940*

I often think it would be best to give up psychotherapy. It is impossible within a world where everything produces neurosis and refuses to remove its fundaments.

11 July 1940

There is surely nothing more difficult than working in a vacuum and knowing for sure that the world in which you live and strive cannot accept you. All you see is gaping hopelessness!

As long as I can still hear the creativeness of a Beethoven or a Mozart on the radio, I will not despair, because this implies that there are still people for whom the music is being played.

12 July 1940

Have I discovered the Basic Law of nature? Or am I just a dreamer? No, I cannot deny the phenomena. They exist.

TO EVA REICH
2 August 1940

My dear Evchen,

Ilse and I are living here in almost complete isolation in a cabin in the forest on Lake Mooselookmeguntic(!).* The lake is right in front of the door. It is cool and it is such a pleasure to lie in the sun. For days on end we don't see a soul. The beach is rocky and you can jump right into deep water. The whole area is secluded forest, with just a few camps. We really could not have found a better spot. Rabbits, deer, squirrels, etc., scamper around all over the place. There are supposed to be bears in the area. The war, the emotional plague of mankind,† and all the usual filth are so far away that it is almost impossible to believe that in two weeks' time we will be back in it again. The area is very reminiscent of Norway with its gentle mountain ridges, the coniferous forests, the lakes. There are still Indian trails. Strange to think that Indians lived here not that long ago.

And you, Evchen? Have you at least been able to have a proper holiday, away from all the duties and "sociability"?

4–8 August 1940
Observed the starry sky and clouds. Moon in first quarter.

1. The blue of the atmosphere in front of mountains shimmering in the distance on sunny days ("fine weather").

Assumption: Orgone, which absorbs and emits the blue color from light, sits uniformly distributed at the lower level. If the mountains appear close up and clearly visible, "it's going to rain"—i.e., the orgone is mixed in the higher regions of the atmosphere and forms the clouds through magnetization and charging of the water vapor.

2. Observations of dark clouds at night: By staring at a point on the edge of a dark cloud, one sees grayish-blue flickering light phenomena. When looked at through a slit, the phenomenon is more

---

*A large lake in the Rangeley Lakes region of Maine.
†Human malevolence, which results from genital frustration, is so widespread in social relationships and institutions that Reich likened it to a plague, an emotional plague.

obvious. Clouds are strongly orgone-charged accumulations of moisture. Lightning is the electrical discharge of orgone energy. The light
phenomena in the clouds are the same as those occurring on the
fluorescent screen of the orgonoscope.

3. In the clear night sky, streaks and dots of blue light can be
(faintly) seen between the stars, especially in the area of the Milky
Way.

4. Grass and rock luminate more brightly (through a slit) than
without a slit. The slit space shimmers clearly and strongly.

5. Assumptions: Orgone is an energy that fills outer space, and it
is more strongly concentrated in the vicinity of bodies. It is not the
same as light, but rather it is the medium for transmitting light waves.
(Difference in rates.)

6. Assumptions: Orgone could be the energy of which solar matter
is composed. Magnetism and electricity are just functions of this
energy (electricity = discharge at high concentration; magnetism =
reaction in metals).

20 August 1940

Back from Maine, Lake Mooselookmeguntic, after three weeks,
very tan and young.

Telegram from Elsa in Sweden. She is constantly on my mind.
Finished dictating orgone book.

Studied astronomy.

23 August 1940

Crazy idea!

Is it conceivable, possible, that orgone light is emitted from the
viewer's eye onto the object? That this is the essential act of seeing:
seeing = irradiating the object, and the object itself emits light.

There is no doubt about the observation. A dark stone observed
through the tube produces a bright spot.

30 August 1940

Objection: Brighter is an illusion. Light in the tube is reflected.
That makes the opening appear lighter. (?)

In the micro-spectroscope, dark lines appear along the spectrum when microscopic dots are in the light. Today a protozoan, as a "dot," exhibited a shift of violet and blue into gray. (?)

21 September 1940

Today, I succeeded in producing a rough model of a sky orgonoscope.

6-foot-long metal tube.

Two lenses at the front, one enlarging, the second placed behind the magnifying lens, no flicker disc, front aperture about ½ cm.

Strong flickering and flashing!

Today there was a downpour following three days of humid heat, 90 percent relative humidity, temperature 70°.

After the rain, flashing and flickering could be seen over thousands of miles in the dark starry sky—even with the naked eye.

On the beeches, the orgone energy flickered more strongly than yesterday.

Assumption: Clouds are formed through a composition of orgone and water vapor ⟶ less free orgone. After rain, moisture is gone. There is pure orgone energy free in the atmosphere.

27 September 1940

6 p.m.

1. Today I was able to control the direction of the orgone rays!!

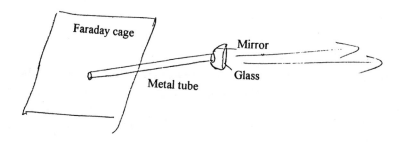

On the film screen, about 5 m away, the shift in the orgone rays could be clearly seen. Placing a hand in the path of the rays changes the weight of the hand?

2. I hit upon the idea of using green, subdued light. The flickering can be seen better in weak light. (Cf. flickering of the atmosphere.)

3. In addition, today I was finally able to observe orgone under the microscope. In the fluoroscope, I replaced the X-ray tube with a cellulose disc. The rays which flickered at low magnification proved to be individual, thin, bright rays at a magnification of 70×. They penetrate matte glass, but are effectively screened out by a violet filter.

27 September 1940

Midnight Outside, there is a bright, blue, clear, starry sky. The stars are glittering. In the blue between the glittering stars, bluish, moving cloudiness and occasionally flashing streaks can be clearly seen.

As far as I am concerned, no matter how much I resist the consequence of such thoughts, there is no doubt that men and animals live at the bottom of an ocean of orgone energy. The air which we breathe is in reality orgone energy. The oxygen which the plants and trees are said to give off is orgone energy which during the day was taken up from the sun. Therefore, it is healthier to live in the countryside than in the city.

Living organisms are matter that enclose orgone, which is moving, and in the movement creates sensations and feelings.

I must build an apparatus which merely demonstrates to me the orgone in the atmosphere. I am amazed that so far nobody has seen the lumination in the calm, cloudless atmosphere.

A storm is the discharge of orgone. Cloud formation is the concentration of orgone. The reaction of living organisms to storms is understandable. The orgone mechanism reacts to changes in the concentration of orgone in the atmosphere.

Seeing involves contact of eye orgone with object orgone. There is still much that is unexplained.

7 October 1940

a. Dark green light causes the blue-gray radiation in the orgone accumulator to show up distinctly.

b. The cancer and T-mice clearly show a positive reaction to orgone radiation.

7 *October 1940*

1 p.m. An air balloon (air-filled) which had been balanced on a scale in the other room shows lift after one hour when placed above accumulator box 1 in the orgone room.

It is growing lighter in weight! Radiation pressure? Absorption of orgone involving change in weight? Completely crazy idea! If psychic sensation, as demonstrated, is functionally identical with orgone energy processes, then a great deal of importance can be attached to the expression "to feel light and buoyant" or "to feel heavy and weighed down."

Does orgone charge actually make something lighter—i.e., does it overcome gravity (weight)? I am afraid to think it, but I must consider all eventualities. If it is not the direct radiation pressure, then it must be an energy which works against gravity.

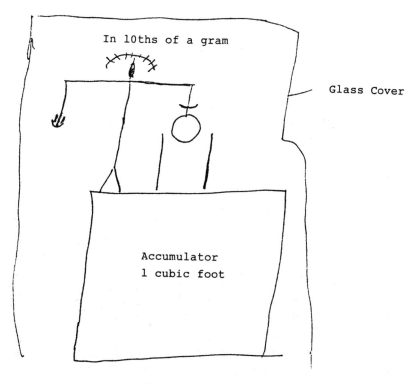

Balloon Measuring Scale

In this regard, the lightness of floating, orgone-charged people, expanding space—

Can it be thermal lift? Simple proof of thermal emanation? There is still the puzzle why heated air becomes lighter! When I took the scales with the balloon into the adjoining ventilated room, the balloon suddenly became about three times lighter.

4 p.m. Balanced the scales with 0.85 g. The air in the balloon weighs 0.3 g and the balloon hasn't shrunk, so loss of air would not account for the difference in weight.

8 October 1940

10:20 a.m. Experiment repeated.

a. Empty balloon with string and wire weighs 4.2 g.

b. Inflated balloon weighs 4.5 g. Balloon therefore contains 0.3 g of air.

c. *11:30 a.m.* (1 hr. 10 min. elapsed.) Again, *balloon has risen* over the center of orgone accumulator 1.

Balanced scales as follows:

+0.05 on the balloon side

+0.1

−0.05

0.1 g Weight loss equals 0.1 g.

d. In the ventilated room, a further weight loss of approximately 0.01 g occurred.

So radiation pressure doesn't explain it.

e. Over orgone accumulator 1 again. Uncorrected with 4.5 g on the weight side and 0.1 g on the balloon side.

October 1940

There must be some force which counteracts gravity, which "lifts" the spirit, makes our hearts "light," lends us "wings," sends us into "seventh heaven," makes us fly in our dreams and "brightens" our waking hours. That which counteracts this force and chains us to the ground is a "heavy heart," "depression" (i.e., being "downcast"), the "leaden fatigue"—in short, that which is conservative, preservative—calcium! calcification!—ossification.

❖ *11 October 1940*

a. Two mice from March and April treated with orgone serum lost their tumors. On one mouse the tumor on throat, previously cherry, and disappeared, came back—bean. Daily one hour in orgone rays made it disappear again.

b. Children of cancer mice got tumors. Orgone rays diminished them.

c. Yesterday two healthy mice injected with 0.2 cc T-bacillus in 0.3 cc NaCl. A half hour later both were very ill. One came into the orgone screen. She is healthy today. The other, untreated, is dying.

Now—orgone screens for human beings.

14 October 1940

Great day!

This logic is uncanny. Four years ago, I had the idea of distinguishing between black and blue bions when I saw that the blue immobilize the black.

Now I know that the blue bions were orgonotic bions, that it was the orgone that killed the black T-bacilli.

Today, I injected four mice with strong doses of T-bacilli (0.3–0.5 cc). Two were placed immediately in orgone accumulator 2. The other two mice fell ill 5 to 10 minutes after the injection and are now dying at around midnight. The two other blue-red mice are *healthy*.

I don't give a damn about all the stuffed shirts.

Such successes achieved by the experiments make up for all the meanness inflicted by my poor contemporaries. I am very happy.

28 October 1940

There is much to be solved, even more to be dissolved: old, useless, oppressive things! Socialists, psychologists—it's going under—let it go. Ever since I saw life energy sparkling in the sky, I no longer feel the need to be recognized, only the urge to bring matters to a decent conclusion. So much no longer matters, so much has expanded, expanded to such proportions that it frightens me. If I am spared the necessity of becoming indecent, I shall be grateful, grateful to that strange God who claims to have created the world in seven days, a God who does not perceive the void but knows only movement.

October 1940

If we fail in the present, we must draw on the past and look to the future.

T O   A .   S .   N E I L L
❖ 7 November 1940

My dear Neill:

It is good that you seem pretty safe in the place where you are, and are still able to carry on the work. You can imagine how closely we watch the events over there. The reelection of Roosevelt seems to me of tremendous importance. I learn more and more how this so-called bourgeois society has done more in the course of seven years under capitalistic rules in the field of social security than any communist in Russia would dream of getting. This is only to indicate that, being quite firm in all my scientific convictions, I feel myself completely confused and inclined to revise most of the things I ever learned in Europe about what socialism should be. I can only hope that the roots of my special work will prevent me from becoming reactionary. If you hear from socialists and communists coming over here and claiming that Roosevelt is a dictator or a fascist, then your stomach simply turns around. I started to hate them. They seem to me a complete nuisance in their lack of any ability to think a thought to the end or to do any kind of work. But it may be that a part of this feeling is mere disappointment.

You are quite right that the personal matters come more and more into the background in order to make place for the social matters. But that should not mean that you forget the personal matters, but that you look upon them as expressions of a definite social situation.

Elsa is still in Norway and striving hard to come over here— in other words, to accomplish a matter which she could have had easily a year and a half ago. But this comes from the misinterpreted Selbstständigkeit.

TO ELSA LINDENBERG
8 November 1940

Dear Elsa,

Your letter of 18 September arrived yesterday. I could say an awful lot in reply, but I will keep my letter short.

1. Everything is being done at this end to guarantee that you can come. Apart from all the personal aspects, the strongest reason is the rational one—namely, that you will be collaborating with me in my work. All the necessary papers are in order and will be sent to the consulate at the beginning of next week. You must merely follow the instructions. I cannot predict how you will fare here personally and financially. One has to struggle hard. But the working group is in the process of forming and will help you. I already wrote and told you that.

2. You asked where I stand with regard to you and the future. I do not know. I have suffered very much from everything that has happened and I am undergoing a gigantic metamorphosis, the outcome of which I cannot predict. There is much in my life which I need to revise, in particular my relationships to human beings. In that area, I made many mistakes, although with the best of intentions. Since I haven't seen you for so long I don't know how you are, and you don't know how I am. But it would be senseless to make your coming here dependent on that. I can't commit myself to anything. The fact that the old problem—you know what I mean—still has not been cleared up is a contributing factor. In the last one and a half years I have, if anything, become even more afraid of other human beings than I was before. Sometimes I see people running around just grimacing, hiding behind masks, artificial, false, full of promises and empty words, unreliable, deceptive, childishly cruel, and I am alone just as much as before. This does not prevent me from having dealings and being popular with many people. But my old love of mankind has gone. I have learned a great deal from the many disappointments and I know that there is nobody who is really there [for me], and apart from my work there is *nothing*. I even doubt whether I will ever be able to love women again the way I used to. This means that I am not as tender and warm as I was. I live without love and I am not prepared to give myself to someone else as I once did. I will be happy

if you can establish your life again here, if I have the chance to see you again. But I cannot satisfy your wish that I should tell whether and how there can be anything between us. You will not possess me in the way that you did in the past, although you still live on inside me. It is a tragedy that it took such catastrophic events to make you realize how you really feel about me. And I no longer want to engage in the old battles. I am right in the middle of some earth-shattering work which calls for all my strength and levelheadedness.

Since the spring I have received only two letters from you, each arriving after a wait of two to three months. I was always very happy whenever anything came and I did not feel any resentment toward you; I am your good friend, as before, and you can count on me.

Ilse has turned out to be an extremely valuable and good friend. But it is not the same between me and her as it was between you and me. Her help and kindness, however, has become an important part of my life. I would like to stress that I do *not* belong to anyone and that I do not allow anyone to make claims on me, not even my children. A new kind of interpersonal relationship is developing here; the modalities are not clear, but they are new and good, and fundamentally different from the old forms. You will have to get used to this if you want to, or you can try out any of the infinite variety of exciting ways of relating to other people which are possible in the U.S.A. I think you will like it.

In my work I am struggling with tremendous difficulties. Not only have I had to revise many of my judgments and opinions—for example, about the value of the saviors of mankind—but also because I still do not have a publisher, I cannot publish anything; I am faced with the task of having to introduce something new; I have to adapt myself to the American mentality; I am struggling with my children, who up until recently were firmly convinced that I was mad; I am financially still not out of the hole, etc. . . . The worst thing is the bitter feeling of being intellectually alone; the fact that after fifteen years of teaching I have still not seen one independent thought expressed in the work done by my students. On top of that, there is the war and the enormous problems which beset one.

I assume that, if everything goes well, you can be here in about six to eight weeks. Send us a wire to let us know how things stand. The main thing now is that you should come. Everything else will fall into place in the American way—that is to say, "with good human sense," cleanly and simply, without any great to-do. You will also be able to buy yourself good, decent clothes here at low prices, and you will also be able to recover from everything that you have gone through.

I hope this letter reaches you soon. Write as soon as you can. All my love.

November 1940

Before undertaking a great and difficult task one must set one's own house in order, find clarity within oneself.

We have—*without exception*—so much dirt, filth, and sickness within us that we must first give ourselves a thorough airing out before making a decision on how to handle a certain truth. I was just reading about the dispute over abiogenesis. Both sides were equally influenced by emotionalism and irrationalism. The one side made unconditional assertions on matters which cannot be grasped without knowledge of orgone energy. The others, like Pasteur, were Christians and compulsion neurotics who refused to accept the truth for what it is.

We must absolutely and at all cost find a way out of this impasse. They are simply unwilling!

Wonder whether it's possible to be cleverer and more cunning?

If the flashes in those boxes in the cellar weren't so obvious, it would make matters much easier.

11 November 1940

Once again I am completely happy, in the mainstream of this wonderful life. Eva attends my lectures, I speak almost exclusively for her and to her. It's peculiar, this experiencing of oneself in the external world! The moment she begins to speak I already know what she is going to say. She is fighting her way through courageously! My students understand and love me. I put into words what they have always thought.

I have cured several mice of cancer solely through the inhalation of radiation, and I am convinced that the orgone will change a part of this world. Nevertheless, Eva's opinion of me is more important than the effect of the orgone.

T O   C L A R A   M E Y E R [*]
❖ *11 November 1940*

Dear Miss Meyer:

This is to answer your letter, which I received last Tuesday evening. If you think that the attendance will be worthwhile, then I would propose repeating my general lecture course as outlined under No. 97 in unchanged form. To let the students attend this lecture course only by consultation proved to be correct.

The seminar (No. 98) should not be announced again because this seminar will not work well with any new students.

Several of my students, especially writers who are concerned with political and social events, are anxious to have a seminar about the mass psychology of fascism. I worked on this theme several years ago and have published a book under the same title in German. Those students wish to hear how biopsychology can be applied to actual political problems, especially to the problem of fascistic irrationality. I would propose giving a seminar of about five to six evenings on this subject only to such students who have attended the general lecture course. I would appreciate it if you would kindly discuss this matter with Dr. Johnson.[†] I hope to see you on this matter tomorrow evening before my lecture course.

Enclosed please find a preliminary outline.

❖ *18 November 1940*

Today the orgone accumulator for human beings arrived and works very strongly. $150 \times 80 \times 100$ cm.

[*]Administrator at the New School for Social Research.
[†]Alvin Johnson, director of the New School for Social Research.

I sat in it twenty minutes naked to the waist. *And it was very strong.*
Now to test:

1. One rabbit one hour daily
2. Different persons from five to twenty minutes

The rabbit gets dizzy, quick heart.

The mice as well as I get very thirsty after having been in the orgone cage. We have to drink much water.

Why?

There is only one explanation! *The body becomes charged with energy. The need for swelling becomes greater, and therefore fluid is requested.*

Tension ⟶ charge.

Charge ⟶ tension.

20 November 1940

It is horrible to be aware that the genitals are the primary brain when the secondary brain refuses to recognize the fact. This crop of humans is the vilest bunch life has yet spawned. The dependency of the emotions upon the orgone charge of the genitals is a slap in the face to any arrogance.

I would like to fall head over heels in love again! To be one with the body of a woman, *my* woman.

❖ *23 November 1940*

10 p.m. I have just discovered a tremendous mistake in my calculations about the orgone in the orgone room.

I thought that it was necessary to keep the room always closed in order to prevent fresh air from dispersing the orgone within the room. Now I had ventilated for four hours. The room showed 13.5° C and the orgone thermometer 14.3°. *Difference: 0.8°.*

The scintillations in the boxes were much stronger than yesterday. The ammeter showed an increase of 0.3 mA above the normal reading of 0.1 mA.

That means:

1. Fresh air brings in new orgone.
2. The old closed-in air seems to use up the orgone.
3. There must be a connection between the amount of oxygen in the air and the orgone radiation.

❖ *26 November 1940*

Some of the orgone-treated T-mice died. The liver in all cases full of yellowish-white granules, like abscesses (but there were no abscesses).

Today 1 ca Herrlein mouse, orgone-treated, died and showed the same liver symptoms.

The tumor showed dark brownish fluid—hemosiderin? Microse! The same formations of overradiated and conglomerated red cells as in the case where SAPA bions and charged-up blood were injected. The brownish stuff must be orgonotic iron in the red cells causing the cells to disintegrate into blue bions and building out of them new brownish cells. The whole matter means a delay of the fulfillment of the therapeutic work, but definitely proved two things:

1. The air orgone is the same as the earth and SAPA orgone.
2. Cells arise from blue bions.

———

The answer of the experiment is: work out the dosage of orgone.

29 November 1940

Yesterday I found a formula for measuring the orgone tension between the air in the accumulator and the air in the room (based on the observation that touching the electroscope with the finger discharges it).

❖ *4 December 1940*

The speed of discharge of the electroscope remains *slower* in the cellar than in fresh air. Today inside orgone potential was 0.75; outside, 0.6.

Now let's think through the possibilities as to whether it's the (a) electrical ionization of the air or (b) orgone in the air, supposing that orgone and electricity are opposite. Regarding (a): If it were ionization from the sun, then the electroscope would discharge *quicker* when ionization was higher and slower when lower. *In the radiation room the discharge would have to be quicker than in the fresh air.* The fact is the opposite. Therefore no ionization of the air in the orgone room can be responsible for the discharge because here the discharge is slower. Ionization does not explain it, and rather contradicts it.

Regarding (b): The orgone hypothesis explains what the ionization theory contradicts.

8 December 1940

It is now a fact that the energy tension of the orgone accumulator is about twice that of the surrounding room. A principle for the construction of an orgone concentrator can be derived from this: by nesting many orgone accumulators one within another.

15 December 1940

Facts:
Orgone flashes in the box even without any connection to the antenna of the radio.
Orgone flashes also after ventilation.
Orgone flashes also without cultures.
Orgone is thus omnipresent at all times.
Assumption: The universe consists of orgone energy. Fixed stars and planets consist of compressed orgone energy in a highly diluted state. Living organisms are orgone energy concentrated in matter of a certain composition: proteins $(H_1O_{16}C_8N_{12})$ surrounded by membranes. Electrical and magnetic energy are thus simply effects of orgone energy in matter depending on direction and substance. (Lightning is the electrical discharge of orgone energy.) Magnetism and electricity are simply functions of orgone energy. The earth is magnetic because it is filled with orgone.
The assumptions are frightening but necessary.

20 December 1940

To adhere to the truth and to remain honest are very costly attitudes. Business forces people to be so petty and low that a person must be really strong to avoid sinking to the level of others for the sake of his cause.

A person is always smaller than the convictions he carries within himself, smaller by far. I'd like nothing better than to be tolerant and courteous, nonoffensive, and on good terms with everyone. It doesn't work. When you see the exponents of such virtues several years later, you can't believe your eyes. What fate saves a person from plunging into the depths of virtue? It is that wave of sweetness which inundates you whenever you love! The wave of spontaneity and insight!

21 December 1940

When one researches orgone energy for many hours every day, the world recedes, begins to be unimportant because it slowly but surely appears in a different light.

I wanted to write a letter to Einstein, pay him a visit, enlist his aid, but I decided against it. He won't believe it, or will believe it and not understand, or understand and send a second Löwenbach* out to bother me.

❖ 27 December 1940

Today I was asked why I work continuously, without rest. I knew no answer! Now I thought, there is not time left—who knows how long the crazy good-for-nothings will leave quiet and time to work.

29 December 1940

Between 4:35 and 5:30. Ilse drew my attention to an "earthquake," so I went outside. I felt giddy. The earth seemed to rock back and forth in an east-to-west direction.

I hung up two pendulums in the basement. They swung in an east-west direction.

TO ALBERT EINSTEIN
30 December 1940

Dear Professor Einstein,

I would very much like to meet with you to discuss a difficult and urgent scientific matter. I work in the field of biophysics and psychosomatic research. From 1922 to 1930 I was Freud's assistant at the Polyclinic in Vienna, and I now teach experimental and clinical biopsychology at the New School for Social Research in New York.

---

*H. Löwenbach, Berlin physiologist who worked on the bioelectric experiments with Reich in Norway.

Several years ago I discovered a specific, biologically effective energy which in many ways behaves differently from anything that is known about electromagnetic energy. The matter is too complicated and sounds too improbable to be explained clearly in a brief letter. I can only indicate that I have evidence that this energy, which I have called orgone, exists not only in living organisms but also in the soil and in the atmosphere; *it is visible and can be concentrated and measured*, and I am using it with some success in research on cancer therapy.

This matter is becoming too much for me for practical and financial reasons, and broad cooperation is needed. There is some reason to believe that it might be of use in the fight against the fascist plague. Apart from a very brief report written one and a half years ago on the charging of insulators by radiation from (human) bodies and the sun, I have not published anything on the subject. At the moment, two pieces of apparatus are in the process of being patented. The matter is too crucial to expose it to the danger of being destroyed by the workings of irrationalism in the scientific community, as so often happens. It would be good and productive in every sense if I could tell you about this matter before asking you to observe the phenomena in my laboratory. I hesitate to follow the usual route of sending a report to the Academy of Physics, and you may find my caution strange, but it is based on extremely negative experiences.

1941

*"I believe that in America, as elsewhere,
there exists much disastrous hypocrisy,
much unconscious and open fascism. During
the two years of my residence in the U.S.A.
I never doubted that these elements could
be overcome, that the will in the direction
of further democratic development was deep,
honest, and powerful."*

1 January 1941

Dear Elsa,

Your letter of 18 November 1940 has finally arrived. It was good to hear from you again, but less good to read all the sad things that you wrote. It is so difficult to answer letters. What was acute and important two or three months ago now seems comical and will be even more so two or three months hence. But there are things which never lose their importance, the deaths of huge numbers of people, our tragedy, the discovery of radiation . . .

I was sad to hear that you are lonely the way that I always was and still am. All the external successes cannot deceive one into believing otherwise. And such terrible things as your being prevented from coming here are simply unbearable. It is just as terrible as my typical experience of seeing people whom I love resisting with all their might against fully identifying with me—namely, with my work—and of knowing that they will realize this too late; and of not being able to do anything about it except stand by and watch; and then of experiencing their awakening and recognition; and of then having to cope with the feeling that so much was lost, because insights develop so slowly and sometimes not at all.

Now above all, I want to be sure that as far as possible you are well. In the meantime you have heard the news. It will take time until the visa is in order, and then we must both face the major question of the journey (quite apart from the costs!). But let us first wait until you have the visa. However, you must keep in closer contact—i.e., write more often.

A great deal has happened in my life in the last one and one half years. The first volume of *Das Lebendige* [*The Living*] has been translated into English by Wolfe. The second volume on the biological radiation of energy is in preparation.* In the meantime the energy has proved to be visible, measurable, and concentratable. Despite suffering from cancer, some mice have had their lives extended by periods equivalent to about fifteen years of human life. But financially things are not going well. In order to maintain my independence I am staying away from the usual sources of money. I am waiting for the work to take off and develop independently. My lectures are very popular and even acclaimed, but you know how people can show enthusiasm and yet do nothing practically. I am living very quietly and withdrawn. Now and again I get a visit from Eva, who has reverted completely to the old Eva. Lore is very difficult. Annie has behaved very indecently and injected the children with poison against me. I never see her. The children cannot stand her husband. She herself is said to be very unhappy.

In contrast, my house is peaceful and a place of work—good, honest work. Gertrud has turned out magnificently well. She is gradually beginning to sever all her old and useless relationships and is going to study medicine. She will perhaps marry an American and stay here. There was never anything between her and me. She is a very good, understanding, and reliable colleague and will perhaps one day become a proper assistant. She is living here in the house. Ilse has familiarized herself well with the work, has taken a course in bacteriology and is in charge of the "animal department." Over the New Year we had three friends over and had a really nice time together. But I am intellectually and spiritually alone and have no opportunity to talk with people who think along the same lines as myself.

Erna† and Neill have been asking a lot about you. Your picture is hanging in my room and I often look at it with love in my heart. Then I think of my fate which has prevented me from making women permanently happy and has left me torn between my work, with all the human and practical difficulties which it involves, and ordinary coexistence with other human beings.

I have only a few students. An attempt is now being made to obtain a medical license for me without having to take the regular exami-

*Later published as Volumes 1 and 2 of The Discovery of the Orgone: The Function of the Orgasm and The Cancer Biopathy.
†A. S. Neill's wife.

nation. There is a law which entitles me to do this. A group of about twelve workers has already formed.

But the political events overshadow everything. We are very well and objectively informed. We understand clearly how completely mad events are. In fact, people here have progressed much further in this direction of thought than on the other side of the Atlantic. This freshness, which is totally lacking in tradition, is very invigorating. And people are struggling hard and honestly to attain some very important goals.

We have sent your mother some coffee. We shall also try to send you some scientific books.

I hope so very much that we will not lose contact with each other. What has this long time apart done to us? It is a major problem, and I am right in the middle of it; I don't know which way to turn, and the only thing that gives any direction to my life is my research. I have put together a new manuscript on future possibilities and it has turned out quite well. Unfortunately it is only in manuscript form.

24 January 1941

I have been trying to continue this letter for the past three weeks, but I have been so busy that I just did not get around to it. Perhaps it was also because I did not want to say what finally needs to be said about you and your personal life: This war has not only destroyed a great deal already but has also probably made it totally impossible for many years to come to restore old relationships. What I mean, and I say this to you in deepest sadness, is that you should not wait for me. I cannot expect or require it of you, nor should you expect or require it of yourself. Try again, as best you can, to be happy. It might take a very long time before you have the chance to come here. You can't wait all that time without suffering harm; we can't live separated from each other for years. If we ever meet again, heaven knows what will happen if we have both become involved with other partners and yet remain unchanged. It would be stupid to decide that today. Therefore, I do not want you to suffer for my sake. Let us try to accept this as bravely as we can. You know that there is always a place for you in my heart. I know that this is not a comfort in a situation like the present. But please do not stop writing. I need your letters. I must know how things are going for you. If, despite everything, you do manage to get here in the near future, then we will at least know that you are safe. It is so difficult to imagine what life is like for you all now on the other side.

TO　ALBERT　EINSTEIN
8 January 1941

Dear Professor Einstein,

I have received your letter of January 6 and would like to suggest Monday, January 13, at approximately 4 p.m. Please inform me if this date and time does not suit you. I can get away from my duties at any time and be at your disposal, with the exception of Wednesday, when I deliver my lectures.

13 January 1941

1. I am famous as a psychiatrist.
2. I am doubted as a biologist.
3. As a physicist, I am regarded as nothing. Therefore I am going to Einstein.

Practical

a. Medical-biological use ⎫
　　　　　　　　　　　　　⎬ War
b. Meteorological use ⎭

c. Use in physics, mathematics (energy production)

d. Biology

Possibilities

a. Hand over the meteorology and physics elements.
b. Work and assistance, possibly for everything.
c. Remain silent.
d. War industry—biological charge.

　Orgone constitutes the "field" that Einstein is searching for. Electricity, magnetism, gravitation, etc., depend on its functions.

❖ *13 January 1941*

Today I had a four-hour discussion with Einstein at Princeton. He was ready to take on the orgone accumulator and to watch the temperature difference.* When I told him that I wanted to transfer the whole physical work to somebody or to get the proper means to conduct it 100 percent properly, that I was not a physicist but a bio-psychiatrist, he asked me, "*Was machen Sie denn sonst noch?*"†

He saw with great astonishment the scintillations in the orgonoscope, but was not sure whether it was not subjective eye impressions. Pendulum oscillations of the earth not mentioned.

The first genuine and fruitful scientific discussion in ten years!

I left behind my trigonometrical diagram of the spinning wave at Einstein's house. Silly mistake!

15 January 1941

A. *Einstein understood*
   Tension-charge formula‡
   Breakdown of crystals into vesicles
   My experience with the SAPA bions

B. *Did not understand the possibility of*
   Free energy in the atmosphere
   The temperature difference at the accumulator

C. He *immediately saw* the scintillations in the orgonoscope,** said "yes," then—as if shocked—"those must be subjective light phenomena." I explained the fact that the scintillations differ according to the object and that they cannot be seen when the metal covering disc is put in place.

---

*Reich had observed a constant difference between the temperature inside the accumulator and the surrounding air. The higher temperature inside the accumulator without the presence of any known form of energy indicated the existence of an unknown energy.
†"And what else do you do?"
‡The tension-charge or orgasm formula discovered by Reich in his investigation of the orgasm: mechanical tension ➤ bioenergetic charge ➤ bioenergetic discharge ➤ mechanical relaxation.
**A diagram of the orgonoscope is included in the photo inserts.

D. He first wanted to send somebody to my laboratory. I declined. Then he was willing to accept an apparatus to measure the temperature difference and to check the difference; if the findings are correct, he was willing to "support the matter."

He did not comprehend the electroscope experiments because I did not put forward my theory of electroscopic discharge. He felt that if the electroscope were open, the moving air would undergo greater discharge. The humidity would not play a role.

Apparatus for Einstein ⟶ construction
Principle of the apparatus:
1. Generate an energy field between metal and organic matter.
2. Demarcate a certain air space from the atmosphere.
3. Organic matter takes up atmospheric orgone. The metal walls reflect it back, so that the energy particles start to oscillate.
4. The kinetic energy of the radiation is converted into heat, which can best be measured above the upper surface.

T O   A L B E R T   E I N S T E I N
15 January 1941

Dear Professor Einstein,

Today I ordered the apparatus for observing the temperature difference brought about by orgone radiation.* It is going to be smaller than the pieces of apparatus which I use here—namely, ⅔ of a cubic foot rather than 1 cubic foot. It will be equipped with a disc of cellulose ester in the front wall (and a diffuse green light can be switched on inside) for the purpose of making the radiation visible. The apparatus should be finished in about eight days. I shall examine it here to make sure that it works and then bring it over to you.

Once again I would like to thank you very much for your extremely kind willingness to look into this matter. As I have already told you

---

*Reich's design of an experimental orgone accumulator appears in the photo insert section.

orally, I do not want to publish anything about this whole matter until I have a chance to verify the observed phenomena in a way that is 100 percent accurate, using the appropriate means.

Talking to you has meant a great deal to me. You will enjoy using the orgonoscope which I left with you, once you have got used to it. You will be able to observe the scintillations *with* and *without* the disc of cellulose ester. However, the disc brings them out more clearly. The metal screen must always be attached to the orgonoscope when it is not in use, in order to keep sunlight from the cellulose disc. The latter has been coated on the inside with calcium sulfide. However, you can also use zinc sulfide for this purpose or the disc may be used by itself, untreated. Whenever the night sky is cloudless or moonless, the tube on its own is sufficient for observing the radiation.

I left behind at your house a sketch and a roll of illustrations. I shall collect these when I bring the apparatus.

16 January 1941

When I visited Einstein I felt as if I were "at home." That is, I had direct contact with him because he is simple and clear. I sensed his weaknesses ("fame" is one of them) and was aware when his opinions were incorrect, but felt not a trace of gloating. I was proud of myself for that. At the end, after four and a half hours of intense conversation, we were both stimulated. There was a great loneliness in that man out in Princeton. It was as if he began to come to life when I demonstrated that the improbable was indeed probable. Any other man would have stumbled at every serious, decisive point. When I told him, in concluding, that people considered me mad, his reply was "I can believe that."

We parted with a firm handshake.

———

Refutation of the argument advanced by Einstein that the rate of discharge of the electroscope depends on the movement of air.

An electroscope set up indoors and in the open air, with and without a fan, yielded the same final result.

Slept for four hours—during the day—depression. I cannot do it by myself, without money and help.

21 January 1941

Apparatus (orgone accumulator) meant for Einstein works also without an organic covering, also in open air at 4° C ($T_0 - T = 1$° C).[*]

———

First experiment to determine the orgone force field between two metal plates (deflection of a magnetic needle by nonmagnetic metal in a certain position) was successful—i.e., field energy could be measured.

Idea for a test to eliminate gravity by using an orgone field acting in the opposite direction to the earth's gravitational pull.

Basic problem: If gravitational force is so minimal, how is it possible for stars to orbit each other at such great distances? Gravitational force has not yet been discovered.

———

Today I succeeded in proving that there is a force which is not the known magnetic force and which acts in the direction of the magnetic field.

T O　　A L B E R T　　E I N S T E I N
28 January 1941

Dear Mr. Einstein,

Please let me know whether it would suit you if I brought you the temperature-measuring apparatus at the end of this week, Saturday or Sunday at approximately four o'clock in the afternoon, or in the middle of next week, on Wednesday or Thursday at the same time, in order to show you how I use it. It has functioned well here for eight days, and I assume that it will function in the same way in your house.

---

[*]$T_0 - T$ signifies the difference between the temperature in the accumulator and that in the surrounding air.

TO ALEXANDER LOWENSTEIN *
❖ 30 January 1941

Dear Mr. Lowenstein:

After the meeting on Tuesday, 28 January, I have thought very much about the plan to establish further study in mental hygiene by founding consultation centers. I came to the conclusion that for many reasons it would not be advisable for me to undertake this work under the present conditions. In order not to run into the difficulties, which are to be expected, too early and unprepared, the center would have to have a thorough background—in other words, the support of some official institution.

Second, my application for the endorsement of my medical license would have to be granted. Besides, the students would have to be more thoroughly educated (through seminars and other work) to handle the cases properly. Consulting work is a very responsible and difficult job if it is to be done with any meaning at all.

Therefore, I think that we should postpone our plan to a later date when circumstances may become more favorable. I do not believe, of course, that social research in mental hygiene could be inopportune in these times, just the opposite is true. The happenings in the world show that there are few fields of greater importance than the study and handling of human structures.

1 February 1941

Handed over an apparatus to Einstein today.

First test +++ after replacing the thermometers. 1.2° C and, after replacing the thermometer, a difference of 0.9° C between orgone thermometer and control thermometer.

Einstein's doubts: Should the control thermometer be covered up in order to prevent the cooling effect of moving air?

My response: Yes, as long as this does not create the same accu-

*A student of Reich's at the New School for Social Research.

mulating conditions as in the orgone apparatus. *No*, if the covering is capable of accumulating orgone radiation.

————

Today, for the first time in ten years, I am enjoying a strong feeling of deep peacefulness.

I brought the orgone accumulator to Einstein. It worked very well. Einstein wants to keep it for two or three weeks and then send a report to the Academy of Physics. If there hasn't been any hidden mischief in the meantime, *I have been successful in every respect,* sexuality, the bions, cancer research . . .

If! There is still that "if." But Einstein is decent, a very pleasant, sincere person. I had such good, immediate contact with him that I am not too concerned.

Now that a breakthrough is in sight, my task is to think ahead, lay my plans. The object is to crush Hitler scientifically—deal him a final blow.

In the event that everything goes well with Einstein:

a. I will propose elaborating my theory of biological energy with his help—i.e., become his pupil.

b. Write a report entitled "The Discovery of the Orgone."

c. Draw up overall plans for the research with regard to locality and financial arrangements.

d. Withhold English translation (Wolfe) until I have finished working with Einstein.

e. Take care of the patent.*

f. Improve observability of the orgone in order to eliminate debate on subjective seeing.

4 February 1941

Alvin Johnson of the New School today turned down my students' request for establishing a "Center for Social Research of Mental Hygiene." They were very depressed.

———

*Reich had applied for a patent on the orgone accumulator and the orgonoscope.

❖ *No date.*
Response to questionnaire from the
National Committee for Mental Hygiene, 1 February 1941

It is difficult to summarize the deficiencies of today's mental hygiene work in a few sentences. However, I personally fought for about eighteen years in this so important field of human endeavor to make clear that it is necessary to distinguish between natural instincts (sexual and others) and those which are secondary, unnatural drives, created by the social suppression of the natural sexuality in children, adolescents, and grown-ups, such as dissocial sexual behaviors, sadism, masochism, all kinds of asocial behavior and lack of rational thinking and acting. The mental hygiene of today neglects nearly completely the natural biological energy, as expressed most clearly in the *natural,* normal genital instincts. I do not believe that mental hygiene will succeed in reaching its aim—that is, to prevent mental disorders—unless it concentrates its efforts upon the great problem, *how to coordinate natural sexuality with the social demands of civilization.* Mental diseases will continue to be an enemy, destroying working ability, joy of life, and social adjustment in about 80 percent of the population, as long as the contradiction between nature and culture is not destroyed outside and within human beings. I am enclosing copies of a preface to a book to appear in English, which may give the right impression of what I believe is wrong with mental hygiene. I would like to express my appreciation of efforts which are made by mental hygienists in the U.S.A. They exceed tremendously what I experienced in Europe through twenty years of work in the field. But it is not enough. We mental hygienists are dealing with a real mental pest, worse than anything that has harassed human societies. The Hitlerism and its wars are nothing but outbursts of this general mental plague within ordinary human beings.

T O　　A L B E R T　　E I N S T E I N *
6 February 1941

Dear Mr. Einstein,

I have carried out a "check of the control thermometer" here by using *two* control thermometers and covering the mercury-filled tip of one of them with various materials; the thermometers were replaced several times. I found that the two control thermometers indicate *the same* temperature as long as I keep to the rule of hanging them up at least one meter away from any wall and not close to the wall. Covering the tip with a ball of cotton wool or with copper, rubber, or glass produces no difference in temperature, or only a negligible difference ($0.05°$ C). According to my observations up to now, any significant difference in temperature ranging from $0.5°$ C to $2°$ C occurs only if a closed metallic cavity is created and the measurement is carried out *above* the apparatus. The difference in temperature is uniform and also larger if the closed metallic cavity is surrounded by organic material and if the space in which the orgone temperature is measured is closed off from the surrounding air.

Several days ago I followed your advice and initiated systematic attempts to photograph the radiation. I have already obtained some positive results. I shall send you the material as soon as I have succeeded in obtaining satisfactory photographs of the radiation.

May I ask you once more not to stay for longer than one hour continuously in the room containing the apparatus, and to breathe some fresh air for a few minutes afterwards.

7 February 1941

I am actually a decent, self-critical fellow and people who call me a charlatan ought to be ashamed of themselves. Just reviewed my journals on the orgone from two years ago. How precisely I felt my way through all that!! I feel somewhat moved by my own actions. How easy it is for someone to criticize from his high horse, but how difficult it is to overcome the worry, doubt, hesitation, the sleepless

*This letter was not sent.

nights, the feelings of worthlessness, because one's thoughts are so "verboten."

9 February 1941

There has been mischief involved in the business with Einstein* —personified by an "assistant" who traced the temperature difference shown by the orgonometer [electroscope] to the "horizontal panel" which separates the air on the floor from that on the ceiling. It didn't occur to him to place the control thermometer *on that same panel* or mount a panel above the apparatus. I have refuted the argument through an experiment and will write Einstein.

TO ALBERT EINSTEIN
20 February 1941

Dear Mr. Einstein,

I have taken plenty of time to reply to your letter because I wanted to evaluate experimentally what your assistant's objections would mean, in practical terms, for the future progress of the work. We had agreed, of course, to conduct experiments to investigate any objections that might be raised. I did not approach you thoughtlessly or with some commonplace matter. The way my work has evolved through experiments has inured me to accidents such as the "temperature difference at the table top" as the cause of the phenomenon. Naturally, you could not have known this and you had to take the objection seriously. I was just very concerned, because you were willing to give up so soon.

A. *Experimental proof of the existence of a temperature difference,*
   while disproving the objection.

The following shows how the interpretation of the phenomenon of the confirmed temperature difference $(T_0 - T)$ is proved wrong through experiments:

---

*Reich had received a letter from Einstein dated 7 February 1941.

Experiment No. 1 conducted indoors (cf. diagram)

If the orgone box in its *original configuration together with the control thermometer* are positioned ¾ m apart from each other *above* the table top, there is nevertheless still a difference in temperature between the thermometer in the box and the control thermometer. However, because of the radiation from the table top, $T_0 - T$ is simply a little smaller than when the control thermometer is freely suspended. For months, I had used a control thermometer here which was standing on the same table as the apparatus and at a distance of approximately ½ m from it, until I noticed that the radiation of the table top had reduced [the temperature difference], at which point I changed over to attaching the thermometer in such a way that it was freely suspended in the air. Over the entire period of time, a mean temperature difference of approximately 0.6° C prevailed (maximum difference of up to +1.5° C in an apparatus having a volume of 1 cubic foot).

If the test area is covered with a second wooden board, arranged parallel to the lower board [table top] and approximately 1 m above it, which interrupts the hypothetical "convection of heat from the ceiling downward to the table top," the temperature difference nevertheless still exists.

If, instead of the lower wooden board, a metal plate is used, which equalizes the temperature difference above and below more rapidly (a difference of ± and ∓0.1° C), the temperature difference between the apparatus and the air also continues to exist.

The temperature difference $T_0 - T$ even persists if, while retaining its original configuration, the box is *freely* attached in such a way in the room that there is no table top below it, for example within an enclosing metal frame.

This difference persists even if the box is surrounded by a covering which protects the thermometer in the box from all sides. If the control thermometer is surrounded with cotton wool, rubber, metal, or glass, the result is not reduced, or only to a negligible extent. All of the above presupposes that no readings are taken while the outside temperature is rising rapidly.

Experiment No. 2 (measurement in the open air)

For several months in 1940 I had kept a small orgone box buried in the ground in my garden and had observed a constant temperature difference. But it was only a few days ago that I found out how much greater this difference is than the difference measured in enclosed rooms.

On 15 February 1941, which was a sunny, cold day with strong winds, I buried an apparatus two-thirds of the way into the ground in such a way that the thermometer in the box was still *above* ground level. The box, together with the upper thermometer housing, was surrounded by a second box made of cardboard; I filled the lateral and upper spaces between the two boxes with cotton wool and wood wool and covered the whole arrangement with a cotton blanket. (The space in which measurements are taken must naturally be well protected against the lower outside temperature in order to retain the heat which has been produced.) I placed a control thermometer through a hole into a glass container and buried the latter 4 inches deep into the soil, in such a way that the tip of the thermometer was *below* ground level. I placed a second control thermometer with an unprotected tip 1 inch deep into the ground. I also used this second control thermometer for measuring the temperature of the air above ground level, roughly at the same level as that of the thermometer in the box, both with and without a covering protecting it against the wind. The three thermometers were constantly exchanged. The enclosed diagrams relating to experiment No. 2 illustrate the arrangement and the results.

In this arrangement, the value of $T_0 - T$ is much greater than it is in an enclosed room, probably because the effect of the secondary orgonotic radiation at walls, table tops, etc., which reduces the difference in an enclosed room, has been eliminated. $T_0 - T$ *fluctuates by approx.* $\pm 2°$ *C.*

In order to be absolutely sure, I continued experiment No. 2 during the night and the following day, from 16 to 17 February, as follows: I left the apparatus in the open air exactly the way it was but removed the cotton blanket—in other words, I allowed it to be "completely cooled down" by the nighttime frost. At 9:30 a.m. on 17 February, the air temperature was $-1°$ C and the ground temperature was $0°$ C. I took the cotton blanket, which had now cooled down, and wrapped it around the apparatus again and inserted the thermometer, which had just registered an air temperature of $-1°$ C, from above through the hole into the "chimney" of the box. The mercury column rose and after a while indicated 2.3° C above zero, while the air temperature still stood at −1° C and the ground temperature at 0° C. At the same time, the air temperature inside the jar buried in the ground was +0.9° C.

I believe that these facts make a perfectly unambiguous statement.

a) *The ground and the atmospheric air contain a form of energy which can be measured in my apparatus as heat.*

b) *The constant source of heat energy attains high values only if a particular arrangement of materials is used.* This arrangement of the materials—organic on the outside, metallic on the inside—is therefore essential for *increasing* the temperature difference $T_0 - T$.

This complementary test also shows how important is the arrangement of materials in relation to the radiation emitted by the ground and the sun. After the influence of solar radiation has been eliminated by the formation of shadows, the difference $T_0 - T$ compared with all the control measurements falls from a mean temperature of approx. +5° C to, on average, approx. 2° C. The control thermometer, which is surrounded by glass and exposed to very little orgone radiation coming from the ground, shows a difference of only approx. 1° C. The orgone apparatus on the other hand, which has the hitherto most complete set of equipment for capturing and accumulating the energy, shows much higher values—namely, *more than* +2° C!

The *lowering* of the temperature in the open air through frost reaches the thermometer inside the box in spite of the covering and *has an effect*. The difference $(T_0 - T)$ remains nevertheless constant within certain lower and upper limits, in spite of the parallel decrease of T_0 and T over a period of approx. 3 hours, as follows:

T_0	=	11.4°	$T_0 - T$	=	6.8°
T air	=	4.6°			
T_0	=	9.5°	$T_0 - T$	=	6°
T air	=	3.5°			
T_0	=	6.5°	$T_0 - T$	=	5.9°
T air	=	0.6°			

I intend to bury the apparatus completely so that the tip of the thermometer is also completely below ground level and then try to establish by means of experiment how large are the differences T_0 Earth − T Air and T_0 Earth − T Earth. As the ground is frozen right now, I shall carry out the experiment when conditions are more favorable and report to you at that time. Without doubt, there are still many questions to be clarified regarding T_0 − T.

Experiments are needed to explain your table top phenomenon. For the time being, there are only two possible interpretations of this now isolated fact:

a) The interpretation advanced by your assistant—namely, that "heat convection" occurs within the room and is directed vertically downward from the ceiling—or, expressed differently, the interpretation that "the temperature at the upper surface of the table top approaches the temperature at the ceiling of the room."

b) My interpretation that the ground and the atmospheric air radiate orgone energy.

The fact that a *radiation* effect exists at the horizontal wooden table top was known to me and was the reason for suspending the control thermometer freely in the room in order to eliminate the [temperature-]reducing effect of this radiation. Your assistant's interpretation has been disproved by the arrangements employed in experiment No. 1 (metal plate below, wooden board above, control thermometer above the lower [metal] plate). The *"horizontal heat potential,"* without a *source of heat acting laterally,* still exists even after the heat convection from the ceiling to the lower plate has been interrupted. Experiment No. 2 refutes the interpretation even more conclusively.

Overall result of experiments:

1) The original arrangement of the apparatus results, under all circumstances, in a temperature difference between the thermometer in the box and the control thermometer, in the absence of any known kind of constant heat source.

2) Experiment No. 1 refutes the argument that heat convection from the ceiling to the table top is the reason for the phenomenon and demonstrates the existence of a horizontal heat potential below a second upper board, without any visible lateral source of heat.

3) The measurement in the open air proves that there is radiation from the ground which varies in magnitude, depending on the arrangement of the material.

If we assume for a moment that the interpretation given by your assistant is correct, we are faced with some very strange facts which, given my test arrangement, would contradict the known principles of heat theory: An upper board made of wood, which is a poor conductor, positioned at a distance of approx. 1 m above and parallel to the lower metal plate, thus interrupting the "downward convection of heat from the ceiling toward the metal plate," either did not show any difference [in temperature] between above and below the board or the differences were negligibly small. In order to explain the box phenomenon, it would be a giant problem for heat to be radiated from the ceiling of the room downwards through a poor conductor of heat such as air, and through the upper wooden board to the lower metal plate, and for an above-below temperature difference to be constantly maintained at this plate, which is a good conductor of heat.

Since there can be no such thing as horizontal convection of heat, as I have proved in my experiment No. 1, if there is no constantly effective lateral source of heat; since also during my experiments the temperature difference at the lower *metal* plate amounted to only $\pm$ and $\mp$ 0.1°; and since therefore the assumption of your assistant is not valid, the only explanation left is the one which fits into the framework of my other observations regarding orgone radiation. In order to understand the temperature difference at the wooden board, which was observed in your home, we must assume the following:

a) Your wooden table top was thermally influenced from above by the omnidirectional radiation of the apparatus.

b) The radiation from the ground *upwards* is also slowed down by the wooden board and shows up as an increase in temperature at the wooden board, just as the accumulated radiation *inside* my orgone boxes manifests itself as a *higher* temperature above the boxes.

I would find it impossible at this moment to decide which of the two interpretations deserves to be favored.

You will no doubt remember that at the very end of our first four-hour conversation I told you very *reluctantly* that, in my experiments, the temperature *inside* the orgone box (one of my large boxes used for humans) is on average 1°–3° lower than the temperature *above* [the box] in the screened room. You probably also remember that you were very surprised and did not want to believe this information. Now, if my interpretation is correct, this fact, which I divulged so hesitantly at the time, would assume an enormous importance which I originally had not attributed to it.

I failed to understand your assumption that "the *upper* side of your table top was cooled *from below*" and that the temperature at the box vanished *for this reason* when you took it from its outer casing. Besides, a box that has been taken apart harbors too many negative sources of error that cannot be controlled.

Now a few words regarding the relationship of the casing to the metal box. Over a period of time, I have formed the following conclusions, based on my observations:

The metal box on its own also exhibits differences in temperature compared with the ambient air, but they are smaller and understandably fluctuate very strongly. The organic casing first and foremost has the function of separating the heat generated by the metal box from the heat outside—in other words, to make it more constant. The casing also has the function (based on the *electroscopically* established fact that uncharged insulators absorb atmospheric energy) of transmitting the energy to the metal on the inside. The metal walls reflect the energy *both inwards and outwards*. Within the metal walls, the energy is able to oscillate freely without being hampered by absorbent organic matter. This can be *seen* clearly when the interior green light and the lens in the front wall of the metal box are used. The energy radiated outwards is absorbed by the surrounding organic casing and is partially given off as heat into the environment and partially returned to the metal on the inside. This process, too, can be seen in the dark, in the space between the metal and the organic casing, by using a tube and a lens. I therefore theorize that this is how a concentration of orgone energy originates inside the apparatus, compared with the energy tension in the air. It is likely that the *retardation* of the kinetic energy of the radiation at the boards/plates forms the basis of the heat phenomenon. This concentration can presumably be considerably increased through a more complicated design and further intermingling of organic and metallic materials.

These assumptions are supported by the *differences in the rate of discharge of charged electroscopes inside* and *outside* the apparatus. Charged electroscopes *which communicate with the air* discharge *more slowly inside than outside.* It has been proven that these electro-scopic discharges have nothing to do with the humidity of the air, and if the air near the electroscope is circulated, for example with the help of a fan, they occur at roughly the same rate. The rate of discharge depends solely on the orgone tension of the ambient air. The higher this tension compared with the charge of the electro-scope, the more slowly the electroscope can discharge; the lower the tension, the faster the discharge.

It is understandable that I am unable at this point to explain all the phenomena in this new field. Therefore there is much that might have been misunderstood and thus requires correction. But, as the accumulator is based on many interconnected facts and on the as-sumptions derived from them, it is understandable why I place so much emphasis on the *visibility* and the *electroscopic measurability* of the orgone energy in connection with the *temperature difference.*

B. *The biophysical framework of the temperature phenomenon.*

1. In the *atmosphere,* in the *soil,* and in the *living organism* there exists a type of energy which acts in a specifically biological way and which I have called "orgone." With the aid of the orgonoscope, this energy is visible as scintillation in the atmosphere and in the soil as well as on bushes (in the summer); it can be measured electroscop-ically and thermally, and it can be concentrated through a specific arrangement of materials. Several pieces of photographic proof exist, but they have not yet been separated out in unambiguous fashion from the control results. Photographs taken with Kodachrome film show the color *blue* or *blue-gray,* and this is also how the radiation appears subjectively to the viewer.

2. For the time being, the unit of a *quantity of orgone energy* can be taken to be *one org*—i.e., the quantity of energy needed to main-tain a temperature difference $(T_0 - T) = 1°$ C per hour.

3. The living animal organism is surrounded by an energy field which fluctuates within broad or narrow boundaries. This can be proved by means of the oscillograph. Fluctuations of the oscillograph can be produced at a distance of up to 4 m, without any connection via a conductor, for example by moving one's hand in front of a cellulose sheet placed vertically in front of a silver electrode.

4. All living creatures continuously inhale this energy and radiate it back again. Thus an exchange of energy exists between living crea-

tures and the atmospheric orgone energy. In animals, the red blood corpuscles are the essential carriers of this atmospheric energy, and they transport it from the surface of the lungs to the tissues. The hitherto unexplained constant production of heat by living creatures is in all probability the heat produced by the orgone radiation of the organism. The fact that the blood has a high iron content takes on great importance in this context.

5. The sun emits the same kind of hitherto undiscovered energy. This can be proved with a static electroscope, when uncharged insulators (rubber, cellulose, cotton wool, wood, etc.) are charged by means of bright solar radiation in conditions of dry air (relative humidity not exceeding 40 to 50 percent).

6. Certain experimental results (the N pole of a bar magnet glows in the darkness of the orgone chamber; a metal tip emits sparks at a distance of 5 cm from a cellulose sheet which has been rubbed) make it appear very likely that the fluctuations of the earth's magnetism are connected with this energy; the situation is similar in the case of the northern lights (massive iron ore deposits in northern Sweden!) and the so far unexplained phenomena of lightning bolts, which represent giant discharges of atmospheric energy.

7. When one takes into account the inherent nature of orgone energy, which magnetizes insulators, the earth's magnetic field has little or nothing to do with the well-known phenomenon of ferromagnetism. There is *one* experimentally proven fact relating to the problem of why magnetic lines of force run perpendicular to the direction of electric current, but it has not yet been clearly worked out. (Rotation of a magnetic needle either N or S between two parallel metal plates in the orgone room.) It might be possible to gain a new and satisfactory understanding even of the less than clear problem of "static electricity" starting from this premise.

8. For months I have been observing a phenomenon which shows clearly that strange fluctuations in the atmospheric energy tension are disturbing the constant galvanic current in highly stable measuring apparatus (Siemens Pantostat units, which are used for medical purposes). This is reminiscent of the disruptions caused in electrical apparatus by the "electromagnetic storms" in the atmosphere, such as occurred in the early summer of 1940. At the time of the earthquake in New England on 24 December 1940, my measuring arrangement

displayed disturbances of up to +8 mA lasting for days in the Siemens Pantostat (the apparatus had been set at 1 mA of quiescent current).

9. Two years ago I published the finding that cancer cells organize from energy vesicles in decaying and swelling tissue, just as do protozoa in moss which forms vesicles as it decays. (Cf. *Die Bione*, 1938* and "Bion Experiments on the Cancer Problem," 1939.)

Parallel to the fact that a temperature difference exists between the space above and inside the orgone box, a biological effect of the radiation was discovered, not by me but independently by an assistant who is a biologist.

Protozoa develop within two to six days in infusions of moss kept in any kind of room. By contrast, if the same preparations are kept *in the box* from the beginning, the development of protozoa and bacteria in the infusion of moss is severely inhibited. *Above the box* the development of protozoa seems to be favored. Exchanging the preparations confirms this effect. This biological experiment thus confirms the physical phenomenon.

The inhibiting effect of concentrated orgone radiation on the development and movement of protozoa and bacteria has been employed for years in my cancer therapy tests involving cancer mice: If plant and animal tissue is biologically charged, its disintegration into protozoa is prevented and existing bacteria and protozoa, which are similar to foreign bodies, are destroyed. For the time being, I cannot explain the actual contradictory nature of this effect (charging of healthy tissues, destruction of the products of disintegration of animal and plant tissue). *In mice suffering from spontaneously developed malignant tumors, which increase in size and prove fatal in control experiments, tumor growth is inhibited, in many cases the tumor is destroyed, and in most cases the life span of the test mice is lengthened when compared with untreated control mice.* The test mice are exposed to the radiation *inside* the orgone accumulator for half an hour each day. The correct dosage has not yet been worked out. The result up to now, which is preliminary and was obtained using approximately 200 cancer mice, is as follows:

Die Bione (Sexpolverlag, 1938). Published in English as *The Bion Experiments* (New York: Farrar, Straus and Giroux, 1979).

a) The ratio between the mean life span of the treated cancer mice and the life span of untreated cancer mice is approximately 9:3.

b) The longest life span observed in treated cancer mice was so far 8 months. The longest life span of untreated cancer mice is only about 2½ months.

From the point of view of cancer therapy, these results are still very unsatisfactory. I would not publish them at all yet, although they deserve to be published; nor would I state that I am able to cure cancer; but when considered from the point of view that orgone radiation *exists*, this biological fact is an argument that carries *decisive* weight.

For the time being, the clinical and experimentally obtained facts can be condensed into the following opinion, which is of course still contradictory in places and will require correction:

The autonomic life function is dominated by a four-part rhythm: "mechanical tension–bioelectrical charge–bioelectrical discharge–mechanical relaxation." This function is thus based on a *specifically biological* combination of inorganic functions which exist separately in the physical world, without being combined in this way. *According to this, life is no more than a specifically arranged sum of physical functions.* All autonomic organs of the animal organism, such as the cardiac system, the intestines, the urinary bladder, etc., just as in invertebrates such as jellyfish, function according to this same rhythm. As a result of the discovery of the specifically biological energy, life no longer simply exists in the form of a highly complicated protein, as is believed, but instead this *protein is controlled by a special kind of energy that results spontaneously from matter which undergoes swelling and decomposition.* Nonliving protein must therefore be a highly complicated organic substance which has lost or failed to develop the four-beat rhythm of tension-charge-discharge-relaxation. Three years ago I published some observations which make it evident that any matter which was made to swell or was heated to incandescence and then underwent swelling, disintegrates into *energy-charged vesicles* 1–5μ in size which I called energy vesicles or "bions." These energy vesicles are units of life originating directly from inorganic matter which have the capacity of developing into bacteria and cellular protozoal life forms. They exist immediately after the preparations have been made, which means that the possibility of infection with airborne germs, which need at least twenty-four hours to develop, can be excluded. The energy vesicles also furnish the energy which we take into our organism in the form of food (organic matter disintegrating into energy vesicles). Inhaling air and ingesting food are therefore the two main pathways for supplying energy directly from the outside world to the organism.

These facts and opinions are in essence close to the *interrelationship between matter and energy* discovered by you. The relationship of orgone energy to electromagnetic energy is very unclear. According to preliminary observations, it seems to work in the same direction as magnetic force and at a right angle to electrical force.

It was essentially my knowledge of your basic idea of physics which led me years ago to refute the objection that sterile bions are airborne spores or germs; this I did by heating coal dust, soot, crystals, etc., to incandescence. I obtained my "energy vesicles" or "bions" through experiments by *exploding matter* in this way and then causing it to swell. This result was experimentally confirmed in France and was presented by colleagues to the Académie Française, the Sorbonne, and other places, where it is now on record.

As I told you and as I recorded in the protocol at the time of the discovery, orgone radiation was discovered in energy vesicles which had developed after marine sand (*petrified solar energy*) had been heated to incandescence and then swelled up. The structures which you saw on microphotographs could not so far be identified. This particular test was undertaken 16 times, 8 times with a positive result—i.e., radiating bions of the same kind were obtained each time.

I know that this is a great deal to accept all at once, it sounds "mad," and I cannot cope with it by myself. In fact it also seems to be so *new* that for years I have had the impression of being on extremely dangerous ground and have little hope of quickly penetrating the iron ring—i.e., the usual tough defensive barrier which anything new encounters. In the field of psychiatry it took ten years for me to gain acceptance for my views regarding biological energy. However, the logical course of development of the problem of biological energy over a period of about twenty years is in itself a very weighty argument—and a consolation. This development has led me without preconceptions and logically to the purely physical heat phenomenon.

When I visited you for the first time, I conveyed to you my ideas on some facts obtained through experiment and clinical experience which are certainly not easy to accept and which I did not arrive at lightly. I was overwhelmed by the wealth of these new insights and had hoped to establish with you or through you the different kind of cooperation in the field of physics which the cause so richly deserves. It would be understandable if, for lack of time or interest, you yourself no longer wish to deal with this matter. But if I now fail to arouse interest in the world of physics for this biophysical discovery, then I have no hope of being able to push through research into the *physics-related* part of this immense field faster and with less pain, in the interest of studying the cancer problem. In addition, any negative pronouncement on your part would ensure that anyone who firmly believes in authority, and that includes the majority of researchers, would turn uncritically against me. In that case I would have to go on fighting by myself, exposed to malicious rumors which replace arguments, without funds, relying on my modest income as a university teacher—out of which I have for years been spending $300 to $500 a month on the laboratory—and supported by my considerable authority in the field of biopsychological studies and by the many facts which have accumulated logically over the years. It would not be possible any time soon to engage in *broad* research on the effect that the newly discovered biological energy has on the various species of pathological microorganisms; nor would it be possible to let the victims of the war benefit from this effect as quickly as possible.

The incorrect metaphysical-mechanistic assumptions about life held by present-day biology would continue to exist unchallenged—namely:

that life is floating "in the atmosphere" in the form of plasmatic airborne germs, a different germ for each of the millions of species of protozoal life forms, something that has never been proved and has been refuted by me *through experiments*;

that life came to earth from the stars through cold space, something that has not been proved either;

that "life can only come from life" and "the cell only from the cell," which does not explain how life *first* originated, although this does not seem to disturb the scientific conscience;

that our earth is the only planet inhabited by living creatures, etc., etc.

Access to understanding the cancer problem has been closed off by the mechanistic and metaphysical opinions prevalent in biology. The natural organization of bacteria and protozoa from energy vesicles, which result from the vesicular disintegration of both living and nonliving matter, opens up a simple and fruitful access to understanding this endemic disease: *Cancer cells come into being through bionous disintegration of biologically malfunctioning organs and through organization of the cancer cells from tissue which is disintegrating into vesicles. Cancer is, so to speak, an autoinfection of the organism.*

As you can see, Mr. Einstein, the real background of the heat phenomenon is of devastating importance and full of problems. It would be a bitter outcome if *an incorrect* interpretation of *one single* phenomenon, taken from a *large number* of new and enlightening facts, could impede the possibility of making a valuable contribution to understanding an epidemic. This area of biophysics is too new and comprehensive to be confirmed or refuted on the basis of one single point. It would be depressing if the interest which you showed earlier were lost because of this.

Of course the phenomenon of physical heat by itself cannot be the decisive factor, either in a positive or in a negative sense, controlling the entire field of biology. I finally had to admit to myself that the individual facts cannot be understood or followed by outsiders who do not have any knowledge of the problem as a whole and of its development. I have therefore decided to collect together and publish the development of the discovery as well as the entire material, as far as it is available. It seems that, for the time being, I will have to forgo the idea of elaborating the phenomena in a comprehensive and cooperative way prior to publication, if you are still not convinced by the fact that the temperature difference is so large when the measurements are taken in the open air.

The individual facts taken by themselves are impossible to understand—that is the reason for the difficulties I come up against.

When I found out through experiments based on my "tension-charge" formula (1930–35) that pleasure and anxiety correspond to opposing directions of bioelectrical currents inside the organism (toward the periphery: *expansion*-pleasure; toward the center: *contraction*-anxiety), a doctor voiced the "objection" that the skin potentials were not the results of psychosomatic emotions of the whole organism but "only contact potentials between electrode and skin membrane." He did not answer the question why potentials are measured at all in the living organism, if a membrane and an electrode are sufficient.

When, in 1936, I discovered the "bions" (energy vesicles) through the tension-charge function, which has been confirmed by experiments, the objection was raised that these were "spores from the air." I refuted this objection by heating material to incandescence, thereby yielding the energy vesicles in an *incomparably better* way.

When I demanded that the energy vesicles should be examined starting at a magnification of 2,000×, the objection was raised that at magnifications over 1,000× the "structures would no longer be resolvable." I refuted this argument by pointing out that in the case of the energy vesicles the important thing is not to resolve structures but instead to make the delicate movements of expansion and contraction visible. These movements can only be observed at magnifications of between 2,000× and 4,000× and they are a decisive argument against another objection—namely, that the bions exhibit "physical Brownian movement." Anyone who has ever seen bions resulting from coal dust at these magnifications will immediately understand my counterargument that the movement of the energy vesicles originates from *inside* (and not from outside through "molecular collision").

At the beginning of 1937, Professor Lapique, a physiologist at the French Academy, refused to publish anything on the biological character of vesicular movement (*movement impulse originating from inside*) and the fact that the vesicles could be cultivated. He only admitted the *existence of motile bacteria-like forms in a sterile preparation*. I refused to allow my message to the Academy to be published in its *Bulletin*, despite being specifically requested to do so, because what I had written had been arbitrarily cut. Because the movement of the energy vesicles manifests itself as *contraction* and *expansion*, the phenomenon is biophysical and not mechanical in nature. Nor did it make any difference when I proved that these movements are absent in a control preparation which has not been heated to incandescence, and that after a certain amount of time they cease in the bion preparations. The matter was treated with complete silence. *People simply did not want to have anything to do with it.* Total silence was also what greeted the microphotographs which I published and which showed without any doubt the protozoal organization of moss in the process of disintegrating into vesicles. However, reports received from France indicate that this part of my work is slowly being recognized.

At the beginning of 1937, when I discovered the development of cancer cells from animal tissues in the process of disintegrating into vesicles, and when I recognized the analogy between the organization of cancer cells and the organization of protozoa in swelling and disintegrating moss, I turned to the official cancer researchers in Norway. This resulted in a campaign by the press against me which raged for ten months and very nearly ruined my finances. The leaders of the campaign were genetic psychiatrists and a pathologist, and they did not come up with one single factual counterargument. It turned out that the cancer pathologist had never seen a living cancer cell. I did not react to the irrational attack and turned the matter over to a lawyer. At that time, I was working on the *relationship between the blue energy vesicles I had found and cancer.* A year later, while the campaign by my enemies was still reverberating, this work led to the discovery of the radiation and heat phenomena.

When I cultivated living microorganisms approx. 0.25μ in size from putrid decomposed cancer tissue and was able to induce cancerous tumors by injecting these microorganisms into healthy mice, a biologist who had respected my work objected that he had found putrefaction bacteria in the preparation. As I had not yet published the matter, he did not realize that his remark had actually *confirmed* my experiment: The injected organisms (T-bacilli) are indeed products of putrefied, degenerated organic protein. And this is what I have had to put up with, in every possible variation, for many years.

And now, along comes your assistant, who cannot have the slightest idea about the overall work, and he objects that the heat phenomenon is a case of "convection of heat from the ceiling to the table top." As in so many other similar cases, this objection, too, has led to a strengthening and improvement of the factual base—namely, to the discovery of the much greater temperature difference in the open air.

I am writing all this in order to give you some insight, however inadequate, into the goings-on with which you have now come into contact. Of course, only my properly equipped laboratory can give the correct impression.

I know that my discovery destroys many beloved illusions and derails many accepted notions. However, I am also aware that my discovery explains in *simple* terms a multitude of facts, especially in the field of biology, that were not understood up to now, and it provides solutions that have long been sought after. Because it lacks a basic *functional* concept, modern biology is mired in the misery of a complicated way of thinking which is at one and the same time mechanistic *and* metaphysical. Biology could now be supported by the fact that a functional, specifically biologically effective energy exists, for *the bridge from nonliving matter to living matter has been found.* But this is too simple, and hence the resistance.

To speak on behalf of such an enormous problem obliges me to assume full responsibility for the accuracy of my observations, experiments, and conclusions; however, it also obliges me to shed any illusions regarding human reactions both inside and outside the field of science. The reason why orgone energy was not discovered much sooner lies in the irrational human structure, that of the researcher included, to which we all succumb far too often. Forty years ago (and this is still true today) people were afraid to look into the abyss of their unconscious physical urges. My own clinical experience has taught me that human beings have a great fear of perceiving life manifested in themselves and in nature *as a function of the nonliving world.* It is almost as if they were disgusted by their primitive plasmatic origins in the realm of the nonliving. Anybody pursuing the problem inherent in specifically biological energy must not overlook this attitude.

Thus science does not stand outside the irrational sphere in humans, the initial discovery of which linked forever the name of my teacher, Freud, with the developmental history of mankind. My own biological work is only the experimental continuation of Freud's research into the psychic energy ("libido") in the biological foundation of the psychic apparatus. In this context I have learned one thing and, driven by the experience of the international mass outbreak of fascist irrationality, I have been forced to make it my principle to fight lies (including my own!) fiercely in my own field of work, but also to

defend proven truths equally fiercely; that is to say, not to be intim-
idated by the usual reaction of the world to anything new.

It is not to be seen as presumptuousness or lack of humility on my
part when I seek your support in representing this great and good
cause. If any reproach is due, it should be directed at the cause, not
myself! The cause would simply like to achieve a breakthrough to
being generally known and fully elaborated, and it would like this to
happen now, not in fifty years' time, as scientific irrationalism would
prefer. The cause is ready to explain itself, to offer proof of where it
actually exists, and to admit where it is still unclear and doubtful.

No matter what you decide after these explanations, I would like
to thank you most sincerely for the effort that you have made up to
now, which has been extraordinary. Apart from the colleagues with
whom I cooperated in France and Scandinavia, you have been the
only outside researcher of all the ones I have met in the last twelve
years who understood the physical basis of my biophysical theory
regarding the *organic development of vesicles through energy development from matter*. This fact alone means much for me personally and
for the cause. If you are not prepared to help, an important support
will be lost.

If, as was your original intention, you are now willing to help, Mr.
Einstein, and this cause is related in so many ways to your research
work, then many people will be grateful to you—not only valued
researchers and medical doctors but especially the countless cancer
patients who can certainly be helped by orgone energy, once it has
been *completely* and thoroughly researched. In spite of all the irrational hustle and bustle of our time, the old medical adage that healing should be left to nature and science should play only a supporting
role is still valid.

21 February 1941

I am horrified by the thought of already growing "wise." It's not
wisdom I hate, but "being wise." This is how one becomes wise: One
has a theory about life (instead of having life itself) and then one
"looks down at life." One stands "without" and "above," only too
soon to be "below." The fact that my work is dependent upon ex-

tremely primitive reactions will save me from becoming wise prematurely. Reactions like the amazement which strikes me the moment I see the completely rigid, vapid smile on the numbed, masked face of the Queen of England. What a contradiction of nature is hidden behind royalty of this sort! Or when I see how fascism (that is, the life will of rigid worms who can no longer wiggle but only goose-step) is sitting in the very midst of old men who advocate the morality of the past century; or when I realize how a decade of experience with fascism has failed to teach the best minds in the U.S.A. that the plague does not follow legal procedure, as their fear would have them believe. On the contrary, it attacks at night, from within, in one's own home; or when I see that the ignorance of the victims is the most powerful weapon employed by this plague's bacillus.

Learn to wait, that's the motto! Knowledge, watchfulness, attentiveness, observation, understanding—these are the weapons against the plague. To know exactly where unarmored life will begin to resist it, without "organizations," "parties," "secretaries," and "presidents." It will begin to resist when it is on the verge of suffocation. Only then will it break free from its fetters—until it chains itself down anew.

The individuals who pity the "poor masses" are reactionary. One cannot relieve people of the responsibility they have toward themselves. This kind of "pity" is pseudorevolutionary, vanity, nonsense. We must state unequivocally that everyone pays dearly for intellectual dishonesty. It is not true that the millions of working and thinking people do not sense and know what is involved! They are simply too chickenhearted to spout openly about this in the way they spout nonsense openly.

It is not true that it is impossible for people to use the opportunities of a democracy. They are cowards and must be told so.

To pity people because they are poor devils implies setting oneself above them; to load them with complete responsibility for their destiny implies taking them seriously and seeing them as they are.

Who is supposed to save them anyway? No one is capable of that! Whoever promises to save them will be their downfall. Either people will learn to be responsible adults or they will continue to be slaughtered like sheep by the million, time and time again—*and rightly so.*

If someone pulls a knife on me and I simply refuse to see it because it frightens me, then I'm a fool and deserve to be stabbed in the stomach. No one can spare me that, or save me, or comfort me over it. I simply must see the threat myself, register it, and dispose of it.

If I were to rely on the various party bosses, diplomats, politicians, etc., I would be idiotically destroyed for sure.

Therefore, *no excuses or pity for mankind! Make man responsible for everything that's going on in this world.*

22 February 1941

Being alone is very bitter—intellectually and spiritually alone! But it keeps you clean! You simply have to pay a price for cleanliness in this world of rotten business!

24 February 1941

I have absolutely no faith that the matter will be accepted. *It is too much—too new—too much responsibility.* But this matter, *my* matter, is simple, clear, solves riddles, it is honest and vitally spontaneous!! Even if Einstein should fail, the cause is not lost. I must then be strong enough to make it by myself.

26 February 1941

Proposal from Union Settlement House to set up a Mental Hygiene Station.

5 March 1941

Still no answer from Einstein. Possibilities:
a. Phenomenon seen in the open air. Field too large, too "dangerous," search for arguments *against.*
b. Phenomenon seen, attempt to check all data!
c. Threw the whole thing in the waste paper basket.
d. Possibly Einstein is writing the promised report or consulting with others.

8–10.30 p.m. Conference at Union Settlement House, East 104th Street and Second Avenue.

6 March 1941

If the Settlement House business goes through, then all my dreams will be fulfilled:

1. Mental hygiene work
2. Cancer and rheumatism
3. Teaching

If Princeton fails, no matter; if Settlement House says "yes," then I shall get facilities there.

8 *March 1941*

Today I started the first cancer treatment with a cancer patient, Mrs. Pops, using orgone.

TO   CLYDE   MURRAY*
❖ *10 March 1941*

Dear Mr. Murray:

I shall have to discuss the following outline in detail this coming Wednesday with my assistants and students. Therefore, some suggestions may be added later which will change some of it.

I believe that we would have to establish to begin with: Two centers for personal consultation, each once a week. (Two psychiatrists, one doctor of osteopathy, two teachers, and one vocational counselor will be working together at the same time.) One public question-and-answer evening, once monthly, for the discussion of important mental hygiene problems with grown-ups and adolescents together. One small-child guidance clinic could be added later.

As mental hygiene work properly carried through very often implies psychosomatic work, a laboratory and assistantship would be needed. I could provide some of it myself, but not all. I think we can let that matter develop in the course of the events.

We would need at least three rooms, properly equipped, to begin with. Should it be possible to provide brighter rooms in the new premises which you mentioned, that would help our work very much. Bright rooms are very important psychologically.

The public question-and-answer meetings are *very important*. I have to stress this fact: Individual consultation as seen from the stand-

*Director of the Union Settlement House, New York City.

point of the mass production of neuroses and crimes is mostly fruitless if the community does not cooperate and does not learn to understand the problems of mental hygiene and to back up the task of the psychiatrist. We have to be prepared for more or less difficult struggles between this rational scientific approach and all those forces in our social life which create fear, submissiveness, guilt feelings, neuroses, perversions, antisocial behavior, mysticism, etc. Therefore, our mental hygiene work has to be neither authoritarian—that is, imposed upon the population of the district—nor an academic "bringing science to the people." According to my experience, mental hygiene is efficient only when it understands how to pull out of the common human being his own natural understanding and sociability and to use those forces to fight the antisocial and irrational mental habits. I could not, of course, explain this principle thoroughly enough in this letter. I may make myself clear by saying that every man and woman, every boy and girl, has to take their part of responsibility for mental health in close cooperation with the psychiatrist, the social worker, and so forth. We shall have plenty of occasion to discuss these principles.

I am sure that you have understood why I wish to undertake this work: I do not believe in academic teaching alone and every one of us feels that to learn about the causes of the mental plague which is devastating the health of our population, and to learn how to handle these problems practically, is an endless task which has to be continued on and on.

15 March 1941

Mrs. Pops ("6–10 weeks left to live") after 8 days of orgone radiation: weight gain of 1 kg, 35–60 percent hemoglobin, blood count good, feels healthy, pain in back less severe, neck free, full of vigor.

Still no reply from Princeton.

19 March 1941

Second cancer patient has 85 percent hemoglobin instead of 35 percent! No pain!

Re Princeton: My report is obviously too much for them! They don't know what to make of it. They would like it to be true, but are afraid of making serious mistakes, both negative and positive. But I didn't do it, I just discovered it.

20 March 1941

The higher I climb, the farther my eye can see, and the vaster the infinite expanse of this remarkable life becomes, the quieter, lonelier, and more afraid I feel within. I fear for my closeness to the earth, to people and women, I fear for the wildness of my desire. It could carry me off and away from the heights into deep valleys, shaded regions where cooling breezes would stroke my brow. There is an incessant burning within me. No success, not even an answer to the most difficult question, is capable of quenching this flame. I have now given back life—at least for the moment—to three people who were marked for death. And it is as if I had merely performed a natural duty, nothing extraordinary, nothing stunning or singular. The pain caused by meanness is always greater, far greater, than the triumphant feeling of victory. Despite all the logic of my twenty years of work, I cannot grasp the fact that I—yes, I—am the one to be granted such great success. I, the man who has been homeless for thirty years, who has no mother, father, brother, the man they drove out and slandered, the man who so enjoys watching girls in bars, whom the girls are glad to see and sometimes happy to love! The greatest scientific achievement without academic office, title, position, money, or connections.

It's incredible! And it will not be allowed to happen without a disturbance. The officials and academicians will see to that.

How often have I wanted to give up—how often has the breath been knocked out of me; how many nights have I spent toiling to refute idiotic arguments. Actually there are three Nobel Prizes *I will not receive: biology*, for abiogenesis; *medicine*, for cancer vegetotherapy; *physics*, for orgone radiation.

During the last few days while two individuals were being saved from death, I felt as if I were faltering and had to give up, as if all the efforts of these twenty years had suddenly been gathered together and would overwhelm me. As if I couldn't go on. I have one great and dangerous weakness—namely, being deeply insulted when people behave basely and miserably. It shouldn't matter to me. But it does matter! Not even a successful cure for cancer could make up for Annie's rotten behavior. Additionally, I feel the faintest stirrings of hate, indifference, and irrationality.

I want to have children but I must not, after all that has happened. I must not bind anyone to myself, because I have not yet reached my goal. A long, hard road still stretches out before me. True, the two cancer patients do appear to be cured. But I must not—

22 March 1941

Today Lore told me that Annie had conferred with Dr. Kubie, secretary of the Analytic Association, about me, and that "they have me at their mercy."

29 March 1941

Murray from Union Settlement House has declined.

T O　A .　S .　N E I L L
❖ 1 April 1941

My dear Neill:

How is it possible, I ask myself, that as I know I have given birth to a very great knowledge, and that on the other hand all the many people whom I learned to know since about fifteen or twenty years and who know what was accomplished *do not do* something about it. There is one great gap between the understanding of the people who meet my work and the practice of all those people together. Very often I fantasize that if all those who came and have gone or are still there would cooperate and act as usual political party members do, then I may frankly say, the greatest and most efficient political movement which the world has ever seen would be at work and would bring about with perfect security all that Churchill and Roosevelt want, and every man in this world who honestly tries the best, and more than that. There is a gap between the fact that every single living human being in this world knows more or less clearly that the real life process is running on a quite different line than the apparent official process which is called diplomacy and politics. Still, the gap is there and somehow all those millions and millions do not seem to be able to find the proper form and organization for their knowledge of the real life process. Very often, I felt the temptation and even the responsibility "to do something about it"—that is, to organize our knowledge as the political parties organize their nonsense. A definite consideration or rather a feeling always kept me from doing so. The feeling was that the first real step into a partylike organization of real knowledge, truth, decency, and straightforwardness would immediately kill knowledge, truth, decency, and straightforwardness. That is because these activities of living matter are not to be organized, they are alive, and life which is productive, and swelling and acting and moving and making mistakes and correcting them and so forth, cannot be organized.

One of my students here once told me a story: "The devil in hell had heard that human beings have found the truth, the real truth. His advisers were shaken with terror. But the devil told them: Don't be afraid, go there amongst them and let them organize the truth they found." This is a very good and true story. I don't know any answer to this greatest of all problems. You can organize gangs, crooks, profit makers, a railroad, a war machine industry; you cannot organize life and truth.

Now to your questions: You are quite right saying that the orgasm reflex brings about the problem that so few partners can be found if you are perfectly healthy. But that was precisely the point which made me break through into the field of sociology and sex politics in 1927. It was the fact that a sick world is fitted for sick human beings and not for healthy ones; that healthy ones are lost in this world and very often even despised and condemned. Your suggestion about the difference in the sexual structure in the adolescent and the grown-up is also correct.

The problem of women being in the army is very difficult. It is quite clear that, as you write and everyone can observe, the army spoils the character because of sexual starvation and rudeness of the soldiers. Women in the army would settle the problem, but, on the other hand, every militarist will tell you that women in the army could mean a hampering of the most characteristic habit of the army and that is automatic, mechanical discipline. Here again, the incapability of life to be mechanized or organized hits against an institution in the mechanized civilization which is based (and by necessity) upon stiff stomachs, retracted behinds, high chests, rigid musculature.

The essence of all those things is a belief that the natural life process has broken through in our age, striving for release and creating new forms of life and confusing all human beings. The old forms have brought society into the abyss of war and destruction. The new forms are not yet born and nobody knows what they will look like. But one fact is clear: The perversities and lunatic happenings which were brought to the peak by Hitler can only be conquered by life itself. I think we can only try to understand and help as much as we can. There is no authority born yet in this field, and should an authority once be created, then I am afraid a new setback would take place.

11 April 1941

This war will be a war of continents, classes, and races all in one. A war of maniacs against maniacs, a war of individuals against individuals; the millions are waiting! They await the fiery sign of reason. It will burst into flame when irrationality in all camps has consumed itself, burned itself up, and is extinguished. Not a moment sooner will the march of the millions resound nor will that which lives and exists begin to sprout forth. But first this world's pollution must smolder in its own stench. No word, no deed—even the most courageous—will penetrate now. A great barren wasteland and immense quietness will follow the turmoil. And then slowly, ever so slowly, hesitantly, cautiously, and falteringly, a new life will arise.

Truth matures slowly, permeates slowly. Mankind took aeons to develop from elementary forms and the process was marked by error and death. *Must* this be so? I do not know the answer! But I do know that unarmored life cannot be defeated as long as this planet is still suspended in the orgone ocean enveloping it. Should this planet perish and life along with it, then other earths, other worlds will arise and life will go on. It will remain, mature, think, feel, falter, perish —arise again.

Comfort? There is no comfort, only truth! In the depths of an ocean of desolate unconsciousness there exists a spark—am *I* its bearer, or another? It pains *me*—the spark feels not pain—it leaps—it cannot be quenched.

Perhaps—it may be—someday we shall be able to harness the spark, to direct and organize it. Then man will have fathomed himself. Today he can only scream and blunder, as he has done for thousands of years. This view of man and his life is bleak, but true: there can be no mastery of life without cognition.

This development has only just begun. It will require thousands of years. But what significance do even two thousand years have? Was Lenin much further ahead than Jesus? He failed even worse than Jesus because he came two thousand years later.

The only thing remaining is to preserve a part of the truth for future millennia. Is it important that cancer can now be cured? It *was* important but is no longer! It *was* important to exterminate the plague, but is no longer!

All that is of importance is to preserve, to save truth, the fundamentals of truth. For truth is the most important manifestation of life! It is "becoming"—it is life itself! Nature cannot lie.

The convulsions of orgastic pleasure cannot lie. They are either present or not. They cannot be feigned. They are true—i.e., existent and functioning. They are true, even if only *one* body experiences them while millions fear.

The sense of life in human beings, which is an extension of the sense of life in all living matter, has manifested itself in millions of ways. It once existed in truth in each of the following: in music, art, poetry, genuine science. It is still existent, even in the final, rotten phases of alcoholism, in brothels, and, yes, even in constipation. *For suffering is nothing other than perceiving that the pleasure of life is lacking.*

It is conceivable, possible, that now—in 1941 or 1942, after so much suffering—unarmored life will make a great, serious, final, and successful effort.

12 April 1941

Clarity of thought dwells in immense loneliness, in spaces like those separating the stars, billions of light-years wide, so that the bodies do not clash but simply revolve in solitude. Bodies are unhappy and cannot think clearly when they are crowded, where one foot treads upon another. Occasionally they feel impelled toward the crowd, in order to see whether it has changed and whether they still fit in. But the members of the crowd have not changed. They continue to push and shove for a little space. They do not sense, cannot imagine the vast infinities, for they fancy themselves secure when they inhale a neighbor's sweaty scent. Once in a while you find a person who looks as if he were able to imagine the infinities. You speak to him of loneliness and as he listens a glow brightens his face. He *appears* to understand even though he does not. Finally you discover that he is commonplace, extremely banal, narrow, lethargic, vain. He has sighted loneliness *in the mirror*—and he flees—or he accompanies you a part of the way, soars with you, only to crash back down into the crowd—wasted energy! Then you live in solitude once again where you can think and breathe freely.

It is good to dive into the crowd once in a while, to convince oneself that it is a mere shuffling, back and forth, with no purpose or goal, just shuffling, back and forth.

Then you return to breathing the pure, fresh air of the mountains, where it storms and worlds collide. Happy? No! But alive!

T O   L E W I S   G O L D I N G E R *
❖ *16 April 1941*

Dear Mr. Goldinger:

According to our conversation last night I wish to summarize the reasons which make it not only desirable but essential for me to obtain the endorsement of my Viennese medical license:

1. The subject of research and the medical technique which I am teaching here on the basis of my vocation are new in the field of medicine. That means that proper authority should be attached to it in order to fulfill the task of medical teaching.

2. Teaching a definite medical technique to American doctors, without having the license to handle the patients of the students myself in case of emergency, is impossible.

*A New York attorney.

3. It harms the factual authority of my endeavor if my students are licensed to apply my technique and I am not licensed.

4. Having to deal with many medical matters and persons, it is embarrassing to have to answer again and again the same question whether I have the license to practice medicine.

5. In my cancer research I am hampered completely by the fact that the borderline between experiment and treatment cannot be drawn strictly, and that will become more and more so the further the experiment leads into practical medical measures with human beings.

6. I claim the right, according to law, of endorsement of my Viennese medical license, on the basis of my twenty years of experience as physician and teacher, especially in the new branch of medicine which I have developed, and which is appreciated and accepted not only by European but also by American medical men.

You will understand, dear Mr. Goldinger, what I told you and the other students so often, that the situation as it is now is unbearable, and that it may even force me to stop all teaching in order to prevent embarrassing situations. Especially the events of the last four weeks, which seem to prove clearly that the orgone radiation is curing cancer in a surprisingly effective way, make it absolutely necessary that I and all who work in the field have to be legally correctly equipped to accomplish our task.

TO ALBERT EINSTEIN
1 May 1941

Dear Mr. Einstein,

During the last ten weeks, ever since I sent my report to you, events have taken place that are of such crucial importance that I believe I must not keep them from you.

Approximately three weeks after I sent my report to you, the man who looks after my tax affairs for me and thus knew about my tests involving cancer mice, asked me whether I would be prepared to conduct an experiment involving the sister of one of his friends who had been seriously ill in bed with cancer for two years. The doctors had completely given up on her, and she was expected to die any day. She was in severe pain, her spine had been destroyed in two places, and several metastatic tumors (originating from her breast cancer) had been found in her pelvic bone. I decided to conduct an experiment with orgone radiation. For half an hour to an hour (1–2 hours Op*) each day, I exposed the patient to the radiation by placing her inside an orgone accumulator that had been specifically constructed for humans. In the course of approximately three weeks the pain disappeared, the blood hemoglobin rose from 33 percent to a normal level of 85 percent; the X-rays showed that the tumors in her pelvic bone were in the process of dissolving and that the bone which had been destroyed was regenerating itself by putting down calcium deposits. Today the patient can be regarded as *temporarily* healed. She does her work, has taken her children back to live with her after a two-year separation; she feels well and is free of pain. Of course, nobody can predict how long this state of affairs is going to last, because this patient was dying when she was brought—half carried—to me.

When I saw the results I have just described, I decided to perform the experiment on three more cancer patients who had been given up to an imminent death. In these three other cases, orgone radiation again proved to be extraordinarily effective, in particular through biologically charging the red blood corpuscles. In one of the cases, it was possible to observe directly how the tumor on the skull dissolved. In another case, where the esophagus had become almost totally occluded so that the patient could no longer take any food, the ability to transport food via the esophagus was restored after the *second* course of radiation. The choking feeling disappeared, the patient put on three pounds in six days, felt strong, and was once more able to sleep.

In all these cases, every step in the experiment has been registered in detail. Of course, I cannot say how long the patient is going to live or if new tumors will occur. One fact is certain, however, namely that the experiments involving orgone radiation are considerably more accurate in humans than in mice. This is because, first, it is easier to monitor the organism in the case of humans compared to

---

*Op = orgone potential.

mice and, second, because tumors in humans are much smaller in relation to body size than tumors in cancer mice.

News of these results has spread fast; in each case the relatives of the patients are extremely active and helpful. Today the brother of the first patient arrived with the message that yesterday his house had been overrun by the family members of five cancer patients.

To sum up, based on the observations to date, the effects of the experiments on humans are as follows:

Elimination of severe pain

Dissolution of the tumors

Elimination of anemia

Biological charging of red blood corpuscles

These preliminary results in humans are of course in no way proportional to the gigantic problems that arise with every step taken.

1. Is it possible to destroy every kind of tumor?

2. Will it be possible to prevent tumors from recurring?

3. At what stage of the cancer is a cure still possible?

4. How will different patients tolerate the breakdown of the tumor and its elimination from the body?

5. How will brain tumors react?

6. How fast may tumors be dissolved, etc., etc.?

It can be expected that the use of orgone radiation in cancer patients at an *early* stage of the disease, immediately after the growth has been discovered (and not two or three years later, when the metastatic process has spread and destroyed important organs), will have a very favorable effect on the overall work and on the prognosis of the therapy. For the time being, however, I myself regard the results with amazement and hesitation. I have not talked to anybody about this new experience. It is important to wait until more results have been obtained, especially regarding the duration of the effect. I shall then probably have to send a report to the central authority of the cancer-fighting organizations.

I am starting to use specially made tubes to connect the orgone accumulators with metal containers buried in the ground. It is apparent that the orgone energy, in keeping with the experiments which I undertook in response to your letter in February, can best be collected in insulated soil. The design has been simplified, because I now bury only tubes made of sheet metal which are about two to three feet long and have a diameter of approximately one foot, so that the cylindrical space is empty and the soil closely surrounds the outside of the metal tubes.

I assume that these reports will please you, and I send you my greetings.

TO　HARRY　BRISSMAN [*]
❖ 5 May 1941

Dear Mr. Brissman:

All the time since I conducted the orgone experiment with the patients I had the definite feeling that a disaster could happen to this work of mine if I did not succeed in taking the utmost precautions. I emphasized again and again that we should not overrate the apparently great results which we have achieved in the case of your sister and all the other patients. Cancer is a very complicated and grave disease. It is true, we have seen results: diminishing and disappearance of pains, dissolution of tumors, improvement of the blood, gaining in weight and appetite—in one word, the orgone radiation is effective in the sense that it charges up the whole body, reaches every part of it through the blood, and thus stimulates the natural fighting forces of the organism. But just because this is true we have, I think, to do everything in order to provide all the facilities necessary to secure this new type of treatment for mankind, and not to lose our faith in it if one or more of my patients would be unfortunate enough to have come too late and to succumb to the disease. I know you agree with me completely on this particular point, but I know also that it is a different thing to see your relative walk around, feel good, etc., and to agree with me, and it is still another thing to see this beloved relative dead after all. Then the greatest enthusiasm and the deepest conviction which you may have acquired in these months may fade away completely. The greater the enthusiasm before, the greater the disappointment afterwards may be. Of course, such a disappointment would be disastrous for my work. As you know, it is

---

[*] The brother of a cancer patient in treatment with Dr. William Thorburn, one of Reich's students.

pioneer work and has to stand up against tremendous odds on all sides, professional, economical, ideological, and personal. A very hard and difficult fight has led me on through twenty years up to the point where I dared say as a physician: I have definite proof that I am on the best way to conquer the cancer disease. Any unjustified rumor which would arise from any possible death of one or more of those patients that the orgone radiation is worthless and not effective against cancer, would be ruinous not to me as man and physician, but to the hundreds and thousands of cancer patients and others suffering from ailments in this world. Scientific research and experimental work are not to be compared with any other human attempt, especially not with politics. No quick results and no surprising ones are to be obtained in this field if they are *true* results and lasting ones.

Hard work through many, many years has to be done on every level which has been reached in the course of the progress. It took me ten years of clinical and experimental work to understand the cancer disease; it took another five years of hard work full of worries and sacrifices to find and to secure the orgone radiation; it will take probably another ten years of hard and troublesome work until we shall be able to say the cancer disease is definitely conquered.

It would mean very much to you, to the other relatives, and of course to me to see human beings die, with whom you had success so far, an incredible success never heard of before in the history of medicine. It is a great triumph, but I may remind you that when the diphtheria serum was discovered, only 30 percent of the cases were saved, and although the germ which causes tuberculosis was discovered many years ago, medical science has not succeeded up to now in conquering tuberculosis.

I hope very much that the good cooperation which was established between this laboratory and so many valuable human beings will continue even in the case of the death of all of the patients treated at present. Excuse me for this apparent rudeness, but in a war against a pestilence and an enemy you have to be rude, and you have to look ahead. You know, and I don't hesitate to say it, that, according to experimental proof, a wall has been penetrated definitely which has obstructed the path toward the goal of conquering cancer. I dare say also that many roads are open now, since the biological energy has been discovered, to fight many kinds of other diseases. The responsibility is not only mine; it is that of the public which suffers as well. You can be sure of my closest cooperation as a physician, but I may express my sincere hope that what you have seen in these short two months has given you a proper insight into the real nature of the only thing in the world which is worthwhile to live for, science and truth. I know that I ask very much of you and of the others in the case of disaster, but far ahead is something which counts very, very much. The goal is to fight the disease before it starts to devastate the human organism, to crash down spines, destroy the blood, and so forth. There is good hope that it will be possible to prevent the outbreak not only of cancer but of many other diseases, if we only give the newly discovered orgone radiation a chance to prove what it can accomplish under all the necessary circumstances.

T O   A L V I N   J O H N S O N *
❖ 8 *May 1941*

Dear Dr. Johnson:

I wish to inform you about some results achieved in my laboratory of which only very few people know. When I came over to the United States a year and a half ago, I not only brought a well-equipped biophysical laboratory with me but also a rather important discovery. In 1936, still in Norway, I had hit upon a phenomenon in glowing [incandescent] and swelled matter (see *Die Bione*, 1938) which has led me to the discovery of an energy in the atmosphere and in the earth, which proved to be specifically biologically effective. I did not publish a word about it because I thought it would be better to wait until the discovered energy revealed most of its secrets. I called this energy "orgone."

In the course of 1940 I succeeded in measuring, concentrating, and making visible this radiation. Some devices have been built, and patents have been applied for them and have been filed in Washington.

Since the discovery of the radiation I worked in my laboratory on

*Dr. Johnson replied on 14 May 1941. He thanked Reich for the "significant courses" he had given at the college, but advised him that they could not be continued because "your work belongs in a medical college or in your private laboratory, rather than in an institution like ours."

experiments with cancer mice, and after approximately two years of many errors and trials, I succeeded in destroying cancerous tumors in cancer mice, and in prolonging their lives (comparative to non-treated mice as 9:3 prolongation of life span). Although I did not publish anything and spoke to very few people about it, some lay-people had heard about it and asked me whether I would be willing to try the effect of the orgone radiation on human beings who suffer from cancer without hope of recovery.

Eight weeks ago I started with the first experiments on human beings. The radiation proved to be much more effective than on cancer mice, because the tumors in human beings are much smaller in relation to the body than in mice. I succeeded in rescuing several human beings from impending death by charging up the blood, destroying tumors which have been inaccessible to any other kind of treatment, and, furthermore, in removing strong pains and getting the patients out of bed. I could, of course, write much more about it, but I prefer to wait for further development. I do not know yet how long the results will hold.

I have informed only one person of great importance in Princeton about these events, and I thought it proper to let you know about it. The matter will not become publicly known for a long time to come, because publicity could only harm its further development. I should, of course, be glad to give you any further information if you would like to know more about it. Meanwhile I would appreciate it very much if you would not speak about it to anyone.

It may also interest you that I arrived at these results by application of the sociological method of investigation which taught me to see that the educational influence upon the biological functions of the body are of the greatest importance concerning creation of diseases in the autonomic life system. I lectured in part about this at the New School. Tremendous problems are ahead, and, of course, you may understand that there are very few clues as to how to meet them.

❖ 12 May 1941

Conference with Mr. Goldinger, lawyer, about possibility of a trial on a misdemeanor—practicing without a license.

Resolved to go through with it even if all the patients die!

T O　A L B E R T　E I N S T E I N [*]
17 May 1941

Dear Mr. Einstein,

I am wondering why I have still not received any reply to my letters of 20 February and 1 May. For the sake of the matter, I would be grateful if you wrote and told me clearly whether my reports were further investigated or whether they are of no interest. I would not have asked you this question yet, had it not been for the fact that word has got around about my experiments involving the treatment of cancer patients and every day new demands are being made.

22 May 1941
(afterthought to my birthday on 24 March 1941)

It is customary to receive gifts on one's birthday, and to say thank you for them. It is unusual on one's own birthday to hand out presents, and to give thanks for the fact that what is otherwise called providence or fate was kind enough to allow one to offer one's fellow men such a present. The present which I, on my forty-fourth birthday, can offer to my friends, colleagues, children, and many sick people is ready. What is questionable is whether I will soon have the opportunity to thank the world for accepting my present. Between 8 and 24 March, with the aid of orgone radiation, I was able to save the lives—at least temporarily—of two people who were facing certain death from cancer. This was the first time that this has happened in the history of medicine. Whether they are permanently cured, only the future will tell. But at this moment they are without doubt healthier, pain-free, fresh, no longer confined to bed, nor in need of morphine. Their blood is normal.

I admit that even I find this success too fantastic, so that I am unwilling to believe it. It is good that objective scientific analysis forces me to believe in it. The fact that three small children have now got their mother back increases my satisfaction as a physician.

People will ask by what witchcraft I have achieved this. As honest

*This letter was not sent.

as I can be, my reply is: This was no witchery; rather I clung to a scientific theory and a way of thinking which proved their accuracy and reliability by leading me to practical success. Our success can be attributed to a characteristic which is in general feared: *complete lack of respect for human institutions and deepest trust in the infallibility of the natural law.* This is a trust that is very similar to that which the believer puts in God. It is not belief in a world beyond, but the most consistent possible pursuit of the this-worldliness and the earthly reality of our life, feelings, sensation, loving, and suffering. It is the *natural scientific* experiencing of the universe that can compete with any deeply religious experience.

On 24 March 1941, looking back on scientific research since 1919, I counted myself among the luckiest if not exactly the happiest people on this planet. A new medical, biological, and physical science came into being. It is called orgone biophysics and the technique of its use is called orgone therapy.

It is larger, broader, more honest than we humans are capable of being. It seems to me a high privilege to serve this [new science]. In the same way that "nature" is called upon to replace the concept of "God," or at least to merge with it, so the scientist is called upon to replace God's priests. The priest of science must be as close to nature as the genuine priest feels to God. To be a priest of science is probably the greatest [mark of] favor, if we interpret priestliness in the good sense which our forefathers gave it: guardian of nature within us, dominant force over nature outside ourselves; in the human mind not the expression of a mystical force that humiliates us, but the hitherto highest accomplishment of experiencing what even the most primitive bion or plasma structures may experience when they stretch in pleasure. The biological task of science is not only to research what is true but also to combat the general human anxiety of anything cosmic, natural, and simple by providing humans with simple truths. With the victory of nature in humans over fear and the unnatural, much suffering will be eradicated. We are at the beginning of understanding life. That means the beginning of the end of all mentality which seeks the sense of earthly [existence] in killing and in peacock-like life. It also means the end of all senseless ideology of sacrifice and replaces it with the courageous struggle for happiness in life, for which orgone biophysics provides an unshakable scientific foundation. There has been much talk, and there still is, of death rays. For the first time, one is justified in talking of *life rays*. They exist, have been seen, measured, collected, and they can heal cancer. We have reason to be proud—proud to occupy the place which science has prepared for us in this life. Filling this position requires solidarity, courage, good human sense, camaraderie. I hope that I can demonstrate better than before that I will not fail to meet any of these challenges as long as I have the sensation of life in me. This will be my thanks for all the friendship, help, and cooperation which my colleagues and students have shown for the cause in the most desperate situations.

29 *May 1941*

Still no answer from Princeton.

a. They do not intend to reply.

b. They do not understand.

c. They are taking their time in seeing something that is astonishingly simple.

d. They are squabbling with each other.

T O   J U L I U S   W E I N B E R G E R *
❖ *29 May 1941*

Dear Mr. Weinberger:

In order to have the things properly on file and to avoid any possible misunderstandings, I wish to repeat what was the essence of our discussion yesterday.

Having been "my own Rockefeller Foundation" for about fifteen years, I do not think it advisable to enter into a discussion with someone who "strongly suspects that the result would be completely negative" in the case that I would be "the sort of a person who would be willing to try a definite quantitative test proposed by someone else" especially if this person did not try first to make himself acquainted with my work. Of course, such tests could be easily selected. One

*Scientist at the Radio Corporation of America.

could, for instance, transplant tumor substance into 20 mice, expose 10 of them to the orgone radiation and keep the other 10 as controls. One could try the radiation, in a cooperative way, with cancerous human beings. One could repeat some of my own experiments with cancer mice. But I reject being looked upon by some official of a foundation as one of its humble employees.

An institution whose responsibility consists in promoting new scientific discoveries ought to know about the campaign which has been fought in the public from 1937 through 1939 in Scandinavia and in France, when the bions were discovered. I think that my responsibility for the proper conduct of the research ought to be matched by the responsibility of such institutions to know about it. With several cancer patients saved from impending death by the orgone radiation, there is no reason to be afraid of the future.

You know that I am willing *and able* to show the phenomena and the charts and the case histories and my laboratory to everyone who is a real scientist—i.e., who has the definite kind of structure to listen and to see what another scientist has to say. In short, the way in which Mr. Weaver* approached the matter seems rather out of place to me and arrogant. I have enough specific knowledge of biology and biophysics to say that especially this branch of science has no reason at all to be arrogant. I would be much more justified in demanding that the one who wants to test my experiments should first submit himself to a test in my laboratory to show whether he knows, for instance, what the autoclaving of blood indicates in cancer persons compared with that of healthy human beings.

I thank you very heartily for your friendly attempt to help. I could have predicted out of my previous experiences what would happen, but I did not want to discourage your attempt. If it means some consolation to you take comfort in the fact that my work has done very well for nearly two decades with almost no material help from outside and will continue to do so.

I intend now to write down the whole story of the discovery of the orgone radiation, the bions, and the cancer research according to available material and facts, and I shall let the world take it or leave it.

*Warren Weaver, director of the Natural Sciences Program of the Rockefeller Foundation. His specific goal was to fund research that would bring methods of physics and chemistry into the life sciences.

T O   L E W I S   G O L D I N G E R
❖ *1 June 1941*

Dear Mr. Goldinger

You have asked me to write down my position in the matter of my having a child with Ilse Ollendorff without being married.

This letter should not only give you the information concerning our private contract but is also intended as a declaration of principle in the event that some person or organization should start a campaign against my scientific and medical activity.

It is quite possible that sooner or later a bishop or a psychiatrist or a politician will "find out about me." In such a case I would ask you to use this letter in public, be it before a jury, in a newspaper, or anywhere else.

Having gone through such accidents several times, I know very well what arguments will be used against me. One will claim that:

I am destroying the marriage institution, family, and morality

I am committing the crime of adultery

I seduce the youth to immoral habits and actions

I was a communist

One will urge that I be deported, jailed, hanged, or lynched.

One will claim that I am in subversive activity, that I wish to destroy the government, that my bions, the orgone, the cancer experiments are bunk, that I am seducing my students, that I have practiced without a license, that I had left my family, etc., etc. Therefore, this letter will be frank.

I want a child but I do not wish to have it with a marriage license. That is not against the law, as you told me. You and others will ask why I do not comply with the social rules. I do comply with every social rule which is in accordance with human nature, decency, with work, love, and science. *I do not comply with rules which are superimposed upon the people by neurotics.* For instance, I don't go to church. I do not enjoy empty social gatherings. I do not believe in life insurance or in heaping up money in the bank. These are appreciated social rules.

I do not marry because of two reasons:

1. I saw so much misery, psychic suppression, lies, and cheating in marriage during twenty-two years of medical practice that I got to

believe firmly in the freedom from marriage. That does not mean that I wish to forbid or to make it impossible for everyone to marry. I simply wish to keep myself out of it. Marriage is today not a natural alliance of two people who love each other. People marry because they are sex-starved and cannot obtain sexual intercourse easily without a marriage license. When people say that they want to marry, they really mean that they want to sleep together. I do not have to tell you as a lawyer how disastrous that is. This kind of marrying kills the real wish for marriage and partnership. And it kills or harms the children who result from such marriages. I know that one can have a family without running for a license in order to sleep together. I think such kind of marriage is deeply immoral, unnatural, and ill.

2. I was "legally" married for twelve years. I have two nearly grown-up children from this marriage. I regret ever having entered it. When I fought desperately with my first discoveries, she said it was not important.

When I found the pathological role of the family, she objected, feared that I would not support her.

When I urged her to study and to be independent, she was angry. She wanted to be dependent. When I taught her science, psychoanalysis, medicine, independence, she turned everything against me.

I made an honest agreement with her about my children. She tried to steal the love of my children.

When I was thrown out of the Psychoanalytic Society, she was on the side of my enemies.

She filled my children with hatred toward me. She told them that I was crazy. She assisted the crook Fenichel.

She told my children that I did not pay for them, whereas I had paid penny by penny.

3 June 1941

Until now man has produced his intellectual achievements within the framework of a struggle *against* his natural impulses: mathematics, technology, the conquests of Cortez, political conquests, etc.

In doing so he drowns out the screams of nature from which he has fled.

For a short time now people have been involved in discovering nature within themselves, in eliminating the antagonisms between intellect and instinct and helping nature to regain its rights.

A new era of human intellectuality is beginning. When man has found his way "back to nature," his rational mind will be filled with healthy impulsiveness; instinct and rationality welded together will make possible achievements in the coming centuries which no drive-negating intellectuality could ever equal. The achievements will be alive, not mechanical; social relationships will become genuine rather than political; the mental results will be ingenuous, geared to nature, not complicated and contrary to nature.

This occurred to me while watching the clever, directed movements of a large brown beetle.

T O   J U L I U S   W E I N B E R G E R
❖ 6 June 1941

Dear Mr. Weinberger:

I have your letter of 3 June and would like to set you straight on a few points on which you seem to lack the necessary information. My statement that the Rockefeller Foundation ought to be familiar with my work can hardly be called "somewhat extreme" in view of the facts. The facts are, e.g., that I sent the Rockefeller Foundation in Paris reports concerning the first discoveries of the vesicular disintegration of matter and the bion cultures obtained from such preparations. I also contacted the Paris representative of the Rockefeller Foundation when he was in Oslo in 1938. Some time later, the foundation informed me that they were not further interested in my discovery and that they wished me good luck.

Therefore, the fact that the foundation not only *ought to* know about my work, but that its European representative *did* know about it as long as three years ago, is a matter of record.

In addition, the discovery of the bions and the fact that protozoans develop from them, published in 1938, was demonstrated, by way of microfilms, to many members of the French Academy by Dr. Roger du Teil of the Centre Universitaire Méditerranéen in Nice. Lectures on the subject of this discovery were given at the Sorbonne and the Academy in Paris. The discovery was the subject of a violent newspaper campaign in Scandinavia which lasted for many months and resulted in enormous publicity. One of my coworkers was discharged from a French university because of his cooperation in the discovery, which fact caused a great stir among scientists. Furthermore, a great many so-called scientists all over the world know about my work but all they do is decide that I am crazy, so they don't have to bother to look into it. On the other hand, Professor Lapique of the Académie des Sciences as well as the Académie on its own and officially, confirmed the finding of ameboid movement and bacterial forms in my autoclaved—i.e., highly sterilized—preparations. Thus, I am indeed justified in saying that the Rockefeller Foundation *ought* to know about it.

I am surprised by your argument that the Rockefeller Foundation could not know about my work because it was published by a not very well-known publishing house. Well, to get this point straight: In order to keep my work free from the unscientific and irrational procedures which so largely dominate scientific activities, my institute, with the help of my European coworkers, founded a publishing house of its own. Whether this publishing house was very well-known or not is beside the point here. But it is my belief that it is the duty of such institutions as the Rockefeller Foundation to assist the work of the "little man" in science, and not only that of the "big men" who, on the basis of a particular way of social living or good connections, or because of their willingness to sacrifice truth or defend half-truths, have access to very "well-known" publishing houses.

As you know, important discoveries have usually been made just by men who were off the well-trodden path of the "well-known." I wonder what would have happened to the discovery in question if it had been made not by me, a man in fairly good economic circumstance and with an academic standing, but by a little country doctor or some technician in a small-town laboratory. It would have been lost "for humanity," as you say. Such a country doctor or technician could not have founded a publishing house, not even a "not very well-known" one. Neither would he have had the opportunity to lecture about his work at a university, thus making it known to a few people willing to take up the fight for it.

As you know, the discovery of the vesicular disintegration of matter led to the discovery of the orgone radiation and opened a new avenue of approach to the cancer problem. These things are so far removed from the "well-known" and are so much at variance with the customary mechanical thinking in biology that I do not believe that your endeavor could be successful. As you know, I am willing to show everything in my laboratory to anyone. But I am not willing and I am not going to expose my discovery to any unscientific, irrational, or arrogant behavior. I have no time for fruitless discussions, because my work keeps me very busy, day and night.

11 June 1941

I would *so* love to leave the field of sex, become a "pure" scientist, cure "pure" cancer. But it can't be done! Each simple case of cancer, rheumatism, cardiac neurosis, leads straight back to the gigantic problem of the sexual plague. I must be faithful to this conviction if I do not want to become a scientific scoundrel—and that's good!

12 June 1941

The owner [of the house], Mr. Lester Brion, has given me notice to leave (as of 1 November 1941). A neighbor has complained about the mice in the cellar. It is not an easy matter to relocate the laboratory. How would I continue the cancer experiments? Any house owner would throw me out.

It will soon be obvious who the celebrities of this century really are. Still no answer from Einstein.

13 June 1941

When I set out to look for a new house for the laboratory, they asked me whether I was Jewish or Christian. I said, "Imagine if I were to ask a patient whether he was Jewish or Christian before treating his cancer." "But that's different. That's a humanitarian matter, not a social one," replied the bureaucrat. America in 1941!

TO TAGE PHILIPSON*
16 June 1941

Dear Dr. Philipson,

The news about the work in Oslo is very troubling. I really do not understand why there should be any problems with the work, particularly at that location. Nor do I understand why I have had no news for more than eighteen months from over there.

You touch on some very important questions, but I cannot, for example, provide an answer to whether the disease process itself can be regarded as a kind of healing process. Obviously, the cancer tumor is the result of a pathological attempt at healing and is not the disease process itself. To that extent, therefore, you are right. But this problem is too difficult and would have to be verified in each and every case.

I regard some of your comments on the orgone book as extremely felicitous; on the other hand, they to some extent also reflect the typical reaction which physicists have to our work.

When you talk to a physicist, I would recommend that you first of all find out very precisely whether, in addition to his physics, the physicist in question also has any relationship to life functions. Only then will you be able to talk with him about our affairs and not get lost in trivial details into which he will drag you in order to avoid having to say anything about the central issue—namely, that life comes about through the development of energy from matter itself by swelling. Please be patient until my work has matured to the stage where I can organize and answer all the many questions which orgone research has thrown up in the last two years.

Much more important than all the detailed questions is the fact that orgone energy exists in the atmosphere and in the ground; it can be concentrated and it has the ability to destroy cancerous tumors and to biologically charge the organism. In discussions with physicists, I believe that the standpoint to be maintained is that they should first of all disregard everything they have learned and know; they should immerse themselves in the specific characteristics of our biophysics and in particular those of orgone energy; only then should they attempt to estab-

*Danish physician and student of Reich's.

lish the various links and connections to known physical facts. It is never fruitful and very often harmful to consider and judge a new fact immediately from the standpoint of old facts. Whenever I take on a new patient, I do not first of all think of previous patients, but instead I consider him as a new case, independent of other cases, in order to discover his particularities. Only later do I ask myself whether the new characteristics which I have discovered agree with the characteristics of previous patients, or whether they contradict them, etc. I am writing all this in order to give you some idea of the methodology which has so far yielded such enormous research results. It enables one to maintain one's own standpoint more easily and also to understand what one has in common or not with known natural science.

17 June 1941

The pain caused by cancer can be traced to the general contraction of the sympathetic nerves. Life withdraws from the affected point. That is why orgone, which has a vagotonic effect, can help.

Similarly, cachexia must be explained as atrophying degeneration of the tissue. It is the contraction of the life apparatus, and not the tumor, that causes the tissue to shrink.

18 June 1941

A father asked me to treat his eight-month-old child, who is suffering from cancer. He ran off to the AMA and asked them who I am. They said that I was not a doctor and that they would have me arrested.

T O   C A R O L E   B A R N A R D [*]
❖ 7 July 1941

My dear Miss Bernard:

I hope very much that all our patients are doing well and that you did not encounter any difficulties. Please do not fail to inform me

---

[*]Reich's laboratory assistant.

immediately if something unusual should happen. I rely upon your judgment which you acquired in finding out how long a patient can sit in the accumulator. Please make sure that whenever dizziness or headaches appear, the treatment be interrupted.

I also hope that you personally can enjoy some of the free time which you have now at your disposal. Please read the enclosed letter to every single patient.

TO CANCER PATIENTS
❖ 7 July 1941

My dear Mrs. Marcus, Mrs. Entegart, Jacobs, Mr. Kroul, Stein, and Robert (alternately):

I would like to be sure that you have understood that I did not leave the city and you without any good reason and not merely for pleasure purposes. In this year since September 1940 so many things of such tremendous importance have happened that I had to find several weeks of quietness to coordinate and to write down the results achieved so far. It was impossible for me to do this necessary theoretical work and writing in the turmoil of the everyday routine. Those results and writings are in the first line to your benefit even if you may not be ready or able to realize that immediately. An experiment is not to be compared to a walk on a nice established and marked road. It is rather comparable to a difficult searching, climbing and jumping and falling and rising again in the thickness of a wild forest full of swamps, wild animals, and deep abysses. You never know where you are going to break your neck. I have learned so much from what you have experienced that I dare hope to be able to apply your contributions to scientific research upon other sick human beings.

Please let me be assured that every one of you will let me know about how he feels, and that you will not get discouraged if once in a while you are exposed to a setback.

I have done a good deal of work in these ten days of absence and I look forward to seeing you all again happy and healthy.

10 July 1941

I very much fear that the experiment with the weighing scale involves the problem of gravity.

TO TAGE PHILIPSON
21 July 1941

Dear Dr. Philipson:

I am glad that you have received the manuscript. It is very good that you are searching for links with official academic medicine in various journals. I do not doubt that you will find vast amounts of "proof" of the accuracy of our theory. However, I think you are making a slight mistake in regarding these proofs as "proof" of the accuracy of our views. I have not developed a theory which now needs confirmation; instead, the achievement of sexual-economic theory was that the tension-charge formula finally explained the fundamental connection between infinitely many known medical and biological facts. My essay "The Basic Antithesis of Vegetative Life"* is based not on my own findings but instead solely on known physiological facts. What is decisive, therefore, in our new medicine is not the fact in itself, but the application of the basic biological formula to all known facts and those still to be discovered. For example, the report by Christiani about the dissolution of cancer cells by normal serum and the failure of serum from cancer patients to dissolve such cells is in itself interesting, but it is unusable. It will not be usable until we understand energetically *why* the cancer cells act this way in one case and that way in another. In order to answer such an everyday medical question one must concretely determine the corresponding biological properties of the serum, with the help of the tension-charge formula. I am naturally still a long way from being able to answer such questions, but I do stress the methodological principle of research which in the long term will effortlessly solve all these matters. Since you mention the immunity theory, I must comment that up to

---

*Included in *The Bioelectrical Investigation of Sexuality and Anxiety* (New York: Farrar, Straus and Giroux, 1982).

the present the principle behind immunization remains completely unknown. Because of my observations on orgone therapy, I can assume with good reason that they will solve the puzzle of immunity.

You are doubtless correct in stating that infectious diseases also belong in the orgone pathology of the organism, as will probably easily be demonstrated in the case of TB. But before we get too deeply into any more detailed studies, we must ourselves be clear about the most important details of the orgone function in the organism. I can only ask you to be patient until I have reached that point.

Please write frequently in order to maintain contact, and please greet all our friends.

TO J. H. LEUNBACH *
21 July 1941

Dear Leunbach,

I was pleased to receive your letter because I had heard nothing from you for almost two years.

It would be nice if all the workers in our field could get together and make personal contact once more. A great deal has happened in the last two years about which you know nothing. Wolfe is now trying to get our journal going again here; in addition, a large group of laypeople, mainly relatives of cured cancer patients, are very involved in our work. They are very helpful. In fact, I was more or less thrown out of my apartment because I had too many visitors, and I also kept animals there. Now my friends are buying me a house for my work so that it will no longer be dependent on some landlord. Basically, the problems of existence are the same as before, except that here in America it is much easier to get what one needs and to push ahead with the work.

*Danish physician and member of Reich's sex-political organization, Sexpol.

TO   WILLIAM   F.   THORBURN *
❖ 22 July 1941

Dear Dr. Thorburn:

I have your letter of 19 July. I hope very much that the case of Mrs. Pops depresses you from a purely human standpoint and not from the standpoint of our work. The radiation cannot, of course, restitute cracked spines and cannot cure a rather grave neurosis and a miserable marriage. Apart from the personal tragedy of Mrs. Pops, I am inclined to be rather glad that you and all the others who got in contact with sexual economy only a year ago or so are getting the opportunity to look into matters as they really are and not as business or hunger for fame or expectations of miracles would like to have them. Unless one learns to deal just with the odd things as they are and to stand through not one year but twenty years, no success can be achieved, seen from a larger viewpoint. I, at least, have learned from the case of Mrs. Pops more about the connection of the mental plague and the cancer disease than I ever could have gained by reading thousands of books. I still stick to my diagnosis that her pain is a functional one and perhaps only supported by the cracked spine. I do not believe that she will be helped at the Memorial Hospital, but if she is helped, then I shall be only glad for her sake.

TO   MORTON   H.   ZWERLING †
❖ 26 July 1941

My dear Dr. Zwerling:

As I have written you already, I have found some very important and significant features of the atmospheric orgone tension. The atmospheric tension oscillates very strongly between the morning hours and the evening hours, with the high point at about 4 p.m. This was completely new to me, because I had thought before that the tension remains more or less equal through day and night and that it only

*Osteopathic physician and student of Reich's.
†A New York physician.

decreases before bad weather. There are also many other things which became clear here. I not only do not regret spending so much time here, but I am even convinced now that the research work which can be done in quietness here is of the greatest importance for the effectuation of the radiation on sick people. My writings are progressing satisfactorily, and I never could have dreamed how many significant biophysical problems are involved in our work. The calm and quiet and the emotional relaxation which are necessary for concentrating upon such problems are, of course, not fitting very well either into the general world craziness or in the tasks and demands of our everyday worries with our patients. But somehow we have to combine.

I hope to hear from you soon again,

P.S. Are all the things which you observe in the patients noted properly in the case histories? This is very important.

TO LEWIS GOLDINGER
❖ *26 July 1941*

My dear Mr. Goldinger:

I have your bad message about my license,* but I am not surprised at all. In order to prevent that the one or the other of our friends should escape the issue by saying that *I am the one* who is aggressive or provoking aggressiveness, I would like to summarize:

Since about two years in the United States, I have been progressing in my efforts to promote the work calmly, legally and in good faith:

1) I worked five years on a manuscript dealing with a quite new

---

*Reich's application for indorsement of his medical license was denied by the Board of Regents. Mr. Goldinger advised Reich:

"The Board's action is based on an avowed policy to keep out as much competition as possible. In furtherance of this policy the Board refuses to grant any indorsement to anybody and insists upon an examination, probably with the realization that very few doctors could pass an examination after a lapse of so many years since graduation from medical school. The policy of the Board reflects the strong monopoly which the medical profession enjoys and seeks to protect for financial reasons. This is the painful truth as it appears to me. As a result, no foreign applicant can get an indorsement without resorting to the courts."

field of biological energy. Dr. Wolfe was working hard for one year on the translation. The publisher refuses the book, saying that there are too many books of the same title.

2) According to a feeling of duty toward the American public and the world of scholars, I wrote a letter to the head of the university at which I lectured, informing him about the first important results in cancer treatment. I expected at least a discussion, if not some help of the head of the university, to secure the work. He throws me out of the university, wishing me good luck.

3) I informed officials of two great hospitals about the results in the cancer research. No help was achieved.

4) I work calmly in my place, and the landlord throws me out of it. I am forced to jump ahead and to secure a place with much money, which I do not possess, to secure the work.

5) There is a law especially made for people in a situation like mine, providing the endorsement of the medical license of a physician who is a recognized authority in his field, who has contributed important things to the medical profession, which I did, who came to this country on a vocation to teach a new branch of medicine, which I do. Some men, disregarding the habit that we should be governed by laws and not by men with their private interests, decide to heap up nearly unsurmountable obstacles to the one who has the official task to push through a definite kind of work which is to the interest of the American public and people. They refused to endorse my license; that means practically that they are checking my work. I would be glad, of course, to submit to an examination if I knew someone who could judge by an examination what I am doing and how I am doing it. But such an authority does not exist yet.

All those things I took very calmly because I am used to them from my European experiences. I feel no inclination to become aggressive, as I should do, rationally seen. Now I can leave it only to the representatives of the American law, education, and medicine to decide whether my work is wanted and needed here or not. It is the same thing which I told Dr. Wolfe in the presence of Dr. Philipson from Denmark in Oslo, in 1939, before Dr. Wolfe went back to the United States. I told them that I would come to the United States only on a vocation; that is, if my work is needed and wanted. I do not belong to the kind of persons who impose themselves upon their hosts, to be called afterwards impertinent and badly educated. It is now completely in the hands of the American citizens to decide upon the future procedure in the matter of my license. My own future actions will, of course, be dictated by their decision.

TO TAGE PHILIPSON
29 July 1941

Dear Dr. Philipson,

Your letter of 10 July 1941 demonstrated to me that you have misinterpreted my response to your "critique" of the bion book. I did not for one moment doubt your motives. It is something else that bothered me—namely, the remarkable, widespread, disturbing propensity of human beings, scientists not excepted, to have anything new served up in such a fashion that they do not personally have to make any effort to become fully immersed in a new problem by identifying with it and following the argument. Naturally, one does not have to "make things unnecessarily difficult for oneself," but that is not what is involved here. I am concerned with the attitude of the so-called critics, who have been annoying me more and more over the years. But if instead of making it "unnecessarily difficult" for them, we make it *too* easy, then that would be acting contrary to our own views and our own requirement that people should learn to develop their own capability and responsibility for independent thought. Problems of the kind that I deal with are not easy to acquire, not even in one's own rendering. But I am not writing for readers; instead I treat each problem separately, with all its provisional characteristics and lack of clarity. If I merely wanted to pay attention to the reader, I would not advance one step. It is the task of those who also work on the project not to expect me to "make it easy" for them, but (also in the interest of their own independence) to help *me* to solve questionable and unclear points by asking questions and engaging in discussions. That is the only attitude that can be called collegial cooperation. In contrast, the expectation that I should make it very easy for readers not only overestimates my strength and ability but also, what is far worse, it places me in the aloof and unattainably high position of an authority figure, and the readers or students become nothing more than recipients of the message without having to do anything themselves. But that is exactly what we are trying to combat through teaching. If the readers of scientific works develop the attitude which I want to see—namely, that they do not make things too easy for themselves—they will also drop the embarrassing habit of allowing their feeling of weakness to evolve into neurotic carping, of the well-known kind, as if they constantly wanted to assure themselves and the world at large that "I also have my own opinion." You are aware of this human attitude just as well as I am, dear Dr. Philipson. As the senior representative of our work, you could do the cause a great service if you would pay close attention to ensuring that in your circles a distinction is made between neurotic carping born of self-assertion, and cooperative questioning and discussion. That is the only way in which you will succeed in leading the people under your guidance out of the state of intellectual dependence and compensatory neurotic arrogance and to educate them to think independently and rationally.

31 July 1941

When you fell trees, chop wood, dig in the ground, sow—in short, when you allow your body to be active—many things appear in a different light. Very gradually I have begun to realize how senseless it is to spend the kind of energy I have been spending for two decades in winning people over, only to be left in the lurch by them later; to set a good example in regard to material sacrifices only to see how they do nothing in return except admire you; to try to convince the official academic world through painstaking efforts, only to encounter neurotic academic fear of the truth.

I could relax for a change, wait, watch what the others are willing to put forth. I could accomplish the same amount in my hut on my two acres as I could amidst the turmoil, without constantly giving of myself.

This would not constitute a withdrawal into seclusion but would simply leave a part of the responsibility to others.

TO MORTON H. ZWERLING
❖ *2 August 1941*

Dear Dr. Zwerling:

Dr. Wolfe told me about the signs of kidney troubles which appeared in Mrs. Jacobs. It is what is to be expected in any case where the radiation is destroying the tumor. The kidneys seem in an acute state of being clogged up with destruction material. There cannot have taken place as yet any kind of chronic inflammation or of any lasting disturbance of the glomeruli. I think the situation can be helped to a great extent if the patient follows strictly the rules which I have outlined in my letter to her, that is, the body has to be cleared and washed out to the utmost.

I want you to get the deep conviction according to reality that such things as we are attempting to do are not to be had in an easy way. One problem which we solve involves immediately a second one, unknown so far, which has to be solved until a third one appears which has to be conquered again. The first problem of reaching the tumors anywhere in the body and of destroying them seems now to work in all the cases. The prevention of an intoxication of the whole body by unccountable amounts of T-bacilli can be accomplished too, as we see (all the patients would have been dead long ago if they had not come to us, because of T-intoxication). Now we face the new problem of how to fight the secondary consequences brought about by the definite ways in which the detritus of the tumors leaves the body in different phases and in different patients. Only step by step, watching closely every small detail, trying to correct all the different phenomena, we shall be able to accomplish the task of saving the patients in whom the tumors have been destroyed from the results of this destruction.

Utmost patience, skill, and conviction concerning the facts which once have been established will enable us to go to the end of the long and difficult road which is before us.

I look forward to the days when we shall be able to sit together again and talk matters over in this fight against death and destruction.

Dear Dr. Zwerling:

I would like to add some words about the fundamental character of our work at the present time. The main features of it have been summarized in my letter of the beginning of August: We are not conducting these experiments with the aim of curing cancer; we are conducting them only with the aim of learning about the effect of the radiation on sick human beings. Every little bit of experience which we gather now means in some cases nothing to the patients, but it means tremendously much for tens of thousands and more human beings later. That is the character and principle of every kind of fundamental research work. Of course, as physicians we would like first of all to cure, but what is the use of having humane wishes which are not to be fulfilled at the time being? There is no other way, and thus it goes with all kinds of new treatments. We have to learn and to learn and to learn again and again. None of the patients, for instance, on whom the whole psychoanalytic theory and technique of the neurosis was acquired was ever cured. Only many years later, when the fundamental facts about the unconscious and the neurotic mechanism had been gathered, could the pioneers of that time think of developing practical techniques. In the long run, every bad experience counts for hundred of successes. We have learned a great deal on Mrs. Jacobs, as to the kidneys and heart involvements, which according to my knowledge are quite new, because usually cancerous patients die of general deterioration and T-intoxication, and not on the results of clogged kidneys. That we understand now. What you write about the enlarged liver in Robert is another example. I have seen the enlarged livers in many mice. I did not understand them and I don't yet understand them. Mrs. Pops had the same symptom after a few days of orgone treatment, but it became normal again. What we can do now is only to delay the fulfillment of our ambition to cure. Once the effect of the orgone upon the cancerous tumor is made sure, we shall be able to cure cancer also in very progressed cases if we know all that is necessary about the question of its absorption.

Another ambition which we should abandon is to prove anything to anyone. We are not conducting the experiments in order to convince anybody, but only to overcome the real difficulties in cancer treatment.

27 August 1941

Man dreamed of being able to fly long before he learned the technique of flying. When this technique became known, he began to pilot airplanes.

Man has been dreaming of education, statesmanship, international law ever since he began educating, setting entire countries afire, and murdering their inhabitants. He has not yet learned the technique of being civilized. He will only put education and international law into practice when he has learned the technique of unarmored life, the same way he has learned to pilot an airplane today. Just as electricity made it possible for man to fly, the orgone will establish a basis for rational education.

2 September 1941

My third wife just told me that I take things "too seriously." I had been complaining about wasting so much money on the future fathers of the proletariat. Heard the same thing twenty years ago from several superiors. What then *am* I to take seriously if not the so-called saviors of mankind who lead millions astray, whom people believed in and for whom they were willing to sacrifice their lives! If you don't want to lose your faith in people (and losing that means losing everything), then you have to take all their statements seriously, in deadly earnest, nail them down, as it were, hold them to their every word and not let go!

TO ALBERT EINSTEIN
23 September 1941

Dear Mr. Einstein,

During the summer months I have used the relatively dry climate in Maine for the purposes of my experiments. From July 5 to

August 20, between eight o'clock in the morning and midnight, I have performed daily and hourly measurements of the speed of the electroscopic discharges in the open air. The results of these measurements confirm my suspicion that the atmospheric orgone energy is not the same as ionic electricity:

1. During the course of the day, the discharges of the electroscope (which communicates with the air) fluctuate considerably in more or less regular fashion and totally independent of wind and relative humidity of the air. The discharges are at their most rapid in the early morning and late evening; the speed of discharge decreases in a regular curve until approximately 3 p.m. or 5 p.m. and then increases again. Thus the speed obviously depends on the solar radiation. It rises when the concentration of atmospheric energy is low and falls at high concentrations of energy. If the speed of the electroscopic discharge reflects the extent of ionization of the air caused by solar radiation, then logically the discharge should be slower in the morning and the evening than during the hours around noon. Precisely the opposite is the case.

2. Before periods of strong and continuous rainfall, the discharge curve suddenly drops—that is to say, the discharges occur very rapidly; the energy tension in the atmosphere is very low while it rains but rises again when the weather turns brighter.

3. Cloud formation manifests itself in an *acceleration* of the electroscopic discharges. It is as if clouds were formed not just by the removal of atmospheric orgone energy from the area close to the surface of the earth, but also as if the clouds thus formed acted as a kind of umbrella protecting against orgonotic radiation from the sun. Changeable weather, alternating between sunny and cloudy on one and the same day, manifests itself in a correspondingly fluctuating curve for the rates of electroscopic discharge.

4. Simultaneously with the beginning of increased sunspot activity on 5 July the concentration of atmospheric energy fell to a fraction of its average values—that is to say, the electroscopes discharged faster but the fluctuations from day to day remained more or less regular, albeit at a lower level. The attached curves will illustrate what I have just stated. I regarded it as necessary to tell you about these additions to my report of last February.

As far as the technique of carrying out the entire experiment is concerned, I would like to make the following suggestion: In February 1941, I applied to Washington to have patents granted for the orgonoscope and the orgone accumulator, of which you have models. I received a serial number and will have to demonstrate the procedure to the patent examiner in my laboratory by 15 December. I had initiated this whole procedure in order to secure the experimental work financially and to protect it from exploitation by unscrupulous business interests. However, I would be happy if this whole patent business became superfluous, because I am neither able nor willing to turn into an entrepreneur. I would like to remove all restrictions, but at the same time I must not neglect the great financial demands posed by this work. Financial support from official sources would be *the* ideal solution and would spare all concerned the embarrassing patenting proceedings. How this question is resolved will also determine if and when I shall publish the entire body of facts. The patent attorney told me that if a patent was accepted, any comprehensive publication would become impossible, and I do not like that at all. I will therefore delay any further decision in this regard, including publication of the manuscript which has now been written, until I hear from you about the state of this matter.

In the meantime, the ongoing experimental treatment of cancer patients started by me in March is growing in scope; some of the results are surprising, some are pleasing, while some results bring out even more clearly the complicated nature of the problem and the means needed to deal with it.

Looking forward to hearing from you soon, I remain . . .

28 September 1941

One illusion numbers among the prerequisites of all achievement: the lofty feeling of succeeding someday. I am aware, however, that it lies in the nature of all development to turn against itself.

This is a law of nature; it belongs to the knowledge of functional biophysics! According to this, when sex economy spreads, as Marxism, psychoanalysis, and Christianity did, it will be a living corpse. It is not human malice but rather biological degeneration which causes the destruction. Unarmored plasma repeatedly attempts to raise itself to the stature of cosmic functioning by making discoveries, striving "ahead." It's as powerless as a drop of water on a sea of fire. We don't even know what "consciousness" is. Thus we always sink back into lifelessness after our mighty efforts.

Only one thing could suspend this law: a gigantic discovery transcending the cosmic, natural law, like the disclosure of how consciousness perceives *itself*. In other words, a discovery which would put the natural law at mankind's disposal. This will begin with the discovery of the function of self-perception in living plasma. Until then there is no solace.

18 October 1941

If the world knew what I have discovered, conceived of, the cause I advocate, I would be stoned, either literally or by being raised to the rank of a genius who is immobilized. Or I would have to slink off in shame at knowing, sensing, and having achieved so much more than my contemporaries while still remaining exactly as ordinary as they. A voice speaks from within me, a knowledge, which dominates me and whose slave I am. I try to escape this God and cannot. I try to be base, petty, coarse, envious, mistrusting, but *it* will not allow me to be so. I would like to hide myself within the community— coequal with others. But this would be impossible because the community does not sense even the simplest laws of life, and then I would become alienated, belligerent.

T O   A L B E R T   E I N S T E I N *
October 1941

Dear Mr. Einstein,

I do not understand why you are not answering my letters. Until quite recently I was firmly convinced that you were waiting for the results of some test. You will understand that I could not regard your letter of 7 February 1941 as the final word in the matter, because the phenomenon of the temperature difference had been confirmed and

---

*This letter was not sent.

the incorrect interpretation by your assistant was the only item in question, which I clearly refuted through measurements in the open air. Nor can I bring myself to assume that you consider such serious communications as mine frivolous or fraudulent; otherwise you would not have listened to me for four and a half hours with such obvious interest and understanding, nor would you have been prepared to have an apparatus sent to you in order to make your own observations, and to promise to support the matter if the temperature difference is a fact. Taking all this into account, your silence is incomprehensible. If you did not want to continue, you could simply have written to say that you are not interested.

I cannot therefore concede what some people familiar with the strange behavior of academics assume—namely, that you are simply abandoning this serious and far-reaching matter. Nor, after our talk, can I concede that you can be arrogant. You do not need to get out of an important matter in *that* way. For this reason, during all these past months I have rejected any such suspicion as unworthy of all those concerned. Since I firmly believe that the experiment in the open air had convinced you that the interpretation at your end was incorrect, and that you were continuing to work on this matter, I told you about the initial observations involving cancer patients and the formation of weather. Also, I do not work on my own but must always confer with experts and fellow workers. Any further development in the work involving atmospheric orgone energy does not, after all, depend on confirmation by you and certainly not on the incorrect opinions of your assistant, because orgone radiation is becoming more clearly and precisely defined before the eyes of many people with every passing week, and many facts exist which I have not mentioned to you. However, your silence is embarrassing and disconcerting. Your silence is keeping us from making important decisions, for example, whether or not we should inform the English government about the radiation. I therefore ask you, in the interest of all concerned, to tell us what has happened, whatever it may be. Answering letters is, after all, part of civilized human behavior, and besides, I do not particularly want to leave the apparatus at your house.

All I can do is assure you that I would rather not have had to write a letter such as this one. May I ask you now to be totally open with me, even if you have heard malicious rumors. We are not playing games here, nor are we dealing with one of the usual, richly funded "discoveries" that the *Times* announces with great pomp every week. This is not my private affair either, but important work for the sake of humanity. I am just as afraid of the hyenas among scientists as you are. But the fact that the functions of orgone energy take place before everyone's eyes, directly and visibly, is far more important.

5 *November 1941*

Letter to Mrs. Dukas,* Princeton, asking that the apparatus be returned by Einstein.

Einstein has not replied to the third letter.

We do not understand this. He could easily have written that he does not want to have anything to do with the matter.

14 *November 1941*

Apparatus returned by Einstein.

His behavior is inexplicable.

1. He is a coward?

2. He doesn't want to get involved.

3. He was turned against me.

30 *November 1941*

I must finally stop being so terribly angry with physicists, biologists, chemists, etc., for thinking so poorly and incorrectly. I am angry with them because I expect their recognition and endorsement. I would never dream of expecting a psychologist to understand or endorse vegetotherapy. In this field I feel that I am *the* authority. When I feel as experienced and at home in the field of orgone biophysics as I do in psychoanalysis, I will no longer have these expectations and will consequently no longer be furious. Then I will want to bear the full responsibility for those fields of natural science involved and will be *able* to do so as well.

*Einstein's secretary.

TO JULIUS WEINBERGER
3 December 1941

Dear Mr. Weinberger:

I had the impression yesterday that you would expect quick decisions through the experiment in which you want to participate now with your apparatus. But it will take years, as it has taken years already, to understand and to work out the phenomena which I have visualized. These observations cannot be made from the distance or by "being called when the phenomena appear."

I am frank only toward people whom I believe to be principally friendly toward my research. Therefore, I take the liberty of mentioning something which I did not quite understand and which I disliked yesterday. I may add immediately that I have encountered the same thing in other scientists, again and again. As I told you, for the unknown there exist very many words which can be used at liberty. But words do not mean explanation.

1. When I asked you what you would expect from rubbing cellulose on a simple lamp, you said that, according to known facts, you would expect *nothing*. Then suddenly you found the explanation for the phenomenon—namely, that the bulb is becoming ionized and thus causes the light phenomenon. I then removed the bulb from within the lamp, but the light phenomenon still continued to exist. Thus, your explanation was wrong, but you did not seem to be impressed by what had happened. You did not say a word and I had the impression that you avoided further notice of what you had seen.

2. Being not quite familiar with the detailed technicalities of radio technique, I wished to learn from you whether the antenna wire contains some kind of current from within the tubes—i.e., originating in the grid. You said what I expected you to say—namely, that no current whatsoever flows from within the tube through the antenna wire to the outside. When I then told you that I can produce sparks and noise by touching a piece of metal with the end of the antenna (the radio apparatus being in operation), you found the explanation that such a phenomenon may appear in badly adjusted radios. When I stressed the fact that this phenomenon can be produced by any kind and type of radio, you objected at first and then you found *another*

explanation. You thought that some kind of structure within the tube releases electricity through the antenna wire.

I mention this in order to make sure that in the case that your apparatus should show the same disturbance of the galvanic current as mine, the phenomenon should be recognized. In the other case, that your apparatus should not show the phenomenon, it would still be existent in my apparatus, which is an excellent modern Siemens-Schuckert-Berlin apparatus, and we would have to try to find the mechanism of the phenomenon. I am sure you understand well that I am searching for the effects of the atmospheric orgone radiation upon electric apparatus and that this is a very difficult and complicated task. Of course, that may take years. I do not have as yet any explanation for the phenomena which I found, and I am trying hard to find the common mechanism of all the phenomena, within the framework of my orgone research.

I hope you will understand that I would not like to be disturbed in this work by any kind of interference from the outside, but I am sure you will also understand that I am very thankful for every kind of help, suggestion, or objection which you may offer. I sincerely expect your further cooperation in the friendly and kind manner which you showed up to now.

TO   JULIUS   WEINBERGER
5 December 1941

Dear Mr. Weinberger:

I was very glad to receive your answer to my letter. I agree with everything that you say. I am sure that you understand that the discovery of the orgone was not just a happening, but a consequence of the Freudian assumption of the existence of a psychic energy and of my success in demonstrating this psychic energy of Freud to be vegetative bioelectric energy. Bearing the responsibility to demonstrate the facts (some of which already have been demonstrated and others being in the process of elaboration), I think that scientific work has two sides: not only the request to demonstrate but also another which is of the highest importance—namely, to demand that the scientists to whom the facts are demonstrated should not deny them on an irrational basis or on the basis of baseless assumptions. The irrationalism which brings our world to ruin does not, of course, hold before the doors of the scientific laboratories of this planet. It is my great privilege and advantage, having been a psychiatrist originally, to be able to distinguish out of everyday experience between rational and irrational reactions. The temperature difference, for instance, has been affirmed by Einstein, who did not believe that it could be demonstrated before he saw it. But then his assistant found a word to explain it away. But this supposedly high-ranking physicist did not bother at all to control his own explanatory objection. Had he thought of such self-control, he would have fixed the control thermometer at the same level above the table upon which the orgone apparatus was standing, and he would have had to admit that his explanation of heat coming from the ceiling down to the table by convection could not hold water.

Here you see what I mean. And I have the impression that you underestimate the irrational in the behavior of the scientists. You will read much about it exemplified in happenings in the book which is coming forth now, as well as in the second volume, which describes the discovery of the orgone.

Neither your nor my apparatus has shown until now any deviation from the line of the fixed current.

7 December 1941

!!*War*. Japan, America, England.
They will need the orgone.

8 December 1941

There are days when everything goes wrong, when you feel useless and unneeded; when all your thinking is at odds with what is actually happening—i.e., when the final sense in the nonsense is revealed; when your powerlessness grows out of all proportion to your clarity of judgment. These are the days when you wish you didn't exist; this is the moment when weak people commit suicide. For a strong person this escape is barred, as he is bound by a duty to his rational mind. He may not forsake it because it leads him with a sure hand —to torturing insights into misery.

This is the reason why people do not want to do their own thinking but just have someone think for them as they go along.

12 December 1941

2 *a.m.* Arrested by the FBI as a "dangerous enemy alien." Taken to Ellis Island. Fingerprinted, photographed, put behind bars.

13 December 1941

In Room D. No clock in the room, not enough chairs, no proper bed, slept on a stretcher, clothes on the floor. Washing facilities poor. My skin reacts badly.* At midnight I was transferred to the hospital. Dived into the bathtub without noticing how dirty it was.

15 December 1941

10 *a.m.* Visit from Goldinger. He tells me that the FBI had intercepted *Work Democracy*,† tapped my phone, seized letters to Europe. There was a 40 percent chance that I would be deported to a camp for the duration of the war, which would mean several years.

Friends are helping my wife with money. They all feel that I have been treated meanly. I am reminded of Lore's statement a few months ago: "Watch out, Willi. Annie has been discussing something negative about you with Dr. Kubie." I ignored it at the time. Now it is important: *Denunciation*. Cowards who do not dare to confront me directly. The FBI had paid Annie Rubinstein a visit a year ago.

16 December 1941

Wolfe is writing a protest letter to Francis Biddle, U.S. Attorney General, in Washington.

17 December 1941

See Ilse in prison for the first time at 10 a.m. She told the children on Tuesday evening what was happening. Annie is forbidding the

---

*Reich had psoriasis.
†Booklets by Reich: *Arbeitsdemokratie*, Politisch-Psycholog. Schriftenreihe, Nr. 4, Sexpol Verlag, 1937, and *Weitere Probleme der Arbeitsdemokratie*, Politisch-Psycholog. Schriftenreihe, Nr. 5, Sexpol Verlag, 1941.

children to visit Ilse. Eva is very upset, so Ilse says. She sneaks away to an outside telephone to make her calls. But she no longer comes to our house. She was scolded severely by Carole Barnard, the assistant, who told her she "should be ashamed—her place now should be in this house." From that time on, Ilse refuses to talk to Eva. I decide not to receive any more visits from the children and to disinherit them. I do not want any cowards as my children.

3 p.m. My house is searched. Carole reports that she got the impression the FBI agents did not know what they were looking for.*

18 December 1941

Great uncertainty about when the hearing will take place. Some prisoners are expecting to have to wait months. Ilse says that officials in Washington are dismayed. The wife of one of the officials is being treated by Wolfe.

19 December 1941

Agony, waiting, refused permission to be given the German orgone manuscript.

The irrationality of my arrest makes me feel bitter and helpless. I decide not to go on working in the U.S.A. I won't make the discovery of the orgone available anymore. I want to get away from the U.S.A. I find the injustice and the meanness of my arrest intolerable.

24 December 1941

Ilse visits me. I feel very close to her. I feel once more that I belong to a woman. An FBI agent tells me that my hearing is scheduled for Friday at 2 p.m.

*An FBI agent made the following list of materials confiscated from Reich's house. Books:
1. Otto Heller, Siberien ein Anderes Amerika
2. A book written in Russian, with yellow front
3. Various papers written in foreign language + clippings
3a. 1 copy of translations of No. 5 thru p. 23
4. Three periodicals: one on socialism, one on fascism, one on Stalin
4a. Books no. 4 & 5 that Reich wrote
4b. Oslo illustrate (1 copy)
5. Two files of correspondence, one belonging to Dr. Reich personally—one being files for business correspondence.

❖ *Statement for Hearing at Brooklyn Court*

I. Possible Charges and Misunderstandings

1. *Nazi literature in my library.*

Answer: In order to cure a neurosis one has to understand its mechanism. Similarly, to beat Hitlerism (not alone the Hitler machine), one has to understand Nazi thinking and the psychological methods which the Nazis use to subdue people. I was one of the few who, as early as 1930, studied Nazi literature from this point of view.

2. *That I am against democracy.*

Answer: I have been criticizing the European democracies for their serious mistakes and their unconscious sympathies with Hitlerism. The European people will never go back to prewar forms of democracy. Prewar formal democracy will develop into full, real democracy. (There is, for historical reasons, a fundamental difference between American and European democracy, the former having been developed by people who were disgusted with the European forms of democracy, the same ones which led to Hitlerism.)

3. *That I am a "subversive" element.*

Answer: I do not belong to any party or political organization; I am neither a politician nor a leader of any other kind; I make no organized propaganda for my ideas. Should the social process in the world move in the direction of work democracy, then the objective development will prove the correctness of my concepts. Work democracy cannot be brought about by any political means; it can only develop spontaneously.

4. *That I have sent books to Europe and have friends still working there.*

No books were sent to Germany or any Nazi-occupied country. They were sent only to Switzerland and England. Many of my coworkers continue to work in Nazi-occupied countries; they can do so because their work is not political. The growing confidence of the people in the work, as, e.g., in Denmark, shows that it is something which people feel a strong need for.

II. PROOFS THAT I AM AN HONEST ANTIFASCIST, FIGHTING FASCISM THOUGH NOT THE GERMAN PEOPLE

1. I had to flee Berlin suddenly after Hitler seized power. There was an article against me in the *Völkischer Beobachter*. I had to leave all my things behind.

2. My publications, which previously had already been banned by the communists, were forbidden in Germany.

3. Also later, I wrote books and articles against Hitlerism.

4. I fought in anti-Nazi organizations in the days when Hitler seized power, and once narrowly escaped the death penalty.

5. At least five of my friends and students in Scandinavia were arrested and imprisoned by the Gestapo. I know nothing about the fate of friends and coworkers in Germany and Holland.

6. I wrote that "the U.S.A. will probably be a good friend of work democracy."

7. The Norwegian government in exile knows me as an antifascist.

8. German democratic sociologists and leaders of antifascist youth organizations visited me in Scandinavia for advice in their fight against fascism.

9. Antifascists (democrats of all kinds) translated some of my books and wrote about me.

10. I was expelled from the German Psychoanalytic Society because of my antifascist activity and publications.

11. The Norwegian officials who refused the extension of my permit to stay in Norway, Minister of Justice Lie, who betrayed the Norwegian government, and Konstad, chief of police,* were both fascists.

12. I have shown my loyalty to the United States on many occasions.

III. MY ATTITUDE TOWARD THE UNITED STATES

1. My detention in an enemy alien camp would mean:
   a) sure death in the case of exchange of prisoners with Germany;
   b) possible death at the hands of fascists in the camp who would soon learn about my sociological function;

---

*Konstad was executed as a Nazi collaborator by the Norwegian government. [W.R.]

 c) destruction of an important, indispensable part of the fight
 against the pestilence of Hitlerism;
 d) an unexplainable injustice done to an honest, active fighter
 for democracy at the hands of a democratic government.

2. My claim that Hitlerism cannot be beaten by fighting for the
very things which brought about Hitlerism is the same as that made
by many distinguished Americans, as, e.g., Dorothy Thompson.

3. My statement that democracy is not a static thing, but a dynamic
development, is the same concept as that held by the American government. Democracy may assume any number of forms in the future.

4. I admire the social accomplishments of the present administration. I have said to many Americans who complained about it that
no democratic or socialist government of Europe has done as much
for the working population as has the government of the U.S.A.

5. The postwar demands of a united democratic Europe do not
contradict present American democracy. Europe has gone through a
development different from that of America.

6. I am for a "government of the people, by the people, for the
people." I am against politics, because such a goal cannot be reached
by politics or politicos.

7. To beat Hitlerism requires two things:
 a) Hitler's machine must be smashed at all costs.
 b) The European people must be given every possibility of developing their own forms of *self-government*, be it work democracy or something else.

8. My "political" belief, derived from twenty-two years of work as
a biopsychiatrist, is expressed in the sentence: "Love, work, and
knowledge are the wellsprings of our life. They should also govern
it."

9. My special field of work is mental hygiene. Hitlerism is a mental disease of the masses, *not only in Germany*. After Hitler is beaten
the main task will remain: that of eradicating Hitlerism within the
people. This is an educational problem.

10. I have never tried to promulgate the principles of work democracy among the American people. Even when my students asked
me to lecture about it, I refused to do so. At this time, it is an exclusively *European* problem.

11. My only weapon is my knowledge. The aims of work democracy cannot be attained by any means of violence, politics, or propaganda.

12. I do not belong to and do not participate with any political party or any government. I have tried, thus far in vain, to contact the U.S. government with the intention of putting my experimental findings at the service of the government (also through Professor Einstein, who possesses a report on my work on the atmospheric orgone radiation). A patent is pending in Washington.

13. I lost my faith in all forms of European democracies (the Russian experiment included) years ago, when one after the other failed to recognize obvious facts and thus unconsciously helped Hitler along. I regained my faith when I met some specifically American processes of life, which showed the strength and tremendous fruitfulness of *real* democratic endeavors (some films, books, the general way of handling things, the New Deal, etc.). But I believe that in America as elsewhere there exists much disastrous hypocrisy, much unconscious and open fascism. During the two years of my residence in the U.S.A. I never doubted that these elements could be overcome, that the will in the direction of further democratic development was deep, honest, and powerful. That gave back to me much of the hope I had lost, and it strengthened my scientific (and not political) efforts to help also my old country, Europe. I am sure that the life process itself tends toward a great, powerful world democracy.

14. I do not belong to those people who change their human relations, their friends, their beliefs, etc., like shirts. I have lived and taught in many countries. My intention of becoming a full member of the American democracy is by no means at variance with the connections with my European friends and coworkers. My mother tongue is German. I love the mental efforts of German people like Kepler, Planck, Nietzsche, Koch, Freud, Einstein, Beethoven, Mozart, etc., and could never forget them. I hate German militarism, sadism, and imperialism. But my education and my work belong to all people; they originated from the suffering and misery of all the hardworking people, wherever they are. This attitude is not "un-American"; on the contrary; it is in keeping with the true American attitude: to help real freedom, to eradicate irrationalism and human

anxiety, to make all people naturally honest, self-confident, and responsible for the truly democratic way of living.

26 December 1941

5 *p.m.* "Hearing."

Questions: What do I do apart from research and teaching?

Do I receive money from Moscow?

Do I want to bring down the government?

How could I afford a house costing $14,500? (I explain.)

Am I for or against active military service? (I say it depends on who's against whom.)

FBI agent Pugh had brought my *Mass Psychology* and *Work Democracy* with him to the hearing.

I realize that nobody understands why I was arrested.

30 December 1941

Firmly convinced that I will not be released.

31 December 1941

Ilse comes to me and stays for two hours. I ask her if there is anything between her and Wolfe.

Wolfe flew to Washington, spoke to the person handling my case. Papers not yet in Washington.

1942

*"An understanding of the roots of the biological
distortion as seen in the human race
could be the essence of my scientific
work—or might it be madness?"*

2 January 1942

Visit from my wife in jail. I am "dead," my hands are ice-cold. Ilse gets confused, has "lost" me. Wolfe is very decent, "helps her." *Expected release.*

3 January 1942

Washington (Justice Department) ordered my release at 7 p.m. by informing the District Attorney in Brooklyn. District Attorney told Ellis Island. Ellis Island refuses to release me. Wants to hear directly from Washington. Nobody can be reached. My wife spends four hours with District Attorney Smith, who telephones and sends cables without any success. Ellis Island wants to be informed directly by Washington.

5 January 1942

At 2 p.m. Goldinger came. I announced that I would go on a hunger strike if I was not released that same day. District Attorney Smith explains to Goldinger that I should never have been touched. The whole thing was just a piece of completely irrational nonsense. Nobody knows why I have been locked up.

———

Precisely at 4 p.m. Washington telephoned Ellis Island. I am released from detention after three and a half weeks locked up as a dangerous enemy alien. Suspected of being an agent of a foreign power.

Laboratory closed.

Teaching of students stopped until my work can be protected— i.e., by my being protected from further arrests.

Assistant let go.

In the last two years, $10,000 spent on experiments; I have got only $220 left. How can I survive?

FBI Record No. 100 8422 "B-12."

❖

I was called to the U.S.A. to teach my stuff. Dr. Wolfe came to Europe to learn it and to bring it over here. I brought a great discovery to this country, am teaching U.S.A. physicians for nothing. The Department of Justice investigates and knows about me—and I am put into jail by a subdepartment of the Department of Justice. I looked up every day from behind the bars to the Statue of Liberty in New York Harbor. Her light shone brightly into a dark night.

7 January 1942

Serious fight with Ilse. Just when I was getting back to her again, completely, she lost contact with me. The aftereffect of my slow detachment from Elsa, and my hesitation in moving toward Ilse. For several hours we were close to breaking up. Finally it got through to her, strongly and completely, like it happened before with Elsa. I am happy to lose myself again in a woman; somehow, deep inside, a thorn remains—a lack of certainty.

Important experiences in prison

1. Most people accept incarceration like sheep. In their cells they do the same things they always did outside "in freedom": nothing. They play cards all day, tell stupid or dirty jokes, gratefully bow beneath every yoke! The sight of it makes one despair over the possibilities of a real democracy.

2. If you scrape off the unnatural surface, their human and democratic traits emerge. Then they really catch on and you can believe in democracy again.

9 January 1942

Mr. Pugh, the special agent from the FBI who had been handling my case for a *whole year*, did not know what I was suspected of. During the search of my house on 24 December 1941 he did not know what to look for. No one knew exactly why I had sat three weeks in jail—no one—except me. They could have had it so much easier. If they had interrogated me they would have learned that I actually pose a danger for any kind of obscenity. I alone am aware of the significance of my work and of what it will someday overthrow—not today, not tomorrow—someday. I have nothing to hide concerning this and nobody can prosecute me for it. Nobody really understands what I am doing, and since they don't, I appear suspect, the agent of a foreign political power, not the person I really am: *the discoverer of life energy and destroyer of every brand of mysticism!*

10 January 1942

There is no doubt that deprivation of liberty and the infliction of crass injustices affect one's entire system like a dose of poison. Anger must be controlled, tears suppressed, sexual excitation repressed or endured in pain. One's system is subjected to severe strain, to an energy stasis which manifests itself in a cramplike twitching emanating from the solar plexus.

12 January 1942

The longer I think about it, the clearer it becomes that it will not be an easy matter to continue my work.

Renunciation of immediate recognition by the masses is one of the primary prerequisites for great, fundamental achievement. Craving for recognition forces compromise, shallowness, catering to people. And I'm having a damn hard time renouncing it!

TO EVA REICH
❖ 17 January 1942

My dear Eva,

I had your letter on 13 January and Ilse told me about your telephone call. To be frank, I am not in the mood to see anyone, not even you. The incident or "accident," as you may call it, had nothing to do with the outbreak of the war, and nothing either with any "enemy-alienship." There was nothing against me, and nobody knew why I was taken and held for nearly four weeks. There are many indications—including what Lore told me several months ago—that the same cowards who dare not oppose my work in the open field of argument, who resort to proclaiming me crazy, etc., had gone to the FBI and told them some funny stories about me. I have first to try to find out exactly.

Besides, your behavior on that occasion was bad and deeply offending. I am sorry to have learned that you were "not allowed" to visit my wife, who was in deep despair, or to visit me on Ellis Island as other children did with their fathers. It did not make sense to keep away because, as you may have figured out for yourself, you and Lore are clearly on record as my children. I am sorry, and very much so, to embarrass you with my way of existence. I cannot help it. I have always been very patient toward your impoliteness and lack of consideration, *too much* of which you are able to show on other sides. I am afraid not to be able to react to such behavior calmly anymore, and therefore I prefer not to see you or Lore. I am regretting that very much, but I hope that you have learned something now about the nature of my existence. Such accidents did not happen for the first time and they will not be the last ones. Meanwhile I need *real* friends only around me.

I wish you good luck.

29 January 1942

War—silence.
Laboratory dead.
$T_0 - T$ operates with approx. 1.2° difference.
Orgonotic radiation strong.
Wait.
Bring Eva back again.

2 February 1942

Mr. Pugh from the FBI just returned the things that were taken away during the house search. Pugh was embarrassed and apologized to my wife: "The whole thing was very unfortunate," he said. "Dr. Reich seems to be a very deep 'thinker.' It was quite clear that *Work Democracy* is written for postwar Europe. It was very regrettable."

Why did they not know this one year *before* my arrest?

17 February 1942

Today Ilse registered as an "enemy alien." She gave her name as Ilse Ollendorff-Reich; she asked whether she could register like that because, although we are married, we do not have a license.

The official told her, "It's up to you, but you may have trouble obtaining the second papers." She registered as my wife, totally correct.

15 March 1942

4 a.m. Awake until now due to just one question: *Is it possible to be free within this framework?* Am I capable of bearing the responsibility for freedom's victory? If even I meet with such difficulty in keeping my balance, despite my experience and schooling, then how could a person with less experience and training ever manage? Will present and future generations be able to muster the proportionate degree of kindness and firmness necessary to withstand the storm of unleashed secondary instincts? How are we to educate a generation born in the year 2050 if the one born in 2000 isn't functioning?

It is awfully hard to be aware of all this and yet be unable to find one's way out of the contradictions.

T O   A .   S .   N E I L L
❖ *18 March 1942*

My dear Neill:

I had your letter of 18 January at the end of February. It was good to hear that things are quite all right with you.

Our international journal* and my new book are just coming forth. You will receive enough copies through Dr. Wolfe. It would be very important and useful if you could provide our journal with typical and significant descriptions of children's behavior under the circumstances of freedom and not-freedom. We shall print them gladly and I think that it would also help your cause to have them printed. I believe the most important task would be to elaborate the problems

---

International Journal of Sex-Economy and Orgone Research.

which arise in children who were brought up in a more or less disguised authoritative manner and who encounter for the first time freedom of movement, thought, and utterance. We always agreed upon the one point that it is not so much the content of a free life as the fear of freedom which concerns all of us. There would, without doubt, be no dangerous problems in freedom if the people and the children were not afraid of it and if they did not long for authoritarian guidance.

T O   M R S .   H A T T I E   T E M P L E T O N
A N D   C L I S T A   T E M P L E T O N *
❖ 6 April 1942

I was very sorry indeed to hear that our friend is not well. Be sure that whatever in this world of medicine can be done, will be done. The X-ray treatments are capable of stopping the disease for a while but they are not capable of building up biological strength in the body. I spoke to Mr. Templeton last summer about the biological radiation in the air and in the soil which shows some really amazing results in building up especially the biological strength of the blood and in removing pain. I cannot guarantee, of course, whether it will work with Mr. Templeton, but I would suggest that he tries it. In order to do so, have a closet built of thin wood, about 5 feet high, 3 feet deep, and 2½ feet wide, so as to enable one to sit in it comfortably. This wooden closet has a door in the front and in the door is made a small window in order to make breathing possible. The inside walls of the closet are lined completely with thin iron sheets. Between the metal sheets and the wooden inside walls of the closet put an even layer, about ½ inch thick, of either cotton which does not absorb water, or capok or even wood shavings would do. This closet is capable of concentrating the atmospheric orgone radiation in the inside of the metal walls up to four or five times as much as

*Wife and daughter of Herman Templeton, Maine guide and woodsman with whom Reich had established a friendship. Mr. Templeton had cancer.

in the open air. Our friend should sit in this closet every day for about one hour or even more if he stands it. He can also try to sit in twice daily for three-quarters of an hour, breathing deeply in and out all the time. Our experiments show that blood which has become weakened biologically by a disease of any kind gets strongly radiating and built up and is thus capable of fighting in a natural way inflammations of any kind and even infections. It will apply in the case of your father.

The closet could also be built into the soil on a sunny place so as to take up the biological radiation from the soil as well as from the sun. There appears some dizziness in the head after a while of sitting in the closet. Don't let that frighten you, it is completely harmless. If the dizziness in the head becomes too strong, then leave the closet and it will disappear in fresh air. The disease from which Mr. Templeton suffers is not too dangerous at this age and can be reduced to a great extent, perhaps even be cured. It is too bad that it is impossible for me to make the proper blood test which would show the status of the biological strength of his blood, but in any case I would suggest using the orgone-radiating closet until I come to Oquossoc* at about the middle or end of June. Then I shall be able to make some necessary tests and then we shall see further. Let Mr. Templeton please eat only light food, much green vegetables, and drink much juices and water. It may happen that the sore tissue around the prostate which hurts will be dissolved and discharged to the outside through the male organ as a bloody, grayish-brownish stuff. Don't get frightened about that. This would only be good. The main thing is to sit in the closet often and long enough. He will feel warmth, will perhaps perspire and his skin may become reddened. All these are only good signs.

27 April 1942

Eva eighteen years old and in troubles,† not to mention eight years receiving psychoanalytic treatment from an old maid who is con-

---

*A small town in the Rangeley area near Lake Mooselookmeguntic.
†"in troubles" written in English.

vinced that genitality is a "drive"—i.e., asocial—and that incestuous desires should never be conscious.

7 May 1942

Last week, in the "conversation with the electrophysicist"* I had concluded that the magnetic field of the earth has nothing to do with magnetism, but instead represents the orgone energy field of the earth. This orgone energy was hypothetically taken to be equivalent to the gravitational field.

In addition, I was able to provide experimental proof of the fact that the attraction and repulsion phenomena on an orgonotically charged iron sphere have nothing to do with + or − electricity. An orgonotically excited iron sphere attracts organic matter (cotton wool, cork, etc.) and repulses metal (tinfoil). In addition, the first iron sphere orgonotically excites a second iron sphere at a distance of about 2 cm.

Theoretically, from the identity of Coulomb's law, Newton's law of gravity, and the laws of magnetic attraction:

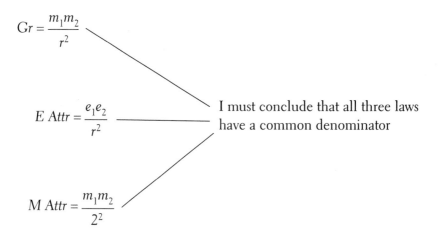

$$Gr = \frac{m_1 m_2}{r^2}$$

$$E\ Attr = \frac{e_1 e_2}{r^2}$$

$$M\ Attr = \frac{m_1 m_2}{2^2}$$

I must conclude that all three laws have a common denominator

Orgone field is the common denominator for gravitation, magnetic attraction, electrical attraction.

---

*"Orgonotic Pulsation: The Differentiation of Orgone Energy from Electromagnetism, Presented in Talks with an Electrophysicist." Published in *Orgonomic Functionalism*, vols. 3–6 (Rangeley, Me.: Wilhelm Reich Infant Trust, 1991–96).

18 May 1942

What conclusions can one draw from the radiation phenomenon?

1. Contact of insulated bodies causes radiation. No radiation without contact.

Conclusion: 2 orgone systems are needed to produce radiation.

2. No radiation outside the orgone box.

Conclusion: Orgone field is essential.

3. No radiation path, or only a short path, outside the accumulator. *Conclusion*: Confirmation of the orgonotic field between parallel plates.

4. Orgone field itself is only a medium. Needed for radiation:

    a. 2 systems and contact of both fields

    b. electromagnetic orgonotic waves

5. Electrical engineers were familiar with the Geissler-tube cathode glow, but they were not familiar with

    a. unipolar radiation

    b. the identity of orgone, static electricity, secondary coil field, cathode glow, and aurora borealis

20 May 1942

I am stuck. It is clear that unipolar radiation is an orgonotic and not an electrical phenomenon. My plan now is to convert the accumulator from stat to orgonomic for therapeutic purposes, to allow the orgone to radiate in the accumulator, with the patients in the middle. It is as if I were to let the patients sit in the middle of the aurora borealis.

From now on I shall concentrate on therapy in the orgonotic radiation field.

21 May 1942

The English edition of *The Discovery of the Orgone* appears, 3,100 copies.

First attempt to produce an orgonotic radiation field in the orgone accumulator is successful.

11 June 1942

Idea.

Organic material differs from metals in that the former attracts and retains the energy, while the latter repels it. The energy *runs* in wire and *radiates* in organic matter. A system that contains organic material and metal mixed together must therefore exert both functions—namely, attraction and repulsion = gravity question.

27 June 1942

Today, for the first time, I succeeded in deflecting a sphere in a moving orgone field. The sphere consisted of a mixture of cotton wool and iron wool that was immersed in water = model of the earth. The sphere was suspended in the orgone field of an accumulator. The field of a radiating gas tube was moved toward this field. The sphere, which swung toward the accumulator, was deflected laterally and executed circular movements. Wolfe witnessed the phenomenon.

29 June 1942

Arrival in Oquossoc.

Templeton very ill; complaining of weakness, numbness in the legs, has lost weight, walks bent over, slowly. I convinced him to construct a box. He has spent $100 on X-ray treatment, altogether $300 at the hospital.

T O   T H E O D O R E   P.   W O L F E
9 July 1942

Dear Dr. Wolfe,

I have just performed a small, but extraordinarily important experiment which will interest you. It confirms that orgone cannot be electricity. You know that spheres are much less able to discharge electrical energy than pointed metal objects. I have known for a long time that orgone acts in exactly the opposite way: Surfaces of all types give off orgone much more quickly than pointed objects, because pointed metal objects absorb orgone from the atmosphere. And now, there is the little experiment which I have just undertaken as a test for planned systematic measurements of atmospheric orgone: Instead of the plate, I introduced into the electroscope a hard rubber rod which is fitted at the top with the tip of a needle. I charged it to 5 org and measured the rate of discharge. After 50 minutes it amounted to about 1 org—i.e., 2 graduations = 1 org discharged in 50 minutes. Immediately after that I fitted the electroscope again with the metal plate, charged it to 5 org and I expected that it would discharge not in 50 but in 30 or in 40 minutes. And what happened? The discharge time with the metal plate lasted just a few org seconds—i.e., the same electroscope eliminated the charge of one org through the tip in 50 minutes, and through the plate in just a few seconds. This means that at the same time that it gives off orgone from the electroscope to the atmosphere, the metal tip also takes up orgone from the atmosphere. The surface of the plate, on the other hand, takes up much less orgone and gives it off much more rapidly. This is a wonderful confirmation of earlier, different experiments on the opposite action of tips and plates on orgone, or electricity. This nice little experiment has the major disadvantage that I must now repeat, using tips, the hourly measurements of atmospheric energy which I undertook last year with surfaces. I do not know what will come out of it. I assume that this small detail will interest you.

TO EVA REICH

14 July 1942

My Dearest Eva,

  Your card arrived the day before yesterday. You must write to us soon to let us know whether you are coming with Jerry* or somebody else. We could arrange the outermost added-on room for you, to sleep two. Ilse and I could have the large room and the adjoining small one. Or, if you prefer, we can try to rent the neighboring cabin 500 feet from us. Let us know which you prefer. I will send you money for the trip so that you can keep your well-earned money for

---

*Jerome Siskind. He married Eva.

yourself. Hitchhiking won't really work this year; it would also take too much time away from the holidays here. You can travel back with us to New York in early September. There is enough room in the car. It will remind us of the Dolomites.

I have been slaving away here for two weeks with a treatise on the structural problem in the struggle for freedom. It is not simple. Ilse is always complaining* that I am thinking too much, but I can't help it. The thinking process goes on all the time and never leaves me in peace.

You won't recognize the cabin. First, because it is summer and everything is green, and there are bushes, and it is warm. Second, because I have cut down a lot of trees, so that there is now less virgin forest and much more open forest.

Also, I have built two miniature orgonoscopes and Ilse always cries out with joy when she looks inside. Also there are sparks when I move a certain glass gas tube quickly through the air or rub it against bushes.

We are also going to get electricity in the cabin, because of the apparatus. Ilse is unhappy about this because, according to her, it will make things "less romantic" for us.

Arrange your holidays so that you really can get some rest.

25 July 1942

Mechanistic technology has rigidified the human organism, mechanized human thinking, and held the natural sciences captive in mechanistic materialism.

The discovery of the orgone will change this. The orgone functions biologically, not mechanistically. Mankind will have to learn to handle orgone. During this process people will have to learn to *think in terms of functioning* and in doing so they themselves will change in their own functioning.

Mysticism is nothing but a sense of unarmored life under conditions of physical rigidity.

---

*That's not true! [Ilse Ollendorff]

5 August 1942

I must make up my mind as to whether I should, for the sake of truth, continue with political psychology based on man's incapability of being free, and reckon with the fact that those who are to be saved are not in the least aware of the work being done for them. Or shall I give up and retire to the green pastures of orgone physics where all that the human heart can desire is beckoning to me?

T O   A N T O N   S W A R O W S K Y *
5 August 1942

Dear Toni,

It is good that you are still searching in the literature. But always remember this: Most of the phenomena observed by us are "known," with the exception, of course, of the main and fundamental fact that orgone energy exists in the atmosphere and everywhere else, and that we live and breathe at the bottom, so to speak, of an ocean of orgone. It is important to note that physicists have developed totally false conceptions of the phenomena outside the realm of wire-conducted electricity and that many things have not been understood at all— e.g., the northern lights. It is becoming clearer every day that the orgone functions according to specific, hitherto unknown laws, such as dissociation, attraction, radiation, etc., laws which still need to be investigated and which will explain a large number of phenomena. I personally am interested in life phenomena—i.e., the manner in which orgone causes a heart or an intestinal tract to pulsate. If you succeed, as you so enthusiastically hope to do, in getting a current that represents electrical energy to flow in wire, and if you make this happen directly from the atmosphere, you will be a rich man. In the meantime, I have personally been able to make a tungsten thread installed in a totally standard electric bulb to glow when I arranged it in a certain way in the orgone field. The wire glows more strongly if one moves one's hand closer to a certain point. It therefore radiates.

*Son of Lia Lassky Swarowsky, to whom Reich was devoted as a medical student in Vienna.

You will be sorry to hear, however, that no ampere reaction is produced.

All gas radiation phenomena can be traced back to the principle of the Geissler tube, except that the field is orgonotic and not electrical. Atmospheric orgone is nothing more than a gigantic, nonmagnetic and nonelectrical, but instead orgonotic field. You should study the summary which I have written on the relationships between orgone, on the one hand, and electricity and magnetism on the other.

Let me know whether the apparatus for producing slow radiation in the form of a sinus curve is coming along well and whether there is any chance of it being completed by the time I am back again in early September.

By the way, I have also managed to detect the electroscopic reaction in the orgonotic radiation field—i.e., I have proved the identity of "static electricity" and "electrical field." Both are the same type of orgone reaction. If you tell that to an orthodox physicist, he will say that you are mad.

14 August 1942

Templeton has had the orgone accumulator for about two weeks. He has put on weight and feels strong. The numbness in his leg has gone away.

I received a notification from the patent office on how to submit a new claim. The stupid lawyer had let the matter lapse.

19 August 1942

Talk with Templeton about building orgone boxes. Priorities by war board = difficulty. No profiteering on orgone; sustainment of research only; payment of costs and wages.

25 August 1942

Proof for the orgone envelope of the planets.

Total eclipse of the moon.

Observed the reduction in size of the ring of the moon in the darkened area; the shadow of the earth makes the orgone envelope invisible.

The moon possesses an orgone envelope.

The surface of the moon is reduced in size by the shadow of the earth = no radiation from the orgone envelope around the moon.

The lumination of the stars is *not* simply "reflected light" but can be ascribed to the radiation of the orgone envelope on which light impinges—i.e., the orgone envelope radiates when it is struck by light; light is transmitted by orgone—orgone is the medium for light.

It is not matter that "reflects light," but the orgone envelope that radiates. The same phenomenon occurs in the orgone box with dark green light.

❖ *30 August 1942*

Grand discussion with Templeton for hours. This man would have become a great natural scientist if he had had the opportunity. He has pus in his urine, dead T, but he walks around, with pain and cystitis. I hope at least to prolong his life and to keep down the suffering from cancer.

I want to live in this country—to have my lab on a farm if possible, to return to my childhood farm days.

1 September 1942

10 p.m. The Milky Way is striking. The orgonoscope clearly reveals stronger flashing in the Milky Way compared with the surroundings. Not brighter but more intensive flashing.

Why should the Milky Way react in such a way if not because of stronger orgone radiation?

3 September 1942

Templeton is healthy, fresh. We visited a 160-acre farm for a laboratory today.

Asking price $5,000.

4 September 1942

In decisive moments the organism thinks spontaneously. It lacks— yes, even opposes—the will and conscious intentionality. Before unarmored life has been completely recognized, before it is stripped of its supernatural character and raised to the universal foundation of all existence, it requires a home where it can be cared for like a newborn babe. It will find such a home in the expanses of Maine. A hundred and sixty acres of land on a soft incline facing south and east, six hundred meters above sea level, covered with a young pine forest, a lake in front and mountains on the horizon. Here truth shall be sought and protected from the plague, here sickness and misery shall be understood and ways discovered for conquering them.

In trying times modesty must yield to duty. If the discovery of nature is connected with a name, then that name does not only co-incide with a person but with a piece of nature itself. It is my will that my ashes be preserved in a rock on this piece of land; my name is to be engraved on the rock so that the plague does not cause me to be forgotten. The symbols of the two laws of nature I have discov-ered shall also be chiseled into the rock

to preserve them for future generations, along with the only slogan which I have to bequeath to the human animal during my lifetime:

Love, work, and knowledge are the wellsprings of our life. They should also govern it.

The name of the home of life research shall be Orgonon.

T O   T H E   N A T I O N A L   R E S E A R C H   C O U N C I L
❖ *26 September 1942*

Dear Sirs:

This laboratory is very anxious to put the discovery of the atmo-spheric orgone energy to the use of the public and the armed forces of the United States. For two years attempts have been made to reach this goal, but without success up to now.

In filling out my questionnaire for the local board of the Selective Service, I tried again to bring the important discovery to the attention of the authorities. A few days ago, I was invited by the director of the medical department of the Selective Service headquarters in New York, Dr. Kopetzki, in response to my report to the local board. Dr. Kopetzki advised me to get in touch with your office. I have also registered with the National Roster of Scientific Personnel in Washington. Two days ago, this laboratory forwarded to you some publications for your information.

This letter is to ask your advice whether you wish a report about the orgone energy and its practical application as far as it has been worked out experimentally to date, and to discuss possible further procedures on the basis of this report.

T O   C L I S T A   T E M P L E T O N
❖ *28 September 1942*

Dear Miss Templeton:

I am writing this letter to you and not directly to your father because I am afraid that he will not do what is needed without your effort.

1. I did not receive as yet any message about his weight, as taken every week.

2. It is necessary that he measure his temperature while being within the orgone accumulator, every time, and also before he goes in. If an increase in temperature takes place in the box, it is important to learn how much it is. This also I would like to know about every two weeks.

3. I hope he continues to drink much water in order to discharge the brownish stuff from the bladder.

Please tell your father that he will receive a letter from me as soon as I have a message from the War Production Board. Tell him also that there are already four orgone accumulators Type B and one orgone accumulator Type C (for children) to be made. I shall send the money for the material and the galvanized-iron sheets as soon as I receive the priority.

I emphasize again the importance of keeping in touch with me at least every two or three weeks with an extensive letter. I hope you are all well, and that you too are using the box regularly every day. We are already in full work speeding ahead. Did you have any talks with Mrs. Love about the farm and what did she say?

29 September 1942

My system senses a social springtime in the air. It is as if I were stretching, stretching toward the future. My organism is preparing for great tasks: formulation of a work-democratic constitution for Orgonon, organization on all levels, summarization, deliberation, foresight.

T O　　L E W I S　　G O L D I N G E R
❖ *5 October 1942*

Dear Mr. Goldinger:

It will interest you to learn that I got into the greatest troubles through Mr. Aaron. When I amended the patent applications I learned from the Commissioner of Patents that both patent applications had been abandoned long ago; that three patents have been cited against the orgonoscope; that specifications of the devices had been asked for and were never answered; that, in short, Mr. Aaron, who was supposed to handle the whole matter in cooperation with me, not only did not inform me about most important actions of the Commissioner of Patents but left me in the belief that the patents were duly pending at a time when one of them was already abandoned. I simply cannot understand how a patent lawyer can receive a communication from the Patent Office that three patents have been cited against one of the applications and not tell me a word about it. All of the questions of the Commissioner of Patents could have been answered most easily. Not that Mr. Aaron did not understand what the patents were about, but that he did not tell me so and that he did not ask me about important questions which he could not answer himself, seems to me a quite extraordinary event. I have withdrawn the power of attorney from Mr. Aaron, and I am conducting the prosecution of the applications myself.

TO THEODORE P. WOLFE
6 October 1942

Dear Dr. Wolfe,

At the moment, I am so overloaded with organizational and administrative work that I don't get around to doing any scientific work outside the hours filled with these other tasks. You will very soon want to start preparing the first issue of Vol. 2* and you asked me what suggestions I had. I will have a better idea of the task involved once you inform me what material you have so far collected for Vol. 2, No. 1. You know that there is an awful lot of unpublished material lying around in my place. There is therefore no need to fear that we cannot fill the journal. But I am interested in getting other people to write and publish material. I believe that we must find ways and means of encouraging the various specialists to learn how to formulate and write down their observations.

Within the next few weeks, I shall probably have completed the basic outline of the work-democratic constitution of our organization, including the planned Orgonon. That would be material for possible inclusion in Vol. 2, No. 1, and would give readers some idea of the form of our work. In addition, I would like also to continue the publications about the orgone. This time, however, I want to include a paper on the results achieved so far in the work on orgone and cancer, or something on "Psychic Emotion and Orgonotic Radiation." Both papers are conceptually ready and only have to be written down. I would prefer the cancer work over the radiation work because it is clinical and practical and therefore more accessible to our readers than the difficult physical radiation.

You can also expect to receive an article on the schizophrenia case,

*Reich is referring to the *International Journal of Sex-Economy and Orgone Research*, published 1942–45.

but only if external circumstances prevent me from continuing the experiment. If I do continue the experiment, then I would wait until it is concluded.

I would propose that we gradually start to examine the criminal-sociological problem associated with neglected youth. The war seems to have considerably exacerbated this problem, especially in New York. You will have read the terrible story about the secondary school teacher who was murdered by two biopathic youths. Would you like to take on this part of the work as well?

The organization of the development of Orgonon is proceeding slowly but well and reliably. The War Production Board has approved the priorities for material, and having given its approval once, it will go on giving its approval in future as well, because the importance of our laboratory work has been acknowledged.

Today, I also received a letter from the Office of Emergency Management, Committee on Medical Research, Washington, in which I am requested to submit a report to them on orgone and its practical application. I hope I manage to write the report in such a way that it does not alarm the people over there and that they do not reject it as too fantastic. (In this connection, can I ask you, please, to keep an exact record of the temperature increases and the subsequent drop in temperature that you experience. I believe that we will learn a lot from that.) So far, I have received orders for about ten orgone accumulators. Some of them have already been paid for. Now we have to wait and see whether Templeton will go ahead with his plan to build the accumulators.

Today, I received my classification as 3A—i.e., I am "deferred." This is good news.

On Saturday I was visited by a young psychoanalyst from New York. It was very interesting. He had spent three years in a training analysis with Cardiner and one year with Rado in control analysis. He complained that he was dissatisfied with the work. When the Horney* group split off, he went with them. When he read your comments about the senselessness of the absolute antithesis of libido and social effect in the foreword to my book, he began to feel uneasy

*Psychoanalysts Abraham Cardiner, Sandor Rado, and Karen Horney.

with the Horney group and found his way to us. He wanted to have control hours but I explained to him that he would get nothing out of it. I suggested he should consider the following proposal: He could train in the normal way to become a vegetotherapist or he could register at the clinic and observe you giving demonstrations from our field of work. He said that he was only speaking for himself, but he indicated that a small group of young analysts was with him in this matter. He will get in touch again and I would like to be able to tell him whether it is feasible for you to give this group of doctors a theoretical introduction to the field of sex economy and vegeto-therapy.

7 October 1942

How difficult it is to decide whether the fascist carriers of the plague should be excluded from the benefits of the orgone!

Last night I was unable to control my own reaction to the plague. Ilse had gone to visit old friends, former German socialists, and had promised to take over the care of a Jewish child whose parents had been deported from France to Poland. She did this without asking me. I protested and made clear that our life is governed by certain rules and that we cannot take a child into our home; just as there are other things which I must do whereas the rest of the world must not.

Ilse said, "These people were so casual and cheerful that it was really refreshing." I reacted poorly. It is indeed true that these people did have the political situation in Germany under their control twelve or fifteen years ago, but they parleyed it and gambled it away. And now they are without feelings of responsibility for the human mess— just simply "nice, harmless, friendly people"!

But that's *exactly* it. I cannot be as "nice, agreeable, and super-ficially cheerful" as they are because I possess a special organ for the plague and its causes—and this plagues me in itself.

Then I became afraid that Ilse might find life here too difficult and go back to her Parisian friends.

8 October 1942

Early today I stopped a racing heartbeat [in myself] by applying orgone-accumulator vagotonia.

With Templeton and his cancer there has been a great turnaround: from having to come to me daily to having an accumulator in his own home.

This will get rid of impossible inconvenience, enable the patient to eliminate pain on a continuous basis, and will be the start of *prophylactic cancer treatment.*

I would offer to reduce the number of cases of cancer to a minimum in any district at all, if I could be allowed to prescribe for the area.

T O   H E R M A N   T E M P L E T O N
❖ *8 October 1942*

Dear Mr. Templeton:

I have your letters of 3 October and 6 October. You know how glad I am that you are doing so well. Please continue to be careful and to take it easy. There is every hope now to conquer the disease completely, and we need you badly just now.

As to Mrs. Love: I know that she is a shrewd woman, as you write, but I am not willing to pay $5,000 for a farm which is assessed at $2,000. The selling of the wood was only a threat, and if she sells it, the property will lose in value. So I think the best would be to let her hang a bit. I would appreciate it if you, according to your experience, would advise the Orgone Institute Laboratories to buy the farm for the amount she asks for it. I am ready now to go up to $3,000 cash on the table. A student of mine is willing and ready to give a loan for this amount to the Orgone Research Fund. Well, try to keep her interested, and tell her a bit more about the purpose for which this land has to be bought. Try, as well as you can, to warm up her heart a bit.

TO E. COWLES ANDRUS*
❖ *12 October 1942*

Dear Dr. Andrus:

Enclosed please find a short outline on the biological and medical characteristics of the atmospheric orgone energy, and a reprint from the *International Journal of Sex-Economy and Orgone Research.*

I assume that for the time being you will be only interested in the practical application of the orgone. The outline contains a few suggestions as to *possible* future applications, which are likely to be expected. The complicated theoretical, physical, and biophysical aspects of the problem involved are arbitrarily omitted in this outline.

Our institution is working on a plan to develop the practical use of the atmospheric orgone on a large scale in the prevention of diseases. This plan could not be carried through without the assistance of state or federal support. I shall be glad to give you any further information about this plan if desired. The existence and visibility of the orgone energy can be demonstrated at any time in my laboratory in Forest Hills.

According to my experiences up to now, the existence and the effectiveness of the newly discovered orgone energy are looked upon as "incredible" and "phantastic." I can only assure you that I, too, experienced these facts as "phantastic" and "incredible" in the beginning. But the fact has been established that orgone shows hitherto undreamed-of biological and medical effects.†

❖ *17 October 1942*

I asked the druggist who declared most of chemical stuff a swindle whether he would testify for me in case of attack by chemists. He said he wouldn't but would perhaps change his mind.

---

*Of the Committee on Medical Research, Washington, D.C.
†Two months later Reich was refused support on the basis that the work was not useful for the war effort.

18 October 1942

Idea: Connection between radiation and the formation of cancer cells.

The cancer cell forms as a result of (a) local and (b) long-lasting radiation in tissues which occurs instead of orgastic radiation of the total organism. It could originate from the buildup of energy in the respective organ as a result of a spasm. This local radiation could be a reaction (an anger reaction) of the cells to the spasm and the asphyxiation.

The orgone cancer therapy would thus be a radiation therapy— that is, restoration of the entire body radiation instead of the local reactive radiation.

24 October 1942

Today Eva moved into her room in our house. Even as an infant she was contemplative. Today she is studying medicine. She was amazed at my microscopes. I told her about cancer tissue. How much this child has suffered because of my work.

25 October 1942

This afternoon I listened to Mahler's First Symphony under Bruno Walter and then to some Schubert and Wagner. I still had the old feeling of contact, but at the same time this world seemed to be going under. The music of the future cannot yet be heard, but one senses the impetus which will someday create it.

26 October 1942

A shoemaker must be aware of the mistakes he makes in his trade and correct them. An engineer must know exactly which miscalculations he might make in order to avoid them. This is the case in every responsible vocation. "Democracy" is supposed to be an achievement of the people. But one never hears anybody raising questions or saying, "People, you are making this or that mistake! People, you're wrong!" Somehow the people always seem to be right. This casts suspicion on history. Isn't this due to the fact that politicians want to flatter the people, lead them astray, arouse their vanity, strip them of their sense of responsibility?

Only when "the people" have the courage to recognize their mistakes (and how enormous their failings and shortcomings are!) will they have acquired the strength to be genuinely democratic.

TO HERMAN TEMPLETON
❖ *31 October 1942*

Dear Mr. Templeton:

You will have the metal sheets about Wednesday or Thursday next week. They will be shipped from New York on Monday. I have also wired to Tibbett* to provide immediately 1,000 square feet of Celotex. And now, please, be ready with the wood, so that no further delay be caused in the delivery of the accumulators. Several of the waiting people are very ill and need it badly.

I wish to inform you that one of my students has offered a loan of $5,000 to buy the property of Mrs. Love. We have to do the following things now:

A) Please give us the name of a lawyer in Farmington or Lewiston or Rumford whom you know as an honest human being and who would make the title search about the property. Let him go ahead immediately, or write to us and we shall communicate with him.

B) See, please, Mrs. Love and offer her $4,000 in cash. Should she not want to take that, then let me know and we shall pay her, without further bargaining, $5,000. I hate this bargaining, and to me and the institute it is worth $1,000 not to have more discussions with a mercenary human being. Of course, it would be proper, then, that the institute treats Mrs. Love, should she come for help, according to her behavior now. When the title is cleared, then we shall pay out the money to Mrs. Love in cash and the papers would have to be sent here for the signatures or the lawyer could sign them for the Orgone Institute, Forest Hills, N.Y., which will be the buyer. The mortgage on the full amount will be secured to Miss Dorothy I. Post.

C) When we have the property we shall immediately go ahead and

*Verd Tibbett, owner of a hardware store in Rangeley.

build a first, primitive workshop on it, to be ready for work early in the spring. Would you kindly think over the estimate of the costs of a workshop about 25 feet wide and, to begin with, 50 or 100 feet long. I leave it to you to make suggestions as to the material and the shape of the building. For this first building we should use the materials which are left on the property. We shall not have to buy any new materials. The only building which will not be taken apart will be the great red barn.

❖ *5 November 1942*

Mrs. Love wants to sell for $4,000.
I buy. Good luck!

6 November 1942

4:30 a.m. Can't sleep. We must take action against the people who are spreading rumors. Zilboorg and Lewin, both psychoanalysts, told a female patient outright that I was "crazy," although Lewin did take it back later. Both stated that the orgone business was "insane" but that I had previously made "good clinical contributions." All this can be traced back to Otto Fenichel. When he was forced to leave Oslo during that whole affair, he proclaimed to the entire world that I was mad. I will ask Wolfe to write an article. *I am afraid of the common human animal.* The more truth and integrity our endeavors reflect, the more dangerously this animal will behave. It is capable of doing anything, of using any means at any time. I fear that the psychiatric profession will trump up charges against me. Naturally, I could make a stupid mistake here or there. In America it's very easy to be committed. A doctor simply has to write out a directive. I must take precautions against this. They are capable of anything when they are reminded of the life they have lost.

A foul-mouthed individual named Sergei Feitelberg announced at a party that I was running an illegal brothel. He is the type of man who boasts in public about how many women he has laid and how often.

TO   THEODORE   P.   WOLFE
12 November 1942

Dear Dr. Wolfe

Today I received the manuscripts and your letter of 10 November together with a letter from the National Research Council in Washington. I mention these two letters deliberately in one breath. The letter from Washington will in all likelihood totally change our existence. My report obviously pleased them a great deal and I was given forms for a contract with the government to expand orgone research. The accompanying letter is very friendly and promising in tone. I now firmly believe that we will get as much money as we need. Even I myself do not know how broadly I should define the scope of our work. I think broader rather than narrower is best. At any rate, I shall submit the plan which we discussed during the summer in Maine. The contract contains data on necessary technical and medical assistance as well as on material and equipment that is required. My plan now is to get Orgonon fully functional within a short period of time. The most difficult thing is the question whether the laboratory should be linked with an already existing hospital or whether it would be better to set up one's own clinic. That needs to be considered. On top of everything else that I have to do now, I also have to come up with a neat and carefully prepared version of the Orgonon plan very quickly. It will therefore not be possible for me to devote so much time as before to writing articles for the journal. For the same reason, would you please overcome your unseemly modesty and prepare yourself to work completely independently on the journal. What you write on the topic of "Rumors and Gossip" is correct, as far as points 1 and 2 are concerned, but can be rapidly and easily overcome. I do not doubt that you will manage the task better than I would. It goes without saying that I would be there to help you if need be.

There is a great deal that could be said about the discussion with Folsom, the professor of sociology at Vassar College. He makes an extremely serious and good impression. He was here together with a woman who is a leading figure in American sex politics, in order to seek my help and advice on founding a new sex-political organization. There is a group of doctors, sociologists, and sex politicians who had read "The Invasion [of Compulsory Sex-Morality]" and "Sexuality in the Cultural Struggle"* years ago; they are in principle very correctly oriented and precisely because of that correct orientation they do not wish to risk going public rapidly and incautiously. They are trying discreetly to build up a sex-political organization which will differ in its principles and goals from the usual organizations. They agree essentially with the European Sexpol. I could not avoid accepting their invitation to attend one of their next sessions and then to take charge of the orientation of the group; one reason was that the old sex politician came alive in me again, after being in a state of decline these last few years. It will soon be obvious whether it might be advantageous to cooperate with this group.

29 November 1942

The sex-political possibilities in the U.S.A. are just as gigantic as the contradictions in its love life. The epitome of petty bourgeois postures and clerical hypocrisy go hand in hand with lectures on birth control for seventeen-year-old girls at Columbia.

But this sexpol is still in its infancy and is struggling with the basic questions of diaphragms and condoms. Legal premarital sex is entirely inconceivable although commonly practiced everywhere.

Just as czarist oppression unleashed the "hunger" revolution in Russia, sexual hypocrisy will unleash the sexual revolution in the U.S.A.

12 December 1942

Idea about the nature of hunger.

Like all organs, the stomach obeys the tension-charge formula. If there is no food in the stomach, then the first beat—mechanical filling—of the four-beat rhythm is lacking and therefore no charging, etc., can occur. "Hunger" is nothing more than the perception of this "emptiness"—that is, the impossibility for charging to occur. Once the stomach is full, it can charge—i.e., initiate peristalsis. Simple but true.

---

*Included in *The Sexual Revolution* (New York: Farrar, Straus and Giroux, 1974).

15 December 1942

I am gradually losing interest in human beings. I have repeatedly discovered that my demanding a rational reaction from people stems from my own cowardice. I fear the responsibility which human irrationality places upon me. I fear the dangers which ensue.

And yet, I am still struggling against complete indifference to people, and even more, I refuse to allow myself to view mankind as a strangely distorted, twisted, miserable mass of plasma. An understanding of the roots of the biological distortion as seen in the human race could be the essence of my scientific work—or might it be madness? It frightens me, it's too much. I do not want the vast loneliness it demands of me. Suppose that mice, as a species, were to run around with rigidified spinal columns and distorted faces as opposed to all other species. It would pose a problem for every biologist. But it does not pose a problem for them when the human species runs around with the same symptoms. It is an illusion to believe that this developmental fault will correct itself in one or two generations. It will require hundreds, perhaps even thousands of years. It doesn't matter! Actually, my tasks are only threefold:

1. Elaboration of the life principle
2. Securing my priorities
3. Preventing myself from being defamed in the annals of science

I have only thirty or forty years left for this work. With each new step I have lost pupils and friends:

a. From psychoanalysis to character analysis
b. From character analysis to vegetotherapy
c. From psychotherapy to biology and orgone therapy

There must be a way for each step to retain its workers without my losing them. There must be a way to hold everything together.

But I must devote myself wholly to biophysics:

Kreiselwelle [spinning wave]

The nature of chemical periodicity

The nature of the N,C,H,O composition of living matter

The cosmic orgone

The origin of matter in general, the functional natural law

I must shake myself loose from present restrictions. Even if it should cause me further grave sacrifices.

18 December 1942

Official sexology reduces the entire problem of sexuality to the question of condoms.

In comparison to this, immersion in the orgastic experience is undoubtedly a cosmic-plasmatic event. We do not understand this as yet. It would be an important achievement if we did.

20 December 1942

I have just finished Sullivan's book on Newton.* It is clear that, with his theory of gravitation, Newton had hit upon the orgone. He regarded gravitation and "God" as identical. Therefore, he always felt himself drawn toward mysticism and religion. His rummaging through biblical history indicates that he had an awareness of the biological-mystical nature of man, of life, and thus of gravitation and the orgone.

Newton was split between mechanism and mysticism, the age-old pitfall threatening all philosophers. Orgone physics unites nature and God, mechanics and "spirit." Its laws apply in both areas. The riddle of the universe and its mechanics will be solved by researching the living—not vice versa, by attempting to comprehend life from the mechanics of the atom, which has been the approach so far. In a certain sense, the ancient philosophers and the book of Genesis are correct: the "soul" is the basis of being—not, however, in the sense of mysticism and metaphysics, but in the sense of orgone physics.

20 December 1942

(While listening to *La Traviata*.) The human animal is torn by his yearning to regress to the amoebic stage and to progress to inconceivable developmental goals. This yearning finds its strongest expression in good music. The dichotomy between progressing and regressing will only be solved through contact with the sentience of plasma. The "purpose" of this lies solely in the function of unarmored life. Since any function can become rigidified and thus exert a restraining influence, the plasma must conquer the "conservative" in order to stride forward. This conflict behooves us to respect the trag-

*J. W. N. Sullivan, *Isaac Newton* (New York: Macmillan, 1938).

edy of unarmored life. It is the "human conflict," the original source
of all tragedy and every struggle!

The real history of culture will only begin with the orgastic potency
of the human animal. Until then, culture will be conservative; until
then, individual lives will be merely a preparation, a preliminary
stage.

Over millions of years the human animal will bring the plasma
function forward to its highest stage of development, to undreamed-
of dimensions which will completely dwarf the paltriness of our day.

The orgone will enable us to visit distant stars and to contact other
beings. It will transform men of German, English, or Chinese "na-
tionality" in such a way that questions of passport or race will no
longer arise. Love will be the driving force of this genuine cosmo-
politanism! Love will be the only religion! It will encompass all that
the sons of the human animal have smashed, wreaked death and
destruction upon, over the past thousands of years.

Other animal races will conquer mankind in the following millions
of years, other types of plasma from other stars will "mount the
throne" and then yield to still other types. In comparison to this, the
emotional plague of earth beings in the twentieth century A.D. will
dwindle to a meaningless nil. This very struggle against "anti-nature,"
however, will unleash the forces which will accelerate and ensure the
continuing turbulent development of unarmored plasma.

It is irrelevant which plasma system senses and grasps the upheaval!
What difference does it make whether I am the one or someone else?

In such moments the concept of "God" is revealed!

26 December 1942

Fifteen years ago I, together with the other rescuers of the people,
believed that "the people" were thirsting for freedom and merely
waiting for a redeemer to save them. So I went and brought them
knowledge, without even feeling like a redeemer.

Then I discovered that "the people" want security—not freedom
—no matter who provides it.

Then I learned that "the people" want security because they fear
freedom—in other words, they want to remain unfree. And finally I
understood the terms "state" and "dictatorship."

I now know that the nature of man erred when it created civilization. If the meaning of life is to function, then life in man ceased to function when he became a machine.

Man is on the verge of discovering his plasma, and this will deliver him from mechanistics. How long will it take? One, two, one hundred generations—a thousand? Who knows.

In order not to be crushed by man one must withdraw when working on plasma. The cardinal objectives then become relentless insight into biological desolation, and freedom from all attachments.

The human animal is neither man nor beast. He is not man because he does not affirm the beast within himself, nor is he beast because he is not human enough to get rid of his fear of himself. The human animal has arrived at an intermediate stage where it dreams of what it has yet to become while destroying that which it still remains.

The function of language is to express feeling, whether this be a matter of intention or simply thought.

Recently Wolfe remarked that 99 percent of all scientific articles could just as well remain unwritten without its changing anything. He's right.

Man cannot use language because his mouth only moves in order to hide the emptiness within. That is why he gossips, babbles, and talks nonsense. He does not speak in order to say something, but simply in order to loosen up his throat muscles.

T O   H E R M A N   T E M P L E T O N
❖ *31 December 1942*

My dear Mr. Templeton:

This letter is to ask a favor of you. For about two months now I have been writing down my experiences about the physical and medical qualities of the orgone energy. It will be published in about March or April. Now, you are one of the main witnesses of the positive qualities of the orgone. Besides that, the way in which you knew about the existence of the small bubbles in the earth and about what you used to call life in the air is of such tremendous importance for the human race that I would be thankful to you if you would give your permission to give an account in this publication about your knowledge of the life energy as well as about how you yourself have experienced its beneficial medical value.

I would also like to mention your name if you would permit it, but that is not absolutely necessary. But it is important that a man who lived all his life in the woods, and who knows life, and growth, and trees and mountains and the sky better than any learned academician, has known for many decades what I have discovered in two decades of hard work by the means of experiments. I hope very much that you will not refuse to be described in this article. I also want to mention that you became the manager of Orgonon because I have to explain how the whole plan of Orgonon came about, and the way in which this institute will try to exterminate cancer and other diseases.

Please let me know quite frankly whether you consent or not. I hope very much you do. It cannot do you any harm, but only good, and I shall be proud to mention the friendship which has developed between us on the basis of common understanding of the nature of what we call life energy and what people experience as "God," who is everywhere and is life and creates life.

A happy New Year and good luck to you and your family.

1943

"I am convinced that only very few of those who fight official medicine would be willing and ready to fight in the right place and for the right thing: the inclusion of the natural process of the orgasm function in the living organism."

10 January 1943
The work on cancer is finished. Seven years of experimenting.

14 January 1943

Fifteen years ago my entire life and activities were anchored in political psychology. In those days it was not wanted. Today, fifteen years later, I have lost all interest in political psychology; the most essential things have been said. Although political psychology is now beginning to take root, I am in an entirely different place: I'm more interested in the radiation of the solar corona than in political psychology. I have become indifferent to man, *he is just too offensive.*

18 January 1943

"Everyone is right somewhere along the line. They just don't know where!" This even holds true for religion, which is doubtless the profoundest form of mysticism—i.e., it has come closest to the *cosmic* orgone. It has grasped the "rational" processes of nature, as distinctly seen in biological functioning and the revolving of the planets. God is the cosmic orgone. The orgone is biological energy. Orgone implies human rationality—as well as the growth of cells.

To function signifies *appropriate* activity. Therefore all orgonotic functioning must be purposeful. The "purpose" lies in the essence of the function itself, not in its "goal"! A bird does not have wings *in order to* fly. The orgonotic function of wings *is* flying itself.

One does not have a brain *in order to* think. The brain's pulsations *are* thought.

Nor a heart *in order to* pump blood. The function of the heart *is* pumping blood.

The function of the genitals *is* orgonotic convulsion.

The function comprises cause, effect, and goal. Functional thought therefore comprises everything that "cause thinking" and "effect thinking" attempted to grasp separately. In this way it renders both mechanistic-causal and utility thinking superfluous.

When men were still animals with undisturbed life functions, writing did not yet exist. Probably there was very little spoken language either. By the time technology arrived man had already forfeited his inner vitality. Thus the various philosophies of life were created, *partial* philosophies because man's ability to grasp the whole had been lost.

The discovery of the sexual function is, of necessity, the discovery of the totality of the organism and of the orgone. For this reason functionalism also resolves the contradictions between mechanism and vitalism, God and the devil, nature and civilization, gravitation and mysticism, science and religion. It eliminates the fragmentation of life, thought, society, etc., etc.

This constitutes a removal of contradictions in the field of principles and theory, not yet, however, in practice.

The practical application of the principle is difficult. One would like to have it easy and thus one misses the mark. Reality is infinitely more complicated than the principle itself. It confuses the principle, frequently seems to be disproving it, is actually imperfect, requires new achievements and correction. But if one loses sight of the principle, then there is no way to update and correct it.

T O   T H E O D O R E   P .   W O L F E
19 January 1943

Dear Dr. Wolfe,

Our influence does in fact seem to be growing a great deal, and I see the following picture emerging. For a while, we will be able to work and publish in peace, perhaps for one or two years. But then the official agencies will be forced to take a position either for or against. *Against* will be extremely difficult for the people, and *for* will mean too much responsibility for them. Thus, a fairly complicated situation will arise which will require the use of all our intelligence, expert knowledge, and flexibility. I would like to discuss all that with you when you are here. At any rate, when the next clash with the public comes, I do not want to be pushed once more to the edge of the abyss; instead I want to be equipped as completely and as well as possible for all eventualities.

In the coming days, I shall give the German cancer manuscript another thorough read-through to see whether I have to make any further deletions or additions. At any rate, there won't be many. I believe that I now have the necessary distance.

Here is something to please you: In the last few days, I have seen the first minimal signs of mechanical oscillations as a result of expansion and contraction of the orgone energy field around metal spheres. This result comes after several years of searching.

January 30, 1943

At approximately 4 p.m. (in the presence of Ernst Kalmus, who is going to build the apparatus) I noticed the following disturbing phenomenon:

For test purposes, we placed a wooden sphere on a vertical shaft which rotated, together with the sphere, at a speed of one rotation every 6 seconds. I held a square piece of copper, then tin, which was hanging on a silk thread about 1 cm away from the equator of the rotating sphere. The piece of metal began to oscillate toward and away from the sphere. If the rotation was stopped, the swinging motion stopped. When the rotation was started again, the swinging motion started up once more. There was *no* swinging motion at the "north pole" of the rotating wooden sphere. From the equator to the north pole the swinging seemed to decrease in intensity (amplitude), but not in the number of swings. To my amazement, when several measurements were carried out with the stopwatch, the number of swings was about 64 per minute—i.e., exactly the number that had been observed several days previously (on the rigid system).

The swinging motion was *regular*, but in air currents it was irregular. There was a not very clear trend for the [piece of metal] to be deflected in the direction of rotation. There can be no doubt about the action of the rotation of the orgone field.

If it should also be verified in a vacuum, after eliminating all the obscuring conditions, this phenomenon would have the following enormous significance:

1. The orgone energy field of rotating bodies pulsates.
2. Bodies in a rotating orgone field start to swing, a motion which is made up of attraction and repulsion.
3. The amplitude varies; the number of swings is constant at 64.
4. Corresponding to 1, can orgone energy be drawn from the air and directly converted into mechanical energy?

TO   ALFRED   KINSEY
❖ *4 February 1943*

My dear Dr. Kinsey:

I have transmitted your request to obtain a copy of my book *The Discovery of the Orgone*, Volume 1, to the Orgone Institute Press, which undoubtedly has forwarded the book to you in the meantime.

I wish to thank you for the reprint of your article on homosexuality. It is my conviction that the question of homosexuality is far from being solved, especially as far as the physiological and biological background is concerned.

20 February 1943

1 a.m. I have without a doubt described the biological pulsation function of the orgone in a strictly physical sense—in the form of a mechanical pendular movement. It is simultaneously a description of attraction and repulsion, of gravitation and the revolutions of the planets.

Over and over again it is *too much, far too much*, amazing, "phantastic." But I will come through, I think, with the simple means of functional thought.

Great difficulties with the organization of the Orgone Institute. Except for me, there are no large contributors. The orgone accumulator will be the basis for orgone research. I must hurry. Have approximately thirty years to live. By then I must have the answers to the following:

1. The gravitation problem
2. The law of natural functioning
3. The spectrum of orgone application in medicine
4. The sociology of the human animal ("Man in the State")

It is constantly getting lonelier, colder, the expanse around me is widening—a horrible but fertile situation, as if eternity and cosmic energy had wed to produce the stuff from which cognition is made, and I am the instrument and observer.

22 February 1943

6:15 a.m. Can't sleep.

From an energetic standpoint the enormous achievement is not "thinking" but rather "not-thinking." An individual with the emotional plague uses more energy than even the greatest thinker. This sounds paradoxical but is nevertheless true. A person with a phobia, who must observe and bear in mind hundreds of precautionary measures in order to avoid a certain street, exerts incomparably more effort than a healthy individual who simply walks down the street. Asceticism, not love, requires the great effort. It is war—namely, the avoidance of simple solutions to the simplest social problems—that requires the staggering effort, not setting up factories and farms, establishing universities and kindergartens.

It is therefore incorrect to believe that good thinkers are exceptions to the rule. It is equally incorrect that the impoverished intellectual activity in the human masses represents a passive nonachievement of some better state of mind. Quite the contrary: this meager intellectual activity of the majority of mankind represents a *gigantic, active achievement* when measured against the simple contact in thought processes. The impotent neurotic always thinks that the erection of the penis is something he must accomplish, whereas in reality he must spend all his energy to suppress this natural process.

Correct thinking only requires effort when there are millions of false thinking techniques which must be overcome or analyzed away in order to arrive at the real topic of thought.

Therefore, to save energy, a good thinker withdraws from the world of deception—i.e., deliberate, complicated obscuring of the truth—in order not to drown in the sea of irrational arguments. Then his thoughts give him joy, like a sport, a great sensation of happiness, no complications, just like riding horseback through the spring countryside.

But in order for the human masses to master their own lives, it is not necessary for them to acquire something or to learn something. Quite the opposite: they must unlearn the tendency to strain, they must put an end to false, complicated thinking past the issue, thinking the issue out of existence.

This alone would safeguard a great portion of the future, a good, full future!

T O　J O S E P H　K .　F O L S O M *
❖ 15 March 1943

My dear Dr. Folsom:
I received your kind letter and your book. I could see at the first glance that I shall enjoy reading it very much.

I am sure that further discussions between us on the problem of sexual sociology will clarify many possible divergencies of opinion regarding the emphasis which should be placed upon the sexual social process as compared with the nonsexual functions.

Please, don't fail to call me up when you happen to be in New York again.

T O　T H E　H E B R E W　H O S P I T A L　A N D
H O M E　F O R　T H E　A G E D †
❖ 16 March 1943

Dear Sirs:
Dr. Batzdorf has informed us that you have agreed to use an orgone accumulator in your Home for experimental observations. The Or-

*Professor of sociology, Vassar College.
†In Brooklyn, N.Y.

gone Institute has, therefore, decided to place accumulator No. 9B at your disposal, free of charge for the duration of one year. The accumulator will be delivered at your Home at the end of this week.

We enclose an instruction sheet on how to use the orgone accumulator, but some more information has been given to Dr. Batzdorf, who, no doubt, will discuss it with you.

We shall be glad to give you any further information about the orgone accumulator, and shall appreciate your cooperation in working out all observations and possible effects.

TO HERMAN AND CLISTA TEMPLETON
❖ 18 March 1943

Dear Mr. Templeton and Miss Templeton:

I am glad to hear that you found someone to help you build the accumulators. Please continue building at least another twenty accumulators, in order to have them at hand when new orders are coming in.

We found out here that a double or triple accumulator is more than twice or three times as strong as a simple one, and might increase the effectiveness of the orgone considerably. I would suggest that Mr. Templeton take the panels which I ordered in my last letter, put them around his accumulator, and try to find out whether he can feel the orgone actually stronger. He will enjoy experimenting a bit.

11 April 1943

Brentano's, the large New York bookshop, carries enormous editions of Napoleon, that stupid ass, in various leather bindings, but it was impossible to round up a copy of Newton's *Principia*. Those scientific parasites!

17 April 1943

Biology will triumph over mechanics and physics. Mechanics may pollute the world, drive entire nations into calamity, destroy lives, while physics produces thieves, cannons, diplomats. The state is powerful through mechanics and physics. It rules, ordains. Dictators are omnipotent, as are the princes of Mammon. Only one thing remains outside their power sphere: No dictator can force a tree to grow. No moneyed prince has the power to evoke the magic of a smile in a child's face when unarmored life is not ready to laugh.

This is the great comfort and the true boon of my orgone biophysics.

18 April 1943

If gravity is caused by "ether" and if ether is orgone, then we can offer proof along the following lines. Bodies are heavier at the equator than at the north pole, and they are heavier at the surface of the earth than at a height of 10,000 miles. Obviously this depends on the density of the orgone. Weight must be greater in a 10× concentrating accumulator.

Einstein's rejection of the existence of the ether was based on a lack of proof—ether was replaced by a mathematical construct, the "gravitational field."

Thus, the question will be answered through experimentation.

10 May 1943

The man of science has a hard road. He must prove his every claim, he must carry on arduous research, must deliberate, recognize his mistakes, screen vicious criticism, understand and refute false theories. He cannot use force. In his struggle against the plague he is without weapons.

The mystic has an easy road. No one demands that he prove his claims. He can allege that God is in heaven and the devil in hell and no one will call him to account for his deceit. The slavelike upbringing of little children assures him the servile faith of the masses.

This is why truth has been defeated.

Keeping creative thoughts pure requires isolation, but bringing them to birth requires gregariousness. (This is the reason for so many lifeless thoughts, for so many stillbirths.)

21 May 1943

The ruination of the human structure has left only two possibilities open for the future:

Either the human masses remain in bondage; more or less good "leaders" misrule society while freedom and truth continue to be illusions.

Or the human masses are caught up in the tide of self-transformation. This is followed by decades, yes, centuries of bloodshed, error, and the discovery of truths. Mankind will murder the very individuals who actually symbolize its own future, the loyal and the true, for it fears and hates the truth. After long periods of such error, full of cruel, bloodstained deeds, the human masses will realize that they have murdered their best friends, the individuals who paved the way for their happiness. Then they will adopt the truths of their victims as their own, will plagiarize them, distort them, comprehend them, reinstate them.

Man will create new saints from the ranks of his victims. New religions will arise—perhaps "religions of truth"—whose priests will be the descendants of those who had been murdered.

One thing is certain: *There will be no peace as long as man is running around sexually unsatisfied with a ramrod down his back.*

22 May 1943

Just finished reading Wendell Willkie's *One World.* Although the man is an internationalist, he views everything from the standpoint of a well-meaning dinner diplomat.

But one must have completely affirmed the communists and participated in their errors in order to understand the fundamentally undemocratic line of their politics.

Likewise one must have identified completely with psychoanalysis in order to grasp the incorrectness of its theories of libido and cultural adjustment.

Only then will new methods, solutions, and hopes arise.

My dear Eva,

It did not occur to me last night to ask you to tell me the name of the person who told you the story about Kammerer painting his animals in order to produce nonexistent results in acquired hereditary characteristics. If such an article about Kammerer exists it would be important to know the author, the title, and the journal where it appeared. Would you kindly ask for the data about this article. I would also like to know the name of the person who informed you.

If this story is not mere gossip, your informant will, I am sure, only be glad to help to find out the truth. It will also be important to you to help to establish facts.

My dear Eva:

Enclosed please find your check for June for $50.

Regarding the matter of the article in question about Kammerer, I would ask you not to bother about it any more as far as I am concerned. It is not customary in scientific circles to make statements anonymously. You either stand for the things you claim or you don't say anything, but you don't hide. And no decent research man would deal with anonymous informers. I also regret very much that I have to withdraw my proposal to show you the documents of appreciation of my discoveries through official institutions and people. I want you to rely on your own judgment and on what you saw yourself. The best thing for you to do would be not to mix with it at all. But please, do not hurt my feelings any more by such unreasonable and irrational behavior.

I hope to see you before I leave. I want you to call up.

2 June 1943

4:30 a.m. In regard to Wolfe: "It's nothing," "It was nothing." It is—and always has been—murder, destruction, wholesale!

In armored humanity we may observe the following behavior: Sexual activity is not an orgonotic, orgastic experience for them. It is a kind of insignificant game one may or may not engage in, entirely optional, an amusement, like a game of bridge or an evening walk, a minor distraction. It is not important to man, not of vital importance, not the essence of his biological being. Therefore "it's nothing" if he plays a little game which the urging of his biological core compels him to do. "It was nothing," and he refuses to take the responsibility for something unimportant. He was just playing around.

But he does it secretly, with a crooked smile and a guilty conscience which he admits neither to himself nor to others. He has no idea that he is playing with fire. Since he is orgastically impotent he has no feeling for this, no sense of *orgonotic seriousness*. When he has spread unhappiness, he slinks away like a coward. After all, "it was nothing."

If it's really "nothing," then why does he do it? If there is nothing to it, then why does he always want some other man's woman, even a man who is his friend or comrade? Because his motive is not love. This is not burning, conscious, responsible action but merely envy, an effort to prove his potency, a compensation for lack of self-esteem.

The orgonotically secure, orgastically potent individual with a genital character does not steal a sexual partner—he either wants her or not. If he wants her he will take up the struggle with his rival, conquer him, and then bear the responsibility for his pleasure. If he does not want her he will not play any little games! If there is "nothing to it" he will remain indifferent. If it is important, he is capable of risking life itself, in contrast to the petty bourgeois. People who are threatened by insanity, by actual madness, live in closer accord with this natural principle than those who are orgastically impotent and find it completely alien. For the one person it means *everything*, for the other "it's nothing."

This phrase "it's nothing" expresses the core of human misery. It promotes death and destruction. It lays human lives to waste. It darkens the world.

And this is only one aspect of orgastic disturbance.

6 June 1943

Anyone who does not find sex economy sufficient in itself and who must have *me* in order to stay in touch with the cause is an unreliable worker.

T O   H A R R Y   O B E R M A Y E R [*]
❖ *7 June 1943*

Dear Mr. Obermayer:

I have your letter of 20 May 1943. Some time ago I let you know that according to our experiences we believe it a waste of time and energy to try to convince people who are laymen in our field, whether they are "specialists" in any other field or not. We really believe that it would be much more important and useful in the long run to put up small and slowly growing laboratories where you can learn to understand and handle the orgone energy in its physical and bio-physical properties. I wonder whether you have tried to build a small accumulator according to my description, in order to visualize the orgone and actually to convince yourself first of the existence of vis-ible radiation in the atmosphere. I understand your eagerness to have many people believe in it, but I doubt whether the energy you spend on it is worth it. Two or three good orgone physicists or biophysicists who have trained themselves for two or three years would account for hundreds of mechanists and mystics in biology, psychology, or physics. We are at present experimenting with more than two dozen accumulators in this country. You will read more about it in the next issue of the journal. It will also take a long time to investigate and understand all the properties of this completely different type of en-ergy.

As to your special interest in the social evaluation of our bio-sociology, I think that special methods of handling larger groups of people without having to submit everyone to vegetotherapy should be carefully developed. An article will be published at the end of this

[*]Political activist living in Palestine. Interested particularly in sexpol and Reich's socio-logical critique.

year or the beginning of the next about the emotional pestilence which stands in the way of comprehending the rational life function within the people themselves. It is the most serious problem and far from being well understood. We firmly believe, furthermore, that quality and depth, and not quantity and superficiality of work, will make it in the long run. We are organizing the institute's work and the journal into the direction of handling the manifold questions, doubts, etc., which are arising constantly in the public. You should not be impatient with the doubters. They will suddenly give in when two or three physicians will have handled only half successfully one or two biopathic diseases.

Would you be so kind as to collect all the arguments you experience there, put them together and make an article out of it for the journal. We shall answer as many of the questions as we possibly can.

One of the most important things for you would be to acquire a microscope which is capable of 3,000× magnification. Without that nothing can be really seen in living matter. And refuse to argue with people, biologists or other, who have never looked into a microscope above 1,500×, and who have not consistently worked with living matter. The common habit of killing living matter and tissue in order to examine it is completely wrong and misleading. As to the orgone, be patient because the articles which have appeared so far contain only a small part of the things which have been found. Many a question and many a doubt by many physicists will be dissolved in the course of the next two years. We ask most of these questions and we doubt most of the same doubts ourselves. But we, in contradistinction to the so-called critics, are doing all we can in effort, money, time, and sacrifice to answer the questions and to clear up the doubtful points.

9 June 1943

5:30 a.m. Overcoming the emotional plague (inside and outside oneself) requires:

1. Basic sexual health.

2. A lovable partner.

3. Acquiring the ability to view people *as animals dressed in clothing, as animals with natural genitality*!

4. Having a wealth of intellectual abilities which not only enable one to be alone but occasionally even force one to be alone in order to set oneself straight, to free oneself from current opinions, even one's own: to take a brief look beyond one's own limitations.

5. Having the patience to think and measure things by an orgonotic scale and not according to the speed of light.

An "orgonotic scale" refers to the *gradual* and (when viewed from the perspective of human life) practically *unending expansion of the life function.* The living corresponds to only a minimal vacillation, a minimal difference in the orgone concentration of a planet as compared to the vast amounts of inanimately functioning orgone. The development of unarmored life from bions to mankind, even the plagued mankind of today, took billions of years. When measured on this scale the cosmic light-years dwindle.

The immense speed of electricity is just a flash. The extreme slowness and gradualness of orgone activity is the basic characteristic identifying it with primal energy. All that is gradual is powerful. Speed is only a sudden flash of that which is normally gradual. Since "orgone" and "God" are identical, man lives on an orgonotic scale by virtue of his religiosity (not the church). No matter how plagued he is by this "church" business it will someday, in orgonotic time reckoning, dawn upon him that not only God and orgonity but also orgonity and genitality are identical. On that day the plague will begin to subside.

15 June 1943

You can find every detail on Beethoven in the biographies: the amount of rent he paid, the number of his manuscripts, dates of birth and death, described in the most exact detail and then described again, his deafness, the pads of paper used during conversations, everything, absolutely everything. There is only one thing which is not described: *the agony of a man whose vegetative harmony with the cosmic orgone destroyed his life with his contemporaries,* the joy of having children of his own, the peace of being provided for in his old age. A man who was periodically overcome with musical inspiration which he was *compelled* to heed if he did not wish to endure great suffering. A man whose joy was in giving, who died from the painful birth of ideas and the strain of elaborating them, who never grumbled and expected neither praise nor reward. And in addition to all this, the pressures of day-to-day existence which contradict all that a man possessed of the spirit thinks, loves, feels, and gives.

Beethoven isolated himself from the inane chatter of this world. He could not, would not, was no longer permitted to listen to it—he became deaf—in the service of the music within.

While his ear still strained to listen, the orgonotic function of hearing from without was to fail him.

You will find nothing about the enormous torments of staggering loneliness—nothing. What you will find, however, are the detailed accounts of his external carelessness, presented with a touch of "the poor fool"! The admiration is not directed toward the struggle of a titan but rather toward a "wonderful man." Wonderful means being full of wonder and "wonder" means "awe"!

16 June 1943

(Orgonon.) The deeds of great, unique individuals have led to almost no progress until now because the pupils, the disciples, the masses, did not internally digest their great thoughts and deeds but simply passed them on in the form of clichés. The in-depth structure has remained untouched. This situation will not change—that is, great thoughts and deeds will remain fruitless—as long as the armoring of the human masses is perpetuated.

TO THEODORE P. WOLFE
17 June 1943

Dear Dr. Wolfe,

It took a few days for me to realize just how tired I was. The tiredness is slowly coming out, but it is a long way from being overcome. You will be interested to hear that Templeton is T-free but, just like Mrs. Pops, has developed a vegetative shrinking with immobility from the abdomen downward. The problem is certainly not due to a lesion in the spinal cord, because mobility exists, albeit with pain and sensitivity. It may sound crazy, but it has been established that the paralysis is purely peripheral, and involves spasm of the bladder sphincter and atrophy of the muscles of the thigh. I am trying to help the family as best I can. The doctors were on the point of killing him with morphine. With a few interventions on my part, I was able to limit the morphine intake to a large extent. I do not know whether I will be able to relieve the bladder muscle spasm. If not, he will sooner or later die because of the shrinking. A terrible problem. The doctor from Lewiston who saw him some time ago established that the prostate is very small.

TO   WILLIAM   F.   THORBURN
❖ 17 June 1943

Dear Dr. Thorburn:

I have your note of 9 June. I want to assure you that I am not disturbed by any doubts, as you put them. The point is not whether one makes mistakes or not. Everyone makes mistakes at every step in new fields. I am, however, concerned about whether I succeeded in convincing those who studied with me that the acquirement of the ability *to realize* when a mistake is made and to correct it is quite indispensable. One great psychotherapist said about twenty years ago: You pay for every important experience with a failure in a case.

18 June 1943

To expect contemporary academicians and "leading" scientists to assist me and bring me general "recognition" implies complete negation of myself. Orgone physics will overthrow three-quarters of all present theories. It must therefore proceed as the conqueror. Can a lion expect to be appreciated by the lamb it is about to devour? The lamb has only one way to save its skin—namely, to bleat so pitiably that the guard comes running with his gun and shoots the lion. But that wouldn't change the fact that lions continue to exist and devour lambs.

5 July 1943

The Marxists lay claim to sex economy for Marxism, and the Freudists for Freudianism. By the same token, the bacteriologists (the successors of Pasteur) and the functionalists of physics (Einsteinians) could claim that orgone physics can be attributed to Galileo or Einstein.

A decent science cites the phases of its development precisely. Orgone biophysics passed through Marxist materialistic dialectics, just as it moved through Galileo's law of the pendulum, Einstein's energy-matter principle, and Freud's theory of infantile sexuality. But this does not link it to materialism, Freud, Galileo, or Einstein. It is a new area in the field of natural science.

8 July 1943

The text of *Work Democracy* is giving me trouble. I use the excuse that I have other, more important things such as orgone physics to occupy me. Just evasions: I have simply grown lazy.

26 July 1943

I can imagine no greater catastrophe than if I were mistaken, and the theory were correct that what I consider secondary instincts or drives are actually primary instincts! Because in that case the emotional plague would rest upon the support of a natural law while its archenemies, truth and sociality, would be relying upon unfounded ethics. Until now both lies and truth have taken recourse to ethics. But only lies have profited because they were able to appear under the guise of truth. Under these circumstances, egoism, theft, petty selfishness, slander, etc., would be the natural rule.

T O   N .   S .   H A N O K A *
❖ *27 July 1943*

Dear Dr. Hanoka:

I have received the book and the pamphlets you have sent me. I have the impression that the description of "diaduction" is directed

---

*Dental surgeon. He had used the accumulator for a malady of his son's.

correctly toward the existence of a specific biological energy. But I had the feeling that it lacked evidence. With that I mean simple, clear-cut demonstration of the force. Very many good physicians and scientists have known in a more or less clear way about the orgone, but somehow, instead of fighting their way through in a practical manner to actually get hold of the life energy, they slipped off into many words or into a kind of mystical praising of a force which surely existed but which could not be mastered by mere wording. That does not mean that I do not admire the intuitively correct thinking of these lonesome fighters. As to the many shortcomings in professional medical education, I also believe that not so much fighting in Congress or other political bodies, but practical, effective, and skillful medical action will do it in the long run. First of all, I think, that the fighters for an improvement of the medical profession ought to keep away the many people who, out of mere mysticism or even profit interests, are joining up in order to fish in troubled waters, as the saying goes.

I am convinced that only very few of those who fight official medicine would be willing and ready to fight in the right place and for the right thing: the inclusion of the natural process of the orgasm function in the living organism. I think that this Cinderella of all officialdom will constitute a clear-cut line of division between what is meant seriously, and what not, in medicine.

1 August 1943

We may assume that natural work democracy will be drawn into the ideological stream. The human personality will not adjust quickly or easily to work democracy. The mechanically armored structure of man has created mechanism and mysticism. People who are only half alive, or have work-democratic ideology alone, will bring about a new social regression. The ideal would be 100 percent work democracy plus 100 percent genital character. For the present this is impossible. New social conflicts will arise from the conflict between knowledge about work democracy and an ideology based upon it but lacking practical application. New pioneers of society will have to further the development where work democracy fails in a practical sense. I wish them luck and success. But they must base their struggle on factual soundness and tangible proof. Otherwise they will simply become "ideological rebels." *Their goal must be the complete genital restructuring of the human masses.* The formation of ideological political parties (instead of work organizations with practical objectives) will be the sign that they are deviating from their course.

TO ELIZABETH BADGELEY*
❖ 4 August 1943

My dear Mrs. Badgeley:

I had the impression from your letter that you have worked yourself up emotionally quite unnecessarily. It is possible to fight through the most difficult decisions in life without so much emotional upheaval, and I am sure that you can manage it if you think it over with your good brain. You are in a period of great changes in your structure, and you don't seem quite to realize that such development always means being and feeling hurt one way or the other. The real difficulty seems to be that you are not quite used to such developmental pains, having lived for so long in an atmosphere of artificial calm and resignation, which, of course, did not settle matters but only covered them up. So, please, take it more easy. You know that you are growing into a social setup on which you can rely, but you have to do your part. I do not doubt you will manage it if only you keep in mind what is at stake, as far as work is concerned.

---

*Patient and student of Reich's.

T O   R O B E R T   O L L E N D O R F F *
13 August 1943

Dear Robert Ollendorff:

Yesterday we received your letter of 5 May. Your exposition is of great interest because the enormous problem of consciousness has been haunting natural philosophers for thousands of years and natural scientists for hundreds of years, without anybody so far finding a solution. I personally regard it as the most difficult and most decisive problem facing all of natural science, for one very simple reason: consciousness is made up of sensations, among which we may also include ideas and perceptions. However, sensation—and in particular organ sensation—is the only door through which we are actively and passively in contact with the outer world. It is, so to speak, the corridor which separates the organized living system from the nonorganized, dead system and at the same time links the two. As you know, there is no natural scientific statement that is not arrived at via sensation. All natural scientific statements are thus of necessity affected by sensation. The schools of the empiricists, mechanists, and vitalists are divided on this point. As you have correctly commented, one of the greatest disadvantages of the Freudian concept was that the apparatus which quite naturally represents the only link with the outside world was approached using a theory borrowed from pathology. Therefore, even analytic psychology withstood poorly the biologically based criticism of natural scientists, and the system of the ego, id, and superego had to be replaced by the energetic-functional system of sex economy and orgone biophysics, consisting of a functional core, a functional periphery, and an orgone energy field. In your attempt to interpret the function of consciousness, I think you are mixing up two incompatible thought systems and concepts. On the one hand, you make the energy system the basis of the thought operation, while on the other hand you introduce the concept of superconsciousness, which is borrowed from the topoi of psychoanalysis—an auxiliary construct born of necessity. I believe that is confusing. Why not simply talk of the system of perception, which must be taken to mean not only internal but also external perceptions. Superconsciousness sounds too

*Ilse Ollendorff's brother, who lived in England.

much like superego and a little bit metaphysical. It is much more likely a sensitive subconsciousness which forms a permanent functional unit with the biological core and the external world and only under certain circumstances expresses itself as self-awareness—i.e., as that which forms the core of the problem of consciousness. I have nothing to say about the problem of self-awareness except for one very important experimental fact. In the chapter on the bioelectrical function of pleasure and anxiety in my book,* I make mention of another fact of eminent importance which is described elsewhere: The quantity of pleasure or anxiety excitation—and this has been experimentally proved—is functionally fully identical with the intensity of its perception. In other words, objective excitation and subjective self-awareness are an indivisible unit. But that is nowhere nearly enough to grasp the phenomenon of consciousness in natural scientific terms.

In my opinion, one can approach the problem of consciousness in two ways. One way is to try to tackle it intellectually—i.e., from the natural-philosophical standpoint, as Bergson did. But this does not seem to offer much hope of success. The other route is more hopeful: One can take as the starting point the experimental facts which are available from the field of specific biological energy and wait until further experiments conducted in orgone biophysics have produced new facts. At some point in time, biophysics will and must encounter the phenomenon of consciousness in a natural scientific way and will solve it, either by making an effort or as if by chance. I think your basic view is correct, but I do not think that it can develop into a useful, i.e. practical, *theory* until more solid facts exist about the functioning of biological energy. It may be useful, and it is certainly of scientific value, to poke around in the area of consciousness, before corresponding facts are available, to see where it will lead. This activity would be preparatory intellectual work which could then be oriented on the facts and verified. I believe, therefore, that you should not drop your particular problem simply because it does not yet have a factual basis. I would like it very much if you would send me your exposition, setting forth in detail your thought processes.

I would like to add a piece of advice. The best guides in the jungle

*Cf. *The Function of the Orgasm*, Chapter 9.

of problems surrounding consciousness are the organ sensations, including in particular orgastic excitation. The changes that take place in the phenomena of consciousness during sexual excitation provide very clear and usable reference points. I am willing to help you as well as I can in your experiments by contributing my experience. In treating armored invalids and in breaking through that armor, one has an extraordinarily good opportunity to study changes in the functions of consciousness. I admit, however, that I cannot see the forest for the trees—i.e., I have not managed to arrange the various phenomena in an understandable way or to read a common fundamental law from them. The functional identity of the quantity of stimulus and the intensity of sensation, which was mentioned earlier, is the only light in the darkness which surrounds consciousness. Your efforts and your interest could therefore be very valuable.

17 August 1943

12:15 a.m. Just finished reading Jack London's *Martin Eden*—a great book! What insight that man had! The end, after the triumph has been reached, is completely logical. "The work has been done." It's horrifying! Martin Eden died when his love of love was extinguished. The consequences of this are harsh, relentless. How I fear those consequences! I fear that my disgust will someday inundate and suffocate me when they come, not to enjoy me personally, but rather my fame. That will be sex economy's final hour.

19 August 1943

I resist "recognition." That is when the weaklings come and throng around you, those whose opinions were formed by other opinions, not by facts or experiences. That's when I'd rather remain unrecognized.

TO A. S. NEILL
❖ *27 August 1943*

My dear Neill:

Your letter of 3 August reached me yesterday. I had felt all the time during the last two months that something had gone wrong. I am glad that you told me about your doubts. Now I want to meet your frankness and be frank myself. You remember that I wrote you several months ago, asking you not to bother yourself with convincing people and getting support from so-called specialists who have nothing whatsoever to do with orgone biophysics. I firmly believe it is your own fault that you got a sense "of failure and frustration" in making my work known. I really don't care whether my work is known or not. I only care about whether what I described is true. I want you to believe what I am saying. I don't care. So please, do not send any journals and any books anymore to anyone. Let people come to you, if they wish to.

As to yourself: I do not understand why you wish to affirm my biological theory. The main thing is whether it makes sense to you. If it does not, why care? If it does, why not rely on your own impression? You say that you are not educated in science. But nobody in this world is as yet educated in orgone biophysics. I really wish, out of our old friendship, that you would not add the troubles of the pioneering work in orgone biophysics—which has nothing to do with electricity—to your own worries in the field of education. I would not like to have our friendship clouded quite unnecessarily. The matter of orgone physics and biophysics is not a question of belief or disbelief; it is a matter of observation and experience. As to the physicists, I have not only lost all the respect I had for physics; I regret to have to say that I would never have dared to imagine how bad their thinking is, how conceited and fruitless their efforts, how wrong their statements are. It is true they can build bridges and machines, but they don't know anything about the most primitive questions of life. I don't hesitate to express my utter bewilderment about the silliness within natural science—with only a few exceptions—which I discover to be ever greater the deeper I penetrate into my own and their field of work with my experiments. You will hear more about this in a year or two, when the inconsistency and lack of logic in the physical theory will be revealed. The same way I revealed the prejudices and the cowardice in the thinking of the psychoanalysts. Do you really believe that this world would look as it does look if it were not so?

I have faced the same experience which you face: Neurotics are the ones who are reading the literature—but not only neurotics. And how do you propose to eliminate neurotics if 80 percent of humankind is biopathic? That is precisely the trouble! The disaster is the result of the general biopathy, and a new world, if at all, will have to be built with neurotic individuals. Again: if that were not so, things would not look as they do.

30 August 1943

Old-school psychiatry condemned neurotics and neurasthenics as "degenerates." That was correct to the extent that it was not a value judgment. However, they overlooked the fact that they themselves were also degenerates and that they advocated educational methods and aired cultural opinions which caused degeneration. A critique of psychiatry was necessary before the biological degeneration of the human animal could be approached.

T O   H A R R Y   O B E R M A Y E R
4 September 1943

Dear Mr. Obermayer:

Your letter of 26 July arrived here yesterday. I would now like to deal with the points which it contains:

The "objections" and questions raised: The questions provide proof of a problem with which we are growing increasingly familiar— namely, the poor training in methodological thinking which is given to technical specialists. One cannot, for example, raise objections if one knows nothing about the field in question. Some of your questions, such as the ones relating to the flickering in the sky, have been dealt with by me in detail in my report. Your people do not seem to have taken the trouble to actually *study* my report; otherwise the person who sat in the dark would have built an orgone accumulator in the manner described. I have explicitly stated that orgone cannot be researched by the known electrical methods and that its own methods are being developed. I was surprised that such decisive statements were simply ignored. Your physical chemist in particular conjured up the following image in my mind: A psychoanalyst tells an experimental psychologist that a child has sexuality. Whereupon the experimental psychologist says, "You can't say that. You must first carry out the Wundt Test Alpha Beta Gamma." Or: A mountaineer attempts to conquer Mount Everest (this is a very good analogy for orgone research); he has to find an entirely new route up the mountain. Another mountaineer hears his report and says, "That's nonsense. Why doesn't he use the railway up the Jungfrau?" This is exactly the kind of objection which your chemist raises.

We will use some of the "objections" and questions in our journal to present the method of correct, scientific discussion. I would recommend very much that you do not use the biophysical publications on orgone, which have appeared in fragmentary fashion probably over more than ten to fifteen years, either as a basis for discussion or as a means of recruiting supporters. A serious person listens to such a thing and waits quietly to see what happens, or he carefully sets about accurately reproducing the given instructions and tries to understand. Anything else is just idle chatter. It is not possible to hold debates or vote on such matters. You will save yourself a lot of annoyance if you follow my advice. Twenty years ago, psychoanalysts firmly declared that they were aware of large numbers of neuroses with full orgastic potency. In ten or twenty years the astronomers and physicists will also be struck dumb and gaze with astonishment at a new world, just like so many psychoanalysts do today with regard to sex economy.

T O   A .   S .   N E I L L
❖ 6 September 1943

My dear Neill,

When I wrote you that the great respect I once had for physicists had vanished completely, it is due to a great experience with Einstein. I don't know whether or when it will be necessary to publish this experience; anyhow, I want it to be on file in a letter to you, so that no future biographer may miss it. Here is the factual story, according to notes in my scientific records of nearly two years ago:

In July 1940, I discovered the light phenomena, i.e., the orgone in the atmosphere. Several months later I constructed the accumulator. Soon after that I found that the temperature, measured by thermometer above the top of the accumulator, was continuously higher than the temperature in the surrounding air and within the accumulator. I knew from physics that such a fact is unbelievable and of tremendous importance, because according to physical law, all temperature differences equalize. If they don't equalize, then there must be some source of energy which creates heat. This temperature difference was not only continuous but it changed exactly with the weather. When the sun was shining it was high, up to 2 degrees, and when it was raining it disappeared completely. The curves I obtained were completely in accordance with electroscopic measurements of the energy concentration within the accumulator. The electroscope, too, showed strong concentration in sunny weather and a great diminishment in rainy weather. I realized the exceedingly important quality of this finding. I wrote to Einstein to have a talk with him. He answered that he would be glad to discuss it. I went to him one day in January 1941 at 3:30 p.m., and we had a rather exciting discussion about the orgone, lasting continuously until 8:30 in the evening. I explained to him the main features of the bionous disintegration of matter, and the discovery of the orgone radiation, first in the SAPA bions and then in the atmosphere, as reported in my articles in the journal. Not only was every single fact new to him but he became increasingly interested and excited. Otherwise he would not have listened for nearly five hours. I did not tell him about the temperature differences, which I knew was an unbelievable fact for a physicist, until I had shown him the rays in the orgonoscope which

I had brought with me. And now, please be attentive: We put out the lights in the room and I gave him the orgonoscope and showed him how to use it. We waited about twenty minutes to accommodate the eyes. Then he looked through it, through the window, and he exclaimed amazed: "Yes, it is there. I can see it." He looked again and again. We put on the light again, and he said: "But I see the flickering all the time. Could it not be in my eyes?"

I was a bit astonished that he withdrew, because the orgonoscope shows the rays in a delineated gray circle, distinguished from black surroundings, and his exclamation was quite genuine and true. In my article about the discovery of the orgone, I had discussed at some length the question of the objectivity of the rays, which are both in the eyes and outside the eyes. The objective proof for the objectivity of the rays is, as I explained, the fact that you cannot magnify impressions in the eye, but you can magnify objective rays. Einstein asked me what else I had observed. Then I told him that I hesitated to tell him about another phenomenon I had observed, because he would not believe it. And I told him about the existence of the continuous temperature difference between the air above the top of the accumulator and within the accumulator and the free air. To that he exclaimed: "That is impossible. Should it be true, it would be a great bomb!" (verbatim). He got rather excited and I too. We discussed it sharply and then he said that I should send him a small accumulator, and if the fact were true, he would support my discovery. Before departing, I told him that now he could understand why people were saying that I was crazy. To this he said: "I can understand all right."

I had a small accumulator specially built for him and brought it over about two weeks later. We agreed to observe the fact of the temperature difference immediately. We put the accumulator up in his cellar, the accumulator being on a table, and a control thermometer hanging about 3 or 4 feet away in the air. After some time he and I could both see that the temperature above the accumulator was higher by about 1 degree than the temperature of the surrounding air. We were both very glad. He wanted to keep the accumulator for about two or three weeks and then write to me. He said he wished to observe the continuity and the average of the temperature difference. After about ten days he wrote me a letter. The letter stated: He had observed the existence of the fact of the temperature difference on the accumulator for several days. Please remember that he, as well as I, thought such a fact to be quite extraordinary—according to his words "a bomb in physics." So he had observed the fact and affirmed it, but now comes that which I have experienced with physicists and other natural scientists again and again: First they deny the fact. When I demonstrate the fact and they cannot deny it any longer, then they try to explain it away by some wild interpretation. That happened, not with Einstein, but with his assistant. I stress again the fact that the possibility of a continuous temperature difference without any visible source of heat seemed impossible to Einstein. Well, now it comes: The assistant, apparently some wise guy, knew all the answers. He told Einstein that in cellars there is a "convection of heat from the ceiling to the table top," and that this must be the cause of the phenomenon which could no longer be denied. Now, it is a law in scientific research that, when you have to confirm a fact and you propose a different explanation of that fact, you are obliged to control your own objection. Einstein's assistant did not do that. He simply "objected" without proof. Einstein took the trouble, as he wrote in his letter, to take the accumulator apart and he discovered that there was a temperature difference between, above and under the table. The fact, mind you, had not been known to Einstein. It seemed to confirm the objection of the assistant, but there were only two ways of finding out whether that objection was correct or not.

Now I shall pause for a moment. The answer is in the next few lines. I want you to think for yourself what you would have done in order to find out whether the temperature rise on the accumulator was due to heat convected down from the ceiling or not.

Here is the experimental answer:

a) You simply take the control thermometer which was in the free air and put it above the table at the same height as the thermometer above the accumulator. If the temperature difference is still there, it cannot be due to the warmth from the ceiling. This is true. I had measured with both thermometers above the table for months, and the temperature difference was always there.

But this experiment is still not pure, because the ceiling of the room is still there. Thus we have the possibility

b) to arrange the experiment in such a way, and to measure the temperature above the accumulator in such a way that no ceiling interferes. In February, for two whole days, I put an accumulator into the soil in the open air. The ceiling was eliminated—and thus also the argument of the assistant. I measured the temperature of the air above the accumulator, in the surrounding earth and in the air. Not only was the phenomenon still present, but more: In the closed room the temperature difference, as confirmed by Einstein, was several deci-degrees—3–6 or 7 on an average. In the open, the difference climbed up to 10 degrees and more in the sunshine, and 20 deci-degrees (i.e., 2 degrees) in shade and cold. The ceiling was not there anymore, but the fact of the temperature difference was still there. So these physicists had not thought, after having confirmed the fact, to control their own objections, whereas for more than two years now I have eliminated the ceiling and have still been able to demonstrate the fact. I wrote the whole story to Einstein, feeling uneasy about this great physicist not having thought of the simple measure—namely, to control the fact in the open air himself. Einstein did not answer to this clear-cut elimination of the objection.

In the beginning, Einstein's whole procedure was correct, but when I had eliminated the objection it was not understandable. I can only assume that some crooked friend of mine from Vienna had, through the rumors put into the world about me, destroyed this great chance. We all had the impression that Einstein wished to wait, and not expose himself.

This experience shattered my confidence not only in practical knowledge but also in the ability of physicists to think, act, and behave correctly where "bombs" in physics are concerned. Einstein and I agreed that this one phenomenon, especially in connection with many others, could not only shatter a great many concepts of physics but that, in addition, it would also lay open a great many black spots in astronomical and physical science to correct answers. So they sit there quietly and are watching, without taking responsibility, my deadly difficult struggle to put these things across. When, after a decade or two, I shall have succeeded and be worn out from frustration, human disappointment, and economic and psychic strain, then they will come—I am sure of that. But I doubt whether I shall accept them then. Einstein is very cautious. I do not doubt that he knows that I am right. He saw the radiation in the orgonoscope and he saw the temperature difference in his house, and he was informed of the much greater creation of heat in the open air, without a ceiling. He well knows that it is a bomb. He also knows about the results obtained so far in cancer.

Now you understand my attitude toward physics and physicists in general. I want you now to join my standpoint that there are no authorities in orgone physics anywhere; that the fight is hard, and that I am on my own. But the facts are coming through slowly, thanks to the conscientious and extensive proofs I have given, most of which are not published yet. The matter is especially hard and difficult because the discovery of the orgone overthrows a great many wrong assumptions and emergency theories in the physical world. The four and one half hours of this intensive discussion with Einstein made him make the remark in the end, when I told him that I was originally a psychiatrist: "What else are you doing?" He had thought that I was originally a physicist.

Well, that is the story. It would be very painful and regrettable if I had to publish it. The temperature difference which meant a bomb to Einstein has been observed now for nearly four years, constantly and in all kinds of variations. It is a bomb because it explains the heat of the earth, which was not understood until now, and it explains the immense quantities of heat of the sun, which had not been understood until now either. They become simple through an understanding of the fact that when the orgone particles which are everywhere are stopped in their motion, they create heat. The body temperature and body heat have not been understood either. They constitute one of the greatest riddles of biology, which is admitted by leading scientists. We don't have to consider the chatter utterances of the small lice in science, who know everything by putting a label, a word, undefined and unununderstood, which means nothing, on every phenomenon.

7 September 1943

Doing orgone research could be compared to swimming the Pacific Ocean. You swim for days, weeks, months, put dozens, even hundreds of miles behind you! And still an infinite stretch always lies ahead. You cannot rest, enjoy your success—onward, onward, always farther, always more! It is like reaching for infinity! The orgone is the basic energy of the universe. How cruel!

8 September 1943

The socialists in Palestine want to make sexpol part of their party platform. It would have been better for me twelve years ago, more timely, though hardly possible. They always come so late. When I am no longer interested in the party, then the party becomes interested in me. When I have lost interest in politics, then politics throws itself at my feet.

What to do if politics should call me? That would be the most horrible moment of my life!

18 October 1943

My objective is to work my way out of a tight spot:

1. I owe my present scientific standing to my political and psychoanalytic work in the past. I am dragging this past along with me.

2. With the discovery of the orgone my activities have made a fresh start. The old line of thought is confusing, it hinders me, it's inhibiting. I must rid myself of it completely. But the world is just beginning to accept the *earlier* findings.

22 October 1943

Conversation with Wolfe: We discussed my disappointment in human beings who have refused for so long (fifteen years) to learn about themselves—they are aware but they remain silent. Also discussed my "well-being" and comfort, which is making me conservative.

Time and time again it's the human structure which renders progress impossible.

I have labored and struggled alone for fifteen years. Now they are coming to me. But now I am tired.

T O   W .   T .   B I D W E L L *

❖ *28 October 1943*

Dear Dr. Bidwell:

I have your letter of 25 October. I would advise you to rent a medium-size type B orgone accumulator with two additional layers,† which increase the concentration of the orgone to twice or three times that of the single-layer accumulator. Would you kindly sign the enclosed agreement which is signed by every consumer of orgone. As you will see from this agreement, the contribution which you are paying to the Orgone Research Fund does not go into any private pocket, but serves solely the purpose of the extension of the field of orgone research, and thus also human health. After a few months' use you can, of course, decide whether you want to continue or not.

I would like to warn you against a too optimistic attitude toward cancer therapy. Some of the results are, of course, marvelous and far ahead of any other kind of treatment, but a very much advanced and nearly dying case with large tumors will not react too well. You can use it for anemia and other blood diseases, in that the orgone has a special affinity to the red blood cells. I would appreciate it highly if you would let me know about your experiences after a few months of use. The accumulator will be sent to you from our workshops in Maine, together with the additional layers. Instructions on how to use the accumulator are enclosed in this letter.

We are using lately with rather good effects a three-fold accumulator of 3 cubic feet with a long pipe and a funnel at one end, to "shoot" orgone at nose and throat in case of colds, and on wounds.

I want you to remember all the time that the accumulator is not yet on the market and is still worked upon experimentally to find out new improvements. You will be notified of any new improvement immediately. Since the delivery of the accumulator takes some time, it would be wise to have the documents signed as soon as possible and returned to the office of the Orgone Institute Laboratories at the above address.

---

*A friend of N. S. Hanoka. Interested in building and using an accumulator.
†Each "layer" or "fold" of an accumulator consists of a combination of metallic and nonmetallic or organic materials.

TO JOHN P. CHANDLER*
❖ 4 November 1943

Dear Mr. Chandler:

I am enclosing the answer of the Examiner of Patents to my application for the orgone accumulator.

As you probably have learned by now, I am quite incapable of understanding mere formalisms and of coping with them. The objection of the Examiner has made upon me, as a humble matter-of-fact research man, a rather peculiar, nonsensical impression. When the first application for the orgone accumulator had been filed, the Examiner made several objections which I have answered. Now, there is a new objection which has no bearing whatsoever on the question whether the orgone accumulator is a useful and operable device. Whether the orgone energy is different from electromagnetism or not has, according to very primitive and basic principles of science, nothing to do whatsoever with the question of the operativeness and utility of the orgone accumulator. The problem of the nature and qualities of the orgone energy is one which may require decades or even centuries of thorough research. That has no bearing on the fact that a human being, a mouse, a grass infusion if put into the orgone accumulator shows definite reactions which they do not show outside of the accumulator. Whether the "X" which is operating within the accumulator is magnetism, electricity, positive or negative, or orgone, or whatever it may be, is irrelevant here.

You may ask now why I have put the sentence about the difference between the orgone and electromagnetism into the application. That has its meaning. Though this difference has no practical effect on the utility of the orgone accumulator, it is, however, important insofar as a framework for the future research on the atmospheric orgone had to be set up. A hypothesis that orgone is identical with electromagnetism would have definitely obstructed any further research. On the other hand, the hypothesis that orgone is basically different from electromagnetism opens many approaches for further investigation. I am not ready and willing to discuss now the facts which show the usefulness of this hypothesis. Whether the orgone accumulator is a

*New York patent attorney.

useful and operable device can be proven by a few simple experiments and by results obtained so far in the experimental treatment of human biopathies.

To you as my lawyer in whom I have invested so much confidence in this matter, I may confess that neither my time nor my strenuous work permit me to enter formalistic and irrational discussions, in order to obtain the patent. It is not only my responsibility that the orgone be protected from exploitation by securing a patent. It is also the responsibility of every public official. As for my part, I can bury the whole discovery with all the documents and proofs. I have no personal economic interest or ambition in this matter. I shall not discuss the connecting links between the orgone and electromagnetism now, for one reason: It would mean to expose and deliver the whole discovery with all its implications without getting anything for it. The orgone energy has disclosed many more qualities than are demonstrated by the orgone accumulator. According to my humble opinion, the demonstrations of the orgone energy which are mentioned in the patent application are sufficient.

20 November 1943

I am straddling the fence. On the one side, I am a pupil and admirer of the great masters whom I studied in 1920: Dreisch, Loeb, Uexküll, Hartwig, Semon, and others. On the other, I am a representative of orgone biophysics. It solves a tremendous number of old puzzles—for example, the motility of unarmored life. It reduces complicated matters to simple principles. It has a unifying effect and makes me an authority over old-school biologists. But my early admiration for the former teachers and masters will not allow me to adjust to an independent position in biology.

It is lamentable how little the average physician, biologist, or physicist knows about methods and theory. This constitutes one of the greatest stumbling blocks for my work. People confuse the word "simple" with "superficial." For them only that which is incomprehensibly complicated is held to be "scientific." This attitude, in turn, means isolation for me and loss of interest in convincing my contemporaries.

21 November 1943

I feel as if biogenesis and its infinite possibilities were constraining me to move only within the narrowest confines of my personal freedom.

In just a few months, Ilse will bear me a child. My concern almost stifles my joy. Shall I be capable of being a father when the boy drags me out to play soccer?

2 December 1943

1 a.m. Took a drive through the lonely streets of the suburbs. Something unthinkably tormenting is bothering me. A young woman comes out of a cinema with her husband; suddenly she turns down a street as if she wanted to run away from him. A lonely, sweet girl slowly strolls along with a heavy tread as if she wanted to be caught up, picked up, yearning for love: a sweet, decent human animal. A prostitute is on the lookout for her victims.

A dark street. The windows and shutters have been closed; behind them are lonely people, women waiting for their men who have gone off to war. Or women who at this very moment are being unfaithful to their absent husbands.

What misery; what nameless, silent, misery!

TO HARRY OBERMAYER
2 December 1943

Dear Mr. Obermayer,

It is very characteristic that in America, as in Europe, *Mass Psychology** is read by many, but it seems that nobody dares to actually accept the sex-economic standpoint that is set out in the book. This is probably the reason why so many publications have appeared on mass psychology which give the impression that my *Mass Psychology*, which appeared very much earlier, did not exist at all.

Massenpsychologie des Fascismus (Sexpolverlag, 1933). Published in English as *The Mass Psychology of Fascism* (New York: Farrar, Straus and Giroux, 1970).

One could write an entire book about the arguments and criticisms of bion research which you have sent us. We will try here to discover the common thread in these arguments and to reply from the standpoint of the orgone biophysics which has already been developed. Some of the topics will appear in the journal, where we will try to answer them as best as we possibly can. In general, I have the impression that the persons engaged in the discussion get ahead of themselves too much. I am astonished that so far nobody has hit upon the idea that, instead of engaging in these highly complicated and theoretical discussions, they should build an orgone accumulator (2–10 cubic feet) according to my specifications, and then spend sufficient time and effort to observe the orgone energy. That would do away with many currently useless debates.

There is only one point about which I would like in principle to state as follows: The challenge issued to me by the mechanists (physicists and biologists) that I should provide proof of my qualifications is not only unjustified, but is a sign that they have exceeded their competence. The discovery of the biological energy of the orgone is not a random discovery in some other field. It is not a departure from the twenty-five years that I have devoted to my field of expertise. On the contrary, it is something that has logically and consistently emerged from these twenty-five years of work on the emotions in the physical and psychic sectors. I assert that no physicist or biologist of the ordinary kind, who by his nature knows nothing and does not wish to know anything about sexuality and emotions, would be qualified or even competent to discover or to comment on biological energy. It is entirely logical that the discovery of the orgone took place in the area of sex economy and not that of electron physics. It is thus the mechanists, and not I, who have to show proof of their competence in the field of emotional and sexual life. There are some major surprises awaiting them here, just like the small surprise of the electroscope reactions which were described in the cancer work. I am deliberately leaving myself a lot of time and opportunity to enjoy setting off the "bombs," which have been created by sex-economic research, and not by me, at the right time and in the right place and with the correct intensity in the field of natural science. The arrogance of fragmented mechanistic natural science, which faces life with a complete lack of understanding, even with hostility, strikes me as unseemly and out of place; and it must be clear to anyone who is seriously concerned with orgone biophysics that we do not expect either credit or recognition from this mechanistic science. That is simply a duty toward a major new discovery.

Logically, little can be expected from so-called verification tests at laboratories which, from the start, are [performed by people who are] either aggressively unwilling to believe in the matter or who approach it with mechanistic conceptions. When a bacteriologist sees a blue vesicle in the microscope, he says "staphylococcus," and that settles the issue as far as he is concerned. If a colloid chemist sees the same structure in the microscope, he says "colloid particle," and again that is the end of it for him. They do not inquire into the origin or the function or the change. They make mechanical use of the words which say nothing about the context of the vesicular nature of all swollen substance. For the last few months a biologist who acquired her doctorate in Vienna has been working in my laboratory. She came to me after she had read the publications and was positively convinced by the simple logic of the functions. Thus, she came here already persuaded. After six weeks of carrying out many hours of intensive experimental work each day at the microscope, under my direction, she admitted to me that she realizes now that she had understood nothing when she first read the publications. It became clear to her that the method of observation and interpretation, the organization of the experiments, and the study at 3,000× magnifications could not readily be acquired without having some contact with our laboratory. It is clear to this biologist, as it is to all of us here at the laboratory, that one must spend many months intensively studying the bions and orgone radiation, in order to free oneself from the mechanistic approach, which so far has so successfully blocked access to the functioning of the living organism.

Regarding the defamation you reported in your letter to Dr. Wolfe: So far, due to personal weakness, I have not taken any action against these plague actions. I am unwilling to wash other people's dirty laundry. However, it may be necessary for me to shake off this weakness and go to court. For your guidance and for the guidance of everybody, I would like to make it explicitly clear here that I have kept up my activity as a medical doctor and researcher without one day's interruption for twenty-five years, that I have never been institutionalized, and that to this day I have borne one of the heaviest scientific and social burdens that can be imposed on a person without allowing it to impair my ability to work or love. I have nothing against and on the contrary I am very much in favor of you and others carrying on the objective struggle against the emotional plague in those analysts who are unable to respond to my discovery in any other way than by becoming secretive and mean-spirited, because they have a bad conscience or are technically helpless. The fact that it is in particular former alleged friends, pupils, and colleagues who have taken up the most hateful means of defamation is just typical of people who have a bad conscience toward this very responsible and promising work. We must check each colleague in good time to determine whether, if he fails structurally or factually, he would be inclined to reply with the specific plague reaction—i.e., if he would stab the proponents of sex economy in the back by defaming them.

I would not have mentioned this personal filth, and in fact I have avoided going into it for almost ten years now, if I did not have to consider the large numbers of specialists now working in the field of sex economy and need to protect them from similar experiences. I am now obliged to reveal all the facts, to drop all consideration and to pillory, which is what they deserve, the biopaths who are spreading the rumor that I am insane. At the appropriate time, this will happen publicly in the journal. I am not the first person who has been treated like this by plague sufferers because of his good achievements. Perhaps it will prove possible this time to restrain these excesses of so-called human nature, which is in fact not natural at all. I believe, in fact, that this is part of our general social task; that we should use such personal experiences to practice how to prevent the emotional plague from being transmitted into the larger social sphere. We can correctly assert that the Hitler plague differs from the plague reactions of a person like Fenichel (i.e., just a minor character) only in magnitude and in its comprehensive destructive effect, but not in principle. All this will be the subject of a detailed objective study of the functions and mechanisms of emotional plague.

Please send me as many "arguments," "criticisms," etc., as possible. Not because I believe that I can answer all these questions, but because they give me a picture of the methodological and factual, educational maturity of friend and foe. The comprehensible problems of the gigantic field of the orgone will not be presented until the second volume of *The Discovery of the Orgone*,* which is in preparation, is published.

In conclusion, I wish to share with you the good news that I am gradually managing to get close to combating the shrinking biopathy which underlies cancer.

Please inform Dr. Lin† that for a year and a half a manuscript has existed here which tries to throw light on the relationships between the orgone and faradic and static electricity. It will appear perhaps in the course of the coming year. I must ask all physicists to be patient until that time.

TO   A.   S.   NEILL
❖ *23 December 1943*

My dear Neill:

This is only a short answer to your letter of 18 November. I do not believe that Einstein was so much afraid of it (though he was afraid too as every other mortal), but more likely some of the pestilent rumors had apparently reached him and obviously he wanted to be careful. I cannot judge this interpretation of mine. I am usually rather inclined to try to understand the actions against me than to be suspicious. I wished I had much more of the paranoic qualities of other fighters who smell an attack before it comes.

Regarding the possible martyrdom of people who are representing my teachings, I very often feel like withdrawing in order not to endanger others. But as I used to say, "I did not make it!" It is not my fault, but rather the fault of the whole setup of thinking and education which endangers the people. It is left to the consideration of every single one to decide whether he wants to meet the emotional pestilence or not. You can be sure that I have never forced anyone, and that I shall never force anyone, to represent my teachings as a politician would do.

*The Cancer Biopathy (New York: Farrar, Straus and Giroux, 1973).
†Dr. Theodor Lin, physicist.

31 December 1943

Quite a way gone since 1919! Twenty-four years.*

I am amazed at how much concentrated energy can be expended in one human life over a twenty-four-year period.

Consider what the world could be like if it weren't for the emotional plague.

*This paragraph was written in English.

1944

"It makes no difference whether the functional law of nature, which I discovered between 1921 and 1944, will be generally regarded as true 10, 100, 1,000 years from now. It is true, proved by logic in the development of the problem, by the succession of tests, and by the coherence of the results."

24 January 1944

It should be possible, by means of electromagnetic waves, to cause concentrated orgone in an accumulator to luminate. If my hypothesis regarding local radiation of light as orgonotic radiation is correct:

What is the relation of orgone to light?

What is the relation of orgone and light to radiation?

31 January 1944

A lot has happened in the last four weeks.

1. The regular oscillation of the pendulum when the sphere is charged.

2. Calculation of the spinning wave.

3. First trigonometrical depiction of the organism.

4. First attempt to harmonize the orgone pendulum law with the spinning law.

TO CLISTA TEMPLETON
❖ *7 February 1944*

My dear Miss Templeton:

I was very sorry to hear what you wrote about your father. As I told you so often, I myself was astonished that he lived so long and on the whole did so well so far. I hope very much that he will get hold of himself again soon. But in the event that this time the end should be coming, the end which we expected several times during the last two years, I would suggest that you make it as easy for him as possible by injecting morphine. Don't do it if you feel that he is not approaching the end but is only having a temporary setback. That will show itself within a few days. Should the symptoms become worse and his face fall in, then you know. I regret very much not to be able to be there to help you, but I don't believe that I could do much.

I want you to keep as cheerful and courageous as possible. Please, do not fail to inform me about his state as often as possible. Also let me know what the physician said. Who was he?

With my kindest regards, especially also to your mother and father.

26 *January 1944*

12:15 a.m. The trajectory of a spinning wave system is not a straight line. Rather, it is curvilinear because the entire system is spinning.

This explains the correct notion that space would appear curved to an observer moving with the wave.

T O   J O H N   P .   C H A N D L E R *
❖ *8 February 1944*

My dear Mr. Chandler:

I wish to repeat in writing what I told you on the telephone last Saturday.

I seem to reach the limits of my strength to cope with the obstacles in getting the most simple formal procedures through. You remember well what I told you, when we first met, about the irrational reactions of human beings to everything that has to do with life problems. I wished you could, in the interest of our cause, develop the conviction that there exists in every human being a terrible fear of spontaneous life functions and, consequently, also of such a thing as specific bi-

*This letter was not sent.

ological energy, called orgone. The behavior of the Patent Commissioner and his saying that he would not grant my patent, no matter what proof I would bring forth, is a clear-cut example and proof of this general attitude. This commissioner was only frank, while others are hiding the same attitude behind all kinds of excuses and arguments.

You suggested that we keep the patent application pending for about two years. Please, do so if there would not be too much effort and work connected with it. Please understand that I cannot do this pioneer research in a quite new field of natural science, pay all the expenses of this research, including the salaries of five people working at it, make the necessary difficult studies, do the writing and thinking, earn my living, and, in addition, should involve myself in irrational reactions and discussions. I therefore prefer, being forced to do so, to withdraw all attempts of incorporation, of obtaining the patent, etc., procedures which I started to begin with in the interest of my American students and the American public. I, personally, can exist economically and scientifically without patent and without incorporation of my institute.

Please do not mistake this attitude for disappointment or evasion of difficulties. It is clear that I do not give up my work. I am only giving up the fight with formalistic irrationalism.

TO THEODORE P. WOLFE
18 February 1944

Dear Dr. Wolfe,

Here is the letter which I promised to write to you after thinking over the embarrassing Einstein affair again.* I would like to summarize this extremely complicated and, from a purely rational, sci-

*On 14 February 1944, after hearing rumors that Einstein had undertaken control experiments with the accumulator and been unable to confirm Reich's findings, Wolfe had written to Einstein advising him that it would be necessary to publish the relevant facts. Einstein replied in a letter dated 15 February 1944. He warned Dr. Wolfe that he had no right to publish his letters without permission and that he would take steps to prevent the misuse of his name "for advertising purposes—especially in a matter that has not my confidence."

entific point of view, incomprehensible affair in a few points, to the best of my understanding.

I. For a start, not answering the detailed letter I wrote to Einstein on 20 February 1941 was and still remains incomprehensible. As I said in a letter to him dated October 1941, which I did not mail, he had the opportunity to say openly that he did not understand the work concerning the orgone or that he did not want to have anything to do with it. That would have been understandable and unassailable. But not to reply to my refutation, which was backed by experiments, of the erroneous interpretation of an established phenomenon was an undeserved insult. I found the fact that my letter and subsequent reports were not answered so impossible to understand, and the thought that Einstein could act irrationally was so repugnant to me, that I consciously and with considerable effort rejected any possibility of this being the case. In the course of my scientific work I have come across plenty of irrational behavior on the part of scientists. But I knew Einstein's work too well, and as usual I had too much respect for true science, so that I had to strictly refrain from any thought that irrational behavior might be involved in this case. I would now like to state that despite all my respect for Einstein's accomplishments, the principle still stands that nobody, no matter who he might be, has the right to insult decent, hardworking people who sacrifice themselves for a gigantic cause. Of course, I would not have given Einstein any additional information regarding orgone research had I accepted the possibility that, after everything that had happened between us, Einstein would be deliberately insulting.

By not replying to my letter, he has simply made matters more difficult. It was not even necessary on his part to avoid stating openly that he wanted nothing to do with this matter. I would not have hesitated to tell the public about such a statement by Einstein, if it was necessary for the sake of the truth, even if such a publication might have turned authority-craving laymen against us and our work. As is now clear to everybody, not answering my letters has led to the present embarrassing situation. I hesitated for more than three years before publishing the temperature measurements in order to avoid an embarrassing situation. That alone proves that not only did I refrain from accepting his help but I also took into account Einstein's position in the world of science. The point is that I knew that Einstein had made a mistake when he checked my experiments. Of course, this mistake in no way lowers Einstein in my opinion, but faced with a world infected by the plague, this mistake could easily have taken on a malicious nature. His mistake was as follows:

If the inventor of the steam locomotive had gone to an Einstein living in the last century in order to demonstrate his locomotive, the demonstration would without a doubt have had the same kind of "bombshell" effect as my demonstration of a temperature difference observed in the case of a simple box without any visible or known constant source of heat. Now, imagine that this 19th-century Einstein establishes without any doubt that the locomotive really moves, but the physical knowledge of the day is ignorant of the existence of steam power. The locomotive appears to be a miracle, or, to put it differently, to the scientist of the last century it appears to be something unlikely and impossible. The 19th-century Einstein, who is not aware that steam power exists, notices, however, that the locomotive moves and wants to find out why. He takes the machine apart and notices that it no longer moves. He also notices that near the locomotive there is a steam phenomenon previously unknown to him, a phenomenon which is just as unexplained as the movement of the locomotive. He now states that the reason why the locomotive moved was due to steam in its vicinity. The only way to decide whether the steam *next to* the locomotive or the steam *inside* the locomotive makes it move is to take the locomotive somewhere where there is no steam in the vicinity. If the locomotive still moves, then its movement has nothing to do with the steam that was found next to the locomotive in its previous location. Let us now transfer this example, which naturally does not entirely fit, to the case of our orgone accumulator:

The fact that a simple box—made of metallic material inside and of organic material outside—can produce a temperature difference compared with the ambient air, appeared to Einstein so impossible and strange, so unbelievable and unlikely, that he not only spoke of a "bombshell" in the field of physics, if it was confirmed by him, but when he did have to confirm that it was real, he also took the box apart out of understandable curiosity in order to discover how the phenomenon came about. This is the only way I can explain on a purely human level why Einstein failed to think of leaving the accumulator alone and why he did not observe it exactly the way it was, *in the open air*, where there was neither a ceiling nor a tabletop. Naturally, taking measurements in the open air would have caused him much less trouble than the complicated dismantling of the box, in the way he describes in his letter.

The only understandable interpretation of Einstein's behavior is the above-mentioned human psychological reaction. The experiment itself is crystal clear. Objectively and rationally Einstein should have replied to my detailed exposé stating his agreement and acknowledgment. To this day I am convinced, despite all that has happened, that he is fully aware that I am right. His attitude in this matter is thus all the more incomprehensible. For three years I felt it correct to maintain a considerate attitude while criminally neglecting the interests of orgone research; then the affair took a new turn:

II. A physician who visited me and who had heard a great deal about orgone research told me that Dr. Edith Jacobsohn, who had worked with me in Berlin and later turned into an enemy because of her guilty conscience, had told him that Einstein had been unable to confirm the phenomenon I had claimed existed. This is not in accordance with the facts, because Einstein had confirmed the phenomenon, even though his interpretation was at first different. We would have been very well within our rights to correct this rumor in public without informing Einstein beforehand. To achieve this purpose, it would not even have been necessary to print his letter to me; instead, merely printing my letter to him and my letter to Neill dated 6 September would have been sufficient. We therefore did not need his permission at all. We were at first respectful and polite enough to tell him, despite his behavior in the preceding three years, which we did not understand but now take as an insult, that we intended to counter the rumor. I suggested this course of action at the time with the conscious intention of giving Einstein a chance to express his opinion. Einstein now replies to our politeness and consideration with new rudeness and insult. He intimates that we want to misuse his name for propaganda purposes, as if we were manufacturers of hair restorers or electric lightbulbs. On this subject, I would like to state the following—please believe me—in an entirely objective and calm way:

a) As you know, I have engaged in much less propaganda for my own discoveries than was generated for Einstein's discoveries. I do not want to quarrel about the difference in importance between the discoveries concerned.

b) Einstein learned from me in person during our talk and from my long written exposé, and it was also reported in the journal, that no considerations of profit are connected with orgone research and that, measured by normal standards, I have made incredible sacrifices in the interest of the cause.

c) There is a world of difference between the propaganda in which our institute engages for our discoveries and the propaganda of a firm such as General Electric, which for them is perfectly correct behavior, given also their financial possibilities.

In light of this, the new insult added by Einstein to his previous attitude in this matter is all the greater, and all the more incomprehensible and painful. I do not believe that we should put up with such insults, no matter who they come from.

III. It is totally immaterial whether or not Einstein has any confidence in orgone research and why he has no confidence. Orgone energy exists independently of his opinion, and its existence will be recognized sooner or later, in one way or another, and there is no way this can be stopped.

a) The steps that the Orgone Institute has undertaken or will be forced to undertake in the future are not aimed at forcing a confirmation from Einstein, and I would like to emphasize this point. I could have achieved that goal as long as three years ago. I did not pursue it, because it would have been a dirty business and because orgone research does not need to rely on Einstein.

b) The publication by the institute concerning the Einstein affair is aimed solely at refuting malicious rumors, which have no foundation in truth. Their only function is to discredit us, especially by relying on Einstein's authority in matters of physics. Strictly from the standpoint of objectivity and truth, Einstein should turn against the rumormongers who misuse his name to discredit us, and not against the likes of us, who up to now have shown the utmost consideration and politeness toward him and are determined to continue doing so. We are caught in a conflict which is difficult to resolve. We cannot counter the rudeness or irrational behavior of others by becoming rude and irrational ourselves. We are doing it not because we are afraid of Einstein's authority. We are doing it because, the way things are, we want to, we can, and we must manage without Einstein actually confirming the phenomenon. However, it is unthinkable that irrational human reactions should be able to hinder the course of events simply because an authority in physics is involved. The discovery of the orgone is much more important to the world than any authority or any other consideration. This is not a question of confidence or lack of confidence in this or that; the only question to be answered is whether or not the difference in temperature exists without a visible or known source of heat. Although we do not need Einstein's confirmation of the phenomenon and do not want to enlist it, we must not on the other hand allow misuse of his authority to be turned against us by the forces of the emotional plague. Let us keep those two aspects strictly separate. In the first instance, we are determined to go on respecting Einstein's wishes. In the second instance, we are equally determined to place consideration for orgone research ahead of everything else.

IV. However, after careful thought it seems to me that the whole affair goes back to something more profound than merely a personal conflict between Einstein and myself. Looking at the matter more closely, it appears that in effect, and entirely logically, *two worlds of science have collided in this conflict.* Einstein was cast in the role of representing inorganic physics, and it fell to me, often much to my regret, to represent a kind of energy which controls both the inorganic sector and the living. Neither Einstein's personality nor my own is involved here. It is no coincidence that orgone energy—that is to say, the basic cosmic energy which controls life—was discovered not in the context of the physics of dead matter but in the context of psychiatry, the emotions. In making the discovery, I did not in any way depart from the field of biopsychiatry. The relationship between the physical-mathematical sciences and the life sciences is simply being reversed: Up to now, biology and medicine, etc., were pursuing chemistry and physics and were attempting, in an entirely wrongheaded way, to place on a scientific basis the laws which had been discovered in the field of inorganic physics. The discovery of the orgone reverses the relationship. Now the functions of the living organism provide the model for research into a basic energy. This will be used not only for research into orgone energy but for much more than this: The many gaps and contradictions in the fields of chemistry and physics will be resolved solely by the facts that emerge from orgone research. From now on, and this I can safely predict, it will no longer be the role of biology and psychiatry to pursue physics and chemistry, but the roles will be reversed, and it will be physics and chemistry which will pursue biology and psychiatry, in order to place themselves on a better and more exact scientific basis. This is also true in another, deeper epistemological sense.

Those working in the fields of natural science and natural philosophy have known for centuries that the door to any kind of knowledge of nature—in other words, the point of communication between the individual and the world—is formed solely through sensations which the outside world generates in the individual. The dispute between all natural philosophies in the past regarding the nature of things revolved around the question of correctness and objectivity of sensations which formed the only means of gaining knowledge of nature. For the first time in the history of natural science a wide breach has been created in the nature of sensations. It is not surprising and, on the contrary, entirely logical and consistent that it was a specialized biopsychiatric field—namely, that of sexual economy—using emotions and sensations, that tracked down the cosmic basic energy. My publications bear witness to this fact through the logical progression of their development.

I hope that I have expressed myself sufficiently clearly. The struggle between the physics of life, with its relations to cosmic physics, and the physics of dead matter will be hard and life-threatening. I do not want there to be any illusions on that score. Sooner or later mechanistic physics will draw its lifeblood from orgone physics, regardless of whether I am its representative or someone else is. This is the present state of affairs: The main representatives of mechanistic theory hold power and have the mechanistic human structure on their side. By contrast, we are very much at a disadvantage. Our scientific work cannot rely on the routine knowledge of centuries. Our work must conquer the new territory it discovers amidst severe dangers and upheavals in the course of organic development. As you know, fear of orgasm—i.e., the fear of being aware of organic sensations—has been the main reason for orgone energy not being discovered earlier. In addition to the uncertainties I am subjected to in orgone research, I

must now also deal with these irrational human reactions and a world
of power and influence poised against me. Often it is tempting to
lose heart, but each time I walk through my laboratory, I regain my
sense of certainty which the cause requires. The facts that have accumulated over the years fit together in miraculous ways. I often have
difficulty following the logic. We can therefore say that what we have
here is a powerful example of factual truth.

I have good reason for mentioning the more profound meaning of
the conflict. The following catastrophic misunderstanding exists and
it can become dangerous, unless we constantly provide elucidation.
It is being said that, if it exists, orgone energy belongs in the realm
of physics. Einstein is the leading physicist of the century. Therefore
his opinion is valid over any other opinion. May I just mention in
passing that this misunderstanding is based on man's obsession with
authority and fear of responsibility. Nobody disputes that Einstein
commands supreme authority in the physics of dead matter. However,
he does not possess the slightest authority or any knowledge regarding
the energy of life—namely, the orgone. All the facts that I gave him
during our talk in 1941, which lasted four and a half hours, were
new to him; in some cases he found them extremely surprising, but
conceivable in principle, otherwise he would not have made such an
effort. Authority in the field of orgone physics and orgone biophysics
must be earned by anybody who wishes to make statements on the
subject—this is something we must state in public again and again.
This requirement is necessary for the simple reason that the laws of
orgone physics are fundamentally different from the laws of mechanics and from the theory of electricity, etc. In this context it is sufficient
for me to remind you of one fact—namely, that according to the laws
of the physics of dead matter, energy regularly flows from the stronger
system to the weaker one; in orgone physics, by contrast, the stronger
system attracts the weaker one or withdraws energy from it. You will
understand what I am driving at here. The idea has been mentioned
that Einstein, with his authority in the field of physics, could easily
destroy the cause of orgone physics for a long time to come. He
certainly could, if he relied on his own irrationalism and on that of
others. But he will not be able to do it as long as we clearly distinguish
where he is an authority and where he is not. These discussions do
not factually involve complicated formulae nor theories about outer

space, but relate to the simplest, most banal, basic facts of nature, such as the existence and distribution of heat, the production of heat in organisms, the function of insulators, the medium of radio waves, etc.

It will take a decade or even longer before I have reached the stage where I can answer the most essential simple questions concerning physics—i.e., Einstein's field. The confrontation between orgone physics and mechanistic physics of dead matter cannot and should not be avoided. However, the confrontation must under all circumstances be kept within the realm of the rational. What must absolutely not happen is that power and influence decide what is the truth, as has so often been the case in science.

I am preparing a detailed publication regarding the irrational way in which phenomena of life and consequently also orgone biophysics are treated. In this publication I will also have to deal with the Einstein affair. The opportunity will present itself, because Einstein's theory of a "field" and of the relationship between matter and energy materially calls for the existence of a fundamental cosmic energy which penetrates and controls everything. We will therefore see a repetition of something which has already taken place during the confrontation with the systems of Marx and Freud: I will in all likelihood have to represent Einstein's theory against Einstein himself.

I shall leave it to you whether you want to reply to Einstein's insulting letter, and how you do it. One alternative would be not to reply at all or merely to refute the suspicions in an objective and serious manner.

TO ALBERT EINSTEIN

20 February 1944

Dear Mr. Einstein,

Dr. Wolfe sent me a copy of your letter. As the responsible leader of a group of decent scientists engaged in work of great importance, I must protest against the insult inflicted by you.

At first you agreed entirely voluntarily to support our work, provided that the phenomenon of the temperature difference, which you described as a bombshell in the field of physics, could be proven to exist. The truth of the phenomenon and its existence were proven before your very eyes. Your assistant produced an incorrect interpretation which I refuted through experiments. You did not reply to my long letter in which I told you about this. In the meantime, I put great trust in you when I informed you about some enormously important facts and assumptions which had not yet been published. At that point, enemies of my work started to misuse your authority in matters of physics against me by falsifying truths and putting out rumors, all according to well-known patterns. After holding back for more than three years on publishing the facts that I told you about in 1941, we are now forced to publish corrections. I asked Dr. Wolfe to advise you in advance of the necessity of publishing; in other words, I exercised the utmost consideration. You replied to this in an insulting fashion by portraying us as profiteers out to use your name for propaganda purposes. The fundamental facts of orgone physics are too serious and too well-founded to be advanced by shabby means. They have so far managed to find acceptance without any confirmation by you, and they will continue to do so.

You do not have the right to insult hardworking, honest people who are making the utmost personal and financial sacrifices for the sake of scientific research. I have told you, and there is documentary evidence to back me up, that far from generating any profits, orgone research on the contrary swallows up immense sums of money.

Your conduct is incomprehensible to me. If you want to prevent your name being misused, turn on the rumormongers and not on us.

TO THEODORE P. WOLFE
25 February 1944

Dear Dr. Wolfe,
    Today I received a letter from Einstein which read as follows:

    Dear Dr. Reich,
        You are doing me a great injustice by maintaining that I have circulated unfavorable opinions about your endeavors. The reason

why I have not replied to your last letter is that I have formed an opinion, to the best of my ability, and am not able to spend more time on this matter. I must also ask you to treat my spoken and written statements with discretion, in the same way in which I have always treated yours.

Yours sincerely,
Albert Einstein

This puts an end to the matter, for the time being favorably for us. As Einstein promises in so many words to treat my communications to him with discretion, as he does not reject my specific claim that he has confirmed the phenomenon of the temperature difference (which is tantamount to agreement), as he assures me furthermore that he has not put out any unfavorable opinions regarding our work, I believe that we should respect his wish that discussions and written communications addressed to me should be treated with discretion. Of course, this does not preclude some "plague mouth" trying sooner or later to misuse Einstein's name against us, as Dr. Edith Jacobsohn has done. If this happens, we shall have to cope with the problem once more. In any event, the matter has now been clarified, and we know what Einstein really thinks. I ask you to treat the conflict between Einstein and myself with absolute discretion. Consequently we shall not publish anything on Einstein for the time being.

Please let me know if your opinion on this matter contradicts mine or if you have any doubts.

26 February 1944

For three days, I have been attempting to calculate the spinning impulse. It is very difficult. It may derive from the angle created by the vector of centrifugal force and the actual trajectory that results. Or from the principle of inertia of uniform motion and actual trajectory.

Undated

The Riddle

Einstein's behavior has remained a riddle to this day. Why did he not reply? Why did he break a promise which he had given? There

were many opinions about this in our circle. Some believed that he
might have regarded the whole orgone affair as humbug. This ran
counter to the understanding which he demonstrated in our conversation. Others thought he might be influenced by certain industrial
interests which did not welcome the idea of the discovery of the
orgone being confirmed by Einstein. This ran counter to the fact that
Einstein had no need to defer to such interests.

To my mind two other versions seemed more likely. As Einstein
himself hinted in his letter, he did not understand the orgone. It
contradicted firmly rooted fundamental views of physics. He also did
not want to put himself into an exposed position but preferred to wait
and see. The second interpretation seemed more brutal but closer to
the truth. According to this version, Einstein fully understood that
the ether had finally been discovered as something actually tangible.
Einstein, however, had based his whole relativity theory on the assumption that the ether did not exist at all and was not even necessary
for the solution of cosmic problems. It was believed that these problems could be solved by purely mathematical means, and this belief
was supported through the confirmation of his theories by observation. It was understandable on a human and a scientific level that
Einstein did not want to contribute to the collapse of his life's work,
although this would have been demanded by strict scientific objectivity. The existence of a real ether need not by itself have disturbed
Einstein's vision of nature. Einstein's theory would only be shattered,
because it would have become redundant, if a new cosmogony could
be deduced from the properties of the newly discovered ether. I would
therefore have to take back my contention in the letter to Neill—
namely, that my discovery supports Einstein's field theory.

I do not know if all these thoughts are correct or incorrect. Einstein
had caused the confusion himself by pulling out in such an unpleasant way. However, the "issue" was compelling and clear. It is possible
that Einstein underestimated the scope of my discovery and its consequences. In short, I can only surmise but cannot assert anything
with certainty. As the years went by, I increasingly tended toward the
opinion that the meeting on 13 January 1941 was an encounter between two completely hostile worlds: *mechanistic* and *functional
astrophysics*—the former a giant with infinite means of waging battle

and wielding power, the latter a mere baby that had only just been born. The newborn baby held in one fist the fact "cosmic energy" and in the other fist the fact "sentient matter." This is enough to scare even the most courageous man.

TO JOHN P. CHANDLER
❖ 7 March 1944

Dear Mr. Chandler:

Enclosed please find the answer to the Commissioner of Patents signed by me. The promise to bring the equipment to Richmond for additional proof, however, seems to be difficult to carry through. I would have to bring to Richmond a dozen mice, a microscope, an autoclave, an electroscope, an orgone accumulator for mice and one for human beings, three thermometers, and so forth—i.e., half of my laboratory equipment. Apart from that, proving the biological effectiveness of the orgone energy would take several weeks (it took several months with one of my assistants who was a biologist), but I think we shall leave this question until later.

The reason why I wanted to conduct the patent affair myself was, as you know, the fact that my first patent lawyer conducted the matter for about one year without any understanding of the thing. I leave it completely to you whether you find it more advisable to have the power of attorney or not.

I hope you don't mind if I add a personal remark to this matter. This patent affair goes on now for almost four years. It gave me so much annoyance and has cost me so much money that I am thoroughly fed up with it, especially since my interest is fully absorbed by highly complicated and theoretical orgone biophysical problems. I really do not know whether to continue with this mess of affairs or not. It is only distressing to see official beings like Einstein or the Patent Commissioner of the American government act irrationally as they do. The worst is that I have no ambitions in this matter, except the one to work out orgone physics properly.

18 March 1944

3 a.m. How am I to cope with the pain which even the best people cause me? They injure me, and trust me—innocently! How amazed they would be if I informed them that they had just crucified me. Innocence is the best protection! Such is the plague!

One cannot respond with revenge without becoming infected with the plague oneself. One cannot take it lightly without being called a fool or a "poor sucker"!

And yet the plague's very intention is to render its victims helpless—and then to triumph.

20 March 1944

I have been ruminating on a speech called "Listen, Little (Common) Man." Whence this burning desire to "instruct" the "little man"? He has often done me serious damage. Am I a redeemer? No.

Life has taught me to experience the little "common man" as "little" and "common," to *hate* him, to view him as the carrier and not merely the victim of the emotional plague—the carrier, defender, and lover of the emotional plague. That's the way it is.

The common man comes out in and is exploited by every sadist due to his little, common, petty traits. These produce the 'isms and wars which cause the big man, the great individual, to suffer. The champions of truth and beauty are destroyed by the carriers of the plague.

Truth and beauty are the basic functions of unarmored life like breathing and the orgasm. Unarmored life wants to safeguard its basic functions; it therefore combats pettiness in both little and great individuals.

If the little, common man were not petty and common there would be no lies, no war, no sadism. Therefore the struggle is necessary to unveil whatever truth, simplicity, and greatness lie within the little man himself.

23 March 1944

Armored human animals sense that research and the pursuit of truth have always and unerringly been directed toward the discovery of the great secret of cosmic energy. This poses a threat to science.

Diagram: Orgonoscope

C: cellulose disk, outside surface dull
W.m.: wire mesh, on both sides of disk
M: metal cylinder, about 4″ long, 2″ wide
L: biconvex lens, about 5x, focused on disk
T: telescopic tube, 1 to 2 feet long, about 2″ wide
E.p.: eye-piece, 5-10x, for additional magnification

Orgonoscope

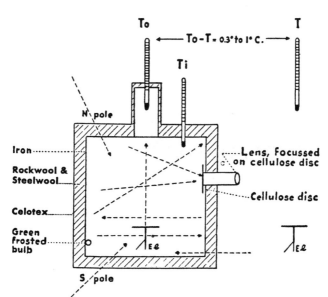

BASIC DESIGN OF EXPERIMENTAL ORGONE ACCUMULATOR. SECTION.

To = temperature above accumulator; Ti = temperature within accumulator; T = control (temperature of air in room). El = electroscope. - - - - → = direction of radiation. Size: 1 cubic foot.

Accumulator

Wilhelm Reich, 1944

Students' Laboratory at Orgonon

◄

Reich at Orgonotic Lodge, summer 1942

Reich in the lab at Orgonon, 1946

►

Wilhelm Reich, May 1946.
"This is my real expression, the one I live with!
Wolfe called it 'grim'—and that it is!"

Reich and A. E. Hamilton's baby, 1946

Eva Reich, Jerome Siskind, Peter Reich, Wilhelm Reich, Ilse Ollendorff in Maine

Wilhelm Reich with his son Peter, Maine, 1947

The path was (and still is) blocked by fear of the orgasm, fear of life itself.

25 March 1944

It is tragic to see human reactions (including one's own) too clearly. It leads to great loneliness. Each person satisfies his own interests to some small extent, but who would bear my interests in mind if he weren't on my payroll.

31 March 1944

Ilse is in labor. The child could mean immense joy and a profound change in my life. For days I have been in conflict: Can I, should I, may I lead this child along *my* path? Will the world change? Or will my child have to go through the terrible struggle with himself and with contemporary irrationalism, the same struggle I have had? Alternatives: Armor fully against pain and pleasure, or experience fully and become transformed. It is a staggering responsibility to protect a child from impotence and the plague and yet still allow it to exist in this world.

3 April 1944

A new member of society: Ernst Peter Robert Reich, my son. Born at 1 a.m. after great pain.

His facial expression is "earnest" and "pensive." I hope he remains that way. Eva and the nurses claim that he's very much like me.

He immediately began nursing with quiet eagerness. No difficulties at all. In utero he experienced many a wave of his parents' orgastic pleasure.

Numerous interrelated facts have given rise to my conviction that sexual lifelessness in a mother is harmful to the child in her womb. Conversely, I feel that experiencing the pleasure of the mother's body is natural and promotes a child's development.

18 April 1944

Today I held six therapy sessions, two of which went unpaid. I have been worn so thin by so much plague that I tend to fly off the handle. After all, I have eleven thousand one hundred and eleven people to support, important research to finance, and no time to think in peace. I literally steal time for my orgone biophysics between therapy sessions, two hours here, three hours there.

T O   W A L T E R   H O P P E *
28 April 1944

Dear Dr. Hoppe,

The lay public is showing an enormous amount of interest in the cancer problem, and I am happy that you have discovered a new path to follow. It would be of great importance for the whole organization if, after you have gathered some experience, you were to send your impressions and your presentation and discussion techniques to the journal so that others can be shown the same path. I must unfortunately inform you that although so far, compared with X-rays and radium, orgone therapy of the fully developed carcinoma has proved to be the superior method, it is still far from being *the* method of cancer treatment. Our animal experiments and experience with humans who have developed cancer give much more hope for a prophylaxis of cancer. And precisely this will require more from the layman than from the physician. The work has also been impaired in every respect by the war. At any rate, your experiments seem to me to be conducted in the direction of general social hygiene and prophylaxis, a direction from which we can probably expect *very much* to come. As you correctly write, not much can be expected from the current generation of physicians because they are mechanistically fixated. On the other hand, the emerging medical generation will probably show a great deal of interest.

---

*Walter Hoppe, M.D., in Palestine, was particularly interested in Reich's work with cancer.

TO A. S. NEILL
❖ 2 May 1944

Dear Neill,

My name, and the subject of sex economy and orgone biophysics have at last been taken up officially among the natural scientists in the Who's Who of natural science, *American Men of Science*, and in the World Almanac. First swallows! Now, of course, people who know damn little about my work will trust me more. It is their shame and not mine. What a world! What an education! What a structure! What a civilization! Make a big noise, boast, make propaganda for yourself, and you will amount to something even if you have nothing to say. On the other hand, live quietly, do a good job, let things speak for themselves, and everybody thinks you are a charlatan. Again, what a world!

I wonder whether you know that I became the father of a third child. It's a boy, called Ernest Peter Robert, a husky strong little fellow, four weeks old, with a strong will, serious in his facial expression, just discovering the world around him and developing together with his mother very nicely. I assure you that after twenty-five years of intensive and extensive psychiatric work, I am discovering for the first time, like a new student of psychiatry, the real nature of a newborn baby. It is amazing and frightening how little this high boasting psychiatry knows about the most primitive things of human life. I hope to be able to write down what I learned during these last three months. Would you ever have imagined that an unborn baby will stop kicking in the mother's womb when it hears good music; that after birth, the same baby has real oral orgasms with twitchings of the face muscles, rolling of the eyes, twitchings of the tongue after a good exciting feast on the breast. I am very happy in spite of the fact that the little fellow has upset my whole schedule, that the quiet is gone, for the meantime at least, to which I was accustomed while working at problems of natural science. I can only hope that we shall at least succeed in making the next war happen not within the next twenty-five years but after the next fifty years, so that this boy won't have to die for liberty, but will be able to live and work for liberty.

8 May 1944

I have been resisting the discovery that Ilse unconsciously and I, somewhat less unconsciously, are going through a crisis because of the child. Ernst has thrown everything into a state of confusion. The "scientific quietude" of our household is gone. We have no help except in the laboratory. A few times I even caught myself hating Ernst. It is important to be aware of such hate impulses. Then the hatred is no longer unconscious and bitter. We will simply have to adjust. The boy is serious and very smart. His complexion is dark like mine. How am I to successfully guide his development if the world remains the way it is? Then he will be a healthy individual but nevertheless an outsider, like myself.

———

When the world has repeatedly given you a beating for your honest efforts, you come to fear further beatings. Such beatings can take the form of public defamation, interruption of proper working conditions, loss of a loved one due to external circumstances, etc. You then fear the world and attempt to change it as quickly as possible so that you no longer need to be afraid. In doing this you become nervous, intolerant, driven.

23 May 1944

Science will only be generally popularized and practiced when a *basic* change in social conditions has taken place. Today science would seem to be a luxurious hobby.

Ever since Ilse has had the boy nothing else matters to her. How strange motherhood is. Does this hold true only for human beings?

30 May 1944

A deeper cosmic meaning lies hidden in all this.* I cannot find it, I'm baffled, yes, despairing. I shall take a rest and wait. I am frightened by Newton's mental illness. Now I can understand it! The cosmic pulse rate (CPR) is close to the square of the cosmic pendu-

———

*Reich was absorbed in astronomical calculations.

lum rate, and this in turn is close to the energy for mass 16 in the *Kreiselwelle*.*

5 June 1944

If suffering itself can be called a sickness, then I have another sickness called "knowledge." An insight which contradicts everyone else's thoughts and actions, but is then proven correct after decades, is the most painful of all. I'd gladly flee from this, in order not to perish.

T O   J O S E P H   K .   F O L S O M
❖ 21 June 1944

Dear Dr. Folsom:

I received your letter of 15 June and the review of our book. Would you be kind enough to enter my subscription to the *American Sociological Review* for one year.

Regarding your caution not to raise too much the latent resistance: My scientific experiences of a period of more than twenty-five years now have taught me that blunt presentation with all consequences and implications rather than consideration and compromise with the irrational resistance to truth is the surer way to victory. But I am ready to grant that everyone has his own way of pushing things ahead. I too hope that we shall be able to meet soon to discuss certain things. The problem of family and sex is, according to my experience, the most burning problem of the present phase of social development, though too deeply rooted to be recognized as such.

I wish to correct one misunderstanding in your review: Orgone is not a hypothetical energy, but a factual force which has been discovered, measured, and used in the medical field for nearly five years now. I wonder whether you received the issues of our journal which

---

*Reich had observed that luminating orgone energy units pursue certain pathways as they move forward through space. These pathways show the form of a *Kreiselwelle* or spinning wave.

brought forth the physical and medical demonstration of the *fact* of orgone. I am enclosing a newly published separatum for further orientation.

With regard to your remarks concerning Maine, I can only say that I feel at home here around Rangeley Lakes, rather than in New York. The Orgone Institute has bought a 160-acre farm on the Dodge Pond near Rangeley, for future establishment of the Orgone Institute Laboratories. The high humidity and the whole climate in the New York area prevent experimentation with the orgone energy during the summer months. Therefore, the fourth summer now, I am experimenting in a provisional setup in a cabin at Mooselookmeguntic Lake. The observations meet the most appropriate climate. It is interesting that you know this country so well. I did not hike much, because I am rather busy, and am not spending my time here on vacation. I love this country and its people. My goal is to transfer the whole institute and the laboratories to the place here, called Orgonon, in the near future. I am enclosing a map of the region where you can find marked with red pencil the place of my cabin and the location of the future laboratories.

I have not been in touch with the methods of Russian sex economy for about the past six years, and have no judgment about the later development. But the whole course of events over there, since about 1934, when I was in close touch with Russian people, institutions, and literature, has imbued me with the deepest distrust and a great fear as to the future role which the Soviet Union may play *against* the development of a *true* democratic society. It may sound impossible, even preposterous or crazy; I could not prove it, and I would not publish it, but the psychosociological development of the Soviet Union during the past ten years gave me the idea of a future war between an America fighting hard for true democracy against a Russia headed by a Czar, one way or the other, called Stalin. The Russian government, originating in truly democratic Marxian principles, has, forced by circumstances, taken a course which has created a very bad conscience. And such bad social conscience of state leaders as to principles and goals is a very dangerous fact. The Christian inquisition of the Middle Ages is a very good example of what I mean.

26 June 1944

Clear west-to-east movement of the waves in the orgone envelope of the earth. Cf. Jupiter's changes at the surface; cf. sun, more rapid rotation at the equator than at higher degrees of latitude.

Hypothesis: The rotation of the orgone envelope is a vestige of the primordial spinning; it is not the earth that takes the ether with it, but "as the ether rotates, it takes the earth with it."

Problem: The rate of this rotation must be *measurable*. Technically difficult.

If it is possible to demonstrate, then it is also proved that

a. Orgone is primordial energy which, when concentrated, gave birth to the planet earth.

b. Orgone rotates faster than the earth.

c. As it rotates, the orgone envelope takes the earth with it.

d. The direction of rotation is identical with the direction of rotation of the earth.

e. Problem: Which planets have rotating orgone envelopes?

4 July 1944

(Orgonon) Everyone around me is "arranging his life." They "settle down" as the English say.

Wolfe is earning so much money with vegetotherapy that he has no time to work on the journal, which is responsible for his lucrative practice.

Ilse wanted to have a child and got one. Ever since then I have had no assistant in the laboratory, no secretary, no comrade. My work was important but now it seems ridiculously interwoven with the necessity of washing a child's diapers.

And here I am in the midst of it all! (I am settling down too.)

5 July 1944

I am faulting my child for my own inability to work. I've lived through phases devoid of ideas even before Peter arrived. But now I have a scapegoat. Wonder whether I sometimes purposely do not work and have no ideas in order to prove that Peter disturbs me?

T O   P E N N Y   W A R R E N [*]
❖ 7 July 1944

Dear Penny:

I received your letter. I shall need somebody to take care of the laboratory, to keep it in proper order, and to do some continuous control of our quantitative measurements. Since you got acquainted with this work, I would prefer you to somebody else, a new one or a stranger. The question is only whether your studies would interfere with the lab work. Would you kindly let me know at which time you would have to leave each evening. It may be necessary to arrange the working hours a bit later, say from ten to six or so. When I shall know more exactly about your schedule, we can make definite arrangements.

Your questions were clever and interesting. Penicillin is, no doubt, a bionous substance. You can provide a sample and study it in our laboratory. Write down all that occurs to you concerning the orgone in its connection with chemistry, radiology, etc. It is important to have these things present all the time. The telescope proved itself not only useful but absolutely necessary. You can see the atmospheric orgone quite clearly with it in daytime and one can even distinguish a preference of motion from west to east. And it can be proven that it is not the air which moves.

The more you learn of *fundamental* facts in natural science, the better you equip yourself for the understanding of orgone biophysics.

18 July 1944

In order to carry out orgonometry of space, I must transfer the Keplerian and Newtonian laws, which are valid for circles and ellipses, to the spinning wave. Since these laws are correct, they must also be correct in the KR [Kreiselwelle].

I must find further proof that they are correct, and why. The Keplerian law of harmony, for example, is simple to demonstrate in a circle, but difficult in the KR.

*Theodore P. Wolfe's stepdaughter.

Questions: 1) How much or how large is a circle in the KR?
2) What is the relationship between the season 365^{25} and the KR?

18–19 July 1944

The west-to-east direction of the orgone remains, only the speed changes.

Problem: Is orgone movement or movement of the air primary?

Probably orgone takes air with it, not the other way around.

Exceptions: Orgone movement produces heat. Movement of matter consumes heat.

Re the "heat death of the universe": The formation of matter consumes heat and tends very much toward heat death; but at the same time matter breaks down (plants, animals, exploding stars). There is constant orgone radiation, so that equilibrium is assured.

Question: Does the breakdown of matter balance out the formation of matter?

22 July 1944

As long as the expansive force is greater than the contractive force, the spinning wave continues to exist. When the expansive force declines in favor of the contractive, the spinning wave changes to a circular motion; the movement slows down, curved space.

Model = orgone pulsation.

The energy of radiation and expansion needs to be calculated from the E_{Kr} movement.

23 July 1944

Theoretical summation of the principle of orgone physics:
Task of natural science:

  a. Reduction of facts to a common denominator
  b. Reduction of events to energy processes
  c. Reduction of all forms of energy to a common primal energy

Re a. *Result:* Reduction of suppression to emotions

          . . . of emotion to pleasure and anxiety
          . . . of pleasure and anxiety to expansion and contraction

> . . . of expansion and contraction to pulsation
> . . . of pulsation to biological energy

Re b.   *Discovery of the orgone:*
              Start of research on its properties

Re c.   *Pulsation is immanent property of primal energy:*
              Pulsation of organisms
              Pulsation of the cosmic bodies
              Reduction of heat, magnetism, electricity, light to orgone functions.

25 July 1944

They may be biochemists, biophysicists, biologists, etc., but I am still the only one to have researched unarmored life. I alone, in the vast field of natural science, know unarmored life as it manifests itself in the sucking of a nursing infant, in the movement of a caterpillar, in a girl's sigh of pleasure, and in the rhythm of Beethoven.

Who is the authority?

Energy is measured by accomplishment. Orgone energy could be measured according to the work accomplished by the pulsation of a heart muscle or by the movement of a celestial body in a certain period of time.

31 July 1944

I need collaborators, but they want to be executives, henchmen.

They say the human masses are still too close to the animal kingdom to be human. Only very few of them ever reach the "top."

I wish the human masses *were* close to the animal kingdom. The tragedy is not their closeness to animals but the fact that they deny this. This denial turns the animal into a beast and obstructs the animal development.

2 August 1944

Can't make a go of it: voluntary professional work amidst this slavery—surrounded by human structures which are incapable of freedom—impossible.

Can't use the whip either. One can't accomplish work on unarmored life with a switch in one's hand.

TO   A.   S.   NEILL
❖ *6 August 1944*

My dear Neill:

I have your letter of 15 July. I am glad you began to do vegeto-therapy, and especially that you tried with adolescents. Since all grown-ups are more or less hopeless, as far as basic change of structure is concerned, the only hope is, I firmly believe, establishment of rationality in children and adolescents when the biophysical reactions still can be molded. As to your inquiry: The amount of weekly sessions depends entirely on the rigidity and structure of the muscular and character armor. I have some grown-ups who will not yield unless I take them four to five times weekly. But they are the minority. In the average case I am coming through with three sessions a week. I wish to stress that these sessions are not as rigidly applied as in psycho-analysis. It happens often, that, after thirty minutes of good work the patient is exhausted. Other times, it may be necessary to add some time. In some rather severe biopathic cases, I have succeeded completely with only one session a week. It depends entirely on the vegetative intelligence of the one you treat. I would advise you to be most flexible in applying your time.

The term "resistance" is still valid, but in quite a different way than used in psychoanalytic technique. If a patient "resists," it means that you did not find the correct words and actions on specific places on his body, which correspond to this specific emotional situation. For instance: You may have released a bit of the masklike stiffness of the facial expression. An impulse to bite may be on the point of breaking through. To this biophysical emotion the patient may react, as a protection, with a withdrawal in his shoulders, a kind of holding back. Now, you cannot get out the biting impulse in the mouth unless you release first the auxiliary muscular armoring in the shoulders, by bringing the shoulders forward. It is always a matter of observing the patient in such a relaxed manner that you learn to realize where a muscular defense (which is of course identical with the character defense) appears anew when the muscular defense on which you were working was just on the point of yielding!

I would be glad if you would care to let me know from time to time how you are getting along with adolescents. The main thing in all vegetotherapy is to know unshakingly that the main obstacle to progress is always a tremendous fear of yielding to involuntary uncontrolled motion and emotional currents. There is always destructive energy blocking love emotions.

Peter is prospering. He did not have a cold or diarrhea yet in the four first months of his life. He is absolutely healthy, happy, eager, curious, and interested in everything. During the last two or three weeks now he shows me that he wants to walk. I hold him above the floor and he marches right ahead. Then he may for hours march with his legs in the air while lying in bed. I never would have guessed how little we know about newborn babies, how completely developed they are biophysically, and, accordingly, how stupid and preposterous this whole educational setup of our society appears—now even more than it did ten years ago. I am learning very, very much, and many important things. I hope to be able to present them at a later date in a useful and helpful manner.

I cannot help getting more and more convinced that our views on education of children and on what follows in consequence of it are 100 percent wrong and upside down. I had even to correct some of my own basic assumptions—that is, to correct them in the sense that I was not true enough nor courageous enough to stand for what I thought with all the vigor at my disposal. I feel now that I had a bad conscience, that I was inclined to compromise, that I was hanging on too long to theories which, deeply in myself, I knew were wrong. I should not have wasted nearly fourteen years with psychoanalysis and its sublimation and false child psychology. You may be astonished, but a baby of three months is not autistic whatsoever. It has its interest in its surroundings fully developed. I have to assume now that the contention of the psychoanalysts of the autistic character of the baby is an artifact. This artifact is apparently due to the armoring of the analysts which does not permit them to develop a full and natural contact with a newborn baby. We easily forget that a child has millions of different emotions and desires, but only one way, in the beginning, of trying to make itself understood—namely, crying. It took me several weeks to learn to understand what the boy wanted when he cried. I did not apply any scientific knowledge—the more I did so, the less I succeeded. The only thing that worked was identifying myself with his expression and then I knew what he wanted. What psychoanalysis calls identification seems to be rooted very deeply in what I might call the contact of the orgonotic system of a grown-up with that of the baby. Animals, if not domesticated, show this motion language very clearly to me now. It is a very vast and most important field of human life which I have just begun to look into.

8 August 1944

The orgonotic pulsation can be exactly observed on surfaces of water unruffled by the wind. Pulsation as the fundamental characteristic of cosmic energy explains the wave character of the universe, of light, of sound waves, of electricity, of the KR, of plasma.

August 1944

It makes no difference whether the functional law of nature, which I discovered between 1921 and 1944, will be generally regarded as true 10, 100, 1,000 years from now. *It is true*, proved by logic in the development of the problem, by the succession of tests, and by the coherence of the results. The functional law of nature means the defeat, the final defeat, and the end of mechanism and mysticism.

I experienced this process in deep humility and reverent respect. I experienced and understood nature. As in a giant symphony, the natural events and phenomena sounded harmoniously together, from the bion all the way through to the expanding universe. Not God, but the fundamental principle of life was the key to the universe. I was only its inadequate servant. I succeeded in reducing time to space and in reducing time-space to the pulsatory function of the individual orgone particle. My life's task is fulfilled.

It is now up to my fellow humans to enjoy the fruits of this labor. The orgonotic awareness of nature is a frightening but uplifting journey into the wide expanse of nature. Sooner or later, the dream of space travel will come true; and that will put an end—forever—to the narrowness of the human spirit!

TO   WALTER   HOPPE
14 August 1944

Dear Dr. Hoppe,

I have long had the impression that the urge to have our work "officially recognized" is very great, and not just in your sector. It is in the nature of the matter that "recognition" in the usual sense— namely, that some university professors will sit down and repeat the experiments, and confirm them, and then award me a triple Nobel Prize—is quite out of the question. It is not as simple as that because functional thought in the natural sciences, which we are introducing and still need to do a lot of work on, is in its early stages and needs to be learned. However, it is precisely the functional method that gives us such fruitful results, and although the relevant experiments could be mechanically repeated, they could not be understood if one did not master the overall method and the theory. This is probably clear. Orgone biophysics will no doubt gain acceptance, but slowly and quite differently from the way in which discoveries usually gain official recognition. It may therefore help you and others to know that sex economy and orgone biophysics were included and published last year, under my name together with that of the Orgone Institute and the Orgone and Cancer Research Lab, in the most recent edition of the American Who's Who of Science, *American Men of Science*, the official list. I did not ask for this. Instead, the request came to me from the editor of the American scientific journal *Science*. There are other indications in the everyday course of events that we are no longer, or not yet back again, in the opposition but instead are being carried along in the general flow of scientific efforts. Without any difficulty, the institute was granted approval to procure material that was otherwise on the restricted list. The War Production Board gave the laboratory a serial number and recently also granted approval to construct workrooms.

There is thus no reason to attract supporters by political-ideological means or by going to great personal lengths. We need fewer supporters and more practical coworkers. It is without doubt useful and and a great honor when an Arnold Zweig, or people of similar stature, are won over to our cause, but I believe that, in the main, the important thing is that we develop and diversify our work in a practical manner. On the basis of the published facts, the orgone accumulator, for example, can already be used by any physician. Such practical work (vegetotherapy, orgone therapy) will in the long term have a much greater effect than any other kind of propaganda. I would like to explicitly stress that I do not regard scientific presentations on the nature of our work as political-ideological means of gaining new friends.

I hope very much that you will succeed in finding an amicable solution to the conflict with Obermayer. I regard Obermayer as an extremely gifted person who will without doubt prove himself a very able sociologist. The conflict between the sociological-political urge toward propaganda and slogging away slowly on the scientific front will in the long term cause our organization severe pain and be a threat to it. But, as consciously socially oriented scientists and physicians, we cannot exclude sociology if we do not wish to experience the same fate that was suffered by psychoanalysis. However, it is still a complete mystery to me how we can keep such differently functioning systems as sociology and science under one roof and still maintain peace. I know this conflict very well from my own experience. I hope to hear from you soon about how your work is developing.

30 August 1944

Over the course of fifteen years of rapid world developments, I have lost numerous friends. This was neither my "fault" nor theirs. Since my field of research had raced far ahead of the social process, I was easily able to keep abreast of events while my friends seemed somewhat too slow.

My enemies, on the other hand, were trapped in one detail or another of the overall development, in keeping with the motto: "It's not much but it's mine." By this I mean some small fragment of character analysis, or the relationship of psychoanalysis to sociology, or the role of sexuality in the etiology of neurosis.

That is why they didn't join me, but became enemies instead, and some of them turned really mean. Today they are lagging far behind what is happening, while I have forged way ahead by virtue of orgone biophysics. I understand them, but they do not understand me. The events rush past them but haven't even caught up with me. Isn't this "lagging behind events" due, in a great degree, to their motto: "It's not much but it's mine"? In my opinion it is one of the most important reasons.

3 September 1944

Eureka! Gravitation is the same as acceleration in free fall. The acceleration increases with the distance of a mass from the center of gravity, while the weight decreases. Newton discovered *that* this is so; I discovered *why* it is so.

T O   W A L T E R   H O P P E
5 September 1944

Dear Dr. Hoppe,

I have received your positive letter of 5 August 1944. The results which you are getting there are the same as those we are obtaining here.* I would like to stress the following in particular: It is precisely the fact that the results are fantastically good that is the obstacle. I have been holding back for several years on publishing these observations because I know that, given the situation, it smells of charlatanism. According to everything that we have discovered through experiment and theorizing, the atmospheric orgone energy must have the strongest effect at the equator; therefore, it could be the case that the therapeutic effects differ somewhat from each other at the various latitudes.

The attitude of the two physicians about whom you report is typical. I saved a woman here from a serious leukemic blood condition from which she had suffered for twelve years. The doctor treating her saw the successful outcome with his own eyes and confirmed it with his own mouth. But he is not getting involved. The reason for this is

*Dr. Hoppe reported on initial positive results obtained through the use of the accumulator and on the skepticism of other physicians.

that doctors, with their mechanistic-chemical schooling, simply *cannot* comprehend how the orgone works. Now, since you have started to work with the orgone, I must ask you in the interest of the cause, and in the interest of your own personal safety, to be extremely cautious how you deal with people, particularly specialists. We can encounter the emotional plague reaction everywhere and unexpectedly. It must be treated with deadly earnest because it is based on the fear of the rigidified organisms when faced with the events that we are discovering, describing, and learning to handle. I can only stress once more, be careful. The cause will no doubt gain acceptance, but only very slowly and from small centers. The first traces of the influence of the discovery of the orgone are beginning to show up here in the natural philosophical and natural scientific literature. Now, to answer your questions: The orgone has been tested by me with good success not only on cancer but also and above all on a few cases of vascular hypertonia. When conducted through long tubes, it also has a healing effect on burns, inflammations, wounds, etc. It does not work on processes which have already resulted in structural changes in the organism—e.g., hardening of the arteries, arthritic processes, etc. I observed a brightening of the field of vision in a case of apoplectic hemorrhaging at the back of the eye. In some skin diseases one notices good effects, in other cases no effect at all, or even inflammatory irritation. The orgone works best on diseases of the blood system, anemia, etc. In several cases, a tendency toward colds, catarrhal conditions, etc., was eliminated.

We must be careful where cancer therapy is concerned. In the first number of Volume 4 of the journal, an article by me will appear which attempts to explain a further piece of the shrinking process. With orgone therapy, you can heal small and medium-sized breast tumors and tumors of the skeletal system, but you do not heal the cancer, since the biopathic shrinking continues to work in the background and leads to death, possibly without tumors. At this point, our vegetotherapeutic attempts are applied to complement the orgone therapy. The prospects are good. I managed to save two cases of cancer biopathy from the shrinking state. It is advisable to stress the still unsolved problems compared with the potential that has already been achieved with cancer therapy, in order to avoid disappointments.

22 September 1944

Einstein's world is lifeless—a few electrons distributed over great distances on the surface of a soap bubble. My world is alive—it is *functioning* in the macro- as well as the microcosm. In my world, man is capable of finding his place and functioning, which he cannot do in the inanimate shadow world of abstract mathematics.*

29 September 1944

Eddington† said it openly: physics operates with shadows, it lacks a connection with the world of the senses. Physicists lack the orgone in every step they take. Their number is four. They have the pulse of the world but have no notion of the orgone. I discovered the number four *and* the pulse without any idea that this was exactly what they were lacking. I'm proud of that.

The "world of shadows" will come alive. Present life will go to ruin, new people, children, cities, and thoughts will blossom, as fresh as Nietzsche's mistral wind which blows aside all that contradicts the meaning of life. We have only just begun. The world has yet to be born. Are these not the pains of labor? Does a mother know how her child will smile, how it will love or hate? Does the artist know how his painting will enchant the eye, or the scientist what will result from his research?

The world of today knows just as little about the world of tomorrow. *Only one thing is certain: that which opposes life will perish.*

The choice lies between taking an uncompromising stand for the sake of complete victory at some future date (never mind when) or doing whatever is possible and concealing one's rapid progress in the pages of a testamentary confession.

---

*Einstein succeeded in fascinating the first half of the twentieth century just because he had emptied space. Emptying space, reducing the whole universe to a static nothing, was the only theory that could satisfy the desertlike character structure of man of this age. Empty, immobile space and a desert character structure fit well together. It was a last attempt on the part of armored man to withstand and withhold knowledge of a universe full of life energy, pulsating in many rhythms, always in a state of development and change; in one word, functional and not mechanistic, mystical, or relativistic. It was the last barrier, in scientific terms, to the final breakdown of the human armoring. [W.R., 22 December 1952]

†A. S. Eddington, theoretical physicist, author of *The Nature of the Physical World.*

No one will be able to bear all of it; I am amazed that I can bear even the consciousness of it all.

Whatever has been achieved in its essentials is no longer of interest to me. Onward, ever onward, forward into new and unknown realms. As I get older, this urge increases rather than decreases. I am not growing "wise"—I know too much for that!—and I know far too little to be able to conquer.

30 September 1944

A late insight: The relationship with my work is the only one in which I have not been betrayed. It has lovingly returned all I have lovingly given.

TO JOHN P. CHANDLER
❖ 10 October 1944

Dear Mr. Chandler:

With regard to the patent, I am rather shocked at the attitude of the Patent Commissioner. It appears to me unscientific, irrational, and prejudiced. I do not know yet whether I would care to carry through the expensive fight in the courts, since I, personally, am not interested in the economic exploitation of my discovery. As you know, the main reason for filing the patent application was that I intended to secure the use of the cosmic orgone energy for everybody, and to exclude profiteering. I myself feel neither fit nor inclined to control the business side of this tremendous task. I have much more impor-tant things to do, and, as I have expressed it on several occasions, I feel that I did my share in the responsible job, and that it is up to the public *too* to do something about it. The Commissioner of Patents is a part of it. The way out of the mess is, I think, this:

Let the Patent Commissioner deny the application. In that case, everybody can build orgone accumulators and nobody else can take out a patent. The same principle of application and refusal of it would be carried through, in due time, in all countries. Thus, my primary purpose of securing the orgone energy for public use without profit by a single concern would be fulfilled. Now, the question is: In case, say, England or Sweden would grant the patent, could they then apply for an international patent? I hope to be able to confer with you about this important point very soon.

17 October 1944

(On the occasion of a visit by Lore.)

People are supposedly talking about me, saying that I am "peculiar," not "sociable" like other "normal" people.

Not only are matters upside down, people actually believe that they are right side up.

They view their compulsive sociability as friendly human interaction. They see no connection between their "ideas" and this murderous war. They are naively happy and yet how desperately unhappy.

They attribute strangeness to the person who is bearing the burden of understanding their misery, who took upon himself the enormous task of plumbing their deadly naiveté, the person who manifests the most normal reaction of all—namely, concern.

19 October 1944

I have never been a head of state but I suspect that it is far easier to rule an entire nation than to analyze away even a single one of the human animal's peculiar reactions.

26 October 1944

A calculating, reserved, mercenary individual cannot be a *genuine* natural scientist, for a genuine scientific researcher must bear the characteristics of nature itself in order to grasp it. Nature has bestowed an overabundance of gifts. A genuine research scientist must also be able to give naively. Nature expects no gratitude. The genuine natural scientist expects no thanks either. Nature is not calculating, it knows no reservations. The genuine natural scientist is equally ingenuous. The genuine scientist continues to give freely even where he may expect betrayal. He is aware that traitors will be the losers in the long run.

6 November 1944

4:30 p.m. Just saw the film *The Hitler Gang.*

The disgrace is all the greater in view of the fact that a small band of scoundrels was able to plunge the entire world into misery. A disgrace for this "best of all possible worlds." Hitler is not at fault, *we are all at fault.*

9 November 1944

When one stops naively storming citadels in the belief that their fall will free the world, one begins to grow tired. Even ten conquered citadels would not be enough because the citadels of hatred for life number in the millions. Such knowledge is paralyzing but I continue to write nevertheless, as if the revolution could break out tomorrow, but without inner conviction. I have been made to wait too long.

12 November 1944

Great internal conflict: I have discovered that I am losing friends and coworkers because the *results of energetic functionalism are too simple and logical.* They might be compared with an airplane ride or a wonderful meal where the passengers or guests do not know how the plane has been constructed or the food prepared. Two dangers arise from this:

1. Repetition of clichés
2. Failure at the slightest practical undertaking and then giving up

I must decide whether to operate with my usual reserve and inconspicuous authority or whether I should draw my pupils into the difficulties of the workshop.

I shall place three issues before them. Objectives of the workshop:

1. Work on oneself
2. Research methods, our own and those of others
3. Accomplishment of the daily practical tasks, from which the "wonderfully lucid" results flow.

That's demanding a lot!

22 November 1944

In connection with submitting our papers for American naturalization, the question arose as to whether we would be committing a crime—that is, breaking a law—if we viewed ourselves as married by common law.

23 November 1944

Thanksgiving Day. I do not carry on research "for mankind," I research the processes of nature. If one adheres to one's "duty toward mankind," one experiences "mankind" but loses the desire to fulfill the duty. One cannot put one's heart into research and simultaneously despise the people who enjoy the fruits of those labors.

The less one can accomplish for man as he is, the more vivid becomes the vision of working for the new, or the future, generation. I recoil in horror at the thought that decent newly born beings will become "citizens of the contemporary world" and wish that I could prevent this mutilation. That is why I work on life, for the new life, the coming, future life! Only vanity and ambition cause productive individuals to work for their contemporaries who neither desire nor deserve their efforts. One grows embittered when one works for mankind. In order to maintain the joy of working one must vault the confines of the present, place oneself in decent, natural surroundings as yet untouched by man, and function in a harmony of consciousness and action. Only under such conditions is creative work possible.

TO LORE REICH
❖ *11 December 1944*

My dear Lore:

I read a letter which you wrote to Mr. and Mrs. Rubinstein concerning your coming to New York for Christmas. In this letter I found the following sentence in the first paragraph: "I will try to get the money from <u>Reich and pay you back</u>" (underlined by me). This sentence shows clearly your attitude toward your father, confirming similar behavior on many other previous occasions. Now, as your father, I must take a step in this matter *in your interest*. According to my convictions and according to the general rules of decent behavior, it is *utterly indecent and dishonorable* to accept money from people whom you dislike, to take advantage of people in money matters. I would not do and I never did such a thing, and I would not keep company with anyone who does such things. I shall not pay any money anymore for your college, and I do not wish to see you as long as this attitude on your part lasts. You have the mistaken belief that a father is legally or morally obliged to pay for college studies. This is not the case.

I want you to realize the seriousness of this matter. I do not know who taught you this parasitic way of life. As my daughter you will fight your way through, accepting money only from people whom you trust and whom you like, or none at all.

15 December 1944

I must master the organizational problems of sex-economic work in a proper, practical way or else the best achievements will be lost, and I along with them.

The conflict with Wolfe's "Nazi" personality structure has been a latent issue for months. It occasionally expresses itself in ugly, apparently insignificant incidents. The general complaint is that one cannot make contact with Wolfe, that he "pooh-poohs" everything, belittles everything. Peter rejected Wolfe from the very beginning: W. has a ramrod down his spine, and is incapable of genuine love, both of which clash severely with his knowledge and the objectives of the work. The reason why W. is offensive is that some deep part of him is sick. Yesterday he really annoyed me, though the incident was laughable. The institute building has had a new coat of paint. The surfaces of the windowsills in one room were not smooth but grained. W.: "That is not nice, that is *fake*." My first thought was: "And you call yourself secretary of the institute when others do the work is *not* fake?"* The matter has deep roots. Work with Wolfe has shown that it costs him an effort to participate. The cause is tailored to his intellect but not to his emotional structure. He has a keen, clever mind but is envious because he is not doing "exactly the same" work as I. He's a faultfinder, a censor, shrugs everything off, writes good criticism of others purely out of joy in degrading people. He is

---

*The sentence was written in English.

not a discerning person. Calls people "nigger" or "Jew" anytime he has a chance. He is still impotent orgastically. Emotionally he has been a "beaten dog" from childhood onward and behaves poorly. It is uncomfortable to show him any warmth because there is no response.

He is aware of all this but somehow he cannot succeed in eliminating this basic attitude. He knows it, and even says himself that it is a "Nazi" attitude.

He will not hold out unless he is successfully restored in the orgastic sense.

He would like to have a lot of titles but none of the stress or strain. He has handed the publishing over to someone else. Understandable! He only did the translations under strong inner protest. If I did not fill two-thirds of every journal he would be hopelessly lost. When the first issue appeared he had childishly had *his* name printed in larger type than *mine*. He treats his women brutally.

It is incredibly difficult because in spite of all this he is a valuable person.

His only choice is between breaking with his "Nazi" intolerance and going his own way, either within or outside the framework of the institute.

He is pathologically struggling for independence.

The case of Wolfe raises a question of a very general nature:

Is the organization of sex-economic work possible at all under the prevailing conditions of social and human structure?

Am I circumspect enough to build and lead such an organization? Isn't it all two hundred years too early? Human structure, as it is presently constituted, must be transformed.

At this very moment the question of the incorporation of the Orgone Institute in the state of New York hangs in the balance. I must wait.

I almost feel as if my life would run its entire course amidst this enervating struggle between work and the world, recognition and defamation, the giant task and the dwarfed political possibilities.

The rigidified human animal simply will not allow his rigidity to be treated scientifically. But he will also not forgo the pleasure of love.

It's as if the present organization of human society rested upon dignified formality, as if procedure based upon facts were an impossibility.

Social responsibility. I was born in the camp of security, under the protection of the ruling class. The lack of responsibility of this class toward the community turned me into a revolutionary. As a natural scientist I give the community what it has always deserved from the very beginning: knowledge about its existence.

In a deadlock: things don't work out with pupils who were formerly patients. These are sick individuals who, once they have been cured, must learn to function. But with other people—those who come to me as pupils and not as patients—it doesn't work either, for without processing there can be no progress! And truly healthy individuals don't come at all because they live their lives apart from the plague. The practical problem of suitable coworkers is difficult, unsolvable.

TO A. E. HAMILTON*

❖ 22 December 1944

Dear Mr. Hamilton:

I have your kind letter of 19 December.† Whenever you feel ready to discuss things, please call my office. There is, in my judgment, and you surely agree with me, no more important subject of discussion in these days of world disaster than the question of human structure and education of small children. Therefore, please do feel quite free to call on me whenever you wish.

---

*Founder of the Hamilton School in New York City.
†Mr. Hamilton had told Reich, "It leaves no room for doubt that what you have given to the world, and are giving, is of immense, immediate, applicable value to anyone in the field of education who is capable of grasping its significance and has the courage to apply what he has grasped." He would like to read everything by Reich that was in English before asking for an appointment to meet him.

31 December 1944

Place children up to four years of age under sex economy and the world will have peace. The pedagogic efforts of good educators of the present and the past have fallen on unfertile soil like seed on the sands. The emotional structure of a child is not capable of assimilating progressive education, of digesting it and interpreting it in ten different ways. Sex economy therefore demands natural structuring of infants and the restructuring of adults in order to prepare the emotional soil for the seeds of knowledge and the arts.

1945

"Did Columbus found Chicago and New York? Did he build San Francisco and the great West? He 'only' discovered America. I have only discovered the orgasm."

1 January 1945

On the whole, I am lacking an important key which would explain the relationship of the rotation of the heavenly bodies to the length of the spinning wave of the orgone particles. It is still too early to put everything together systematically.

TO BRENTANO'S BOOKSTORE
❖ *2 January 1945*

Dear Madam:

Kindly let us know if you have or can find the following books in either German or English:

Copernicus: about the motions of the heavenly bodies

Kepler: main works

Maxwell: theory of electromagnetic waves (exact title not known)

Galileo: *Dialogues on Two World Systems*

Your information will be appreciated.

7 January 1945

They want international peace while preserving customs barriers and national borders.

They want education without a previous change in human structure enabling it to absorb that education.

They have laws to protect the state but none to protect life.

They have the state's rights over the lives of its citizens but the citizens have no rights in controlling the state.

They want the joy of life without potency, and love without responsibility, or responsibility without love.

8 January 1944

I will not find peace until I have put into words the very essence of the emotional plague, described it in such a way that every child will unfailingly recognize it for thousands of year to come.

In a description such as this, one is hampered by the urgent necessity of discussing theoretical questions which, in three hundred to five hundred years from now, will not have the slightest significance.

I must return to the simple principles again. This can only be accomplished by breaking with the vast boisterous world of everyday life.

T O　 A .　 E .　 H A M I L T O N
❖ *9 January 1945*

Dear Mr. Hamilton:

I liked what you wrote in your letter of 7 January very much. Why should you not think that I am a faker, if I myself am not always sure of not being one. Of course, I am seeing in the microscope the aura of the theosophists and mysticists. But is not that exactly what natural science should do? Since everybody is right in some way, it is only a matter of whether he knows or does not know where he is right and what to do with what he knows is right. The analysis of your reaction against my findings is quite common. The only difference is that you among very few people realize where and why you resist.

As to the social implications, my past experience tells me that it is a rather dangerous job. May I therefore suggest that you be utterly careful in the choice of the persons whom you draw into the picture.

10 January 1945

4:30 *a.m.* Last night Ilse came home from consulting an American lawyer on the question of American citizenship. He said: "You are perfectly within the law, living according to your moral code. If you were American citizens, nobody would care; but the law requires that you have a license when you become a citizen. No judge would give you the citizenship when you tell him that you live in a common-law marriage."

The common-law marriage in the state of New York has not been recognized since 1934 on account of some rich people whose sons had common-law wives who claimed their rights as *wives*. In that way a few rich nuisances were able to discard an important law, a common law.

At first a wave of deep disgust overcame me. Is that the democratic way. "I shall not give my formulas about the cosmic energy to the Americans if they treat me by coercion."

But not having the license and thus not becoming a citizen endangers my wife, my child, and my work to better such conditions of life. Under which circumstances, I ask myself, can I do the most good? By refusing to become a citizen or by becoming a citizen and then fighting this type of law all the better, not because it is a "law," but because it is an indecent, cruel law.

First I shall take the license in order to protect my wife and child. Then I shall do it myself *under written protest*.

21 January 1945

The human element in the superhuman individual is his searing disappointment in people and the farewell he must bid them as he departs into the isolation necessary for further accomplishment. The biographers of such destinies portray the tragedy of these accomplishments as "the fate of genius." The departure into isolation represents a flight from the type of human beings who find an evening of conversation or a notice about themselves in a newspaper more important than a principle, be it the principle of truth or freedom, of life or youth.

The superhuman accomplishment, which extends above and beyond man in his contemporary condition, is achieved not out of contempt but for *love* of mankind. The total stupidity one encounters here is responsible for the unbearable pain. It can easily result in scorn, an attitude bearing witness to the fact that one is still deeply concerned.

25 January 1945

4 a.m. Had Freud remained the natural research scientist he was around 1900, his following would have been small. Later all the neurotic metaphysicians who wanted to see a mirage of love rather than the functioning of love itself flocked to him. Functional research science found its home elsewhere, in orgone physics.

26 January 1945

Recently, day and night, I have been going through a deep crisis of my entire intellectual and spiritual being. I am simply experiencing the events of *this* world and at the same time penetrating the laws of cosmic functioning. The simultaneousness of business, politics, gossip, idle talk, German murder, and Russian-type revenge, on the one hand, and the life function of Ernst Peter or the bion, on the other, is unbearable.

My intellectual integrity cannot endure it, cannot understand, cannot grasp completely the vast extent of degeneration in the human animal. To see it in its entirety would be appalling. I am powerless in the face of this realization and must surrender since I do not wish to be Don Quixote. But surrendering is desertion, which is also undesirable. It is tempting to consider becoming a "pure mathematician" but that would be a shame. Shameful indeed to sacrifice oneself when such a sacrifice would come under the heading of insanity. *This is my spiritual crisis.*

It is impossible to make people understand the meaning of such a dilemma today. It is better to write for future generations, for the year 2400. Maybe then I will be understood.

29 January 1945

Of late it has become increasingly common for pupils who already have a practice of their own to approach me with the question of what is happening to them. They find themselves isolated and increasingly alienated from mankind. On the other hand, people have now begun to approach them for help and advice. But they are also felt to be "peculiar" and are resisted. I must emphasize that these pupils are just average people with the usual inclinations, prejudices, and social ties.

The work they are doing causes a change in them and allots to them a fate which I originally considered my own personal neurosis —namely, heavyheartedness.

From about 1917 onward, I have suffered from a "heavy heart," an ever more familiar *yearning* in the region of the solar plexus. My friends and acquaintances do not suffer from this. They are "staid," "normal" human beings of great dignity but with no yearning. I thought this heaviness and yearning were neurotic and entered analysis in order to free myself of it. I tried to kill the best of the human animal so that I would not have to "step out of the ranks"!

Today it is my professional conviction that my yearning and suffering were completely healthy and natural and that the coldness of my friends was pathological. In my children I see, quite distinctly, this yearning of the plasma to break out of its own confines. I hear the call of the wild in the depths of nature! Carry on!

For two weeks I have been fleeing from the great victory, the victory which is not merely one single event bringing a certain state of affairs to conclusion, but rather the victory which lies in the ceaseless development of infinite possibilities, in the struggle itself, in the experiencing of the process of truth!

I wanted to give up because I am losing confidence in man and my love for him; because I can no longer work "for suffering mankind" as I have in the past. Realization of the fact that man is irretrievably lost leaves a deep, burning wound. The maimed individual has sealed his own fate, he does not want to be saved, prefers to have diverse saviors die a torturous death on the cross for his salvation. He wants the saviors to unburden his conscience. I do not want to be a savior. I was only capable of struggling for man as long as I still didn't realize how he crushes his own life. Since he hangs his saviors in order to venerate them after they are thoroughly dead, loving him becomes a crime against life. Let us fight while we are alive and unarmored so that we can live for unarmored life! When mankind becomes unarmored once again it will find itself part of the striving of all unarmored life to experience joy and give of love. Rejecting degenerate man is not rejecting unarmored life. Quite the opposite.

4 February 1945

The New York Board of Regents has rejected incorporation of the Orgone Institute. This is perfectly logical, but it hurts. I still had illusions. Now I will not send in any more requests. Now they will have to come to me.

I can wait another three hundred, five hundred, one thousand years. And if those pedants want anything they will have to pay millions. I must finally come to my senses and give my accomplishments some dignity.

T O   L O R E   R E I C H
❖ 6 February 1945

Dear Lore:

Your letter arrived just at a time when I was engrossed in most difficult situations and problems. I wanted to answer you extensively, but it would take a whole book to answer all the misunderstandings and wrong assumptions which are compiled in your letter. I suggest that we have a thorough discussion about all you want to know at your next visit to New York. One of the difficulties with you is that you never came to me openly and frankly asking your questions and ventilating your doubts. I hope you will be able to correct your attitude toward me *basically* in order to reach some kind of friendly basis on which we could communicate with each other. I am quite different from what you think I am.

16 February 1945

I am afraid that I have once again arrived at an immense rupture in my life. After the incorporation was rejected, I succeeded in producing protozoa from frozen orgone water.* This widened the gap between my social and my intellectual existence tenfold, a thousand-fold. I no longer believe that this world will be able to accept me and my theories without turning itself entirely inside out. And since

*Reich refers to an experiment, Experiment XX, in which the "freezing of orgonotically highly charged water ('bion water') results in the production of plasmatic flakes. These flakes are capable of growth, development of bions, and small bean-shaped protozoa." *Orgone Energy Bulletin*, Vol. 3, No. 1 (January 1951).

this is not going to happen, it will dispose of me one way or the other. I am deeply concerned, do not trust the situation, and would like to safeguard my wife and my child. No one will stand by in the case of a catastrophe. There are many who would even attack me from behind. I realize that I am exaggerating in my anxiety, but catastrophes in the past and my knowledge of the vulnerable spot in human structure have made me cautious and suspicious. My first scientific blow was aimed too deep, without my realizing it. I cannot move backward—only forward, and forward means . . . ? I shall only be able to move forward alone, and not with my pupils. *It would be too dangerous.*

I am afraid, in the most ordinary, inglorious sense of the word.

21 February 1945

3 a.m. The war of clarification being waged against me continues. The greatest danger for me and for all my followers is my naiveté, which has still not been stamped out. My longing for social contact and open-minded comradeship always tempts me to forget how sick man is; I do not have the courage to perceive, in a full, practical sense, that all mankind has arrived at the edge of an abyss. The downfall of this animal species—whether it takes one thousand or one hundred thousand years—is occurring in myriads of tiny daily events, and in daily life I am like an airplane in a dense forest. Thus I continue to await support for my work from the same social agencies whose sentiments and thought systems I vehemently combat and unmask as pathological. I am still awaiting financial assistance for my research from the same sources whose commercial pollution and theoretical helplessness I simultaneously reveal as the basis for the miserable state of scientific thinking. I continue to hope for a "working people" whose contamination by the emotional plague I myself discovered and described.

Why do these illusions exist in my otherwise quite logical mind? Because I am afraid and cannot find a practical approach to the immediate future.

I am afraid of the gigantic responsibility which has become my lot through my work. My forced isolation has even robbed me of the possibility of having a friend (as in Oslo) with whom I could discuss matters. In a practical sense, I am confronted with the choice of either ceasing all work and withdrawing into "theory" (which is exactly what my archenemies would like me to do) or, together with a handful of people who have just been cured and are socially inexperienced, waging a frantic, dismal war against the officials of completely befuddled nations, against the church, human nature, and perhaps even nature in general. It's as if there were no room for *truth* in this system of nature and society (which I, of course, do not assume is true for nature).

I am afraid to realize that I am sitting on a high, quiet rock, surrounded by deep ravines into which there is no descent except to plummet. I climbed and climbed, and have apparently gone astray. Nothing, absolutely nothing far and wide which could lend me practical support. My patients are not the healthy warriors I would need by the thousand in order to have even a chance of success. My pupils are hardly out of their diapers with regard to the fight against the plague. And the six years of war have once again interrupted connections and developments such as those in France, Holland, etc.

Apparently I do not dare to realize how brave I was to climb that high, lonely rock. I wouldn't have succeeded had I known exactly what I was doing. What now?

Since the road of political power has been excluded and since science, although indeed able to understand this world better, will not direct and teach it any better for a long time to come, the outlook is gloomy.

Someday, somehow, through someone, the emotional plague will strike.

It might suddenly gain the victory over me. Things do not look good for me personally. I cannot even console myself with heroic illusions, for the work was not accomplished through heroism but approximately the way a child builds a castle out of building blocks, in utter seriousness, except that the castle of the science of the life function was erected in reality. The orgone was discovered in the same way, like a game, in complete innocence.

A heroic pose is ill suited to this, even if I do occasionally assume one.

TO A. E. HAMILTON
❖ *21 February 1945*

My dear Mr. Hamilton:

I wish to say a few words in regard to your plan to use my book "as a framework for our parent program next year." I hope you don't mind if this word will be one of warning again. You may well say that you are grown-up enough to know what you are doing, and that it should not be my business to interfere with your plans. Though I am thoroughly convinced by now that you understand the problem of human structure emotionally and deeply, I feel obliged to point out the great dangers and risks which are involved in using our knowledge practically.

This enthusiasm of the people for our publications should not lead us astray. The enthusiasm is a clear expression of the deep longing for happiness and freedom which comes out of the biological core. But decades of experience have shown that this enthusiasm in the long run does not keep its promises and very often even turns into hatred, putrid and pestilent, against us, if the inability to take responsibility for happiness and freedom is not removed or absent. This inability is an expression of the armor which surrounds the longing biological core and renders the organism helpless. The later hatred toward our work is always, with no exception, a disappointment reaction projected on the work, but it originates primarily in the inability to overcome inner and outer obstacles to freedom and happiness because of rigidity.

The use of our literature as a means of social endeavor on a broader scale, therefore, requires a definite caution based on this contradiction in human nature, a caution which must be applied in the way one chooses people and in observing their early reactions. There is, for instance, the necessity not to entrust people with any kind of responsible work in this field who do not live in some kind of sexual happiness or who even may deny it to children and adolescents. They may be intellectually sympathetic, even enthusiastic; they may even go with us emotionally to a definite degree; but a later hatred reaction is unavoidable because no one can stand the idea of happiness for mankind with all its prerequisites without enjoying it himself. Please, believe me that I have paid dearly in the past for this one experience alone.

28 February 1945

Bedbugs versus the northern lights: Science is the natural enemy of pedantry. I mean genuine natural science, not the thoughts of pedants at the universities. In this sense genuine science is the archenemy of all pettiness. Under its rays the petty bourgeoisie die as quickly as bacteria in glaring sunlight. There are bedbugs and there are northern lights; both are natural phenomena. We are flying through space at approximately four hundred and fifty miles per second, and in a thousand places mothers are demanding that their children should not breathe through their mouths.

On the earth's surface we are revolving at a speed of approximately six hundred meters per second, a speed which would make people faint if it were perceived as such. Somewhere in a New York hotel people are staging an adultery scene in order to get a divorce because two human beings of different sexes cannot separate without a court decision involving complicated and costly proceedings.

Somewhere in a doorway a young man strains to seduce a girl; she is afraid of him, has both desire and guilt feelings simultaneously. Love, you see, is forbidden by law during the age of blossoming sexuality. At the same moment, in nature, millions of cells are twitching in copulation, dividing into quadrillions of new cells; millions of couples are performing the most singular act of nature, superimposition.

And millions of light-years across the universe the arms of a spiral nebula stretch out in the same process of superimposition.

Members of Parliament are struggling to pass a bill which will deny Negroes the right to vote,* close bars at twelve o'clock instead of three, give Russia a piece of Poland, give Poland a piece of Germany, and all "for the sake of justice." At the same time an aurora glows because the earth's orgone envelope has reached a speed which produces irradiation.

14 March 1945

If a goal cannot be reached through truth it had better remain unreached. The path, from one point to the next, determines the

---

*Hatred of Negroes stems from the same source as the hatred which plague-stricken individuals bear toward nature, toward love. [W.R., 1945]

character of the goal. The goal is a functional unification of all points along the way.

Therefore, true peace can never result from belligerent actions, nor can a true work democracy be attained by force.

It is indeed possible to defend a peacefully acquired plot of ground against violent entry and force. But it is not possible to enjoy a violently acquired plot of ground in peace.

It is possible to let a tree grow and then destroy it, but it is not possible to destroy a tree and then have it grow again afterward.

It is possible to be true to the principle of truth, and occasionally protect oneself against the attacks of the emotional plague through an untruth. But it is not possible to go through life telling tactical lies, and then face the emotional plague with faithfulness to the truth.

It is possible to allow a child to grow up free and later occasionally to restrict it. It is not possible to raise a child under oppression and then expect it to live freely.

This too is a part of the natural orgonotic law.

20 March 1945

The kiss of truth is at first a painful kiss. You feel the pain of man's world and are incapable of separating yourself from it. You love man more, in a better and more practical way than before, because you suffer over his being as he is, and you have a painful desire for him to be different.

You feel the revolving movement in your own emotions. In the heart region there are perpetual pangs of yearning, as if one wanted to grow and strive upward and outward, beyond oneself. At first one thinks that this heaviness of the heart is an illness. On the contrary, it is the best, most fertile part of the human animal.

The kiss of truth also leaves its mark upon a man's face. Under the prevailing conditions of life, it is an expression of painful knowledge, sorrowful utterance, and burning desire for things to be different, better, happier.

Beethoven, Galileo, Leonardo da Vinci, Freud, etc.—the countenance of each of them showed traces of the kiss of truth.

There is no return to indifference once you have been kissed by truth, just as there is no return to life once pulsation has ceased.

There is no escape into illusions or feelings of power. You are irrevocably delivered up to the truth. The profound happiness of finding truth is only granted when one finds a field of productive activity for one's yearning.

All of this is revealed in the facial expression: *suffering* without masochism, *determination* without sadistic harshness, *kindness* without weakness, *knowledge* without vanity, *love* without profit or reward.

21 March 1945

Basically, the functional law of nature finds its formulation in the functional identity of the orgasm, the formation of matter, and the spiral nebulae. The details are now only a question of time, of exerting an effort, of lonely perseverance.

TO WALTER HOPPE
2 April 1945

Dear Dr. Hoppe,

I would like to report something which even I find incredible. However, there is no doubting the facts, which are as follows:

So far, in word and writing, I have represented the view that orgone energy is not able to influence disease processes in the organism which have led to fixed structural changes; that is, arteriosclerosis, arthritis, calcified TB foci, multiple sclerosis, etc., would be inaccessible. Now the following has occurred: A test patient in Maine informed me that after using the accumulator regularly for a few months he is no longer bedridden with arthritis, which he had been for several years. I saw the patient last year and can attest that he was almost totally restricted in his mobility. I refused to believe his report, which I received only recently. And now, a female patient who is receiving vegetotherapy from me has reported that the most recent X-ray of her lungs shows that the calcification shadows of an earlier case of TB have simply disappeared. The doctor told her that himself. Is it therefore possible that orgone therapy can make calcifications disappear? It would be good if you could direct your attention to this problem. I cannot understand in what way orgone-charged blood or tissue should be able to dissolve a focus of calcification. If further confirmation should be obtained of this point, it would be enormously important and should therefore not be carelessly ignored.

I heard that, among other things, some socialist politicians feel abandoned by me. It is regrettable that these zealous people should have such little sense of reality that they do not notice how much more concretely the work-democratic relationships of people represent their dream than does the dream of socialism itself. I ask myself whether it would be possible to save the good elements among these socialists for practical work. Or should it prove to be true that political discussion is more important than practical work achievement?

3 April 1945

Peter is exactly one year old.

I know a man who has thirty-five relatives to support. Here we see the purpose that family ideology so often serves.

I would very probably not have discovered the orgone if the death of my parents during the earliest years of my puberty had not catapulted me on a course toward independence. The sighting of the orgone required an especially high degree of intellectual independence.

4 April 1945

MARRIAGE CONTRACT
between
Ilse Ollendorff
and
Dr. Wilhelm Reich

We confirm with our signatures the following agreement:

1. We consider ourselves as having been married since 1939. We decided to have the marriage certificate issued in order to satisfy the requirements of the American naturalization authorities, because Ilse Ollendorff's American citizenship must be assured. In consideration of the deep-rooted immorality of the compulsory marriage laws, we obtained the marriage certificate under protest after five years of marriage, and in fear of the temptations to commit impropriety, which the immorality of the matrimonial law is suited to impose. This pro-

test is the basis of this marriage contract, which only came about due to the necessity imposed by social compulsion.

2. We declare herewith our agreement that if one of the partners desires a separation, the other party must acquiesce, because we feel that compulsorily enforcing the state of matrimony is immoral.

3. Since alimony paid to a divorced woman who is capable of work is equivalent to blackmailing a man, Ilse Ollendorff renounces any claim to alimony in the event of a separation.

4. In the event of a separation, Wilhelm Reich agrees to do everything possible to ensure that Ilse Ollendorff will continue to receive her present income from the Orgone Research Fund, in return for appropriate work on her part.

5. We agree that our son Peter should be educated according to the principles of self-regulation, and in a sex-positive manner, to protect him from any family influence and, in the event of a separation, to allow him to decide with which parent he wishes to live. The spouses state explicitly that it is indecent and immoral for one of them to keep a child against his will or to influence that child against the other parent. It is the obligation of both parents to bear the costs of looking after the child. However, the major share of the education costs shall be borne by the parent who is financially better off.

6. Each of the two marital partners shall retain the property that he/she acquired through his/her income from any source. The possibility of donating [property to the other partner] remains.

7. The blame for any separation that may occur cannot be borne by just one of the partners. We agree that in any case both parties must declare their responsibility for the need to separate.

Signatures: Ilse Ollendorff
Wilhelm Reich

5 April 1945

Just picked up our "marriage license"—after six years of marriage and a one-year-old child. What deep immorality, what a mess these marriage laws are—the ones so recently ratified by the "revolutionary proletariat."

What lifelessness in those halls where love is identified with a test for syphilis and marriage is equated with economic extortion. A country where such legislation is considered holy has no right to try to save the world. *America, first save yourself.*

All this is the work of the little man! "Of the people and by the people!"*

They don't dare to love, and since they are only accustomed to fucking they are *incapable* of love.

People's happiness in their love lives has become too unimportant while cosmic energy has become too important for me to make a big affair of the license. When I left the courthouse I could have puked! My wife too!

I will tell them the truth, these petty bourgeois people who are ruining the world. I will explain my attitude in no uncertain terms in a document that will leave an indelible mark, a documentary of their disgrace. Since I now know that my work will stand in the foreground of the future history of mankind and since, furthermore, I have no desire for fame here and now, I *want* to, I *can*, and I *will* tell them the truth.

Compulsory marriage provokes: economic exploitation, forcing of personal inclinations, intervention of outsiders in personal affairs. This "public opinion" was created by sick individuals. To bow to this is equal to confirming the views that there are superior and inferior races, that God exists, etc.

The prerequisite for genuine accomplishment today is renunciation of all recognition by representatives of the present, and even more, a feeling of disgust for their recognition—those filthy, greasy, cowardly, lying, plague-ridden gossipers.

I must remain faithful to my sense of the truth, even when truth betrays me, and still continue listening to radio commercials to keep in touch with reality.

*This phrase was written in English.

10 April 1945

Dear Leunbach:

I must say that I am extremely disappointed at, and indeed cannot comprehend, the behavior of the Scandinavian coworkers of the institute. We have waited here for years to get any news, we were very concerned, we took the articles that appeared in Scandinavia and translated and published them in the international journal. I sent manuscripts and letters in order to maintain contact, and the result is a lax and indifferent relationship which is extremely discouraging. In the meantime, the work here has made enormous strides and there was reason to fear that the many years of interrupted contact would result in alienation. We started out in 1936 as a serious, responsible, scientific organization and it was assumed that each individual who at that time signed on as a founder of the institute would do everything possible to keep the cause going. This was not the case, because, once the mail links were reestablished with Sweden, it was naturally the first duty of the people there to send us detailed reports about everything worth knowing so that we could ensure the further development of the work. Since Philipson and Hoel and others have preferred, for two years, not to make use of the possibilities of written communication, it is naturally difficult to have any understanding, and also all opportunity is lost to maintain the cohesion which is so necessary. Sex economy and orgone research are proceeding and making great progress. It is now up to the Scandinavians to restore the contact which they have allowed to lapse in a way which strikes me as very ugly. This is a very serious matter. I ask you or Philipson or anybody else to send a clear, detailed, and honest report on the situation in Scandinavia, how strong the will is to work together with the international institute, and to identify with my work. Whether and which names will appear after the war on the title page of the international journal as representatives of the international movement which I founded will depend on this.

I do not want there to be any doubt that to my personal disappointment are added some decisive factual considerations and I must have complete clarity on the relationship of the Scandinavian col-

leagues toward the institute. The sketchy reports sent to Leistikow*
on chiefly personal matters and affairs are naturally not a substitute
for proper, sober, factual work reports. It is also important that we
here learn how many serious sex-economic educators and physicians
are working according to our way of thinking; whether there is any
intention to resurrect the Scandinavian journal; which sex-economic
works were translated and into what languages; what new and independent material has been published; whether any steps can be taken
in Scandinavia to have the literature sent from here to there, etc.,
etc. The world did not stop existing and functioning along with Hitler. On the contrary, I regard it as one of our main functions to
survive such Hitlerian world-scale catastrophes and to overcome them
through serious work. Each of us is naturally very interested in personal reports, but it is impossible to regard a personal report as a
fulfillment of the task which a specialist in our area has to perform.
When I had to flee Germany in 1933, and spent two years as an
outlaw, I nevertheless founded a publishing house, published literature, wrote books, launched a journal, and among other things set up
a promising Scandinavian work group. I would like to know what
remains of all that. Naturally, there can be no talk of a conference
until the necessary contacts have been established and sufficient preliminary technical work has been done.

Do you have any news about what happened to August Lange and
Oeverland?† Please write immediately to let me know.

❖ 14 April 1945

Address before the scientific workers of the Orgone Institute:
Friends!

We are not participating in the Franklin Roosevelt death holiday.
We have gathered here as usual for scientific work just as the workers
gather in the factories to do their job. We belong to those strata of
society who do not try to overcome social misery by prayers and fes-

*Gunnar Leistikow, Scandinavian journalist.
†August Lange, sociologist, and Arnulf Oeverland, Norwegian poet laureate.

tivities alone but foremost by thinking away the veil that obscures human life and by working hard, continuously and resolutely, to unravel the secrets of life. It is due to these unsolved riddles of life, to the existence of mystical ideas, that Hitler, the exponent of the emotional plague, could seize power twelve years ago, that he was able to threaten two billion working people of this earth with utter disaster, and that Franklin D. Roosevelt had to interrupt his great social endeavor and to replace positive social actions by mobilization of the population, by turning from production of goods to the production of killing devices—in short, that utter confusion and desolation overcame our lives.

Roosevelt fell, so it was stated correctly in public, as a victim of this war, and with that, as a victim of the emotional plague. That may sound strange or exaggerated. But it is true. Roosevelt was a great man and a true friend of the people. He proved that fact by his actions. "Great man"—what is that? Look at the well-known faces of so-called great men, and you will, if you look with open eyes, discover the secret of great men. Their faces show sorrow, deep, devastating sorrow! It is the suffering of the one who looked deeply into the tragedy of the animal man and did not keep aloof.

I saw Roosevelt's face in a movie picture soon after the Yalta Conference, and I knew that he was utterly depressed and sick and would probably die soon.

We may not have agreed with some forms in Roosevelt's actions which were dictated by the political setup of our social system. But we certainly agreed fully with the general trend of his leadership. We agreed because this trend made it possible to at least *develop* truths. Those who blame Roosevelt for not having accomplished the paradise on earth immediately should try themselves to be in his place.

T O   A R T H U R   G A R F I E L D   H A Y S [*]
❖ *16 April 1945*

Dear Mr. Hays:

At our discussion on 9 April, you expressed your willingness to function as the lawyer of the Orgone Institute in case that I, as the leading representative of its work, should be dragged into some kind of court action. I am expecting a major attack from the quarters of the organized emotional plague any day. Such an attack may or may not come. At any rate, I would like to prepare for it in order not to be caught unawares.

The literature which I am having sent to you by the Orgone Institute Press will provide the necessary information in regard to the substance of my scientific position as well as in regard to some of the attitudes and actions of the foes of this work which I experienced in the past. I would appreciate it if you would kindly inform me whether, after taking cognizance of the subject matter, you would be inclined or not to function as our lawyer.

I gained confidence in you when I witnessed your attitude in questions of social morals and modes of living of the people at the radio. He who does not feel and suffer from the deep immorality and social disasters caused by the ancient cultural laws concerning human private, and especially sexual, living, cannot understand the burning scientific impetus to investigate the effects and to find the ways of betterment in this field of terrible human suffering.

Please say frankly yes or no after having read the few articles which I have marked with red pencil. In case of a court action I would, of course, be my own defender and would turn my defense into an attack as far as scientific matters go, but since the emotional plague does not dare to face issues squarely and take a stand in a matter of truth, since it prefers to use underhanded methods of defamation, framing, etc., a skilled and open-minded lawyer is needed to take care of the merely formal legal procedures in close cooperation with the large factual issues. In case you would not be willing or free to accept this function, could you recommend somebody else suitable

---

[*]This letter was not sent.

for this purpose? The Orgone Research Fund is in a financial position good enough to remunerate the services of a lawyer.

I am sure that the literature will not fail to convey the conviction that major social issues are involved.

21 April 1945

The social exigency of the masses of human animals will not be eliminated until the sadness of deeply moving music dwells in their hearts. Only when they mourn over themselves will the impulse arise to secure a happy life for all.

Mankind's innate desire to dance for joy will have to arise and conquer the body and the mind in order to reawaken the joyous spirit of life.

I played with my son for an hour and felt the pulse of life once again. One must live with healthy children to understand what life is all about!

24 April 1945

One must learn to read *functions* from numbers and formulae, just as one perceives the expression of a movement.

3 May 1945

Orgone physics obviously is developing a new type of mathematical thinking, functional orgonometry.

7 May 1945

The end in Europe. The German army has capitulated. People are celebrating the victory over fascism and have no inkling of the fascism within themselves.

The next wars:

a. American democracy vs. Russian fascism
b. American fascism vs. Russian fascism
c. English Tory capitalism vs. Russian fascism

8 May 1945

The Western democracies differ from the dictatorships in Russia and Germany in that they offer at least the possibility of conceiving peace for men. The danger lies in confusing this possibility with real peace.

TO THE AMERICAN CIVIL LIBERTIES UNION
❖ *8 May 1945*

Gentlemen:

I received your invitation to the meeting on World Freedom of Speech and Press. May I be permitted to say a few words, being unable to attend the meeting.

Freedom of speech and press are usually and unconsciously being misinterpreted in the sense that irrationalism should have the same freedom of expression as rationalism, and that the lie should have the same freedom of speech as the truth. This misconception of freedom has led the European world into the disaster because the present human character structure is more afraid of the truth than of the lie, and more inclined to irrational than to rational reactions. If real peace and democracy should have a chance of growth, I believe, a thorough distinction between rational and irrational, truthful and deceitful human action and expression should be made, and that freedom of speech and press should not be granted to fascist lie and irrationalism, wherever and by whomever it is expressed. I do not, of course, overlook the tremendous implications and difficulties of such a change in the concept of human freedom.

T O   H E L E N E   L I N D E N B E R G*
12 May 1945

Dear Mrs. Lindenberg,

I just received your letter of 16 April. I am sorry that you have been unwell. Are you completely recovered now? Today I am again sending you a food package through CARE. Write again soon.

T O   E L S A   L I N D E N B E R G
14 May 1945

Dear Elsa,

I have received your letter of 9 April and thank you. In this letter, I just want to stress one point with you and ask you to hammer it as quickly and as emphatically as possible into the heads of the other friends and coworkers of the institute: For reasons which are completely incomprehensible, the manuscripts which I sent to Scandinavia more than two years ago on the discovery of the orgone in the atmosphere, on the orgone accumulator, and on its medical therapeutic significance have been ignored. I can only assume that even my former close friends have decided to believe the rumors that I am mad. Now, the fact of the matter is that I am not in the least bit mad, but on the contrary over the last five years I have smashed a deep breach in the problem of organic diseases such as cancer and other biopathies. The orgone accumulator is already in use far and wide here, also in Palestine, and it is extremely important, in fact it would even be a crime, if we did not try to use the new means of biological energy to combat the massive health problem in Europe. I regard it as the duty of every member of the institute to initiate the construction of orgone accumulators everywhere in Europe in order to help restore the health, in particular, of the poor strata of the population. I wish to stress that further cooperation depends on the fulfillment of this self-evident social duty. I am deadly serious about this. By return post, I would like to be informed of who possesses the two manu-

*Elsa's mother in Berlin.

scripts entitled "The Discovery of the Orgone" and "The Cancer Shrinking Biopathy." They were sent in 1942 to Ingrid Klackenberg in Sweden.

In the meantime, the Orgone Institute Research Laboratories have been incorporated in the state of New York, and thus for all America and other countries, as a nonprofit corporation. If there is anybody there who undertakes to construct and distribute orgone accumulators among the population in order to charge blood and tissues, he would automatically become an American institution on the basis of this incorporation. Discuss the matter with Nic, Sigurd,* and others. Try to arrange it that our literature can be sent to Sweden. There is a terrible amount to do in this misery. Politicking by itself will not do it. What we must above all achieve is mental-hygienic clarification and the application of orgone energy to increase resistance to disease among the population.

One more thing: If you ever meet Evang,† let him know in no uncertain terms what a disgusting thing he did, spreading the rumor everywhere that I had been locked up over here because I was mentally ill. Please write to me in detail and immediately. We must get the international work going again as soon as possible.

I would recommend that "The Function of the Orgasm" should be published. However, wait until you receive the English edition, because, for obvious reasons, when I sent the manuscript I did not include two important chapters—namely, the foreword and a chapter on fascism.

Please ensure that everybody writes to me and that a summary work report is sent to me. Stay in touch. I would also like to know exactly, with precise details of their respective fates, which of our friends ended up in concentration camps, because I want to publish these facts.

---

*Nic and Sigurd Hoel, Norwegian psychiatrist and writer.
†Karl Evang, Surgeon General of Public Health Services in Norway.

T O   R O G E R   N .   B A L D W I N[*]

❖ *16 May 1945*

Dear Mr. Baldwin:

I am in agreement with your statements in your answer to my letter to such an extent that the apparent disagreement serves as an excellent example of democratic ventilation of opinion:

Of course, we cannot entrust the power to suppress the evils of free speech to anybody. In my publications I have again and again stressed the point that power and truth are mutually exclusive. But the point is this: The existence of a Civil Liberties Union which fights bravely and strenuously against political irrationalism proves that the truth has not the same right as the lie. I would like to see things reversed; there should exist a "Lie and Racial Hatreds Liberties Union," with the plight to defend itself against well-established and unshakable civil liberties. Truth should not have a lesser but a greater chance than the lie. There are untold numbers of democratic committees on this and that; why not establish a committee for the investigation of objective differences between rationalism and irrationalism, mechanisms of lie and mechanisms of truth? During the past forty years science has provided many tools of knowledge to distinguish irrationalism from rationalism. The possibility to incorporate this new knowledge into the total framework of democratic endeavors is thus given.

I would like to mention only one great distinction between rationalism and irrationalism, the *life positive* and the *life negative* functions within our society.

I did not mean to say that "Europe went fascist because of free speech," but that Europe went fascist because of the lack of such distinctions in social thinking. I also firmly believe in the democratic instincts of the people to decide what is right and what is wrong; but these democratic instincts will not become effective unless the power of organized irrationalism is matched by unrestricted and protected freedom of truth all over the world.

[*]Official of the American Civil Liberties Union.

TO MRS. RICHARD STERN*
❖ 25 May 1945

Dear Mrs. Stern:

I received your letter of 19 May through the Orgone Institute Press. There can be no doubt that what the Indian people called *prāna* for so long is the same as what orgone biophysics calls orgone. But I would like to stress the decisive difference: Orgone biophysics learns to use the life energy in a practical manner, to demonstrate it objectively, to determine the amount of energy at work, its specific characteristics, etc.; in other words, it is natural science.

Before Sigmund Freud taught us the technique to reveal and to handle the unconscious psychic processes, very many people knew that there exists an unconscious psychic life. But only when the psychoanalytic technique was established were we able to handle it. It is clear that the living organism knows about the life energy. But only now does it become possible to deal with it in a practical scientific manner.

The orgone is inhaled over the whole body surface. The intake is not restricted to special places. Orgone is stronger at the sea and in pine forests than, for instance, in a city. It is not yet possible to measure definite amounts of absorption on different places of the skin.

I appreciate your comments, and I hope you will keep in touch with our literature.

30 May 1945

In Orgonotic Lodge,† Maine. Alone, lonely, desolate, hopeless, with gigantic solutions to gigantic questions in a sick, lifeless, murdering world.

4–5 June 1945

Kepler epitomes contain everything about the orgonotic cosmic function except a correct description of the orgone.

*Mrs. Stern had written to Reich in response to one of his articles.
†Name given by Reich to his cabin.

TO JANE DARLEY COATES[*]
❖ 9 June 1945

Dear Mrs. Coates:

Your letter of 5 June reached me here today. Your objection is excellent; but I have made this objection myself in my article "Orgone Therapy of the Cancer Biopathy" in 1942. It would, of course, be an almost criminal offense against the principles of truth to claim that the orgone application can remove the cancer scourge. The cancer scourge will not be erased from the earth unless the sex-economic principle of living has been established for children and adolescents. We have to keep that straight in focus. On the other hand, nobody with good sense will refuse to alleviate the pains, and, if possible, the tumor and rotting process in cancer patients by means of orgone, because there is a greater principle involved. We have to do both things: do the possible now and fight for the principle at the same time.

TO HERBERT HARVEY[†]
❖ 9 June 1945

My dear Mr. Harvey:

I have read your letter of 31 May with great interest. I intended to write the following short answer: Why don't the physicists, instead of having millions of objections and arguments, simply construct orgone accumulators, study the most visible orgone phenomenon, and do all the other things which I described in my articles. Interpretations could be discussed later; and also the question of whether I know about physics or not could be delayed. At any rate, it must have some significance that those who know physics did not discover the orgone, while a biopsychiatrist who, according to the current views in science, is not supposed to know physics, *did* discover the orgone.

---

*English woman who had been in analysis with a former student of Reich.
†Herbert Harvey had introduced himself in a letter to Reich as "not a professional physicist" but "orthodox" in physics. Reich, he said, knew nothing about physics.

You won't mind if I tell you that you underestimate my scientific conscientiousness. In the published article on orgonotic pulsation I dealt with the common opinions among everyday physicists, whether right or wrong. In the following second part I shall have to deal with highly specified physical theories and theorists, as for instance Jeans, Eddington, Millikan, Einstein, and others. Just my familiarity with physical basic theory requests utter humbleness on all parts. I would like to emphasize the fact that there are no authorities as yet in the field in which I am working. If you deny the most clearly established experimental facts, no further discussion is possible at all, and a great war in natural science will be unavoidable. If, on the other hand, you and other physicists agree as to the *existence of these new phenomena and facts*, it will be a matter of long, decent and elaborate discussion as to whether the established mechanistic views of electrophysics or my functional attempts are the better ones. The condition for any discussion remains: acknowledgment of the facts and objective, friendly cooperation in the attempt to incorporate these new facts into our world picture. If my functional interpretation is wrong, and if, at the same time, mechanistic electrophysics are not applicable, some quite new type of working hypothesis will have to be developed. If, however, my method of energetic functionalism proves to be correct, the mechanistic viewpoint will be shattered and remain true only within a circumscribed realm. I have no ambitions in any of these directions. All I am trying to do is to keep my experiments in the process of development; I am happy to say that I was successful so far in the course of about twelve years. I do not intend to engineer a permanent divorce between my research and other objective sciences, as you state. I am ready and waiting eagerly for cooperation. But the world of mechanistic physics will have to take a different standpoint from that expressed, for instance, in Eddington's works. The life process is *inside* and not *outside* the realm of the physical sciences. For the first time in the history of natural science, the link between the living and the nonliving world is secured by the discovery of the orgone and its functional and not mechanistic properties. I refuse to believe that the framework in natural scientific thinking has been set already to provide for the objective judges. That will take a lot of time and hard work. I can assure you that one of the highest authorities in the world of physics was free and objective enough to confess ignorance about the phenomenon of the orgone energy. We both know, and every high-ranking physicist knows, that the mechanistic physical picture of the world has left us in bad shape since the principle of absolute causal determination has been punctured. I can assure you, furthermore, that the attempts of energetic functionalism which are made on the basis of the discovery of the orgone, to fill the gaps and, first of all, to bring the living plasm within the boundaries of natural science, find ample support in the writings and concepts of very many acknowledged first-rank natural scientists, Demokritos, Kepler, Newton, Freud, etc. Nobody knows as yet which way this process of new insights may turn. I would like to suggest great caution. I hope to have shown my extreme caution and carefulness in my work; whether I am doing my job well or badly, only the future will tell.

TO THEODORE P. WOLFE
10 June 1945

Dear Dr. Wolfe,

I am uncertain in what form the remainder of the (numerous) results of physical orgone research should be published. There are three possibilities.

a. Publication of the experimental facts *by themselves* (swinging of pendulum, west-to-east movement, Experiment XX, the formation of bions and protozoans from concentrated orgone in water, etc.), without interpretation, as a provisional report.

b. Publication of Part II of "Conversations with the Electrophysicist," in which the working hypothesis of the spinning wave is submitted in rough terms, *without* any mathematical proof.

c. Extensive and detailed publication of all experimental results and relationships achieved so far, as Volume 2 of *The Discovery of the Orgone*.

I do not know which form, which sequence would be the best. I would like to leave myself a lot of time in publishing the comprehensive context. Against this there is the fact that if physicists are not informed of the total context, they lose their nerve (see Lin!). The question is difficult. Would you please be good enough to help me decide it. We can discuss the matter when you are here. There can be no doubt that repeatedly presenting the *same* phenomena each time from a different viewpoint and context would be one modus agendi.

Although recognition by the world of mechanists is not important to me, I would nevertheless not like to make it difficult or even impossible to obtain such recognition. I am also influenced by a feeling of resentment regarding Einstein's behavior (failure to reply to letters)—i.e., I have a great desire to be rude and not to tolerate any more insolent remarks. The mechanists do not know how to respond to my facts, except to try to explain them away. In their camp, the facts about the orgone have an effect similar to that of a pike in a quiet pond of self-satisfied carp.

TO THEODORE P. WOLFE
20 June 1945

Dear Dr. Wolfe,

Construction is slowly getting going here. We hope that the building will be up in about six weeks.* In the meantime, we are working with the oscillograph in the small shed so that we will have completed the preliminary work by the time that proper experimentation can start with the atmospheric pulse in the large building. Kepler described the orgone as the driving force of the heavenly bodies, in the same way that Newton described the orgone as ether. It is unbelievable that nothing can be found about this in the physics textbooks.

20 June 1945

When a creative individual produces thousands of wonderful things, thousands of people insult him. If he utters even one single nonsensical word, he has a following of millions. This too is a part

*A laboratory was under construction at Orgonon.

of the human animal's tragedy, a symptom of his emotional plague.

He allowed Marx to starve because of his discovery of the value of labor, but he followed, by the millions, the "dictatorship of the proletariat," one of Marx's horrible errors.

He murdered Socrates because Socrates denied the gods. He idolizes the generals who denied all human rights, his *own* included.

He persecuted and scorned Freud when the man pointed out to him the misery of his childhood, but he rejoiced over the nonsense of the death instinct.

This all proves that I have not yet uttered any obvious nonsense, for until now very few have followed me.

If one wishes to overcome one's inhibiting timidity and paralyzing adoration of great men, one must study them carefully. One will find their simpleness just as redeeming as the loopholes in their knowledge and the greatness of their thoughts.

TO   NIC   HOEL
22 June 1945

Dear Nic,

We were very happy here to receive news from you. It is good, both in personal terms and otherwise, that you have survived this dangerous war in Europe. I was particularly touched to learn that you now know, from personal experience, the unspeakable problems with which I had to cope at the time when I was forced to leave Germany and reestablish the work. Particularly in the light of these human experiences, it seems to me all the more tragic that serious conflicts have obviously developed in Scandinavia between individual members of the institute. I do not know whether you will ever manage to get a grip on things to the extent that the work over there will survive and not collapse. Philipson writes that he wants a conference "at a neutral place in England, where Neill lives." Neill is proposing London. I have written to tell Philipson that there is no chance of holding a meeting until the necessary preparatory work has been done. I think the following preparations are required:

1. News must be received here from all the Scandinavian mem-

bers of the institute dating from 1939. So far, I have heard nothing from Raknes, Siersted, Sigurd, and Odd Havrevold. Despite having the opportunity, Philipson and Leunbach let more than two years pass without writing. To this day, I do not know how much of the organization still exists and is working in Denmark, and what was added in Sweden. Receipt of manuscripts which I sent to Sweden was never confirmed and the manuscripts were never commented on. We did not receive any clinical or organizational reports. We should first of all know on what basis such a meeting would take place. What papers, reports, etc., would be presented.

2. How many of the ten members from 1939 desire such a meeting and are ready to travel?

3. A meeting would be a catastrophe if all the institute members referred to above were not first of all familiarized with at least the theme of the work which has been carried out here since 1939. The American journal and the other publications should be available over there and it should be clear whether anybody, and who, agrees with this development. Much has changed. This does not mean that it is necessary for orgone biophysics to be accepted or understood, but it must be clear that nowadays sex economy and vegetotherapy constitute only part of the main work, which since 1942 has been proceeding under the publicly adopted name "Orgone Biophysics."

4. If it takes place, should the meeting include only the ten members, or should each working group bring with them anybody they wish? In the latter case, the names, professions, and workplaces of all participants should be submitted here beforehand.

5. Someone in Scandinavia or England must be willing to organize the meeting.

There are many other questions that could be asked, but these seem to me the most important ones.

25 June 1945

There no doubt exist unconscious considerations which are equal in every way to the conscious ones.

At first, with no conscious thought, I arranged the length of the orgonotic pendular swing in such a way that the length of the swing represented the atomic weight. I would not have been able to offer an explanation for this had anyone inquired at the time (1942). Only three full years later, when this experimental arrangement had revealed the gravitation formulas so very important to me: $gr = 10^2\pi^2$ and $l = 25t''^2$, and only when I was able to account for the original equation of the length of the swing and inert mass ($l = mgr$) (and *had* to account for it if my theory were to survive), only then did the significance of this explanation emerge. I had been considering the problem of the transformation of energy into mass for years, and above all the question of whether and how orgone energy represents the cosmic proto-matter from which the chemical elements developed. Now it has become clear that energy is determined by the number of wavelengths and oscillations per unit of time, whereas mass is determined by gravity.

If, therefore, mass developed out of oscillating energy, then the original length of the energy wave must appear in the weight of the mass. In this manner, the great conclusion emerged which states that what we today call the gravitational attraction of mass (gr = acceleration) was originally an oscillating wavelength ($gr = r^2w$).

T O   N I C   H O E L
28 June 1945

My dear Nic,

I wish to add the following, more personal comments to my more factual letter.

There have probably been a great many changes in the lives of all the people who founded the International Sex Economic Institute in 1936. I do not know whether these changes in the personal development of individuals are such that they permit any further practical cooperation or whether we can only remain personal friends, or possibly even whether some of us might become enemies. I would therefore just like to state briefly what changes have taken place in my life since 1939. I am coming increasingly close to Karl Marx and therefore I am moving further and further away from current political socialism and communism. I no longer believe in a future of politics if fundamental principles have to be modified. I now only believe in the possibility that the rational functions of *love, work,* and *knowledge,* something which I call "natural work democracy," can make a gigantic effort to create those conditions which we all desire, each in his special way, according to his special experiences or structure. (Naturally, I am not talking here of the political reaction.) Because I have finally come to accept the full consequence of the insight that the only person responsible in the chaos is the average "little man"; because no Hitler and no Mussolini could ever achieve anything without the approval of the masses; because, in addition, I have no answer to the question how one can socially bring about a rational position in the masses of working people without once more promoting political irrationalism, I live very withdrawn and work mainly in the field of natural science, and I only become socially involved to the extent that I have a clear understanding of social problems. In 1941, I was placed under detention here for three and a half weeks on suspicion of being a German spy, but I was unconditionally acquitted on that count. You come right from being engaged in the work—currently illegal—which I got to know and had a taste of about ten years earlier. Will we understand each other? I would like to know how you see the long-term social problems. I mean the development toward *true* democracy, how you stand with regard to the various parties, their errors of judgment, their lack of understanding of the psychology of the masses and their coalitions. When I say that I live a lonely life, that does not mean that I do not closely follow the social events and do not pay close attention to any sign that points in the direction of achieving the truly democratic goals of society. In contrast to my life in Norway and Germany, I do not on principle cultivate any personal, social contact with pupils or patients. The difficulties of personal relationships are too great and the work suffers as a result. I have come to realize that many errors were committed in this personal, social interaction. In addition, there is the following consideration: It is only recently, after going through long and difficult internal struggles, that I have been forced to acknowledge that I am somehow different, I react differently, feel and think differently, and also work more effectively than the average individual, even among the best anywhere. I have resisted this realization for twenty years so as not to lose contact with friends and the circles in which

I move. But it has now transpired that my reluctance to recognize my state of being different and my greater performance capability has always led me into a situation where I naturally expect my colleagues and friends to behave exactly as I do—namely, to work just as hard, to spend just as much money on research and social efforts, and to remain as true to the cause as I do. Due to my false assessment of democracy, I placed everybody else on the same level of achievement as myself, and this had two negative effects: One was that a friend or colleague felt equal to me and tried to achieve as much as me without being able to do so. As a result, he regularly competed with me. This was irrational and inevitably had to end in enmity. The second serious effect was that, due to my excessive expectations, I was disappointed and committed various stupid errors. Another point which I must openly make is the following: The sex-hungry people around me tend, in a mystical way, to expect me to create a paradise on earth. In the case of women, this very often gave rise to some extremely difficult situations. This was another decisive reason for me to withdraw from all social contact and to live my life with my wife and child. I believe I am immune against becoming a bourgeois or a reactionary because the problems which I have raised, and certain answers which I have given, have carried me far beyond myself. I could not become reactionary without sacrificing much, indeed perhaps most, of what I have achieved through severe personal sacrifice in the course of twenty-six years of my life. It is naturally not impossible, but since I am not entirely stupid I would myself notice if any such change was occurring. I believe quite honestly that (not myself but) the natural scientific discipline which I have founded will in the long term be far more revolutionary than the views and moods of everyday revolutionaries, whom I admire very much for their courage. But my life has been no less endangered for the past thirty years and it will remain that way. I know that you will not misunderstand me. The conflict between long-term, deep-rooted natural science and short-term political requirements is just as unresolved as ever. Quite apart from that I am more than overburdened with experimental work on the cosmic orgone energy.

I believe that the foregoing will give you an impression of me and will enable you to help reestablish contact with the Scandinavian friends of 1939. If it were up to me, I would get together with all of you and spend a few wonderful evenings engaged in lively, genuine, and friendly discussions.

1 July 1945

When one has grown accustomed to work which requires great perseverance and devotion, one inclines to be overly loyal toward people. Work produces results. Loyalty toward people is a painful, disappointing attitude. The prerequisite of this loyalty is the false assumption that man is as faithful as work.

3 July 1945

The harmony of the KR law of nature gives me a feeling of intoxication. How satisfying it would now be not to be forced to have anything to do with people, neuroses, perversions, etc. But I must pay for my independence.

I am standing on the crest of an enormous mountain with deep chasms on all sides. May no one follow me! From these heights the world below looks small. Its political concerns are miserable. How narrow the deep valley appears.

6 July 1945

Start (after ten days of preparation) of tests with the cathode-ray oscillograph to determine cosmic orgone pulses.

July 1945

1. The gravitational center of Copernican astronomy is not fixed but moves in space. This movement is proved by the gradual change in the position of the planetary orbit relative to a selected fixed star.

2. The movement of the gravitational center radically changes the pattern of movement of the planetary system:

In reality, the planets do not describe Copernican circles or even Keplerian ellipses around the gravitational center. They describe orbits similar to those of a rotating top, as "spinning waves" in a certain, regular relationship to the moving central body.

3. The planets spin—i.e., they *rotate* about their own axes in the direction of their movement in space. The movement relative to the

central body is functionally merged with the movement of rotation about their own axes. In reality, however, only *one* type of movement, the spinning movement, exists. For purposes of orgonometric study, it is permitted and advantageous to break this uniform spinning motion down into its components—namely, the rotation of a planet around its own axis and the circling relative to the gravitational center. It should not be forgotten that this breakdown of the motion is an arbitrary act and does not correspond to reality.

4. Movement in space, circling, and spinning flow together in one functional unit. The form of movement $\overline{\mathcal{F}}_{\curvearrowright}$ is a dynamic resultant of all three movements; or, more correctly put: F can be broken down into constituent movements.

$$\overline{\mathcal{F}}_{\curvearrowright} \, f \!\!\! \mathcal{K} \!\!\! \longrightarrow \, + \!\! \mathcal{K} \! a \, \, \digamma$$

Therefore, the spinning impulse $\mathcal{V}_{\curvearrowright}$ must contain not only the impulse of the straight-line movement (which will need to be corrected, but is provisionally allowed here) but also the impulse of the circling motion. The spinning impulse $\mathcal{V}_{\curvearrowright}$ in reality determines movement and rotation simultaneously.

Classical astrophysics operates only with the three components, but not with the true movement $\curvearrowright$. It calculates separately [axial] rotation, circling around the sun, and movement in space. The consequence of this functional unification of the three components to form the true movement is that we must regard the rotational impulse $\mathcal{V}a$ as the causative agent of the movement in space as well as of the circling and the spinning along a curved path $\curvearrowright\!\!\!\curvearrowright\!\!\!\curvearrowright$.

A planetary system whose individual bodies rotate in *one* plane and in the same direction therefore offers an ideal starting point for functionally and also genetically resolving the pull of the mass attraction of the gravitational center.

Functionally by replacing the mass attraction of the gravitational center by the rotational impulse.

Genetically because the mass attraction must once have emerged from rotating energy: because it is bound to mass and therefore cannot have existed before the existence of mass; because ultimately it must have formed when rotating, oscillating energy was transformed into mass and must therefore be expressed as functionally identical with this oscillating energy. It is essential to assume that the transformation of oscillating energy into mass is continuing unabated, and mass is also unabated [sentence not complete].

July 1945

Problems

The gravitational attraction between the sun and the planets behaves as if the earth was mechanically linked to the sun. This concept of a "cord" linking the two is very incorrect. But we have no better idea to set in its place.

The basic question relating to the gravitation of the planets is as follows:

What holds the earth and the other planets in their orbit around the sun if they are not mechanically linked and if we exclude an attractive force acting directly from the sun on the planets, as was assumed by Kepler and then formulated by Newton? What is the nature of the energy that maintains these distances? Could it be that the sun and planets are held together in the *same* way by a *third factor*? The idea that the sun attracts the planets to itself would be redundant! Is it conceivable that the sun itself is held in a row with its planets?

We will have to embark on a long and difficult journey to find an answer to this question.

TO A. S. NEILL
❖ *12 July 1945*

My dear Neill:

I gave myself several days' time to let matters sink in. Now, after rereading my letter to you I think it is right to send it, and I would like to add a few more things about my standpoint. I am ready to work in a factual, rational, work-democratic setup of cooperation. But I shall not enter any fights with "lines" which have already been drawn up, with "fronts," etc. It seems as if the principle of politics to unite easily and smoothly for war, but to be incapable of unity for

practical rational peace aims, applies already to the old institute of
1936. I am ready to give freedom to everybody to do what he wants,
but he cannot spit on my table when he wants to and still expect me
to refuse my right to freely accept or refuse his spitting. We know
from spoiled children how easily they mistake real freedom for license, and how easily they think they behave freely, when they only
behave badly. There is a difference between the idea of freedom in
a fish who was caught on the bank of a river, trying hard to get into
the water again, and the other, the real freedom which functions in
a fish who is swimming in the water. Freedom to my life and work
and concept of living does not mean that you can do whatever you
want, but that you can choose among numberless free possibilities to
do best to a definite end.

I cannot judge how far apart the members of the old institute have
drifted from each other. If you can do something to correct the situation in the sense that there is rational cooperation, and not in the
sense of license, I shall appreciate it.

13 July 1945

Only a free man can be free.

15 July 1945

It is more important for the progress of natural science, as well as
for life itself, to verify old scientific facts than to deny them.

It was not denial but the natural scientific verification of the soul
which constituted progress. And it will not be the denial but the
natural scientific confirmation of God's existence that will lead us
onward. To deny "divine emotion," which is commonly called "en-
lightenment," means barring one's access to the cosmic orgone and
thus to nature itself.

It was a triumph for me when the orgonometric calculation of
cosmic KR time confirmed the observations of Copernicus from a
further, a third perspective. The correspondence of my KR calculations of the sidereal year with those of Copernicus completely confirms the basic principle of functional orgonometry.

For Copernicus, the sun is the stationary center of the world. In orgonometry, the sun moves according to KR laws. Copernicus' observations were correct but his theories were not. I have not observed the motion of the sun but I have theorized correctly. This is why my cosmic system of thought corresponds with Copernicus' facts—with a difference of 8.08 seconds per 33,660.747.8 seconds.

This additionally proves that graphic, functional thinking is capable of great achievements through simple algebra and simple differential calculus without the application of complex, abstract mathematics.

TO HERBERT HARVEY
❖ 22 July 1945

My dear Mr. Harvey:

I agree completely with the main trend of thoughts in your letter, and, especially, with the distinction you make between true and false science. Unfortunately, what we are meeting in the *practical* life process of true science as severe hindrances are mostly pseudoscientific statements and ideas which are propounded the more authoritatively, and which are the more widespread the falser they are. I don't believe that this statement is exaggerated. In order to avoid any dealings with pseudophysics and pseudobiology, true science would have to hide completely if it does not prefer to fight pseudoknowledge as hard as I found it necessary to do. It cannot be bypassed under any circumstances.

There are, of course, not only "millions" of objections, but also millions of productive questions, observations, trends of methods, etc., to be discussed and worked out. I shall look forward to seeing you in New York in my laboratory at Forest Hills when I return in the beginning of October.

Naturally, establishment of contact of two fields of natural science, especially in a strange case as that of orgone physics, is not easy. In order to make it easier, I would like to point out a certain fact which, I believe, is confusing you because you don't know it: You had the impression from my publications so far that I am misjudging, mistreating or misunderstanding established physics. This is due to the fact that I did not publish as yet any of the *basic* and new *physical* facts concerning my discovery. You will understand the reason why I hesitated for years to publish the most clearly established facts: They have to sink in, to be corroborated from many sides and through many experiments. And they not only have to fit my own line of research, but they must also not contradict well-established facts of classical physics. For more than twenty-five years, I have rigidly followed the principle to form my research methods independently, in order to arrive at my own conclusions, and thus to become certain of the correctness of my method of thinking and investigation. Once a conclusion is reached, I check it against established and well-known facts, as distinguished from ideas about or interpretations of facts. To illustrate: My claim is to have discovered the specific biological energy—i.e., that energy which governs the life process. Should this energy not be conceived of as being metaphysical, the claim must be extended: The specific biological energy must be also functioning in the nonliving realm of nature. (Here is the point where you may disagree on principle.) The orgone then must of necessity be a basic cosmic energy. To check this contention, I decided to make my test on a definite astronomical problem. If this problem could be solved, then the fact would be irrevocably established that orgone is a physical cosmic energy. The problem itself has been dealt with by Copernicus and Kepler. I postponed studying their works in the original text until I had solved my problem. I reached a definite result, and then I read Copernicus and Kepler. And here it was! My result was in accordance with a definite calculation of Copernicus—established beyond doubt since it was within a close space of 8.08 seconds within the time of a whole year. I tell you this not for reasons of sensationalism or a wish to impress. I tell you this for the sole reason that it is extremely important for the one who wishes to establish contact with orgone physics to be very cautious in his statements. I have stressed this point in my first letter to you without substantiating it. Now I did substantiate it, in order to say clearly: If orgonometry, quite on its own, could establish such a contact with classical physical astronomy, it is impossible that it should be basically wrong in its evaluation of classical physics. It may be pleasant for you to hear that so far the basic laws about work, energy, etc., of classical physics are not in contradiction with the results of orgonometry. It was one of my greatest worries for years that this could be the case. I may say, *fortunately*, it is not. But there are plenty of surprises in store for the physical and astronomical world, and probably some more to come. I feel myself only as a humble servant in this process of discovery.

Thus, if you still wish to establish contact, and to do your share in discussing and elaborating the new facts, and their incorporation into a quite new world picture which is not mechanistic and not mystic, but *functional* as all true science is, I am ready for it. I want you to understand that, just as I have to avoid unnecessary and fruitless discussions (I am awfully busy and have my hands full of work), I am eager for free and fruitful discussions of this importance.

2 August 1945

Paul Goodman* proclaims sex economy as the psychology of the revolution, and Freudian psychology as the psychology of the post-revolutionary era. Therefore: In order to stage the "revolution" they will give youth sex economy. But afterward they will return to sublimation!

Such false thinking arouses bitter agitation. Since there are millions of Goodmans, every revolutionary movement fails. The Goodmans have no ill intentions; they do, however, represent a cultural about-face because they fear the masses!

In view of the tremendous intellectual repercussions, I should, and must, acquire an attitude of fatherly, casual concern in my reactions. These dangerous derailments of my train of thought leave me far too overwrought.

5 August 1945

Unarmored life possesses genius in the sense that the sick little man uses the word to describe great intellectual achievement. Genius is nothing but the wide, natural expansion of a being. The opposite of this is the restricted, "confined," unfree individual.

What a newborn infant accomplishes is tremendous. Just think what it requires to keep one's balance when first learning to walk.

*American author and social philosopher.

Even its naiveté in walking, climbing, bears witness to genius. Thus man, the individual whom they call a "genius," rushes out into the truths, the horrors, and the grandeur to be found in this world.

7 August 1945

They are rejoicing over the atom bomb. Only now, they claim, is eternal peace dawning. For who would dare to provoke the use of such bombs?

How miserable, how blind, and incapable of learning from experience are these human animals. *Out of the fear of death* they proclaim everlasting peace. Once again they are only seeing mirror images. The proclamation of everlasting peace was preceded by the news of the first atom bombs being dropped on the population of Japan.

How blind they are:

1. Bombs are manufactured in order to be sold. They are purchased in order to be dropped. The rigid profit process acts as an obligation to kill.

2. The Japanese will also soon know how to manufacture atomic bombs.

3. Never has a more menacing weapon enhanced the possibilities for peace.

4. There are no guarantees against American militarism. Militarism is by nature a machine of murder. It was contrived and invented for this purpose and is also maintained and supported for the same reason.

Rigidified human animals are incapable of orgastic convulsions but are detonating atomic bombs with the explosive power of two thousand tons of dynamite! That is the truth.

TO A. E. HAMILTON
❖ *11 August 1945*

My dear Mr. Hamilton:

You would not believe how much I enjoyed your letter of 9 August, revealing the effects of the "Revolution." There is nothing left over to wish for after what you conceded to the dreadful Revolution. You made only one mistake, if I may say so. You overlooked my emphasis that this kind of revolution has nothing to do with shooting and the like (pages xii to xv).* And that we have been living through this revolution, consciously or unconsciously, for about ten years now. You also seem to forget that, if you object to the dreadful collectivization of children's education, you ought to close your own school and that of Neill. Wasn't the patriarch a bit too much concerned about himself? and that to such an extent that he overlooked the many dozens of parents who bring their children to your collective terror chamber every day and that these families still exist. That goes for Neill too and for thousands and thousands of other schools of collective education.

Now, I shall tell you a little story about myself. For the first two months we spent here we could not find a place to leave our child and to do our work. Consequences: My wife could not help me in my work and could not do her own work for the institute. I could not work either, because my boy, whom I love dearly, chose to climb on my knee just at the moment when I had to find out in how many seconds the earth rushes through the orgone ocean of the universe on a stretch of so many centimeters. Mind you, that goes into the trillions of centimeters. Further consequence: I felt inclined to be patriarchal to my boy, but he, fortunately, did not understand. He thought I was joking, but I meant it seriously. Result: I had to flee my family in order to do my work. That meant sitting grudging and foaming in a little cabin at Orgonon, carrying all my notes, books, to and fro every day, spending about an hour or two to transform myself from an outraged patriarch into a decent, quiet orgonometrician. And my boy? Well, after about four weeks of disturbing his parents he found out that he can moan and thus achieve all his goals. He also found out that we would neither beat him, as millions of parents do in such situations, nor would we shout at him too often. Finally, we found out that we all three were miserable until we found a local family where there is a little girl of about the age of my boy and we decided to bring him there every day for collective education. This revolutionary action of ours did not shock anyone. On the contrary,

*Reich refers to his book *The Sexual Revolution*.

it made us all happy again. You won't believe it, but I assure you that I, the bloodthirsty revolutionist, disliked the idea of not seeing my boy for six hours a day very strongly. (My wife being much more revolutionary than I, did not care at all.) I understood thoroughly the emotional obstacle to a full realization of the bloody revolution we are all in. It will interest you that my boy did not moan when being collectivized, but during the first days began to moan promptly as soon as he saw us. It vanished after a few days. You are lucky to have a kindergarten where you don't have to send your children to other people for collectivization.

This is our revolutionary evolution so far. But I confess that I would not object to having a few well-armed guards on towers around our collectivized children's camps to keep away for good dissatisfied mothers, growling aunts with shrill voices who frighten the children, and older siblings who live out their frustrations on the little ones. And I know it will be difficult to believe that I, the old versed destroyer of the holy institution of the family, cannot stand being away from them for longer than a day. I doubt that this is good, but I cannot help it.

Did I succeed in clearing myself in the eyes of all patriarchs? I firmly believe that the revolution of collectivization of children's education has improved and not destroyed family relationships, as can be seen from the difference of family setups of today and forty years ago. And if somebody would try to grab children away from parents by force, I would object loudly with all my authority in the field, just as I am going to do in the matter of the killing of several hundred thousand women and children with one stroke by a single bomb. I think a demonstration of the effectiveness of this bomb in an uninhabited space would have been sufficient to finish the war. But this is revolutionary again, and I believe 90 percent of all Americans are revolutionary in this sense, including yourself. I would suggest making a deal: I shall profess to stress the evolutionary element in this revolution much more than I did fifteen years ago (when I wrote this terrible book in the midst of famine, exploitation, social crimes, etc.) and that you stress the fact that you are a dangerous revolutionist much more than you do. Agreed?

I hope you are all well, enjoying your well-deserved rest, and anticipating the pleasure of a new baby to come into my clutches.

How about coming up for a few days, together with the new baby and its protector?

2 September 1945

Eva has opened her neurotic cupboard:

In 1940, shortly after my arrival in New York, Berta Bornstein* told her that she would simply have to accept the fact that *she has a sick father.* She claimed I was sick because I did not fit into society, said that I only wanted to change society's morality because I had experienced a "trauma with my mother."

This is a case of the perilous obstinacy of these social democrats of depth psychology:

a. Society is absolute, and I don't fit in, am not "adjusted."

b. My views on life have been determined by my experiences.

Both of these claims presuppose that infantile experiences alone are the determining factors, and not society. A further claim:

Only when one rejects society and wants to change it can the infantile trauma be held responsible, but not if one supports social morality. Therefore:

Annie Pink† was a compulsion neurotic and could not find a husband because her mother was a compulsion neurotic and frigid. The last question she asked on her deathbed was: "You don't have a boyfriend, do you?" That is why Annie supported morality. *That is supposed to be good.*

Wilhelm Reich overcame the social hazards of his upbringing and was able to make a lot of girls quite happy. He changed social mores because his mother was a victim of this morality. *This is supposed to be bad.*

Thus the infantile trauma explanation only holds good if it preserves the unfortunate conditions—it is bad if it removes them.

Such are the workings of the plague on human thought.

I am building the organization for orgone biophysics in Maine, the most conservative area of the U.S.A. In the middle of the enemy

---

*Austrian psychoanalyst with whom Eva was in treatment.
†The maiden name of Reich's first wife, Annie Reich Rubinstein.

camp? Nonsense! The respect with which I have been received here shows that even conservatives have truly revolutionary hearts and that they honor work and love more than many a socialist.

I shall have to depict my personal background in a separate personal statement in order to prevent the emotional plague from using the reverses which my work has encountered against the truth which I myself derived as a means to counter this very plague.

For example, that people are living a lie when they try to maintain a bad marriage. Annie Pink already knew in 1923, one year after we were married, that it "was not going to work." (Eva told me this.) But in 1933, ten years later, she was still struggling tooth and nail against a divorce.

One should not—if one values one's life and work—live out a lie.

4 September 1945

Yesterday Eva experienced the orgone and saw it clearly. She was frightened by it and understood that everyone is afraid of the orgone, its discoverer included.

Her comment: "The orgone will also carry the orgasm theory through to success. You must concentrate everything on the orgone."

Her mother still believes that I am sick. "Only a physicist could have discovered the orgone."

Eva wrote her husband saying that I am an asocial genius. "Which of the two is asocial," I asked, "the person who devotes his life to work such as this, or the person who attends social gatherings and does nothing else?" Her idea of "asocial" is based on a girl's traditional definition of the word.

The most painful thing is man himself!

TO   A.   S.   N E I L L
❖ *10 September 1945*

My dear Neill:

I had several inquiries regarding the relationship of orgone to the atomic bomb. Orgone is, as far as I can see, subatomic energy in its natural form out of which chemical elements arise. The atomic bomb

energy is obtained by smashing matter. We are gathering the cosmic
energy naturally. I don't believe that the mechanists will ever succeed
in slowing up the process of smashing up matter to such a degree
that the energy could be used beneficially. Somebody said the other
day that the orgone energy is the only real counteractor to the deathly
atom bomb energy.

15 September 1945

Einstein is indecent. When I conferred with him in January 1941,
he was in the midst of the atomic bomb project. He wanted to know
what I had to contribute toward the advancement of the murder.
Since I had nothing to offer, he stopped answering my letters.

25 September 1945

I am struggling so that the rest of my life, thirty to forty years, may
be orderly. I don't want to make any more glaring blunders. I dare
not.

Above all: I *am* different from other people; I have known that I
am different ever since I began to think. I was afraid to admit this
fact to myself and to others because I feared the loneliness. But now
I must and I shall live according to my own uniqueness:

It will save me the annoyance I feel when others do not love,
produce, or think as I do.

No further financial sacrifices "for others" (an illusion).

No expectations, no disappointments, withdrawal.

How can I raise the three hundred dollars a month I would need
in order to be able to work independently?

29 September 1945

I am growing wise through experience, gradually. People's stub-
bornness is no longer a flaming arrow burning in my soul—I "register" it—will no longer be victimized by it, am withdrawing to my own
positions.

(What does the poor man do who has no positions to which he
can withdraw?)

One reacts to human meanness and pettiness the way one does to a set of false teeth:

 a. One feels the misery in one's stomach as well as in one's mouth.

 b. The first reaction to both is rage.

 c. One grows accustomed to both. They gradually cease to be something foreign.

I am on the verge of becoming wise, in many respects.

And I am also finding myself out: I was too chickenhearted to be internally as alone as I was in a professional sense.

That is why I was always so furious when people didn't want to be and live as I do—so that I wouldn't be alone. In vain.

I was afraid of having to live like "everyone else," no longer living the way I wanted to.

Now I've discovered that I needn't make concessions, that I can retain my own uniqueness if I just give up the illusion that everyone else has my capabilities.

I have accomplished more than others, *that* is why I'm different.

One needn't despise people when one knows their deep weaknesses.

Needn't hate them for not being good, perfect, diligent, etc.

Needn't fear them, despite the fact that one knows the abysmal bestiality stemming from their lack of satisfaction.

Mine is the *privilege* of rejoicing over the glow in a person's eyes which bears witness to the extent they have understood a portion of the truth I have to offer.

The discovery of the orgone settles all debts I have incurred to mankind over the course of my life.

T O   T H E   S T .   J O H N ' S   C O L L E G E   B O O K S T O R E *
❖ *1 October 1945*

Dear Sirs:

I received your price list of September 1945 and would like to order the following books:

---

*St. John's College in Annapolis, Maryland.

Hippocrates: Selected Works	$1.00
Gilbert: On the Lodestone	3.00
Cervantes: Don Quixote	.95
Constitution of the U.S.	1.00
Dedekind: Essays on the Theory of Numbers	1.00
Faraday: Experimental Researches in Electricity	.95
Harvey: Motion of the Heart	1.00
Leibnitz: Discourse on Metaphysics	.60
Rousseau: Social Contract	.95
Spinoza: Ethics	.95
Swift: Gulliver's Travels	.95
	$12.35

2 October 1945

Report: People are referring to me as the "crazy man who discovered the blue lights."

Mass orders for books are coming in from the West Coast.

At the New School for Social Research they have announced a seminar concerning me and my work—for ten psychiatrists.

In England they're arguing about whether I am a charlatan or the greatest living reformer.

In Norway my students held a convention.

In Palestine the accumulators are beginning to be used.

The question of time has been answered in agreement with Copernicus.

The answer to the chaos is present in principle.

What a responsibility! Shall I be able to bear it?

13 October 1945

4:15 a.m. Can't sleep. Am tired of being uncertain. An old world is collapsing without being aware of it. People think that the atom bomb has brought about the change. No, the discovery of cosmic energy in outer space has done it—my orgone. Overnight I became involved in the struggle for the new world through the politics of the atom bomb, through simply possessing a key to cosmic energy. The allied military powers and big financiers know nothing of this. But the world has begun a search for

a. protection from the atom bomb

b. peaceful uses of atomic energy (which cannot be expected from atom bomb energy)

c. solution of the chaos through peaceful means

All this presses toward the "discovery of the orgone." Now by the world itself. (Even Wolfe in his negativism later ceded this point.)

The constellation of events has led me down the path of responsibility for part of the present and the yet unborn future. In an emotional sense I am not quite prepared for that.

I shall probably have to defend my standpoint in public and win the argument. For this I must drop all illusions, false expectations, petty considerations.

I shall have to walk my path quietly with a clear head, without too much anxiety. I shall have to adjust to the possibilities of my work bearing fruit in ten years or in five hundred.

Cosmic orgone energy will doubtless put the mechanists' murderous atomic energy out of use.

When? How? With what sacrifices? To what ends?

15 October 1945

Rousseau: "Man is born free, and everywhere he is in chains . . . How did this change come about? I do not know."

I found the answer to the source of the misery, but I have no answer to the question of what form an organization should take in order to eliminate it.

6 November 1945

After six years of gigantic renewed effort things are going awry again:

The Scandinavians are refusing to be members of the cooperative. No news, no articles. Therefore the *International Journal of Sex-Economy* will have to be discontinued. Wolfe is failing as an editor. Has no ability to inspire people to publish.

The New Yorkers are doing well because they are still under my direct influence. But earning money with orgone therapy is all too easy. The money is becoming (and already is) more important than anything else.

People can imitate my prices (twenty dollars per session) but not my abilities.

They imitate my four-month absence from New York but not the work, the hard work I do over the summer.

People want to learn all about the laboratory without putting anything into it.

TO   WALTER   HOPPE
13 November 1945

Dear Dr. Hoppe,

I have received your letter of 4 November. Thank you for the photograph. I will pass on your report about the orgone accumulator to Dr. Wolfe for publication.

As regards your inquiry about the prospect of using orgone treatment in cases of ascites, I can only provide an uncertain reply. Ascites is obviously the symptom of anorgonia in the abdominal segments. I am very pessimistic about the prospects in cases where the cessation of pulsation is so advanced. However, I would like to add a word of encouragement: Once you reach the point where you have distributed dozens of accumulators, the negative results are balanced out by numerous cases in which, surprisingly and pleasantly, cures are reported. Orgone therapy using the accumulator is already quite widespread and well known here in America. In New York, on the West Coast, and in the extreme Northeast, people are talking about this method of treatment as if it were a miracle. And, in fact, wonderful things are happening. It is scarcely credible that an ulcus varicosus can be healed or that there is improvement in a case of arthritis which has lasted many years. Orgone therapy can be used not only to treat cancer but probably can also be used mainly in other areas of the autonomic life apparatus.

With regard to your inquiry about the energy of the atom bomb: I personally do not believe that it is possible to use this energy for peaceful purposes. Even if it should prove technically possible to slow down the reactions, these possibilities would never be exploited, because the spirit which created and administers the atom bomb is not in the least bit interested in peaceful applications. The situation is catastrophic, and as long as militarism and scientific mechanism hold our fate in their hands, cannons will fire and atom bombs will explode.

The conversion of orgone energy into matter has so far only been theoretically proved in terms of orgone physics, but the proof is flawless. I cannot predict whether it will be possible to produce matter with the help of energy. I can only say that the principle of such production was found in an abstract, theoretical manner. However, I would need at least half a million dollars in the fund in order to test even the possibility of practically implementing the theory.

It would be extraordinarily interesting and important to know whether you have got anywhere with the microscopic work relating to orgone biophysics and if so, how far. I am currently giving a practical course in which five assistants are taking part to learn the technique of microscopic orgone biophysics to the point where they can become instructors. Why don't you come and visit us next summer.

TO   TAGE   PHILIPSON
16 November 1945

Dear Dr. Philipson,

I have received your letter of 31 October. I am hastening to answer it because, given the present state of social suffering, the most important thing as far as I am concerned, in addition to finding a new way to educate small children, is for the orgone accumulators to gain acceptance in Europe. I am glad that you are getting down to tackling the matter of the accumulators. As a doctor, you will obtain an extraordinary amount of satisfaction from this work. However, based on my experience, I would recommend that you hold back on treating serious diseases until you have convinced yourself, for example, that all cases of anemia can be cured by orgone treatment; that wounds can be made to heal extremely rapidly by directly applying orgone by means of metal tubes; that colds can be arrested, etc. I am in the process of summarizing my experience with orgone therapy in various major and minor areas. Dr. Walter Hoppe in Palestine has already had a number of positive results with the therapy.

And now to your questions: So far, I have always lined the inner walls just with thin iron sheeting. I have so far no experience with aluminum or copper or with any other metals, as far as therapy is concerned. But as a general theory, *any* metal should fulfill the purpose of accumulating atmospheric orgone inside the box. The thickness of the layer does not play a role; it can be quite thin. The metal wall must be continuous; a mesh will not work. At the start, in 1940, I tried to dose the application of orgone using very complicated electroscopic measurements. Over the course of time, it was discovered that the patients themselves know exactly when they have had enough. Once the body temperature has been increased, it starts to become unpleasant to be in the accumulator, and the patient simply gets out. The radiation time is shortened, of course, if one uses two- or three-layer accumulators. The time varies greatly from individual to individual. I have had enough after just ten minutes; anorgonotic patients with a poor skin charge can sit in the accumulator for three-quarters to a full hour without feeling anything. It takes weeks of regular daily radiation exposure before the time is shortened and the patients begin to feel the warmth and the tingling.

As regards the indications: It is not easy to deal with that problem in a letter. In Maine, I have a patient who was immobilized in bed for several years with severe arthritis and muscle contractions. After two months of using the accumulator, he was able to get out of bed again. I have no experience with pulmonary tuberculosis, but since orgone biologically charges the organism, I anticipate success. Disseminated sclerosis could yield to treatment. You will first of all, with great patience, have to feel the orgone effects yourself, and then you must try to learn the orgonotic blood tests and gradually acquire your own experience. The results are often so astonishingly good that I have not dared to publish them. I would recommend that you start with two- to three-layer accumulators. We are at present building a new accumulator which is covered on the outside with wood-plastic; its inner walls are made of thin iron sheeting and it has an intermediate layer about one inch thick consisting of a mixture of metal wool and rock wool (as an insulation against the cold). In the enclosure I am sending you some specimens of forms of the kind that we use here.

I am naturally willing to provide any other information that you need, because I believe that the further the misery progresses, the more importance our orgone accumulator will gain, both medically and ideologically, in the struggle against the danger of the atom bomb.

You are probably unaware that you have paid me a great compliment by writing that my work is so simple that it can only be understood by absolute ignoramuses, and that it is so deeply theoretical that only someone with an enormous amount of knowledge can comprehend it. I cannot write for the ordinary scientist and physician because his way of thinking and his language are wrong and he will have to learn to think differently. Such a fundamentally new discovery as cosmic orgone energy brings with it new terminology and a new methodology. As regards cancer: I wish to inform you that we are working here mainly on developing a prophylactic treatment. The elimination of the pathways for getting rid of detritus is a problem that has not yet been solved. I believe that the task of healing fully developed cancer is just as hopeless as trying to treat fully developed character neuroses. You know that for twenty years I have been concentrating almost exclusively on preventive treatment and that I have had some success in that area.

As regards your intention to come here: We have built a large laboratory at Orgonon in Maine and next year we intend to set up an introductory course on orgone therapy.

22 November 1945

I am learning from my little son. He teaches me to see life the way it is before civilization disturbs it.

He is now nineteen months old. He does not tear books but carefully inspects each page. He is orderly and tidy without having been raised to be so. One day he discovered the potty all by himself and asked to use it. He does not wet his bed, is happy, neat, clean, loves me madly and calls me Igor, for some unknown reason. He listens attentively and tries to understand when something is explained to him. He likes a gentle tone of voice and rebels against severity and force. He eats by himself, has a good healthy appetite.

Ernst Peter has convinced me that all rearing of infants would be simple and easy if the biopathies of adults did not deflect the functions of unarmored life from the very beginning.

27 November 1945

I have lived under the constant pressure of a demand. True, no one demands anything of me; nevertheless the demand was present. I have been obeying it for thirty years and I cannot escape it. Where does it come from, what is it, who is placing it upon me?

It stems from the development of my work.

Today, thirteen years after its publication, my *Character Analysis* is sought after and is being widely read. I was therefore thirteen years ahead.

This has happened with other books as well.

What will the world be willing to accept in twenty years that it would not accept today?

For three years I have been wrestling with the task of describing the little man in actual proportion to his future environment. I just can't make it.

In ten or twenty years people will be demanding it just the way they are ordering *Mass Psychology* today.

Now that I have somehow been called to a position of leadership, my enthusiasm fails me. They have smashed and broken it. I had to wait fifteen perilous years until "Sexualität im Kulturkampf"* was generally accepted as valid.

Making a living—and illness—were never matters of concern in my life. Even during the worst times I was earning, and was basically healthy. The only thing that continually dejected me was the riddle of man's relationship to nature, and of society to man himself.

---

*"Sexuality in the Cultural Struggle." Published as Part 1 of *The Sexual Revolution*.

T O   P A U L   G O O D M A N *
❖ *30 November 1945*

Dear Mr. Goodman:

I was kept informed about the articles and discussions in different magazines in various countries for quite some time. Such discussions are not new to me; I know that my natural scientific position, as it developed over the past twenty-five years, has put human emotions on fire again and again in many countries. I appreciate your endeavors very much, but I cannot relieve you of your position, into which you have put yourself of your own free will. You are wrong in assuming that I should "take up my own defense." First, because I am not defending myself at all, but, on the contrary, I am fighting a human disease, called emotional pestilence by me, which has ravaged human society for more than four thousand years. As a natural scientist who has, for the first time, discovered this sickness and its mechanisms, I do not offend and I do not defend, I simply reveal facts. And in this capacity, I have been standing "on the firing line" for about twenty years.

If I can be of any help to you in any way, please call on me. I think I know how difficult your position is.

Finally, I would like to stress the fact that I wish to stay out of all political and ideological organizations and groupings, and that I, therefore, do not wish to be presented to the public by any kind of label which does not fit, be it Marxist, anarchist, syndicalist, liberal, etc. My work is beyond such narrow and merely ideological political restrictions and organizations. Restriction of this work to a definite political group by way of a label is only apt to impede its general influence on the social process. As I once tried to formulate it, I am neither left nor right, but *forward*.

7 December 1945

The enervating struggle against the emotional plague continues without interruption. If I were to apply in everyday life the insights I

---

*This letter was not sent.

have gained on the emotional plague in my consulting room, it would be impossible to go on, impossible to trust a single soul.

The secret techniques of the emotional plague cannot be put into words and therefore are one of its mainstays.

The pioneer of truth becomes exhausted because he feels only his powerlessness to make a breakthrough and does not understand why his road is blocked.

If he becomes pliant and flexible, his name may well become known but not his cause.

Interpersonal communication only transpires peacefully on the levels of superficial social etiquette.* This kind of communication *cannot* approach the core of a matter because this would require passing through the chaotic strata of the emotional plague which lie between. For this reason all discussion remains confined to a superficial level and, even with the best of intentions, can never penetrate to the heart of the matter in question. Realization of the existence of such intermediate plague strata in the human animal leads without fail to chaotic consequences when one tries to probe the depths and arrive at *real* insight. Expressed in terms of society this means:

Society will have to pass through a phase of chaotic events, including mass murder and killing, before it arrives at a social order based upon the human animal's biological core.

Twentieth-century fascism is the organizational expression of the chaos of the middle layer following the removal and elimination of the superficial courtesies of liberalism.

These insights have been firmly established; they are necessary, concise, and inexorable.

However, it is impossible to make headway in a practical sense because of the little man's fear of life. This is partially a fear of the passage through the hell, the inferno of the middle layer of the emotional plague. Dante's fantasies and Freud's realities of the unconscious are respectively the poetic and scientific expressions of insight into the emotional plague.

The discovery of the biological core of the human animal offers us hope, but it also reveals the necessity of passing through this in-

---

*Reich's clinical research revealed three layers in the human structure: the periphery or superficial, the middle or secondary layer, and the biological core.

ferno of the middle layer in order to arrive at the core. Exactly the
way it happens in therapy.

15 December 1945

Only to the few is it granted to taste of the sweetness of life. Nav-
igating the horrible narrows is a hard-won skill.

19 December 1945

It is Beethoven, always this great, simple, honest Beethoven, who
shows me the joy of eternity and the eternal misery of the sons of
men.

It was so much easier to grasp, to portray, to explain the little man,
the oppressed animal, in music than to document him scientifically.

It is always Beethoven who brings man and the universe into harmony for me, who reassures me that man made a grievous error when
he created his religious and his political concepts.

The error will indeed be corrected but it will cost the blood of
millions.

Centuries will pass before a man like Beethoven is understood.

Lost in the vast universe of its life sensations, a poor animal called
the "human being" strays about, driven by fear and longing, by feelings of pleasure and guilt.

Someday when this life has arisen from its dark and bewildered
past, it will also find itself again within mankind. Then it will discern
its own harmony and no longer experience it as a sinful burden.

Someday men like Beethoven and Wilhelm Reich will walk the
city streets with their heads held high. They will be the models for
youth, and no longer ostracized; as loved as they are today, but not
as dishonored; models of the kind of life which harmonizes with itself,
with creation and the universe.

Geniuses like Beethoven will then no longer be exceptions, curious
phenomena, but reflections of a good clear world!

21 December 1945

Hoppe once wrote me saying that the difficulty of my position lay
in the fact that I had solved too many natural scientific problems of
too vast a scope.

Sex economy, abiogenesis, cancer, cosmic energy, etc.

In reality I have dealt with and solved only one problem, the *phenomenon of the orgasm*. The fact that it proved to be the key to the vast realm of cosmic energy and subsequently to the understanding of abiogenesis, cancer, etc., is comparable to Columbus' landing on the coast of America. Did Columbus found Chicago and New York? Did he build San Francisco and the great West? He "only" discovered America.

I have only discovered the orgasm.

24 December 1945

12 p.m. No accomplishment, no matter how great, is able to dispel my feeling that our understanding of what caused man's downfall should be even deeper, fuller, more complete.

In the process of superimposition—material, sexual, and cosmic—the great question of the meaning of life exhausts itself for me.

If I succeed in writing the last movement of the grand symphony of unarmored life (in a proper, decent form so that it will endure for as long as life springs forth upon this planet), then, when that final movement has been written, my life task will be fulfilled.

Others will have to master the practical problems resulting from my work. *There can be no doubt that the discovery of the cosmic orgone has opened the gates for interplanetary travel.*

It's a pity that I was born in this twentieth century. My life would have been a more mature one, happier, fuller in the thirtieth or the fortieth century.

My son will live to see the beginning of the twenty-first century. I want to continue growing through him, no matter whether he becomes a musician or a scientist.

I am filled with pride at the fact that I succeeded in avoiding the beat of the world's drum, in accomplishing so much in utter silence, with no rigamarole, no medals, no uniform, no cannons.

Great and unrewarded is science!

1946

"Avarice and strategy are such integral parts of human structure, especially American structure, that honest motives are inconceivable and as a consequence my teachings have often resulted in chaos."

3:30 *a.m.* Worries, enormous worries. Can't sleep!

Sex economy now seems to be prevailing everywhere, even on the "highest" levels. And with it the orgone theory. This gives me joy and satisfaction but also great concern. For example, I just awoke under the pressure of a silly question which had never occurred to me before: "What practical measures would you take if you were the director of a social agency and were opposed by Bishop Spellman? Or the communists, or the Freudists! What measures would you, *could* you take on a large public scale in order to implement your social hygiene program?"

I must constantly remind myself of how gigantic my responsibilities are. To be overly aware of it at all times would mean forfeiting the spontaneity of my thoughts and actions. Bearing it in mind too little would mean making mistakes.

I ought to reintroduce instruction evenings. Or should I intervene through active assistance? Experience warns me: The more reserved I am, the more they will accept and respect me. But respect alone, although it is necessary, serves no purpose. They must really *understand* the cause and work *correctly*.

To organize on an international scale under my direction would not work. The cause must be decontrolled, must be completely free. But it does require some journal which can correct false views, set them apart from the cause. One must simply let life run free and have confidence in it.

5 January 1946

Psychiatrists from American state hospitals with ten thousand mental patients are recognizing my vegetotherapy. Several are coming for treatment.

6 January 1946

The road I have walked is long, extremely long. I began my journey through life as a young boy of only seventeen. From one province of Austria to the next, then graduation from the gymnasium, the war, medicine, natural science, love, suffering, illness, marriage, a child, then another child, a profession, a career, the discovery of the orgasm, the conflict with Freud, illness, more strife, flight to Berlin, the founding of social psychology, war with the communists, conflict with the fascists, flight from Berlin, conflict with the psychoanalysts, conflict on all sides, loss of the children, loss of my high position in the International Psychoanalytic Association, defamation, conflict with the mechanists, conflict with the genetic psychiatrists, flight from Norway, discovery and founding of abiogenesis, then cancer, the orgone, the spinning wave, cosmic orgonometry. Too much! Too much?

Was the discovery of America, was the discovery of fire "too much"?

TO   WALTER   HOPPE
8 January 1946

Dear Dr. Hoppe,

We are in receipt of your letter of 26 December regarding the patent matter. The Patent Office here has raised the same objection.* We have filed an appeal and a final hearing is scheduled for September 1946. However, we do not wish to force the matter in any way. The most important thing for us is to obtain confirmation from the Patent Office that the accumulator cannot be patented, because that would automatically mean that nobody else can acquire the patent, and that is exactly what we are trying to achieve. We would therefore recommend that you do not try to force matters over there either. As long as nobody can build up an exclusively profit-oriented business

---

*The Patent Office in Palestine's objection related to the layering of metallic and non-metallic materials in the accumulator as, it claimed, similar layering is used for other purposes. Therefore, the accumulator constituted a "discovery," not a patentable "invention."

with the accumulators (based on a patent), we also benefit from having our patent rejected.

TO A. S. NEILL
❖ *12 January 1946*

My dear Neill:

On the one hand, I am developing more and more the conviction that any kind of strict organization would be bad in the case of my work. I am a bad police dog, and I don't like to supervise. Seen from this side, anybody can go ahead and do what he wants. I can only hope that he does not do foolish things, that he knows the dangers and the scope of the work, and that he is prepared to be rebuffed by me publicly in my journal, in case he is doing damage to the total effort. Seen from the other side, it would seem advisable, and according to most primitive rules of cooperation and living, that whoever wishes to spread knowledge communicate with and take advice from the one who has the most and the best of experiences. When I was a young doctor, it was quite beyond doubt and beyond question that I listened to what my teacher had to say. But somehow times seem to have changed, and people won their independence everywhere and by all means. I talked the matter over with Wolfe. He seemed to object, but having no means of forcing anybody, I would say let them go ahead and let's hope for the best. There is only one wish I would insist upon being fulfilled. They should not use the words sex economy or orgone biophysics in the title of their journal, unless they are ready to cooperate with the Orgone Institute very closely, as Dr. Hoppe in Palestine and others in other countries do.

All this sounds a bit confused, but this confusion is not due to me, but to a confused situation on the whole.

I believe you are still adhering to an old antithesis of capitalist world and socialist world, which is a dead past. You say, your feelings are with Russia against the imperialist idea. I wonder why you don't see that Russia is as imperialistic as any capitalistic country could be and that the American government has divided up the big estates in Bavaria. I also believe that you underestimate the truly democratic

trends and forces in the U.S.A., the hate of imperialism and dictatorship. I wish we would have time enough to discuss these things
thoroughly.

12 January 1946

2 a.m. On 10 January 1946 I had my hearing in the Brooklyn
court for U.S. citizenship. They had a thick dossier full of documents
(the whole Ellis Island affair). The judge told me that they had received a report on me before I arrived in the United States in 1939.
His main line of inquiry was: had I ever been a German official, a
fascist, or a communist. There was a slight clash with the judge. He
was an overly ambitious young man who was trying to make himself
important. If I had shoved my honorary membership in the Mark
Twain Society under his nose, he would surely have backed right
down.

I did not avail myself of my fame to impress this judge or other
obstacles in life. Man is not honest to you if you are famous. To learn
about human nature one must always keep hidden among the miserable multitudes of the human species.

I shudder to think of what one is dependent upon: he was annoyed
that my library contained books by Lenin and Trotsky. I told him I
also had Buddha, Hitler, and all the rest. But what do biology and
physics have to do with Lenin and Trotsky? he inquired. He also said
that one was not an M.D. if one hadn't passed an examination by
the State Board. In other words, no physicians outside of the AMA!

How small, petty, inflated!

There is a possibility that I will not be granted citizenship, that
these underlings will set a new "investigation" in motion, that I will
have to move on again. But *I am so tired!*

Travel again? Where to? Experience again how each person thinks
only of himself? How they want the raisins, but not the parching sun.

If I only had enough money to live without having to work so hard
and could devote my time to thinking, to biology and physics.

American capitalism arose in a society of small laborers and trades-
men; it did not come about through the division of labor. The mass
character of the tradesman created it; due to the busyness and naiveté

of the workers it was tolerated and allowed to grow—until Morgan appeared.

In this way capitalism developed out of a character structure.

I first had to work my way out of all the mistakes of Freudian psychologisms and discover the loophole in Marx before I could see human character as the origin of an economic development. *Character is structural history, active reproduction of history.*

In the U.S.A. the little man reproduces capitalism.

25 January 1946

12 p.m. The next phase of social development will be determined by the struggle of unarmored life against everything which obstructs and destroys life. Therefore, in essence, it will be a struggle of work against politics, to the extent that these politics fail to stem from the wellsprings of life.

Human society is currently involved in a revolutionary movement toward certain goals.

These goals will first be characterized by negation—of the state, of war, of militarism, of capitalism. Only during the elimination process of these institutions and their supporting ideologies will human society become aware of its positive objectives. In its attempt to fulfill these tasks, society will encounter the weaknesses of human character. In this manner the danger of a restoration of the political state will arise. The purging and rational structuring of human character through education and social concern will require centuries. At the beginning of the process of self-government men will commit numerous atrocities. They will murder those who remind them of their weaknesses. They will confuse fucking with loving until millions of physical collapses force upon them the proper attitudes in questions of love. They will repeatedly create a "Führer," whom the masses will follow, only to be misled anew.

The following basic laws will gradually emerge:

A law for the protection of unarmored life.

A law for the protection of children and adolescents against the educational crimes of their teachers.

A law against calumny and gossip.

A law for the protection of one's own intellectual acquisitions.

A law against war, exploitation, and pornography.

26 January 1946

The psychoanalysts in New York have developed a new form of defense. They exclaim: Ah, Reich, excellent! His book *Character Analysis* is a "magnificent contribution" to psychoanalysis (a "contribution" they call it)—stimulating, fecund thought, a good clinician, that Wilhelm Reich. But what he's been doing since then is all wrong. He has unfortunately lost his footing, poor fellow. It's a pity about him.

You scientific philistines forget your own decency and intelligence whenever you find it convenient. So you agree with character analysis, do you? Then why did you hush it up for twelve years and not make one comment, discuss it, or even sniff at it?

It was your own press that printed it, although it wasn't published there in the end. You were afraid, horribly afraid of truth in distress, and now you are praising my book which you tried so long to dispose of.

14 February 1946

I am generally acclaimed as the "top man of psychiatry in the world." As the foremost psychiatrist. I, however, view myself as a natural scientist who has enriched psychiatry, sexology, biology, physics, sociology, astronomy. I have been assured that orgone physics is no longer hidden in obscurity but has assumed its position within the framework of the natural sciences.

My responsibility is gigantic.

16 February 1946

Death lurks in the difficulty with my throat. My throat segment sometimes contracts, a condition which I am the only physician in the world to understand. The contraction is accompanied by cold sweats in this segment, palpitation of the heart, frequently up to 180 beats per minute—heart is apparently affected through paralysis of the vagus or irritation of the sympathetic nervous system. The damage is located somewhere in the medulla oblongata near the breathing center, because sometimes when I cough to remove mucus from my throat or upper bronchial tubes, I lose consciousness for a second and my head nods or I collapse.

I will treat this ugly business with bion-earth, once a day for one minute.

This "death in my throat" does not mean that I am going to die tomorrow. It only means that the nature of my death is already indicated if I do not heal myself:

a. suffocation due to paralysis of the respiratory center

b. heart failure through overstimulation

c. glottis spasm

d. edema of the throat segment due to anorgonia

20 February 1946

I found out that Otto Fenichel died of a heart attack three weeks ago.

That man died of his structural cowardice. I cannot judge whether my publication of his misdeed which appeared in April 1945* gave him a push. In his book he plagiarized absolutely everything from me and since he was aware of this it must have been a terrible ordeal for him.

One must be courageous and remain so if one wishes to survive!

International Universities Press is publishing an anthology entitled *The Psychoanalytic Reader* (edited by Dr. Robert Fliess), containing three monographs by me.

Fourteen years after the publication of *Character Analysis* they are discovering character analysis, but *without* the orgasm theory.

8 March 1946

Sixteen years ago my mass psychology was an innovation. At that time I received praise but no recognition. Today my triumphs have become general knowledge. Few people are aware that *I* was the innovator in the area where psychology and sociology clashed.

They can no longer keep it a secret and therefore elevate me as the great psychiatric authority, along with Rado, Horney, Adler, all of whom have fled from the subject of sex.

My parentage in the entire field of modern mass psychology suffered under the sexual core of the question. That is why Fromm had

---

*Cf. Chapter 16 in *Character Analysis* (New York: Farrar, Straus and Giroux, 1972).

an easier time, although he arrived on the scene later than I and accomplished a lot less.

That is why Horney, who first discovered her social sentiments in America, is considered *the* mass psychologist: she denies sexual needs altogether.

People flock to anyone as long as he does not touch upon the confounded sexual needs of the masses.

T O   V .   D .   C O L L I N S *
❖ *13 March 1946*

Dear Mr. Collins:

As I wrote you before, apart from the addition to the small cabin at Orgonon (which will be taken care of by the Orgone Institute Research Laboratories, Inc.), we need a small summer dwelling for us privately. I am enclosing a rough sketch of what we would need, and I would appreciate it very much if you could let me know as soon as possible whether you think you will be able to get the necessary material to build this cabin early this spring. The cabin could stand on cement posts as a foundation, and would be erected somewhere near the well which you cemented last year. Would you also please let me have an estimate on how much such a cabin of 20 × 32 feet would cost, complete with electric wiring, plumbing installation.

In case you cannot see your way clear whether you will be able to get the material to build, we would try to buy a prefabricated house. In that case I would like to know whether you could take care of the erection of such a house, the foundation work, and all the other additional work that has to be done. We would then get a complete blueprint from the company which makes the house, would send it to you for an estimate of the cost to have it completed.

I would appreciate it greatly if you could let me have the information as quickly as possible. There are quite a number of people coming up to Orgonon this summer for work, and we would have to

*Building contractor in Rangeley.

start working early and need the living accommodation. Thanking you for a prompt reply, and with best wishes.

TO OLA RAKNES
13 March 1946

Dear Dr. Raknes,

The relations between the American Orgone Institute and the staff of the Scandinavian Sex-Economy Institute from the year 1939 are too complicated and too important to be correctly dealt with in a letter. In the following, I have provisionally summarized a few of the points relating to the coworkers in Copenhagen and those in Oslo which seem important to me. Would you please therefore transmit the contents of this letter to Copenhagen and to Nic Waal and Havrevold.*

1. As regards the "improvement of my technique of character analysis" by Dr. Philipson: I already heard about this, over a year ago, but to this day I do not know what it is actually all about, because nobody has given me a detailed description of the "criticism" and of the "improvements." In 1935 I myself improved my character analysis by introducing the vegetotherapeutic technique, and further progress has been made since the discovery of the organismic orgone energy. However, this progress is being made more and more in the direction of the underlying biophysical conditions of neuroses. The work is confirming and defining more precisely the old formulations of the orgasm reflex as the core of the overall question. I do not know whether Dr. Philipson's improvements are aimed in the same direction or whether they lead away from it.

It is clear that I cannot accept any technique as an improvement of my character analysis if that technique leads away from the central question of the orgasm reflex and the biophysical importance of the function of the orgasm. I do not say this in order immediately to reject Dr. Philipson. On the contrary, I am eager to hear what he has to say. I brought it up in order to give you an idea of the direction

---

*Nic Waal Hoel and Odd Havrevold, Norwegian physicians and students of Reich's.

in which my work is developing because you have decided to come to the United States and continue working with me for a short while. Since, according to what you write, you have accepted Dr. Philipson's technique, it would be a great disappointment for you, and one that would involve great sacrifice, if you were to come here and discover that the improvements in my technique, which I have been implementing since 1939, pointed in a direction that was unacceptable to you. The case histories of my patients, in particular those relating to cancer biopathy published in the journal, give an approximately correct picture of the status of my current work.

As long as I do not have a detailed description of the changes which have been made to the technique, I must leave everything up in the air. It will interest you to learn that for about a year and a half, in addition to my routine work which is known to you, I have been trying to break through the character armor in a rapid and concentrated way in order to prepare the patient for character analysis in a shorter period of time. These experiments are very promising.

2. On the matter of the Scandinavian journal, I did not understand the following point: You wrote that a Scandinavian journal could not appear until a sufficient number of scientific articles were available. Why are the new papers from the institute not translated into Norwegian and published in the Scandinavian journal? We have, as a matter of course, taken the articles which appeared in Scandinavia and had them translated and published in English here. I believe it is the duty of a section of the institute to prepare its publications. Since there has been no personal or work-related contact between us for almost seven years now, I am afraid to say any more because I do not know how things really are in Scandinavia, whether or not a Scandinavian Section of the *present* Orgone Institute still exists and is operational. This question also I must leave until I can discuss it in person with you or another coworker.

3. The orgone biophysics which has developed in America since 1939 is not a new area of research but a legitimate continuation of the old sex-economic research into the area of biology and physics. For the first time in the history of biopsychiatry, our ideas about energetic processes in the organism are no longer hanging in the air but have been anchored in experiment and microscopic observation.

Sex economy is nowadays only a special area of the much wider field of orgone biophysics to which it has led.

TO GERTRUD GREISSLE *
25 March 1946

Dear Mrs. Greissle,

I have received your letter of 23 March. Why is it so important to you that the bion research should be "recognized"? Official medicine is just as incapable of "recognizing" bion research as the manufacturers of gas lamps were incapable of recognizing electric bulbs. In the same way that electric bulbs are superior to and have replaced gas lighting, so will orgone therapy doubtlessly replace sulfa drugs and similar stuff. How quickly orgone energy finds general application is a part of the responsibility that devolves on human beings.

3 April 1946

My son, Peter, is my best teacher when it comes to unarmored life. I have never seen life develop and function so clearly. He inspires me with confidence in life, in unspoiled life. Today he was two years old and knew that it was his birthday.

I want to reenter life, leave this rigid isolation into which I was placed by people's craving for an authority.

They are proclaiming me the genius of the century, another Newton, Galileo, the man who surpassed Einstein.

But I want only one thing: mutuality in my human relationships, understanding for my work. *Give and take*, not "only take."†

Even the greatest man could grow stale and shallow in this age of physics and chemistry.

---

*A patient of Dr. Thorburn's.
†This sentence was written in English.

It is a dying, spoiled, desiccated world in which only fresh young life has any future prospects.

One must hold fast to the "foolishness" of one's youth if one wishes to stay young.

Youth is rare. Youth has no limits. There is no such thing as youth anymore!

They all want secure positions as bank clerks.

4 April 1946

4 a.m. Last night I collapsed again after a coughing attack: glottis spasm, loss of consciousness, collapse.

I understand the glottis spasm but not the fainting.

Glottis damage stems from the years between 1928 and 1932 when I gave a lecture every night and became hoarse—and from being denied the right to speak since 1933.

But whence the blackout? Epilepsy? No! Petit mal? No! Paralysis of the respiratory center in the medulla oblongata? Possible!

General surrender to being "completely drained"? Probable!

5 April 1946

Examined my sputum at night. No malignancy, no TB. This is a functional death. Respiratory paralysis? But I must draw up a will, must make provisions for Ilse and Peter—and for Eva—the manuscripts, instruments, archives, books, scientific testimony.

TO NIC HOEL
8 April 1946

Dear Nic,

I have received your letter of 1 April together with the two short manuscripts. I am afraid that events and the long time that has elapsed since 1939 have driven us too far apart. You presume to criticize things which you have not been involved in, which you have not studied, and which you have not understood, and it is all too evident from your letter that you are afraid of being criticized by your friends and that you are writing with a guilty conscience.

As early as 1930, in my *Mass Psychology of Fascism*,* I wrote that fascism is not a party but a basic, human, reactionary attitude. At the time, you agreed with this view, and you yourself say in this letter that one can be culturally fascist and yet politically antifascist. That is completely correct and confirms my standpoint. The socialists in Norway—namely, Scharffenberg, Kreyberg, Mohr—and many other members of the workers' party, who attacked me in a mean way, are completely fascistically oriented as genetic psychiatrists and theoreticians, whatever their convictions might otherwise be, because this basic mental attitude will certainly lead to renewed fascism twenty years from now, whether these people want to be socialists, communists, or whatever.

We are accustomed here to rejecting any criticism that is not based on active participation in the research work. And we do not recognize anybody as a coworker who is not engaged practically in work on our problems, continuously and with total dedication.

Your remarks that I give the impression of being schizophrenic are irrational and are based on your—to me—well-known fear of losing contact with people and with things which, given your cleverness, you have inwardly long since come to terms with. Although I did not agree with much of it, I have handed over your article on educating people for democracy to Wolfe for publication. I agree with you that only a very detailed discussion could perhaps eliminate the major problems that have developed between us. However, such an exchange of views would only be fruitful if it was based, on your side, on practical experience with the orgone energy, and if you were free from anxiety about what Mr. Scharffenberg or Mr. Kreyberg or other gentlemen would say about it. Orgone research is proceeding in this country and in other countries. It is not my fault if the coworkers from 1939 were left behind. But I must protest against being criticized out of thin air by people who have not taken the trouble to put in even one thousandth of the enormous amount of effort that I have had to make. I can surely expect that people who regard themselves as my coworkers understand what is involved, and that scientific work is more important to them than politics. What I have published in the last few years is new, comprehensive, and important. Anything

The Mass Psychology of Fascism (New York: Farrar, Straus and Giroux, 1970).

the politicians have said during these years was known to me in 1914 and 1918. The political line of thought has led to the monstrosity of the atomic bomb, while my line of thought has led to practical results which promote life, in a practical, visible, tangible way, and which are recognized not only in America but elsewhere in the world.

Please understand that I cannot let meanness of the sort committed against me in Norway pass without comment, not just for my sake but for the sake of the cause. And I have every reason to be angry when we have done everything possible here to preserve what had been laboriously built up in Scandinavia, while Philipson for years failed to reply to manuscripts, Dr. Raknes did not find it worth the effort to write a letter once postal communication was reestablished, and others, instead of fighting on my side, got involved in everyday politics, which would have been far better left to other politicians. We need good physicians, teachers, educators of small children, sociologists, but not political wafflers. I regard it as a medical crime that people have failed to immediately introduce orgone research and orgone accumulators to strengthen human organisms in Europe in this chaos of meanness, hunger, and malice. Therefore, instead of having people speculate on whether my scientific work in recent years has attained a high or low standard of excellence, or on whether or not it appears schizophrenic, I must now *demand* that accumulators be built and that the effects be tested in hospitals, as Dr. Hoppe in Palestine, also physicists in England, doctors in America, and people in Canada are doing. This, and nothing else, is the criterion for determining whether one can be regarded as a coworker.

14 April 1946

I do not feel that I will die soon. I feel as young as an eighteen-year-old and hope to reach ninety.

I have now arrived once again at one of those great turning points in my life where new horizons are opening up. I am going to limit my medical practice to two or three hours a day and devote the remainder of my time to reflecting upon and elaborating the functional laws of nature.

The quiet will do me good. One cannot accomplish anything intellectually in just one undisturbed hour a day—9–10 a.m.—as has been the case until now.

My path leads off into the natural sciences, equipped with psychiatric knowledge. I am not leaving psychiatry, but only the individual patients. I am continuing to adhere to the cause of man as the exponent of his society. In all other respects I wish to associate myself with unarmored life.

19 April 1946

This mundane world with its senseless political clamor is becoming increasingly remote from me. It is making room for another wider, larger world where the laws governing the living hold sway. Here there is no sickness, no distorted faces, no stinking, warped human souls but rather the harmony of numbers, processes, principles, a harmony one can only come to know through pain, far, far removed from daily life.

I don't want the mentally ill about me anymore, want only to be surrounded by healthy life, plants, animals, newborn human beings! In brief, life unspoiled! No more Nics and Philipsons!

1 May 1946

When I founded sex economy (1923–29) I felt that I was formulating banalities which everyone knew.

When I elaborated sexual physiology—i.e., discovered the orgasm reflex—I thought I had made some "small discovery with which everyone would be delighted."

When I discovered the bions I was still naive and unsuspecting.

When I received the first blows between 1934 and 1938, I realized that I had disturbed the "slumber of the world."

Today, however, as I put into words the functional law of nature, I know that I am helping to construct the thought patterns of the future. The great responsibility involved makes the task more difficult, rather than easier.

7 May 1946

When Dr. Thomas died I suffered for twenty-four hours from paroxysmic cardiac arrhythmia (pulse rate up to 180 beats per minute).

My strong heart couldn't stand it. Thomas was a physician whom I was treating for cancer, a decisive case. I was defeated.

However, there was something else which I can never forget: I observed Thomas in the process of dying. First he was unconscious but then he opened his eyes for a few moments—in the course of his death rattle—recognized me, smiled faintly, and gave me a completely lucid look as if he were trying to tell me something. So people *know* when they are dying!

18 May 1946

Oath for American citizenship set for Tuesday, 28 May 1946.

Very gradually and cautiously I am realizing that I understand infinitely more about the real processes of nature than the conventional physicists do.

19 May 1946

Incorrect thinking kills.

A deer that misjudges a ditch before jumping over it will break a leg.

Thinking is a function of the entire body. One thinks with the whole body and not just with the brain, just as one hears, feels, rages, and loves.

An armored individual thinks incorrectly, in principle and in every respect.

But the incorrectness is not due to loopholes in his knowledge. It is due to his fear of thinking correctly. And incorrect thought is always deadly, sooner or later, consciously or unconsciously.

Fascists murder millions of people, not because the murder is intended but because they are driven to such action by incorrect thinking, because they believe they can find justice through murder.

26 May 1946

There is only one reason for writing about serious matters and it lies in the nature of one's being, in the structure of one's needs. One does not write for the public, the journal, the publisher, or for money. One does not write for hate unless the hate has become a part of one's rational nature. A passing hatred will only move a pen pusher, a person like Scharffenberg,* or a third-class journalist to write. I personally do not write for human beings, I write about humanity. I write because I must and not because I want to.

28 May 1946

Peter has been put into a home for children until we fetch him again in four weeks. We have no room for him. The cabin on the lake is too near the water. There is nothing at Orgonon, except the laboratory and workrooms. For the money I have invested in research I could have built my son a home at Orgonon long ago.

And all this effort—for whom? "Humanity"?

The boy went quietly to Randi with no resistance. The sadness in his eyes was his only expression of suffering.

———

Half an hour ago I took the oath for American citizenship. An important formality, especially in my case.

30 May 1946

Back at Orgonon. My wife is exhausted, overworked, as I am. No salaried employee can know how difficult administration is.

I am growing frightfully indifferent to people. This is helpful in my work but it's also dangerous—amazing in comparison to my earlier behavior.

8 June 1946

A hardworking thinking apparatus needs weeks in order to come to rest and enjoy it. It needs rest just like every other machine. This rest consists of not-thinking. But the resting is only peripheral. Inside, in the core, new intellectual deeds are being prepared, just as the shoots of a plant fill with strength before springtime and then blossom forth in splendid green.

9 June 1946

Ilse has driven to New York to fetch Peter. I am listening to Beethoven's Fifth Symphony and mulling over my article "The Living

———

*Johan Scharffenberg, Norwegian psychiatrist with a particular interest in genetics. He was one of the leaders in the opposition to Reich in Norway.

Orgonome."* An honest work which at first will even be incomprehensible to the best of them. Maybe even to Wolfe.

The gypsy-like quality of my life is a part of its nature. Thirty years ago, in 1916, I was wandering alone around Austria as an Austrian soldier. Homeless, without parents, brothers, far removed from any homelike, family atmosphere. Wandering, wandering, thinking while I wandered, probing, thinking away the fog.

I am very aware of being highly decent. All the more pain caused by the defamation I experienced through sick friends who could not soar with me, yes, and even through a woman with whom I lived for ten years and who bore me two children.

17 June 1946

Received another letter from Philipson in Copenhagen. It is full of insolence to boost his ego. He remarks that I am "still psychologist enough" to understand, accuses me of making "presumptuous suggestions," etc. I will not write back. All they want is a "more vegetative private life." I must free myself from psychiatry and the psychiatrists. Deeper issues are at stake, e.g., the human thought process, cosmic energy, new hope for medicine. This involves still greater isolation. Humanity is the issue, not man himself.

T O   T H E   S T.   J O H N ' S   C O L L E G E   B O O K S T O R E
❖ *19 June 1946*

Gentlemen:

I intend to copy in our journal (*Journal for Orgone Biophysics*) that part of Kepler's *Epitome of Copernican Astronomy* which deals with "Vis Animalis" as the common force of the planetary system. Kepler's view, though animistic in the old sense, has a rational core which can be detected in connection with orgone physical investigations. It is therefore of importance to us to quote Kepler extensively, and, in addition to that, to pay tribute to a man who was so much misun-

*Included in *Cosmic Superimposition* (New York: Farrar, Straus & Giroux, 1973).

derstood in one of his most important astronomical statements— namely, in the numerical law of harmony of the universe.

I would therefore appreciate it very much if you would be kind enough to grant us permission to copy from the above book, Volume 1, pp. 74 to 109.

21 June 1946
Despite hundreds of different but concurring results of orgonomy, I still have doubts as to the overall concept. It is too *simple*: sexual, chemical, and sidereal superimpositions are essentially one.

TO A. S. NEILL
❖ *Late June or early July 1946*

My dear Neill:

I have your letter of 19 June. The things you say about one's worries in regard to the future fate of one's labor are so very true. I can understand them perfectly, being in a similar position. One's own children are very rarely the ones to carry on. One's disciples are apt to split their head mutually over who is the best follower. It often happened that it was just an apparent opponent who really carries on . . . but his way, and not mine or your way. I believe your school as such will not continue. But it will stand for all times as an example of what education should be. And that is more than the walls and the kids in it. As to Orgonon, I intend to establish a scientific research foundation carrying my name (it seems vain but the name promises stability to certain central ideas!), a foundation which will house the whole archives and will be devoted to orgone science. Should my son grow into it, all the better. But my children should build up their own lives.

On 28 May I became an American citizen "with the privilege to vote and to function as a juror." I told the officer that I hope to be of more important service by taking the constitution *wörtlich*.

1 July 1946

I am happy—because Eva is happy. She is living with her husband in my cabin on Lake Mooselookmeguntic. I always dreamed of owning a cabin in the woods where Eva could be happy. And now it has come true. Despite her miserable mother!

T O　A .　E .　H A M I L T O N
❖ *3 July 1946*

My dear Mr. Hamilton:

I hope you do not mind if I don't answer your letters instantly or if I do not answer every single letter. I enjoy them tremendously and I only wished you would keep on writing letters to me.

I understand perfectly well the conflict you are in between the facts of actual life and the task of safeguarding the life process by thought and action. I could tell you a long dramatic story about a man who was once just living, enjoying life thoroughly, until he detected that life was hated and persecuted everywhere with the most terrible and most unrecognized weapons, how he at first fought to defend his own life process, how in the process of this defense he realized the general nature of the struggle, how he who loved and adored his children was cut off from them because they loved him, how out of this personal fight for the right to live developed the fight for the recognition of the living process in general, how amazed he was to find that from ancient times honest serious people have been struggling for the same purpose, how futile their attempts were, how finally everything ended up in the atmosphere of the atomic bomb test. It is a long and sad story.

All I wanted to say with this was that I understand your trouble perfectly well. Living yourself and struggling for the living of all are two different and too often opposite things impeding each other. You are one of the very few to realize the basic difference between the discovery of the gamma rays and that of the orgone energy. It is not necessary to be restructured for work with the orgone, but most people are afraid of the physical force which creates and governs them. It is biophysical unity. The orgone is your *own* force, the gamma rays are foreign to you. Therefore people like to work with the gamma rays and not with the orgone.

5 July 1946

Recently I have felt perfectly happy with Eva, Peter, Ilse, the laboratory, and the assistant. In the back of my mind I hear my conscience prodding me "don't let up," "don't become middle-class," "carry on"—isolated, distant, a loner. But I seem to be slipping back into this world again. My main achievement, the long road from Freud to the cosmic orgone, is behind me. Only isolated skirmishes, elaborations, and a long life lie ahead. At the age of almost fifty I feel young, energetic, daring, even though the possibility of a disaster is not to be excluded. Some plague-stricken soul could still cause damage. And yet, my world is built on firm ground, my theories are being taught and applied. Now I can aim for the comfort I deserve after having given of myself for twenty years. Building Orgonon is a beautiful, rewarding task. Having Eva again brings me joy, great joy. Watching Peter grow—this intelligent, healthy child of my new world—is elevating. He is both my best teacher and the most beautiful proof of my theories. Life with Ilse is peaceful and right. I don't think that I will become a petty bourgeois. The autumn of my life ought to be mellow.

Is this the aging process? I am no longer *so* concerned that people around me function, work, think, or feel the way I do. I have grown accustomed to the fact that I am really "different" from other people, a fact I resisted for so long. The dangers for me now lie in cynicism and reactionary mannerisms.

A danger: the possibility of being destroyed by the aunts, nephews, and cousins of my pupils, should an organization really come into being.

And if I remain alone—the possibility of failure.

It is difficult to succeed and not be slaughtered scientifically. The fate of Marx or Freud demonstrates this. They were understood but bowdlerized by the little man.

With sex economy the danger is even greater. I fear the changes to which I find myself subjected. Will I retain or lose my straightforwardness, my human qualities, my harmony with the world? Will my productivity increase or decrease?

21 July 1946

They call me a "genius" and I can make no sense of it. My accomplishments only appear so gigantic against the background of mankind's miserable acts. In themselves they are simple, clear, accessible, and understandable to all. It is still beyond my grasp how people can be or think differently.

When I see myself returning to "life as it is" I fear for my intellectual future. Returning to what? To some genuine family life: good. To some comfort after twenty years of wandering: good. But not back to the situation I fled thirty years ago, not back to a petrified life.

I must be extremely careful about "leeches," parasites on my life. One must pay the ghastly price of alienation if one wishes to partake of a bit of comfort.

Is it unavoidable that one should suffer when one tries to adhere to the central issues? Must this be so?

And where is the next towering summit of the mountainous massif for me to climb? It is the peak called cosmic harmony, and the path leads through horrible loneliness, from a lucrative practice of treating life's pathology to genuine care for life's health.

If there were no pathology in life there would be little effort involved in protecting happiness. It would be assimilated by the general stream of the living. Today, however, life's pathology prevails and the struggle is bitter.

22 July 1946

Tolerance is only appropriate when rational processes are involved. When it comes to the plague we must be just as intolerant as we are of murder or the seduction of children.

When the wind howls around my cabin in the mountains, I hear the music of creation sounding in harmony with the law of nature.

When my two-year-old son looks at me with his dark eyes and his deep understanding of my very being, I realize what cosmic energy is telling me.

23 July 1946

There is a certain kind of enthusiasm for the orgasm theory which is far more dangerous than overt, threatening animosity. This enthusiasm—let us call it "redeemer enthusiasm"—does not result from an unarmored organism's understanding of the human animal's biological misery; it is not sustained by awareness of the massive social maliciousness which prevents a correction of human character structure and which therefore lacks the perseverance necessary in the struggle for the self-regulation of life functions. This redeemer enthusiasm is not willing to make any sacrifices or limit its demands in any way.

Redeemer enthusiasm is dangerous because it views orgasm theory as a new doctrine of salvation and expects that universal and individual sexual happiness are now simply going to be distributed and allotted by a physician or educator. It overlooks the fact that organisms which have been trained for decades to negate the joy of life and love have consequently not only lost their ability to give and take in the process of loving but have made loving itself an object of a deadly fear, and can frequently no longer be rendered capable of experiencing joy. It is exactly this structural incapacity for pleasure which turns the individuals involved into redemption enthusiasts and gives rise to their hopes that salvation has now arrived on the scene.

When the therapist is unable to fulfill these all too lofty expectations, the enthusiasm regularly turns into a hatred of life and into an intense desire to slander the therapist. The time has come to issue a word of warning about such enthusiasm.

The orgasm theory never claimed that chronic orgasm disturbances based on completely armored character structures could be healed. On the contrary, I repeatedly emphasized that a majority of individuals belonging to the present generation have little to expect with regard to achieving sexual happiness and that the primary objective now is to fight a determined fight for the sexual rights of children and adolescents. In other words, prevention of biopathic illnesses based on armoring and chronic sexual stasis.

Orgone biophysics has nothing to do with redemption. It emphasizes the staggering proportions of the hindrances to a happy life among the masses of the world population. It demands responsibility and perseverance in the personal and social struggle for the self-regulation of unarmored life.

Orgone therapists must therefore keep a constant and close watch for the redeemer enthusiasts.

T O   A R N I M   B E R E G I *
14 August 1946

Dear Mr. Beregi,

It was with great interest that I read your letter of 27 June regarding Experiment XX. A young physicist who is currently studying here at Orgonon was given the task of answering your objections, in order to gain some experience in theoretical debates on orgone-biophysical problems. The attached exposition provides the answer, with which I in principle agree. I have just one small, but fundamentally important detail to add:

When we study fundamentally new areas of nature, we have no choice but to proceed totally free of any preconceptions. I try to drum it into my students that all facts acquired by classical natural science should be accepted, but all interpretations and theories should be forgotten. Accordingly, we can do nothing at all with the atoms and molecules of physics because they are hypotheses which themselves require explanation. No one has so far seen an atom or a molecule. But we can observe bions and energy vesicles. It is likely that the atomic theory will be explained or corrected by the bion theory. When Freud discovered suppression, he would have been wrong if he had made use of Wundt's theories. It seems to me that you are making the mistake of trying to interpret the very new facts of Experiment XX by means of the molecular theory. On the other hand, I interpret the new facts independendently of all classical theory, but I am always ready to modify that interpretation if it should prove necessary to do so.

However, your contributions are important and interesting. Carry

*An engineer in Palestine.

on. Any interpretation and objection, even if incorrect, helps us make a little more progress.

19 August 1946

For twenty-five years I have been slave to a stupid error: I searched for the living which I felt within myself in the little man, the very place where it barely manages to survive.

My great restlessness was apparently an attempt to escape, to flee from sickness and search for a healthy life.

I encountered unarmored life only in its distorted or perverse manifestations, but I sensed health behind the facade of pathology. I even discovered the "biological core" behind and within Freud's "unconscious," the human being in Hitler, and the exigency of the masses behind Stalin.

I discovered the emotional plague within myself at the age of eighteen, after four years of inner turmoil. Freud confused the mental illness he found in life with the intactness behind it—i.e., with *real* life. That was his big mistake.

Freud's biology is completely hopeless. One can apply it neither to an amoeba nor to any other creature.

It offers no explanation of how life was able to exist in a perverse way.

America's beautiful women are images of a healthy life, in the form of marionettes, where the realities of biopathy and pornography are avoided. Russia has been frightened by pornography and has murdered the living.

If one oppresses people they suffer.

If one gives them freedom they become insolent. Where does the answer lie?

29 August 1946

The theory of the living, of unarmored life, will perish if it is not sustained by genitally healthy individuals who are capable of love. Sick or "cured" individuals can at best only be good helpers, but they will never be the advocates and representatives of unarmored life. For in such people life impulses are deflected or distorted while passing through the organism.

I have nothing to champion but unarmored life itself, and its science, orgonomy. Not psychiatry, not socialism, not the "future" or the past.

30–31 August 1946

3 *a.m.* Beautiful aurora as on 26 July (which I did not see).

This evening I observed the following facts:

1. Aurora visible = radiation of the orgone envelope.
2. Not understood: Why is it strongest from the north?
3. Radiation is *pulsed*—discontinuous in broad, undulating areas, like in an argon tube.*
4. Why is the center at the zenith?

Is there an aurora in the Southern Hemisphere?

Problem: Why does radiation emanate from the North Pole?

What causes the radiation precisely in August?

1 September 1946

My end will be old age and loneliness after a life full of youthfulness and rich in human relationships. My past life will appear radically different from that of most other people, but my future will be the same.

Beautiful young women still desire me, although I look fifty-four, and am actually forty-nine. But none can follow me into that immense loneliness and stay with me permanently. That is why the end will be solitary. That is why all—at least all of my kind—spend their last days in loneliness or madness.

Outwardly I am fifty-four instead of forty-nine, and inwardly I am fourteen or sixteen. The fire of youth will burn within me for another thirty years—I am certain of it—just as it burns today and burned thirty years ago. My life work will surely be accomplished. A large

---

*Reich reported in *Cosmic Superimposition* that "this motion is of the same kind that can be obtained in highly orgone-charged argon gas tubes through excitation by a moving orgone energy field derived from the body or the hair."

part of this work will have been the overcoming of my perpetually erring contemporaries.

TO WALTER HOPPE
6 September 1946

Dear Dr. Hoppe,

Experience has shown that the prognosis for stomach cancer, even in the early stage, is poor. The occurrence of a tumor in the intestinal tract is itself evidence of a high degree of anorgonia in the organism. Usually, the disease has been present for many years before the tumor appears. The resorptive capacity is greatly reduced. This applies more or less to all types of malignant tumors, based on the experience that has been gathered in recent years, with the exception of tumors in the breast and in the bones, where there are no vital organs that are easily damaged in the vicinity of the tumor. For these reasons, the emphasis has been shifted toward early diagnosis of general anorgonia and toward the very promising method of preventing tumor growth. I absolutely refuse to take on any more advanced cases of cancer for treatment. However, a clinic could certainly do a lot even with such cases, in combination with surgical measures. That will come with time.

I would recommend that you build a twentyfold accumulator. We have one in Maine. The results are much better than those obtained with the twofold one. I have seen a serious case of Parkinsonism yield to treatment. We must work with much stronger accumulators. The possibilities are far from being exhausted. Unfortunately, the heavy twentyfold accumulators cannot be loaned out. Everything cries out for a clinic. Perhaps I will succeed in building it here in a few years' time.

There is nothing to prevent accumulators from being dispatched to the four corners of the globe. On the contrary, that would be desirable.

The bion sack acts locally and intensely with secondary radiation. The accumulator acts generally and much more gently with primary orgone. The application depends on the type and location of the functional disturbance.

We have had a good, but new kind of working summer. There were many physicians here and I was able to demonstrate patients who have been cured. They were highly impressed, but not sufficiently so to speak out loudly in favor of what we are doing. Psychiatrists are coming in droves.

An article on my sociology appeared in the official organ of the University of Sydney. A long paper, in which a report is given about my article on cancer, was published in the official journal of homeopathic physicians.

Dr. Ola Raknes is arriving here today from Norway and will no doubt have a great deal of important news to relate. Experiments with the accumulator are already being conducted in Norway and Denmark.

11 September 1946

It is painfully obvious that I am involved in a new crisis involving my entire personal and spiritual existence:

During my conversation with Raknes I realized that I can expect nothing, absolutely nothing from my pupils—nothing at all. I see that it is the fate of such achievement to simply be taken, ingested, and then passed out again as waste.

If there is nothing I can count on, then I must take a little better care of myself. Mustn't give of myself so freely.

Furthermore: It is clear that Ilse and I are very, very close friends but that, as husband and wife, we only make it with difficulty. Our love for each other as human beings is now becoming detached from sexual attraction. Where will this lead?

13 September 1946

Minutes can be as long as days, and days as long as weeks when you are waiting for someone you love.

All the people who come to me offering help end up *taking* from me. Ilse came as a laboratory worker and a personal aide. There ensued beautiful years of her helping me.

But then the child arrived, and then the marriage license, and she stopped writing letters for me, and the manuscripts were kept waiting for a long time—and then I was alone again. Now I have begun to search anew. The more people who come, the less they help me personally. Each one, after a longer or shorter period of enthusiasm, begins to think of his family, his party, his career, his income.

No one thinks of the work.

That is why I'm searching again.

And each person making a living from my work wants me to live like a saint so that he can use me as a showpiece. This tempts me to make "stupid mistakes." I plunge down into "life" and soil myself. Or have I become a moralist, as people inform me?

TO MELVIN AVRAMY * †

❖ *25 September 1946*

Dear Melvin Avramy:

It is too bad that in the pursuit of serious scientific matters so many personal and irrational motives are involved so often. I think that personally you reached the level on which you can go on by yourself. As far as orgone research is concerned, I feel that your approach has been not sufficiently serious. You did not even care to study carefully the publications which appeared until now about the orgone energy. If you had done so you would have discovered that it is not a matter of Reichenbach's Ode, or a matter of sensitive and nonsensitive persons, and not a matter of suggestion, and so forth, but that it is the matter of the discovery of the long-sought-for "ether" in the *strict physical* sense, with all its consequences for physics, astronomy, and other sciences. If you had read all publications carefully you would also have understood that I cannot permit myself to enter discussions which have nothing to do with the core of my experimental and theoretical work. All that, of course, is due to the mixing up of personal and factual relations. But I am sure that by separating yourself

*Professor of physics, Columbia University.
†This letter was not sent.

from me for a while you will be able to separate the personal from the factual, and that you will study the published material and arrive at your own judgment this way or the other way.

Please, don't fail to call on me whenever you feel in need of a talk either personally or factually. But I would suggest to let several months pass by.

TO A. S. NEILL
❖ *14 October 1946*

My dear Neill:

I just received your letter of 4 October. I find that you are in the same terrible mood as I found myself in already for months. You are quite right, there is no use in writing good books, true books, if the Stalins have the ways and means to keep the man in the street in their power and pocket. I would only correct the following: I don't think that *The Sexual Revolution, The Function of the Orgasm,* and even *The Mass Psychology of Fascism* are too difficult for the man in the street. I think we should begin to look at the man in the street more closely and to see him as he really is. We must ask why he listens to trash rather than to truth, to fanfares rather than to sensible things. Somebody has to do the thinking and the heavy writing. That things are not so simple and become rather complicated is, among other things, due to the little man's unwillingness and inability to sit down and think things over. After four years of bellyache, I finally succeeded in writing down my "Speech to the Little Man." This speech is true and it tells him exactly how he brings about fascism. But I won't dare to publish it. I just cannot step out and tell the little man in his own language what he is, how he looks, how badly he thinks, how cowardly he is, and how he promotes all the rot in the world. You simply cannot do it, though you ought to.

TO WALTER STRAUS*
❖ 24 October 1946

Dear Dr. Straus:

It was a pleasure to hear that there exists another group of students of our literature. I appreciated your frankness in regard to your re-action as a medical student in 1933. We know from thorough clinical experience that between the acting human being and his biological interests there is always the inhibiting force of fear of life as its func-tions. It is to my mind also a typical mass-psychological phenomenon that the results of scientific endeavors are not realized by the mass of the people for whom they are meant, until catastrophic events force the people to see the truth. There is nothing, I am afraid, one can do about it, but try to search for the forces of fear that prevent people from drawing the right conclusions *in time*.

I am afraid that you misunderstood my evaluation of Russia's de-velopment. The reproach is not that the Russian leaders failed to eradicate the damages of six thousand years in the twenty-nine years of their existence. But there is the justified reproach that they have reestablished the patriarchal, authoritarian way of life to a terrible degree.

I had the feeling from your letter that the "impatience" is not on my, but on your side. As biopsychiatrists we realize the abyss of hu-man existence, and we have to muster the forces to stand the impact of fright in contradistinction to most people who don't want to realize this abyss and who are doing everything in their power to prevent anybody from seeing and mastering it.

As far as Shaw† is concerned, I think that he saw through a great deal of our misery. But I am afraid that people misused the humorous way in which he presented human misery to eliminate the impact of the insight.

---

*Walter Straus, M.D., had formed a study group in New Jersey. They studied *The Sexual Revolution, Character Analysis,* and *The Mass Psychology of Fascism,* as well as works by George Bernard Shaw.
†George Bernard Shaw.

T O   A E N N E   M O R S E T H *
28 October 1946

Dear Aenne:

This is an addendum to my last letter dealing with your inquiry about the American and the British attitude toward the Germans. I believe that this attitude is born of a general misunderstanding. Fascism is usually linked with the Germans and the Japanese. The point is overlooked that fascism is a character trait that can be found among people everywhere in the world—i.e., among Americans just as much as among Germans. The indiscriminate identification of fascism with the German nation, as wrong as it may be, is the basic reason behind the *punitive* attitude. We are fighting hard against this misinterpretation, but it is very deep-rooted. It is also up to you whether and how quickly the numerous false views of what constitutes fascism disappear from the world. I believe that there is nothing more important today than to discover the human side of plague-ridden people and to contrast it with the fascist plague in the same people.

T O   W A L T E R   H O P P E
1 November 1946

Dear Dr. Hoppe,

I am hurrying to reply to your letter of 17 October as well as to the letter of Arnim Beregi to you and me dated 6 September.

With regard to your question about the chances of success in treating testicular cancer: I have long held the view that the appearance of fist-sized tumors is indicative of a very advanced stage of death of the organism. Where operation on such tumors is still possible, such as in the case of testicular cancer, I would unreservedly recommend an operation to spare the organism the need of having to cope with the detritus of the orgone-treated tumor. However, since we know that the tumor itself is not the disease but one of its symptoms

*A student of Reich's in Germany.

and that the disease itself consists of a functional disturbance of the entire organism, orgone treatment following the operation is essential. Although radium treatment cannot be combined with orgone treatment, the radical operation will probably be compatible with subsequent orgone treatment.

I will write directly to Beregi. I understand him very well. It is dangerous to abandon an ancient, respected theory of cosmic function, which is thousands of years old, if one does not have the slightest guiding principle for replacing it with anything better. The atomic theory is now two and a half thousand years old and has served us well. I understand that Beregi is trying to base the orgone phenomena on the atomic theory. But he does not know yet that, at a very particular, practical point, atomic theory inevitably applies the brakes to any further research—namely, at a point which I have already indicated: Atomic theory assumes, without being able to prove it, that the primordial element in the cosmos is the particle of matter—i.e., the atom—which in turn is made up of other particles, that is to say electrons, neutrons, etc. In contrast, orgone research already possesses absolutely convincing material which states that the primordial element in the cosmos is not material or electrical in nature but is orgonotically functional. Electricity and matter, as well as all other forms of mechanical energy are obviously specific variants of the primordial orgone. I am fully aware of all the responsibility that goes with making such statements. I know what it means to put a two-thousand-year-old hypothesis out of action. The seriousness which characterizes the discovery of the orgone guarantees that I do not act rashly. On the basis of Experiment XX, I have at my disposal, among other things, an orgonometric theory regarding the formation of life-specific chemical substances from orgone energy, a theory which I cannot yet publish, but which has already been elaborated and written down.

I leave it to you, as someone who knows Beregi better than I do, to make him aware of this circumstance. When we talk of the orgone, we mean primordial, cosmic energy from which all forms of mechanical energy and the chemical substances emerge. Thus, the primary element is orgone and not the molecule, atom, or electron. Without this working hypothesis I could not take one further step.

I suggest to Beregi that he should provide a theoretical summary of his views and publish this in the *Annals*.* The further progress of the work will decide everything. Do you think that Beregi is loyal and already deeply enough imbued in the matter to help us solve a chemical problem, which I am not equipped to cope with practically? I can only indicate the problem to you: There is no question that in Experiment XX not only plasmatic material but also fat, sugar, and carbon were newly formed from free orgone energy. I know that, once more, this sounds mad. This fact has such enormous practical dimensions that I must first look around me carefully before I start to work things out in practical terms. A chemist like Beregi would probably be the ideal man to solve the problem. Please write and let me have your opinion on this.

14 November 1946

Ilse, wonderful soul that she is, has grown tired of me. For seven years she has been bound to the entire situation. She wants to take a six-week rest in England with Neill and her mother and brother. She really ought to.

18 November 1946

Marriage licenses are immoral documents because they presuppose irresponsibility and licentiousness among the individuals involved. Furthermore, they are immoral because of the restrictions they place upon free nature and because of the venom of divorce.

How much more important morality is to the world than the health of our children! At least you still don't need a license to have children.

People stay in one place, they settle down, make no sustained effort to accomplish anything; they jeopardize an achiever by attaching themselves to him.

So few people have a structural understanding of a serious, working organism's need for development, for *inner freedom*, freedom from the sordid world of business.

Annals of the Orgone Institute, a journal published by Reich in 1947.

It is inexplicable why the emotional plague's influence on mankind should be so much greater than the influence of truth and unarmored life. The main reason for this is unarmored life's naiveté and lightheartedness.

————

Adolf Meyer, Professor of Psychiatry, has asked for information about me and my writings. Meyer is the patriarch of psychiatry and introduced psychoanalysis into the U.S.A. forty years ago.

19 November 1946

Further changes. I have been told that "everyone" in New York is talking about my work. "Everyone"!

The Soviet Russians news agency, Tass, has ordered a copy of *The Mass Psychology of Fascism* for a book review.

There is a new movement among church people: away from the church toward social work on diseased mankind!

Until now antireligious mechanism and religious mysticism were in direct opposition. In the U.S.S.R. the conflict was clear and outspoken.

Now, through the discovery of the orgone, a unification of natural science and religion has become possible. Natural science will have to accept the existence of emotional or biological energy, and religion will have to accept the existence of orgonity.*

The age-old conflict which divided me against myself for twenty-five years was that between science and politics. Today, in 1946, this conflict has manifested itself socially in the form of a clash between Wolfe, who favors the strictly scientific, and the church people, who incline toward social work.

One cannot dismiss this invasion of sex economy into the church (as Wolfe does) simply because one is against the church!

Wolfe and Gladys Meyer, his wife, do not want Protestant ministers to be trained as sex-economic social workers. Meyer herself was once a member of the church and now hates it. They feel that the important thing is the orgone, and that people are only a secondary con-

---

*In a glossary, Reich defined *orgonity* as "the condition of containing orgone energy; the quantity of orgone energy contained."

sideration. The ministers, they say, should leave the church if they want to work in the field of sex economy.

Today I invited Wolfe to have a talk. His reply was: "I don't feel there's any sense in it under the present circumstances." What are the "present circumstances"? Just today I sent Wolfe two patients.

T O   J .   H .   L E U N B A C H
❖ *27 November 1946*

My dear Leunbach:

Some time ago I received a letter from Mr. Stig Bang, the lawyer in Copenhagen, and a document about the establishment of a Danish institute, to be co-signed by me. I am returning the bylaws to you unsigned for the following reasons:

1. The "International Institute for Sex-Economy and Orgone Research" has, according to the development of the work during the past few years, been replaced by the "Orgone Institute." The Orgone Institute has been registered as my private undertaking in the United States. It consists solely of myself and those workers whom I choose as my personal helpers and assistants either here or abroad. It is not incorporated, has no members, and is not an association. The Orgone Institute has no branches outside of the United States except work represented by my personal assistants, as for instance Dr. Hoppe in Palestine.

2. The "Orgone Institute Research Laboratories, Inc.," which does the actual research in orgone physics, is incorporated as a nonprofit corporation. The title which you put into the bylaws, "International Orgone Research, Inc.," is therefore wrong.

3. Orgone research is being carried on in different countries at first without affiliation with the Orgone Institute until it reaches a point of maturity where its recognition by the Orgone Institute in the United States is justified. Only when this functioning is secured in cooperation with the Orgone Institute for a period of time may the foreign research stations incorporate as Orgone Institute Research Laboratories, Inc., in their respective countries.

4. The patent application is made in my name. If it is granted, I

will lease the patent rights to the respective research laboratories for $1.00 per year. If the patent is not granted, then the aim has been reached that nobody else can take out a patent. This is enough to safeguard against outside exploitation of the orgone. In no case can the patent be taken out in somebody else's name, be it a person or an institution, since the orgone is my discovery. To make it quite clear: I am not donating my invention to anybody, but I am granting its free use with the right to withdraw the permission whenever I think it advisable.

5. Because of this present structure of the organization of my work, I do not consent to the founding of an institute or of a department of the American institute in Denmark. The first prerequisite for the establishment of a section of the American Orgone Institute Research Laboratories, Inc., in Denmark would be close cooperation and proof of fruitful work over a period of years. Dr. Philipson has not shown his willingness and ability for such cooperation. Furthermore, it is a strict requirement for this cooperation in orgone research that the basic principles of sex economy are being followed. This is not the case with Dr. Philipson, according to reliable reports by Scandinavian workers. The orgasm theory and the basic elements of orgone biophysics are inseparable. What I said above does not impede in any way the prosecution of the patent application in Denmark or the prosecution of serious research in orgone biophysics.

26 November 1946

Today, in 1946, a positive attitude toward sex is becoming increasingly prevalent. From 1922 to 1930 I was alone in this respect. Lindsey,* Malinowski,† and others *tolerated* sex but were not *sex positive*. Malinowski affirms sexuality for Trobriand children but not for European children.

People today are not aware of this. But since I am the only one receiving the blows I would also like to assure my priority.

---

*Judge Ben B. Lindsey, coauthor with Wainwright Evans of *The Revolt of Modern Youth* (New York: Boni and Liveright, 1925).
†Bronislaw Malinowski, Polish anthropologist and author of *The Sexual Life of Savages* and other works concerning his study of the mores in the Trobriand Islands.

27 November 1946

A new transition is occurring in my life, this time due to the break-through of sex economy on a large scale. The press is selling an average of 350–400 books per month. And again, people who were important have remained behind. This time they have poisoned the atmosphere less. It is still unclear whether the direction taken will be sexology or physics, or both simultaneously. All this is happening in a world situation which only arouses fear and trembling. One meets with inane chatter and the fear of truth everywhere. This is one of the reasons why my fifteen-year-old books are now making a breakthrough. People are tired of idle talk and beating around the bush. I would probably not have been able to write my books under present conditions. My friends would be the very ones who would prevent me. An example: I wanted to get rid of my marriage license since my own conscience is sufficient for me. But that won't work, because in America one partner has to sue the other for a divorce. Separation on the basis of mutual consent does not exist. My fame has spread far and wide and my name would get into the newspapers. My intention of then continuing to live with the woman I have divorced is blocked by my progressive students' fear of my being libeled for "living in sin." Instead of putting up a vehement struggle against these filthy laws, they quickly yield like a swampy marsh.

Even before I am in a "position of power" I have already been forbidden to be free and to determine my own life. They fear the same public opinion which they plan to overthrow as incorrect. Apparently this is the way reversal of all progress begins. Whereas I once had to struggle against the enemies of my work, I must now be wary of my own pupils and allies.

29 November 1946

I do not desire, like Wolfe, to be "proven correct." He'd like to prove he is "right" before he has gone through the filth himself and understands why it is so ghastly.

Freud was "right" when he opposed the communists; but he did not learn about the mass psychology of fascism. The fascists are "right" that people are worthless; but they did not write a "talk to the little man."* I'd rather be wrong and learn from experience.

My controversies with conventional thinking and lifestyles are apparently a part of my research. If unarmored life intends to revamp its modes of existence, it will have to develop them organically while struggling to free itself from traditions.

While doing this it is damned hard to keep one's own emotional sensory apparatus pure.

To stay in touch with the old way of life and protect oneself from it, while developing the new and keeping it alive, is a damned hard job.

1 December 1946

Other people have a lot of time for diplomacy. I have neither the time nor the ability. This is why it is so difficult for me to make progress. Granted, in the end I will win out, but with what a staggering effort.

Other people sway like reeds in the wind as soon as a magnet comes near them. But I do not want to attract them to myself in that way. I want them as independent individuals who join me in a common effort.

I have completed the talk to the little man. It's as if a weight had fallen from me. I have freed myself from my irrational attachment to the little man without becoming reactionary. I have separated his human from his inhuman qualities.

When I look back over the past thirty years, I am amazed that I have circumnavigated hundreds of rocks unharmed. Each rock was the "good advice" of some "well-meaning" friend. Under the guise of being concerned about me or my work, they looked after their own shortsighted peace of mind.

Thus I resisted the advice to marry rich when I was twenty-two years old

the advice "not to be so aggressive"

the advice not to take everything so seriously

*Listen, Little Man! (New York: Farrar, Straus and Giroux, 1974).

the advice not to trust people and not to expect too much of them

the advice not to formulate the orgasm theory in universally valid terms

the advice to limit character analysis

the advice not to tackle problems that did not belong in my field

the advice to stay away from "politics"

the advice not to "attack the family"

the advice not to affirm infantile sexuality but simply to tolerate it.

Every single piece of advice was correct on a short-term basis but would have been a catastrophe had I followed it in the long run. Cosmic energy would have remained undiscovered, the mechanism of the emotional plague would have continued to go unrecognized, if I had not exceeded my own limits and exposed myself to the mortal dangers of politics and the plague.

To whom do I owe my thanks for being saved this time?

I am now being told that I should push people away who are connected with the church, when they come offering help.

This is probably the first time in the history of the church that its emotional foundations have been recognized. Sex economy attacks the heart of religion. The ancient mystic religion which transcendentalized life will someday be replaced by another kind of religion, a religion of the living, of unarmored life.

We are now experiencing the first germinal beginnings. They are pregnant with the future. Intellectual, mechanistic Marxism will not touch the masses emotionally. The mystic church is collapsing. A new religion of life will arise, based on knowledge of life energy. Reverting to mysticism will only be easy as long as the enigma of self-perception in unarmored life has not been solved. Until this happens we will not have natural-scientific knowledge of how sensation occurs. The mystic religions undoubtedly drew their great power over human beings from the organ sensations of unarmored life.

Centuries of ideological struggles over the essence of unarmored life lie ahead. Only extremely clear and courageous thought will make it possible to prevent reversion to mysticism. However, religious people will be among the chief advocates and founders of the new religion of life. From them, from the many, from the majority of the earth's population, we may expect more than from the desiccated materialists and Marxists or from the rebellious, neurotically infected intellectuals.

Energetic functionalism rejects both the mysticism of the church and mechanism. It includes the living—i.e., motility plus sensation.

4 December 1946

Avarice and strategy are such integral parts of human structure, especially American structure, that honest motives are inconceivable and as a consequence my teachings have often resulted in chaos.

7 December 1946

Happy events:

1. Report from Wolfe: American intelligentsia is fully informed on the work.

2. Dr. Gordon, chief of Marlboro State Hospital,* who was previously hostile, has inquired about the therapy.

3. The head of the New Jersey Medical Board has received a report on orgone therapy.

4. Approximately two hundred copies of the publications are being sold per week.

5. *The New Republic* printed a review of *Mass Psychology*. Caution: I must be cautious. The medical technique is gaining ground. People's interest: earning a lot of money. But the essential point—namely, prevention of neurosis—is being forgotten.

8 December 1946

I have been aware of it for months but haven't dared to face the problem in a way that would require action.

My reputation in the world is on an upward swing, while at home things are on the decline.

1. Penny Warren has left. Granted, she left because of her husband's nagging, but still, she left, and would not have done so if my situation were not what it is.

---

*In Marlboro, New Jersey.

2. Jimmie Innis* is no longer working. She wants to get back into "therapy." She is not a worker.

3. Ilse is tired of everything and wants a vacation, two months in Europe. I understand her completely. The child, the work, and I have been too much for her.

4. Wolfe is "on strike" again. The journal is simply not getting on. He advises me to withdraw to academics, "orgone biophysics exclusively." He overlooks the fact that dissension at a meeting of medical specialists is also orgone research. In short, they all get stuck somewhere, sometime, are inflexible, stop developing. I cannot, must not follow their advice, so that I don't stagnate myself.

I AM COMPLETELY ALONE. CAN'T COUNT ON ANYBODY, *IF I WANT TO PROGRESS!* AND THIS DESPITE, OR BECAUSE OF, THE BREAKTHROUGH. THIS IS FRIGHTFUL.

The old conflict: Politics or science? Man or nature? How to resolve it?

10 December 1946

I have often asked myself why I refuse to penetrate the secrets of "higher mathematics." I'm not interested in them. Is this a "lack of talent for mathematics"? No! My sense of life and my research instinct have guided me well until now.

I avoid "higher mathematics" the way I avoided the biopsy of malignant tissue in cancer research. Both lead away from the living, from functioning. Mathematics leads to a "world of shadows," and the biopsy leads to dead, not living cancer tissue.

This is why mathematicians, as well as cancer researchers, have kept their distance from the orgone and have ended in their respective cul-de-sacs.

No, natural science will have to learn to accept nature *in its living reality*, and no longer only in the form of cadavers or symbols (i.e., mechanical or mystical forms).

I cannot say whether my path will lead to a new kind of mathematics. *Functional equations?*

Parting from the little man is very painful. The preparation of the manuscript took three to four years; writing down sixty pages of truth

*An assistant.

took five months. I am afraid of separating from the little man. He offers the security of the petty bourgeoisie as opposed to the insecurity of that which he calls "genius." "Genius" borders on "insanity," on pathology in unarmored life which stems from incomplete, fragmented knowledge of oneself, from the conflict between rejection of "normal life" and the inability to free oneself from it. My adieu to the little man also has other consequences: I am beginning to notice the dangers which threaten the little man when he is supposed to advocate the living in this "normal" world. *Insanity (schizophrenia) is a knowledge of unarmored life which lacks the courage to bear that knowledge.* "Genius" is knowledge of unarmored life plus the courage which that knowledge produces. A "genius" falls prey to schizophrenia when he does not have sufficient courage to bear the final consequences in the face of the world—i.e., to admit that four thousand years of human thoughts and deeds have led to intellectual bankruptcy; in brief, when he remains dependent upon, attached to the little man. But the "final consequences" of rational thought also lead to the danger of mental illness when the matter is viewed from the other aspect: A "genius" must not succumb to sexual stasis, he must lead a satisfying love life if he is to withstand the blows of isolation and of the little man.

Nietzsche's mental illness was caused by his asceticism.

It is greatness, not pettiness, which drives people insane. A petty person may develop a compulsion neurosis but never schizophrenia.

People develop schizophrenia when the organism cannot bear the high degree of cell irradiation produced by great insights or experiences. I must therefore be more careful about the individuals I accept for work. Either they sense the danger and go berserk or they do not sense it and sink into a life situation which befits them. For me personally, the question of whom I should share my loneliness with remains unanswered. My helpers, the good, decent people surrounding me, see the "final consequences," but only in the mirror. Those who do not turn into enemies simply withdraw. There can be no hope of ever explaining this to an outsider. One must have experienced this conflict oneself in order to understand it, and to experience it approaches taking the "final consequences."

The pettiness of great men, such as Goethe or Freud, presumably begins with the fortification of the ego against the "final consequences." And at this very point their deviation from the truth also began. For truth borders on eternity, and eternity is simply much too grand for man. He can only digest small amounts of it.

Naturally, I am in great danger of mental illness. Either through the fright of reaching the final consequences or through forced abstinence.

As long as I remain capable of assuring my orgastic release I'm probably not in danger. And then too, it decreases with age.

Am I growing "wise"? I used to fear and hate it. Perhaps I'm growing wise from a need to protect myself from the human beast, in particular from the busy psychoanalysts whose peace of mind would profit so greatly by a diagnosis of "schizophrenia."

It is crystal clear, like a great, beautiful light.

It won't even be necessary for me to withdraw completely. One can maintain superficial, deliberately courteous relationships with these animals with their grinning faces while remaining internally detached and without having to become armored oneself.

Thus understanding is helpful in emotional distress.

11 December 1946

I have raised my fee to fifty dollars for physicians studying orgonomy. Numerous physicians tell me that they expect me to charge one hundred dollars. They earn their money back within a month or two. They are overrun with patients who love the technique. A young physician in Newark, who came to me when I charged twenty dollars, was already earning between fifteen hundred and eighteen hundred dollars a month eight months after beginning his studies.

I don't like this moneymaking. But with thirty years of research and achievements I cannot charge twenty dollars when my pupils are charging fifteen dollars after their first year. This is America.

12 December 1946

I am reading a story about Jesus by Papini.* That man was two thousand years ahead of his time. He knew the specific reactions of the plague, knew the secondary drives, and demanded that human

*Giovanni Papini, *Life of Christ* (New York: Harcourt Brace, 1923).

beings be restructured. One issue, however, remains unclear: Did he also condemn natural love along with the "flesh"?

14 December 1946

The time is growing ripe; the hour of departure into greatest isolation is near.

One more look back over a rich life.

One last embrace with a young body.

One last walk through the meadows leading my son by the hand.

But one day I shall have to begin the journey, far away from all that is dear to a human being, far from everyday thoughts, everyday joys, everyday worries.

The journey to the land of numerical harmony.

For one year I have been avoiding orgonometry, in order to rest, to cool down, in order to start anew from the beginning.

20 December 1946

Look back, look back, in order to see ahead more clearly!

Why are people running away?

Certainly not because I have bad manners. They are running away when I'm not present as well. They are running away from themselves.

21 December 1946

Yesterday Dr. Ferrari* told me that after his last session he went to the Psychoanalytic Institute. A psychoanalyst named Lewin asked him, "Have you heard the latest? Reich has been taken to an insane asylum." Ferrari chuckled to himself, didn't mention that he was seeing me.

23 December 1946

Last night the orgonometric picture of rotating cosmic matter began to form once again. I feel insecure, incompetent, as always when a breakthrough to new fields takes place. I felt this way when I overcame Freud; when I entered the field of physiology; when I discov-

*Dr. Guillermo Ferrari Hardoy, Argentinian psychoanalyst and student of Reich's in the United States, 1946–50.

ered the orgone. Each time I was tortured with doubts as to whether I was justified. Looking back, I have been proven magnificently correct, but looking ahead, I still feel insecure. Even if I did do the right thing several times in the past it could go wrong this time. And my work does not allow for any stupid mistakes.

This time the questions are astronomical and I am a "layman" in astronomy, just as I was a layman in physics and biology. I am relying solely on the *logic* of my discovery of orgone energy. It will have to lead me, but I must not slip. The harmony must be achieved.

24 December 1946

Self-examination. I have hold of myself by the scruff of the neck. It is an austere self-examination. A major portion of my "life" had the secret purpose of not losing touch with my contemporaries, of not noticing the fact that I'm "different," of concealing this. Hence all the pain, emotional cramps, the numerous disappointments.

I am still not over it, even after having completed *Little Man*. Must add one more thought:

"Only when truth has kissed you, little man, only when your facial expression reflects the kiss of truth, only then will you understand the man of truth, of art, of achievement."

They sing the praise of Jesus but they have no idea what caused his death. They are still killing him.

———

Frederic Wertham, who wrote the pestilent critique of my *Mass Psychology* in *The New Republic*,* was the man who wanted to discuss my course on fascism with me in 1940. Clara Meyer, the secretary at the New School, advised me to do so, but I refused to be censored. That must have "insulted" Wertham.

25 December 1946

Christian choral music rises emotionally far above the lowlands of secular, naturalistic-mechanistic singing. It represents the cosmic elements in man. Jesus Christ felt and taught the cosmic nature of unarmored life. The church deviated from this and landed in the

———

*In his review (2 December 1946) Wertham called upon "the intellectuals in our time . . . to combat the kind of psycho-fascism which Reich's book exemplifies."

morass, although it deviated no more, perhaps even less, than secular vendors of happiness. The fact that all great things are torn to shreds is not the fault of Jesus' teachings but rather the fault of the sons of man.

Jesus established heavenly joy (= mankind's cosmic awareness) on earth, whereas the church failed in the central question, the joy of love, and moved joy on earth back into heaven. But didn't Jesus sow the seed for this himself? Wasn't Jesus also caught in the tentacles of fear, the fear of unarmored life in its nakedness?

Jesus, Plato, Aristotle, Marx, and Freud were all caught in these tentacles. I also was ensnared, unknowingly, jeopardized without sensing danger (in a positive sense). And when I discovered it I wanted to run away. Flee from the plague of mankind.

To free oneself from the little man completely and still stand by him, that would be the solution to my basic emotional problem.

The Jesus story fascinates me. It exposes all the elements of the emotional plague:

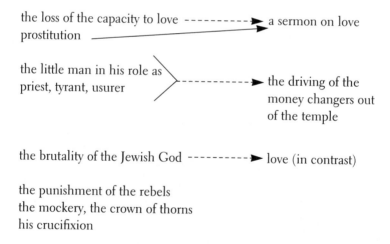

the loss of the capacity to love - - - - - - - - -► a sermon on love
prostitution ⎯⎯⎯⎯⎯⎯⎯⎯⎯⎯

the little man in his role as
priest, tyrant, usurer ⟩- - - - - - - - - -► the driving of the
money changers out
of the temple

the brutality of the Jewish God - - - - - - - - -► love (in contrast)

the punishment of the rebels
the mockery, the crown of thorns
his crucifixion

And the little man at work again as the Catholic Inquisition.

29 December 1946

In spite of my external success I am in the midst of a debacle. Once again my laboratory has gone dead, all the "assistants" except

Ilse have left. I asked Ilse what was going on, whether it was my fault. She said no, it was just that I am too far ahead.

I will probably still have to wait for a long while. Waiting, forever waiting. How far ahead am I actually?

4 p.m. I am plunging into orgonometry again, am concentrating on a demonstration of the functional equation of pendular-oscillation energy, the energy of a falling body, and the energy of mass attraction.

The numbers have been worked out.

This accomplishment will solve the problem of gravitation.

30 December 1946

It is possible that all this confused calculating, just like my "confused experimenting" on the cosmic orgone, will lead qualitatively to a new functional type of quantitative equations.

There is no gravitation—i.e., no falling—in space, but only oscillations in the orgone ocean, in the rotating orgone ocean.

One must free oneself from gravitation in order to understand it.

1947

"They brought me into the public eye in America in a shabby way. I am going to stay in the public eye in a good way. I am going to make the American, French, and Russian constitutions of democracy come true."

1 January 1947

When I am accused of being poor at mathematics my reply is: "True, but your higher mathematical calculations excluded my orgone, whereas my orgone, sooner or later, will include correct mathematics."

I can now calculate oscillation frequency and oscillation duration independent of the duration of planetary revolutions.

4 January 1947

If overcoming the earth's gravity were ever to become a practical possibility, if spaceships were to fly to other planets, classical astronomy would be misleading. For the earth does not revolve around the sun but *oscillates in a relationship to the sun conforming to a natural law*. Its movement is not elliptical but follows a curved, wavy course in space. That is why a spaceship could not return according to the classical concept of space. Spaceships will have to make their calculations according to orgonometric space-time reckoning.

5 January 1947

Have been working on the astronomic second pendulum for eight hours. My mind is aglow. I'm tired.

6 January 1947

6:25 a.m. The g KR* problem and the emotional plague are keeping me awake. Why do I worry about what people will say about me when I'm gone? It should make no difference to me! *But I do not want the hard, honest work of decades to be slandered by a handful of plagued individuals.* Gerö,† for example, who is still living on the fame of having once been a pupil of mine, claims that all of my

*Orgonometric gravitation function.
†George Gerö, a psychoanalyst.

theories, even about the communists, have been proven correct. But that I personally am paranoid. (A "paranoid" is apparently anyone who has worries other than his love of Hungarian *Schnitzel.*)

Therefore I want to make sure that the emotional plague can do as little damage as possible to my work, for the sake of the living.

The more lucid my work becomes, the less children will wail.

A plaguemonger does not understand such motives. All he does is corrode.

T O   W A L T E R   H O P P E
7 January 1947

Dear Dr. Hoppe,

In my view, the cooperation with Beregi will be far more fruitful if, for the time being, we eliminate all theoretical discussions on the nature of orgone energy and restrict ourselves solely to facts. Engineer Beregi comes to the problem of cosmic energy from a background of mechanics and electrical engineering, whereas I come from a background of biology, and, in particular, from the function of the orgasm. This difference in the way we have arrived at the problem is naturally reflected in the interpretations of the phenomena. I can do nothing with mechanical and electrical theories in the fields of biology and psychiatry, and I can only base myself on the *new* laws that have been developed in these fields. I have difficulty in answering his questions because I would have to set aside all my work for weeks and months and develop special experimental setups to answer not just Mr. Beregi's questions but also those of many other people in detail. For reasons of time, I am forced to abide by the principle that every experimenter must gather his own experience. Where experiences diverge, we must leave it to the future to decide which of the views presented is correct and which is false.

I regard the discovery of "iron cancer" as extremely important. In all probability it involves bionous decay and the growth of bion clusters.

The twentyfold accumulator in Maine has yielded new experience. The difference in effect between a single and a twentyfold accumulator is clearly evident. For example, in a case of Parkinsonism, the twentyfold accumulator stopped the shaking of the organism in about fifteen to twenty minutes and also had longer-lasting effects. The accumulator cannot be disassembled. It is made up of five plates on all six sides, each of which contains four layers of organic and metallic material. These plates are simply slipped into a fixed frame so that the strength can, to a certain extent, be regulated. I would very much recommend that you experiment with such an accumulator. I am now gathering some interesting data on the effect of orgone on a case of shell shock (traumatic neurosis).

As regards your inquiry about German publications, I can answer as follows: I have been trying for a long time to establish a German-language branch of the Orgone Institute Press in Europe. It would be too expensive to publish literature in the German language in America for the European market. Would *you* be interested in assuming responsibility for a German-language Orgone Institute publishing house? Could you print the journals and the *Annals* in German in Palestine and send them from there to Europe? One could try to link up with a German-Swiss publishing house—e.g., Huber in Bern or Orell-Füssli in Zürich—to sell the literature. Please let me have your views on this matter as soon as possible.

At this end the work is proceeding well. I am at present training twelve physicians in orgone biophysics and the publishing house is selling on average 400 copies of our literature per month, which is an enormous number given the fact that we are not advertising, etc. All our doctors are overworked, and people all over the place, including in Australia and England, are talking about the work. Dr. Ola Raknes from Oslo spent four months here and returned to Norway with many problems. The greatest concern is and remains the organization of the work. The matter of being granted tax-free status is still pending.

To conclude, I would like to propose that you and Beregi regularly collect your observations and send them in, if possible in English, to be published in the *Annals*. Any practical detail is important.

8 January 1947

A quiet voice which I am resisting is warning me about Wolfe. Not that he is deliberately mean. It is just that he sways like a reed in the breeze, is dependent upon his wife, and has this confounded air of reserve which marks him a snob. He might possibly commit a serious blunder in order to protect "sex economy" from me—"unwittingly," "innocently," "with good intentions." In addition to this he is once again sabotaging the *Annals.*

12 January 1947

4:30 a.m. Keeping a diary and taking notes is growing increasingly important:

It allows me to pour out my heart when there are no friends nearby, or when friends would be too weak to bear the things that keep me awake at night.

It holds each new situation captive.

It safeguards my work against future misinterpretation.

18 January 1947

I awoke from a dream, as if from a long sleep. I am like a train rushing at full speed which must suddenly put on the brakes.

All this is due to the obvious breakthrough of my theories in America, England, Australia, Scandinavia, and elsewhere. They are not being resisted, not being hushed up. People are marveling, commenting, remaining silent, whispering, writing.

I must change my entire strategy of life if I am to adjust to the situation. I have been in the opposition for twenty-five years, involved in a difficult struggle, outnumbered. Now the majority appears to be coming over to my side. And I personally have not yet adjusted to this. Not yet.

I must be more cautious with my pupils. They are interested in money, not in the prevention of neurosis. I cannot, in today's world, fall behind in my earnings if I do not wish to fall behind in my prestige as well. I am now earning approximately fifteen thousand dollars a year (plus returns of about six thousand dollars for the fund through the accumulators).* The youngest of my physician trainees

---

*Income from rental of accumulators went to the Orgone Research Fund.

earns the same amount, albeit working ten hours a day and not three or four as I do. But then he doesn't have the worries of research, of reasoning, of writing which I have. I am doing the research free of charge.

The transition demands:

earning more money: thirty thousand a year,

stopping the outlay for orgone research,

not putting up with insolent pupils anymore,

being a professional authority,

fully accepting my superiority,

no longer forming close relationships with those around me,

controlling my craving to discover more and more. I can let other people handle the application of the orgone in medicine.

I have accomplished enough.

And suffered more than enough under mankind.

19 January 1947

My life situation is too constricting for my urge to work. "Where to turn with this wealth of thoughts?" The problem which always torments me is *overabundance*, and the difficulty of confining and delimiting it.

Some of these limitations are imposed upon me by my most intimate friends and pupils. They want peace and quiet.

T O   A .   S .   N E I L L
❖ *19 January 1947*

My dear Neill:

I see the whole question of prevention of the biopathies going to hell, and I see already fear in the eyes of the workers to deal with the social structure which opposes healthy living. You don't mind, I hope, that I am pouring out my heart to you. Our work, yours as well as mine, is caught right in between money madness and political frenzy. People live their lives in ideologies, and are avoiding the realities involved in honest pioneering. I see, for instance, educators raving with enthusiasm about your writings, but in reality taking no steps to fight the misery of children all around us. What is the use of all this struggle if the common man teacher or physician spills the fruits of hard work when he touches it? Do I exaggerate? Am I pessimistic? They call me a damn optimist, and yet there is reason to be desperate in view of this flattening out of everything that is meant to change our lives in a rational manner. They hail me now because I introduced the understanding of the character. They say it is accepted everywhere, but I know that no one who is not under my immediate control is actually doing anything practical about the core of the problem. They still don't mention the issue: healthy sexual living of children and adolescents!

Ilse is now definitely going over to England. It is difficult to decide whether or not she should take Peter with her. On the one hand, she wants a rest from seven years' exhaustive work. On the other, I am a bad child provider though a great child lover, being buried under a hundred different tasks to handle "human nature."

24 January 1947

Received a letter from L. B. Szekely, a theoretical mathematician in Jerusalem. He informs me that through his critique of mathematical theory he has ascertained that I am *the* psychologist. Presumably because of the energy factor.

26 January 1947

Can't sleep: The little man within me is pleased that a "great" mathematician, a representative of the "greatest," "most precise," "purest" of all sciences, has recognized a "little psychologist" and is willing to include him in the ranks of natural scientists. The little man within me (and it is the primary objective of my natural science to show this little man no mercy) has overlooked the fact that the little psychologist is overthrowing the great science of mathematics, that he is on the verge of formulating the functional law of nature, that his calling and capabilities will even explain the factual existence of "mathematics" as a natural phenomenon.

The mathematician has no idea that his ability to express nature in the form of numerical laws is as yet unexplained. He views himself, in a highly unpsychological way, as the representative of the most advanced and purest language. But the fact that his intellect is capable of calculating the distance of the planet Mercury from the sun—i.e., of conceiving this idea—is a question of consciousness, and therewith a profound problem of natural scientific research itself. To assume the existence of an "absolute" mathematical intellect or an "absolute" numerical harmony of nature is tantamount to introducing the concept of an absolute spirit.

Our task is to explain through natural scientific energetics how the mathematical intellect operates, how it is sustained by orgonotic emotions, and how the natural function is capable of transforming itself into a numerical function in the core of the living orgonotic system.

This is the objective of a "psychology" which should be called orgonology. Its task is to combine the shadow world of mathematics with the real, living world of the cosmos. It must explain the nature of apperception and self-perception, must include the structure of the research scientist in the evaluation of his research findings.

It will probably have to trace the formal elements of logic and mathematics back to form, trace form back to its very creation, and then trace the creation of form to energy processes.

Thus the little psychologist must be aware of what a great task he faces. He must not harbor an all too petty sense of pride over the fact that the mathematician has elevated him, and despite all his modesty must know how not to be too small to adjust to his gargantuan task.

The petty, restricted, armored man still remains the problem.

There is truth in the old research on numerical harmony and we must grasp it.

My approach to numerical harmony in the cosmos is that of a psychologist, not an astronomer. The unity of man and the world is demonstrated by r kr (Radius Kreiselwelle). What a relief! I don't need to act like an astronomer.

My throat section is behaving better than in the spring. I have not collapsed for months, am coughing less and smoking less.

T O   L .   B .   S Z E K E L Y
27 January 1947

Dear Mr. Szekely,

As you can appreciate, your letter of 9 January both interested and pleased me. It is good to hear that mathematical science is successful in advancing useful criteria for scientific theories. And it is pleasing to hear that one's own theory actually meets the strictest criteria of a—for the time being still far from being established—discipline.

As you know, I have worked for more than twenty years on consistently implementing the energy principle in biopsychiatry. It is admittedly something different to mathematically test the correctness of a scientific theory (as you do) and to drive toward energetic formulations—i.e., quantitative determinations of qualitative emotional processes (as I do). This is like building a tunnel from two opposite sides. Let us hope that the two sets of effort will meet somewhere. Then it will be possible to find a practical solution to the problem of human "nature" or, if you wish, of "un-nature." So far, mathematics has looked down on psychology, and psychology, because of its youthful status, has not known what to do with mathematics. However, the subjective world of sensations and the objective physical world must at some point combine into a scientifically useful unit if the dream of unifying all the sciences is to become reality.

I assume that you will be interested in the progress that my work has made over the last twelve years, because it actually deals with the quantities and energy processes in the psychological sphere. My assistant Walter Hoppe, M.D., 56 Ben Jehuda Road, Tel Aviv, will certainly be very happy to get to know you and to show you the work that has been published.

I would be pleased to receive a copy of your publication on the criticism of mathematical theory.

❖ *29 January 1947*

Encounter: A mother in the park pushes and squeezes her one-year-old child into the carriage like a dead cushion. The child cries bitterly. The mother, furious, pushes harder. The older child, standing nearby, begins to cry. The mother slaps her. She cries more. I am standing by with Peter. "Why do you look that way?" the mother asks, a false smile on her face.

"I am a physician who makes his living on children made sick in this manner by mothers like you," I answer.

"It is my child, isn't it? I can do with it what I want."

"You cannot do what you want with your children."

"I shall call a policeman!"

"Call if you please."

"You are one of those refugees who try to make trouble in America!"

"All Americans are refugees."

"Have your hair cut."

"Get a license to be a mother! To beat children! You need a license for everything else."

"I'll call a policeman!"

12 February 1947

Haven't been able to sleep for two hours! Yesterday there were two events which bothered me:

Raknes reported from Norway that Schjelderup* is speaking out against the orgone and that my friends want to have the matter investigated by the "authorities." Who is the authority? Kreyberg?†

Dr. Willie‡ informed me that a patient had called him and said that "Reich had just been taken off to the insane asylum." That's how rumors spread.

And I am on the verge of withdrawing from this plague-stricken world, of fleeing to realms where it cannot follow me.

Ever since I completed Listen, Little Man! there has been turmoil and unrest within me. I am searching for a new, different mode of expression. A novel perhaps? But I am no novelist, am a poor storyteller and poet. And yet I still have the desire somehow to vent my feelings without being bound to the stolid vein of contemporary scientific writing. My belief is that, with the atom bomb, mankind has

*Harold Schjelderup, Norwegian psychoanalyst and student of Reich's.
†Lejv Kreyberg, cancer researcher in Norway, who was hostile to Reich.
‡James Willie, M.D., a student of Reich's.

had enough of science. Nevertheless, I am a scientist—or am I? Is that all I am? I am creating some new form of human existence, of human thought, although it is difficult to foretell just what it will be like. Therefore I must be cautious with final creations. I am returning to man and approaching him from without, so to speak, after having been bound to him for so long.

All the proportions are changing: things appear smaller, while the horizon seems wider. In comparison to the function of the cosmic orgone even the discovery of the electric lightbulb or the phonograph seems trifling. Important, but small. I am beginning to understand the negative outlook on life of the Jesuits—to the extent that it is *real* and not pathological in origin.

It is disquieting to think that these comments could someday be read by a wide public. I want to be able to think and write in private.

I wish I could look back on this present age from the year 3047, from the standpoint of the new man. My own good books such as *Character Analysis* and *Mass Psychology* would then seem very strange to me, would appear small and of limited scope. Nevertheless, they were milestones in this world, not in the cosmic realm.

T O   O L A   R A K N E S
13 February 1947

My dear Dr. Raknes:

I would like to summarize in a few points my attitude in the matter of the "accumulator in Norway." You know very well that I would not interfere in any way with your decisions as to how and when to put the atmospheric orgone to use for the benefit of the Norwegian people. But I am sure you will not mind if I tell you my opinion, about what you wrote in this matter.

1. I would like to warn emphatically against any attempts to have professional people of any kind "control" my experiments with the orgone energy. There is nothing more dangerous than this wrong idea of "control." Scientific discoveries can be controlled only when they fall within a known framework of theory or factual reference—i.e., the controller has to be basically familiar with the problems involved.

This is not the case with any living scientist today in regard to orgone energy. It is an old experience that those scientists and doctors who are corroborating my findings are looked upon as being influenced by me and therefore being "unscientific," as, for instance, Dr. Hoppe, Dr. Wolfe, Du Teil, Raknes, and so many others; whereas those who don't understand a thing of what I am doing and are ready to prove by any means that I am wrong are looked upon as the true scientists.

2. I showed you the documents which prove that even Einstein, the top-notch scientist, has declared his incompetence to judge the orgone, though he has corroborated the fact of the temperature difference, which fact alone overthrows the second law of thermodynamics. This is not a petty thing to deal with in a petty manner. Control is therefore out of the question, and only collaboration in a modest and decent way with you by a few doctors and scientists seems feasible to me. We must not permit anybody to step up as an authority in relation to this work, and we should not let our own friends acknowledge such "authorities." An authority is one who works continuously in the field in question.

3. I had the feeling that we should not speak of introducing the orgone accumulator in a country. The best way proved to be that of working quietly with a few assistants, and letting the accumulator speak for itself, as it does up to now, in the U.S.A., in England, in Argentina, in Palestine, etc.

I hesitated to write this letter, but I did it because I am very much worried about your falling prey to irrational mechanisms in scientific intercourse. I know very well how much alone you are there in Norway, and with what a tremendous task against most terrible odds.

Another point I would like to make is this: My work was capable of fighting its way through in the United States mostly because of one reason: the publication of the total work in the language of the country. Thus many circles in many places were able to form an opinion about the seriousness and the honesty of the total work. The cause of the orgone accumulator in Norway and in Scandinavia would, in my opinion, be helped to a great extent if our literature became well known and widespread over there.

25 February 1947

My worries focus on the fact that my contemporaries do not understand the unity of my science and that they view me as a great psychiatrist but separate my psychiatry from my orgonomy. They do not realize, since their own thoughts are fragmented, that orgonomy and psychiatry are both rooted in nature and that both originated in emotional functions. They still consider the soul something religious, something outside of the body. Dr. Melvin Avramy, professor of physics on the Columbia engineering faculty, recently asked me whether I was not of the opinion that the soul, as a *form*, leaves the body at death and whether there was not after all a kernel of truth in spiritualism. I replied that the death process continues for decades after "death" (i.e., after the heart has stopped beating) and that the orgone leaves the organism only very gradually.

In this one sense there is "no soul," there is nothing but membranes, body fluids, and orgone. One of the functions of this pulsating orgone sack is perception, and this includes the "soul." All spiritual sensations may be traced to organ sensations. As enigmatic as perception still is, its connection with the pulsating orgone within the pulsating sack still remains. The cosmic orgone is definitely capable of being stimulated and excited but *we may hardly assume that it is capable of perception.* In the event that it is factually, practically, and objectively proven at some future date that the atmospheric orgone not only pulsates but *perceives* as well, this would be proof of the existence of God, not a personal God but only the omnipresent God without a personal form, the God Newton sought.

The problem of consciousness would still have to be explained. Probably consciousness will someday be understood as an *extreme expression* of organismic unity, as an act of combining all organ sensations in one ego, as a consciousness of ego boundaries as well as of the unity of the ego and the universe—i.e., the simultaneous existence of both states in one. For I cannot experience myself as a self if I do not differentiate myself from the universe while simultaneously experiencing myself as a part of it. In this dialectic of ego as separate and as part of a whole, in this unification of self-perception and perception of the world, the contradiction between Stirner and Marx will someday be resolved and balanced.

The psychiatry which I founded deals with the delimited ego while orgonometry treats the ego as a part of the universe, as a minute element of a special state of cosmic energy.

When people separate my psychiatry from my orgonometry they reflect an ingrained separation between the ego (here) and the cosmos (there). This is the error of mechanism in science. The absolute opposite of this, the antithesis, is the Catholic religious sense of the self as a part of God. Scientific separation of the self and the world in psychiatry (here) and astronomy (there) and religious-mystical fusion of the self and the cosmos are thus merely particular, detached aspects of the living. These aspects may be combined with a functional mode of thought but nevertheless be kept separate. The self is actually a part of the cosmos. If we place the emphasis on the word "part" we are operating with the self as delimited. If we place the accent on the word "cosmos" we are operating with the religious aspect.

psychiatry   astronomy
science   religion
self   cosmos

The self as simultaneously delimited from and fused as a part of the cosmos.

It follows from these functional facts that when natural science comprehends the world it is operating through the self as a functioning entity. Essentially, science operates through the delimitation of the self from the cosmic orgone. Religion operates with the unity of the self and the cosmos. It understands the cosmic orgone (its "God") when it turns inward ("Jesus within the body"), and the significance of the self—as delimited function—disappears when it is compared to the ego as a part of the cosmos. Natural science therefore cannot attribute consciousness to the cosmos whereas religion is forced to do so.

Mathematics, as a logic of numbers, can only offer a description of objective nature because a unity of self and cosmos exists, because ego and cosmic functions obey the same laws.

mathematics   cosmic events

self *f* cosmos
harmony

Thus psychiatry and orgonometry treat two separate natural functions, ego and world. At the same time, they form a functional unity (historically, thematically, factually) since ego and world form a union.

———

Does the ether impede the progress of objects that move through it, and is there any dragging effect?

The ether moves faster than the objects in it.

Michelson experiment.* Assumption: Ether is motionless; earth moves in the stationary ether; therefore a beam of light traveling in the direction of motion of the earth must take less time than a beam traveling perpendicular to that direction of motion.

Assumption is incorrect: The ether is functionally equal to the orgone ocean. It is not stationary but on the contrary moves faster than the globe.

28 February 1947

Yesterday I finished reading Frank's† biography of Einstein. Einstein was the last offshoot of classical physics as it turned toward functionalism. He encountered all the problems of nature which later became the central questions of orgonomy. But since he replaced the ether with formulas he barred the way to concrete, measurable reality. "Modern" physics was unable to grasp the *functional* characteristics of the ether which fills space and consequently became involved in

———

*Reich refers to the experiment in 1887 by Albert A. Michelson and Edward W. Morley. The results were interpreted to deny the existence of an ether.
†Philipp Frank, *Einstein: His Life and Times* (New York: Alfred A. Knopf, 1947).

the theory of probabilities. The orgone particle spins and therefore has a curve and quantum; when it flies it has no localization, is not a particle but has momentum; when it spins it has localization as a particle but no momentum because it is decelerating.

2 March 1947

10 a.m.–3 p.m. A bomb explodes!

It occurred to me to tackle the problem of gravitation from a new and different angle; not from the relationship of the planets but from their surface rotation.

The rotation of all celestial bodies in the orgone ocean would then be determined exclusively by their mass and would have relatively identical values per second. Gravitation is a problem of the orgone ocean. *The motion of celestial bodies is determined by the waves of the cosmic orgone ocean.*

There is no attraction between sun and planets.

Large masses spin more slowly than small masses. This is why the sun, which is the largest mass among the celestial bodies in our planetary system, has the least momentum. This explains why the planets have 97 percent of all the momentum but constitute only 3 percent of all matter.

The greater the mass, the less the momentum of its rotation.

A large ball on a wave of water rolls more slowly than a small one.

———

So I stagger through time seeking one goal, the living in the universe. The law of the spinning wave reveals the unity of life and the cosmos. People love, laugh, mourn, but there is only one guiding line through all truth and all error: the law of the spinning wave.

3 March 1947

I feel as I did thirty or thirty-five years ago when my parents' fate* catapulted me into the vastness of life. How alone and deserted I was in those days, and how little I was aware of it! I felt only sorrow, boundless melancholy and yearning, but for what?

The living within me refused to realize its misfortune: the social

---

*Reich's mother committed suicide in 1910. His father died four years later from tuberculosis.

catastrophe from 1914 to 1918, as well as the personal catastrophe. They combined in a powerful union to which I owe the theory of unarmored life. It was then that the great search began:

Science, socialism, wife, children, mentors, the human masses.

This was followed by enormous setbacks:

Defeat on all fronts: Freud, wife, children, political parties, associations, errors in my ties with terms, ideas, movements.

Have I finally found *myself*? I don't want to be too isolated! And thus I can understand the herd animal's fear of thinking!

I am expanding as I withdraw from this pseudo-life. But no other earthly human being can understand me. I am clinging to my courage.

7 March 1947

My life, my love, my work, my music, my composers bear the stamp of yearning. Yearning is the sensing of an unarmored, decent future for the sons of men. Beethoven's Choral Symphony impresses such yearning upon the listener's heart.

Do I take my work too seriously? Does cosmic power flow over all human life without pity or mercy? Even the little worm, man, has grasped some small bit of nature, formed, and understood it, albeit mistakenly and haltingly, but grasped it nevertheless, understood it, converted it to music.

The fact that I can hear music, that emotional excitation can be and is transferred to my body through the air, is in itself an important but unsolved riddle. Now it is certain that the *energy* which lies between the source of the music and the ear is capable of excitation, that sound can be relayed over thousands of miles, from New York to Berlin, due to the existence of orgone energy in the cosmos.

9 March 1947

People say that I am working with scientific dynamite. This is why everyone is talking about my work but no one is really willing to handle it. People say that it takes centuries for such accomplishments to gain general validity. I, however, do not want to die without seeing orgone accumulators in use for the prevention of cancer. One small reason for this is that I'd like to live to hear the ring of my well-earned fame, but the main, the honest reason is that so many people are dying unnecessarily.

One of the greatest difficulties of my work has been that since 1919 it has been unable to become anchored in any country for a period of twenty or thirty years under one individual, that it had no place to sink its roots and branch out. It's amazing that it has made even this much progress.

The work is much too large for the form in which it exists, and I am too small for its scope. What a fate!

29 March 1947

There was an article by Brady in *Harper's* magazine which degraded my influence on the younger generation of writers and artists, calling it mystic.*

They do not understand the reality of emotions. We are working with the same material used by mystics but along rational lines.

30 March 1947

4 *a.m.* The great problem of this horrible century definitely remains the "normal man," the human animal with an atom bomb, but without genitals—in short, the petty bourgeois. I experienced him thirty years ago in Vienna and removed him from my life. And now I am experiencing him again in America. I am concerned! A fascist character who will not tolerate Negroes at the Psychiatric Institute in New York is to become president of the American Psychiatric Association. Conservatism is organizing everywhere. This could mean the beginning of new witch hunts.

❖ 31 March 1947

It is a part of my bitter existence that those who know what I want do not write much but earn much money with my knowledge, and that those who know little or badly about my work write much about it.

———

Confirmation of Experiment XX from the university biochemistry laboratory in Williamsburg, Virginia. That is America. It would have been impossible in Europe.

*Mildred Edie Brady, "The New Cult of Sex and Anarchy," *Harper's*, April 1947.

4 April 1947

Went to the cinema with Ilse in the evening. Had a coughing attack with a throat spasm, lost consciousness for one second.

8 April 1947

Ilse leaves for England tomorrow.

T O   P A U L   G O O D M A N *
❖ *14 April 1947*

Dear Mr. Goodman:

I appreciate your note.

I am used to such behavior as you described in *Politics*,* but the worry is not on my part when a writer nails himself down with an opinion about serious work in a magazine without first having learned enough about the subject in question, then sooner or later he is bound to be detected. Miss Goldwater simply knows nothing of the existence of our journal, where the existence of orgone energy has been demonstrated on several hundred pages of print. In the thousands of reviews and articles which have been printed during the last twenty-five years on my work the latent animosity was always of the same design, and I got used to it. But what I do not understand is how progressive people can fail to see the simple facts of human interrelations which are present and functioning everywhere, waiting eagerly to be endowed with social power.

❖ *19 April 1947*

I hear old melodies from my childhood and the first years of manhood. *La Traviata* and the tangos I often danced with so many dear

---

*The editor of *Politics* had asked Paul Goodman to review *The Mass Psychology of Fascism*. Goodman had subsequently asked for and received from Reich permission to make extensive quotations from the book as an essential part of his review. Without consulting Goodman, however, the editor gave the assignment to someone else, Ethel Goldwater.

women. What a pity that those days will never return, and that I have become a "staid, middle-aged gentleman."

TO WILLIAM B. WASHINGTON*
❖ 19 April 1947

Dear Mr. Washington:

Mr. Sharaf has already told me about you and your intentions. It is difficult to reach a decision in regard to your proposition. I shall not be able to accept any students for work during this summer, since I shall be busy with hard work on orgonometry. But I see the possibility that you might help in the development of the mathematical side of orgone physics. The best thing to do would be to have a discussion first. Are you coming to New York during the next four weeks? Or could you come to New York for this purpose? It is too complicated to be expounded in a letter.

TO ALICE RANDALL † ‡
23 April 1947

Dear Mrs. Randall:

I would like to say a few words in connection with the Parent-Teacher Meeting which takes place tonight. My remarks refer to the problem of whether children should or should not fold their hands and pray to God. I would like to explain shortly why I objected to Peter doing so:

1. The idea of God is closely associated in the minds of children with the idea of punishment for sexual activity, especially masturbation. This is a well and safely established fact of clinical psychology. There will be no objection to children appreciating a universal cos-

---

*A man recommended to Reich as a mathematician by Myron Sharaf, a student of Reich's.
†Of the Kew Kiddie School, in Queens, New York.
‡This letter was not sent.

mic force which is responsible for life and creation, but as long as this idea is associated with punishment for sexual activities I find prayers to be damaging to mental health.

2. The healthy individual is absolutely tolerant of any kind of religious belief. Unfortunately, this is not true the other way around. The different religious beliefs are strictly and severely against the natural and healthy manifestations of children and adolescents. This is not an opinion but clinical experience. It is regrettable, but I can do nothing about it. Therefore, I find it necessary, in order to keep my boy healthy and free of emotional and psychosomatic disturbances, to keep him away from the influence of irrational religious beliefs.

Finally, I would like to express my appreciation for the excellent manner in which your school dealt and deals with my boy.

6 May 1947

It is said:

1. I have no sense of humor.

I do have a sense of humor when I'm with a child or the woman I love. I *do not* have a sense of humor when capricious meanness drives millions of people to their death.

2. I repeat myself too often, am "repetitious."

If I had not dealt with the one great theme again and again over the last twenty-eight years cosmic energy would not have been discovered and psychoanalysts would still be preaching sublimation of genitality and the death instinct.

3. I am aggressive (violent).

The little men and the little intellectuals would like to carry on their petty falsity and meanness without interference and I disrupt their questionable activities.

4. I am *almost* paranoid.

The little, pestilent individual would love to persecute, gossip, slander, and plague without the person whom he persecutes, gossips about, slanders, or plagues defending himself. If the person does offer defense then he's "paranoid." In America this diagnosis business prospers especially well. A paranoiac is a person who thinks he is being persecuted while in reality he is not. A person who really *is* persecuted cannot be called paranoid for stating this as a fact.

TO A. E. HAMILTON *
❖ *20 May 1947*

Dear Mr. Hamilton,

I read your letter of 18 May with great care. I also gave Mrs. Hamilton the proofs of an article of mine, which was written about three years ago and which will appear in the *Annals*. I hope this article has cleared up most of your hesitations and doubts as to whether I am a dictator or not. You can rest assured that this work of mine cannot be done by people who are "believing in me" or who are growing up as independent "seedlings." But if I am a sequoia and a seedling of mine claims to be a sequoia seedling and turns out to be a turnip, and if this seedling does not realize he is a turnip and not a sequoia, and in addition to that does not say so publicly, then I have, by the nature of rational judgment, the right to declare that this seedling is not a sequoia but a turnip. Your exposition on scientific independence, with which I agree 100 percent, brought to my attention once more a most miserable fact which I had to experience many times in a very painful way during the past twenty-eight years. The fact is this: The turnips would like very much to enjoy the glamour of the sequoia without taking sequoian pains and risks. Not being able to function like a sequoia, the turnips usually get nasty toward me, if they fail to realize their true nature. To make it short:

Only independent groups and groupings and no association or organization can secure the free growth of orgone biophysics, *but it has to be orgone biophysics* if cooperation and friendly relationships as well as listing in the *Annals* should function. As you proceed in this new endeavor of yours, you will have the same experiences that I have had. If you work on the line of the sequoia, you will see turnips grow around you like mushrooms, claiming that they are sequoias.

*This letter was not sent.

23 May 1947

4 a.m. There was an article by Brady in *The New Republic* (Wallace-Stalinist) entitled "The Strange Case of Wilhelm Reich."

It was typically communist, mudslinging propaganda under the guise of a factual, objective portrayal.

She called for legislation against Reich, as in Norway.

Orgonomy was confused with Mesmerism, chiropractic treatment, and psychoanalysis.

It's obvious this Mrs. Brady believes that I am the only man who could help her to achieve an orgasm, which she so desperately needs. The tragedy is: she is not aware of her need.

A campaign approaches. I must stay calm, be factual and truthful, accept full responsibility, not fear taking risks, be aware of all the negative and positive aspects of the armored human animal.

It must remain clear.

25 May 1947

Brady's article in *The New Republic* is quite thought-provoking:

1. A progressive periodical attacks an important discovery.

2. An intelligent but obviously sex-hungry woman has been able to stir up the mud while I myself can only inform the world of what is motivating her.

3. It is necessary to consider the motivation behind an action.

4. The discovery of cosmic orgone energy is both advocated and abused by "people." This is perfectly logical, for it is a case of the plague *within the masses* which has been wreaking havoc for thousands of years.

5. Could it be possible that the great revolution has now begun? I mean the constructive mastering of the chaos.

6. Or will my work be destroyed together with me and only come to the fore after centuries have passed?

7. I must finish "The Struggle for Unarmored Life" and "An Orgonomic Hypothesis."

Points to be clarified:

1. What mistakes do I make which cause progressive individuals to attack my work?

2. In what way are irrational motives responsible for pestilent behavior?

3. Which of the workers are good and which bad?

Answer: Experience will show me exactly who is good and who is bad.

4. What practical measures can be taken?

5. Keep everything in the public eye.

6. Their motivation is not to clarify, but to *destroy.*

7. Users of the orgone should defend their own interests. I am tempted to take the accumulators away from them.

8. The greatest difficulty lies in the "God-like" character of the orgone.

9. The struggle of the red fascists against the progressive sexual attitude of the Americans. This is an important point.

28 May 1947

11:30. Arrived at Orgonon, tired and depleted from all those people who drain me.

It is peaceful here, and just as lonely as in my own heart.

6 June 1947

Midnight. Alone at Orgonon. Not a soul within miles. It feels good. I can think, even think above and beyond Einstein, the scientific hero of the twentieth century. I can allow my thoughts to soar beyond contemporary mankind; the very best individuals can only understand with their heads, and not with the lower half of their bodies. But the soul (in an emotional sense) rests in the lower half of the body. An embarrassing fact for the majority of the human race.

It's bad when one must conceal basic truths, bad when the simplest things pose a threat.

10 June 1947

I am waiting, waiting, but for what? For the full consequences? For the ideal condition of society? How idiotic!

A night owl is trying with all its might to break through the windowpane and get in.

The first volume of *Annals of the Orgone Institute* has appeared.

14 June 1947

Yesterday Ilse arrived with Peter. I was happy to be reunited with them. Ilse reported that both her brother and Neill are well aware of the importance of the discovery of the orgone and equally of the fact that my life is in danger.

The more success I have, the more I sense that I am in mortal danger. And the more successful I become, the less they will be inclined to spare my life. It can hit me at any time and in any place. Other people are beginning to tell me this also.

T O   W A L T E R   H O P P E
20 June 1947

Dear Dr. Hoppe,

I have received your letter of 7 June and I would like to reply to the questions and points you raise.

1. There has been an immanent internal logic to orgone research for the past twenty years, but it is only in the last few years that it became fully clear to me. This inherent, internal logic in the development is the reason why more and more mathematicians who work with logical problems are starting to show an interest in the work. It will interest you that I have been involved for years in mathematical studies which are concerned with astrophysical questions. Please do not be alarmed and please do not think that this is scientific immodesty. Once again, it is entirely "logical" that I should end up in astrophysics, given that I actually discovered the basic cosmic energy, and that *is* what I have discovered. The logic is thus beyond the realm of my will. I believe that in the course of time a group of young mathematicians and physicists will gather around our work.

2. There is still not enough money to build a cancer clinic. My "competitors" in the field of classical medicine have collected $2 million throughout America and our fund at the moment contains $2,000. It is too bad that this is the way things are distributed. Here we have the solution of the problem without any money, and there we have the money without the solution of the problem. The cancer

book*—i.e., the collection of all past publications together with some additions—will soon be printed and it could move the matter forward.

3. The experiments in Williamsburg have in fact discovered all the phenomena of Experiment XX, with the exception of the development of protozoa from bions. But the young biochemist wrote to tell me that what has been found has created sufficient excitement.

TO A. E. HAMILTON
❖ 28 June 1947

Dear Mr. Hamilton:

I have your letter of 26 June. It is not sure whether Neill will arrive on 15 August, the day for which his ticket to Farmington† is taken, or on the 14th. Since every day will count, I suggest that we try to get him on the train to Farmington on the 14th, in case his boat arrives early enough to make that possible.

What you told in your letter about Alvin Johnson is very interesting. I am sure that the natural scientist Conant‡ would say: I have the greatest admiration for Reich, the sociologist and anthropologist, but as a scientist he is nuts. You see, everybody gets the wrong end of me all the time, and misses the right one, which is his.

I am deeply engrossed in mathematics and have rarely had such a peaceful, quiet time to spread out my thinking.

TO SIMEON J. TROPP**
❖ 10 July 1947

Dear Dr. Tropp:

I thank you for your information about the cases of 4 July. It would be important if these and perhaps other cases could be written up by

*The Cancer Biopathy (Volume 2 of The Discovery of the Orgone) (New York: Farrar, Straus and Giroux, 1973).
†Farmington, Maine, is forty miles from Rangeley.
‡James Bryant Conant, chemist, president of Harvard University 1933–53.
**Physician and student of Reich's.

you for the *Annals*. It is at present not important at all whether we can cure cancer, and what type of cases can be helped. It is too early to demonstrate that. But every single observation, good or bad, is of the utmost importance for the further development of the orgone therapy of cancer in the future. Therefore, the more practical, clinical experiences we gather, the better.

You should read the article by Mildred Brady in *The New Republic* of 26 May, in order to orient yourself about what a nuisance of a freelance writer can do, trying to damage a good cause.

TO L. B. SZEKELY
10 July 1947

Dear Mr. Szekely,

Your letter of 12 May took me quite a bit further into the world of your ideas. With regard to future dealings between us, it will be important for you to know that I am usually several years ahead of my publications when it comes to working on the problems that consistently follow from them. In this case, we are talking about the orgonometric—i.e., the mathematical formulation of the facts of orgone biophysics. In the last six years, I have succeeded in establishing a numerical agreement between independently developed orgonometric research and certain facts taken from the field of classical physics and astrophysics. Naturally, this constitutes a great triumph for the correct natural-scientific formulations of the findings of orgone research. It will take some time, possibly several years, before these orgonometric results are ready for publication. But I believe that the methodological requirements which you mention in your letter coincide fully with the direction which has been almost spontaneously taken by my functional orgone research.

Please let me have further details on your research because, as already mentioned, you have arrived at similar or identical conclusions from a completely different starting point, and this is always a welcome and important fact in natural-scientific research.

As regards the philosophy of nature, I have learned over the past thirty years to be careful. And when making a judgment, proof of practical achievements is always a foremost consideration.

TO LÉON DELPECH[*]
❖ *18 July 1947*

Dear Sir:

Your letter of 9 July 1947 from Toulon was a great surprise and conveyed a great pleasure at the same time. It was a great relief to hear that Dr. Du Teil[†] is back again in life and work. I did not hear from him until now. Would you kindly tell him that I am eagerly waiting for a letter from him?

In regard to your own intentions connected with my work, I should be glad if *The Function of the Orgasm* and the later orgone biophysical research results would become accessible to the French public, where some ten years ago the first important interest arose. I am informing the Orgone Institute Press (157 Christopher Street, New York, 14, N.Y.) to send you the journal of 1945, the first number of the *Annals of the Orgone Institute*, which appeared in 1947, and also the three books which were published in English in 1945 and 1946: *The Mass Psychology of Fascism, Character Analysis,* and *The Sexual Revolution.* The second volume of *The Discovery of the Orgone* will probably appear in the autumn, and will be sent to you at that time.

If I can be of any further help in your endeavors, please don't hesitate to call on me.

21 July 1947
I am overflowing with ideas and brilliant insights on the question of energetic functionalism.

[*]French educator, who had contacted Reich in 1941 when he was a professor at the Lycée in Gap, France.
[†]As professor of philosophy at the Centre Universitaire Méditerranéen in Nice, Roger Du Teil had been interested and involved in Reich's bion experiments. He had disappeared during the war.

26 July 1947

Have completed a description of the development of functional thought technique.

Am on the verge of a mathematical formulation of functionalism.

When once my soul plumbs the source whence my intellectual ability flows, I will find peace.

1 August 1947

Today I wrote down the derivation of the "Two Functional Equations of Gravity." Tomorrow this will be followed by the derivation of l^3t^{-2}.

Great brilliant days and nights.

A stream of relationships.

6 August 1947

The chapter on "Two Functional Equations" is finished. I am content, but not completely. Have begun to rewrite "The Orgonotic Pendulum Law." This time it is much better than it was a year and a half ago. There is no longer such confusion of methodology and factual data. First comes the methodology, second the facts.

"Cosmic Application," etc., will not be published yet; despite the fact that Washington* applied $l = 100t^2$ to Mercury, Mars, Venus, and Saturn with positive results.

I am reading a biography of Darwin. The man was a tactician.

8 August 1947

Today I completed the second and final version of "The Orgonotic Pendulum Law," and along with that, the work on Energetic Functionalism.

I shall publish the following preliminary reports:

1. The Orgonotic Pendulum Law.
2. Observations on searchlights.
3. Observations on divining rods.
4. Observations on cloud formation.

*William B. Washington.

5. X-ray photography of the energy field of the hand.

6. The possible effectiveness of orgone against atom bomb radiation.

9 August 1947

My Geiger-Müller counter has been running amok since yesterday:

At the beginning, in early June 1947, when it arrived, it clicked two to five times on the first day in the room and in the orgone accumulator. Then the Geiger-Müller apparatus was silent for many weeks and *did not show the slightest reaction*. Therefore, I was already starting to think that it was worthless for my orgone research. Yesterday, by chance, out of curiosity, I picked it up again, to see whether it was still dead. When I switched on the power, *the apparatus suddenly burst into life*. The pulse counter *spun round in circles*, about one complete revolution = 100 pulses per second. Today the spectacle repeated itself and I have *no idea* what is happening.

Why does it operate only for one day?

Why was it dead for weeks?

Why does it now race like it has gone mad?

It does *not* indicate cosmic rays. Is it totally drunk on orgone?

Continuation of Geiger-Müller tests:

1. Switching off tube: No humming, but one click each time the high voltage is applied.

2. Questions to Washington on the phone, 2 p.m.

    a. Have you ever worked with such a device?

    b. What is most speedy reaction of Geiger-Müller to radiation?

    c. What is the "normal" reaction to cosmic rays?

    d. Ever seen 100 per second?

3. Measurement with seconds meter + recorder.

In 25 seconds *1,500 pulses!*

60 per second!

Incredible!

Consequences:

1. Wheels are rotated by pulses of orgone energy.

2. It will be possible to power motors with orgone.

3. This use will be risk-free; it will be cheap.

4.20 p.m.

I place the receiver in a threefold orgone accumulator in order to see whether it rises.

Today, 9 August 1947, between 11 a.m. and 5 p.m. *I have discovered the principle of the transformation of orgone energy into mechanical energy by means of the electronic impulses of a Geiger counter.*

Present this afternoon were: Ilse Ollendorff
William Washington, whom I called
Tom Ross, our caretaker

One revolution per second at the counter.

Immediately notified: the Atomic Energy Commission, American Academy of Sciences, French Academy, Patent Office.

T O   W A L T E R   H O P P E
12 August 1947

Dear Dr. Hoppe,

A scientific bomb exploded on 8 August in my Orgonon laboratory. The present document provides the essential information about what happened. This means: Unless there is some error, which is not likely, we have for the first time obtained a motor force from atmospheric orgone—i.e., orgone energy has been transformed into mechanical energy. The mechanical details must first be established. The manufacturers of the instrument and atomic physicists have declared that the highest rate achieved so far for atomic energy was 10 to 50 pulses per second. This means that orgone energy now works about four times as fast—in other words, it develops a much greater motor force.

I shall keep you up to date, and I ask you to take good care of this document for the time being. Please feel free to tell your coworkers about it. I shall probably publish a short report on the matter very soon. However, I do not yet know how to proceed. Should I develop the matter myself or hand it over to somebody else? I would be grateful for any good idea that you have.

14 August 1947

5–6 a.m. It is beginning to become clear to me that the reaction in the impulse counter has nothing to do with the mechanics of cosmic rays. *It is new:*

Orgone is capable of turning a wheel if a counter tube or similar instrument is so excited that an electromagnetic wheel rotates. It seems important that the electrons "excite" the orgone in the tube. It remains to be discovered whether the electrons or the orgone itself is the motor force.

I have simply transformed orgone into electrical energy. The impulse is a simple electromagnetic system.

9 a.m. Proof for orgone = motor force.

I killed the reaction by completely uncovering the counter tube. Reaction 0. As soon as the counter tube is placed in the accumulator or metal housing, the motor on the counter starts to run.

Tasks for orgone motor.

1. Does the orgone motor also work outside the metal-lined room,* with accumulator in the open air or in an orgone-free room?

2. What types of electromagnetic apparatus are caused to move?

3. How much can be eliminated from the structure of the Geiger-Müller without destroying the principle?

4. What are the conditions for obtaining a patent if a Geiger-Müller counter tube is used?

5. Can the motor force be increased, and how?

5 p.m.

I intended to send Washington to an electrophysicist in Boston but gave up the plan because I do not want to experience the animosity again.

I must go back into seclusion where I can think and breathe freely. I can manage this *by myself*—just as I've managed everything before. No one ever helped me.

---

*Reich refers to a room in the laboratory at Orgonon which was lined with metal as an accumulator.

T O   G L A D Y S   M E Y E R   W O L F E
❖ *14 August 1947*

My dear Mrs. Wolfe!

May I ask you not to try to investigate how "the proper people" could best be approached in the matter of my latest discovery. I have secured the phenomenon in today's early morning hours beyond any doubt as an effect of the orgone. I do not wish to expose this important fact to any misinterpretation by nuclear physicists who, as I am assured by Mr. Washington, would not understand anything at all. I prefer to wait and to investigate the matter in detail myself. It has been the fate and duty of orgone research to build its own bridges with its own means up till now, and I am afraid it will remain so for a long time to come.

I was just as excited the last few days about the practical and theoretical impact of the observation of a motor force in orgone energy, visualizing at once the vast consequences, as I was once, in 1936, when I saw the natural organization of protozoa and understood its importance for the understanding of the origin of the cancer cell.

I wish to thank you for your kind offer, once more!

15 August 1947

Neill arrived in New York yesterday. Will be coming to Orgonon tomorrow at noon. The man did not even have enough money to pay for a second-class ticket.

17 August 1947

Spoke with Neill for several hours. He hasn't changed but has no connection with my discovery, other than his belief in me.

20 August 1947

I gladly accept criticism from Neill, while I do not accept it from the little man. For the little man uses criticism of me to raise his own self-esteem and not to further the cause as Neill does.

28 August 1947

Mr. Wood* entered the Students' Laboratory, and when I asked him what he wanted, he said explicitly in approximately these words: "A friend of mine has shown me the article by Mildred Brady in *The New Republic*, and I wanted to look into this matter." I protested immediately and revealed the red fascist origin of the article to Mr. Wood.

Mr. Wood requested to see and was shown my personal academic papers, the numbers of the devices in the building—a thing which he had no right whatsoever to ask for—but when he asked about the matter of my conflict with Freud, I protested and refused to answer since it was none of the business of an administration which deals with foods, drugs, and cosmetics.

30 August 1947

At 4 p.m. Neill left to visit Hamilton. We were both very moved. A good friend was departing. He was bound for seclusion in England while I remained behind in my American isolation. I could joke with him and be natural. He too. We are fairly well agreed in our opinions on people. He despises man somewhat more than I, places less responsibility on him. Neill saw the orgone and comprehended it. On 9 September he will be giving a lecture on behalf of the institute at the New School for Social Research.

TO ARTHUR GARFIELD HAYS
❖ *1 September 1947*

Dear Mr. Hays:

Your office is handling some of the legal affairs of the Orgone Institute, and especially the application for tax exemption of the Orgone Institute Research Laboratories, Inc.

I am writing you this letter on a special matter. The enclosed document gives you some orientation on the following:

The orgone energy has been used up to now only in medical curative experiments with much satisfactory success. On 8 August 1947,

*Charles Wood, an inspector of the Federal Food and Drug Administration.

I discovered a motor force in this same energy. This important discovery has not only brought joy and satisfaction but also some tremendous worries to this laboratory. The reaction of the specific device called Geiger-Müller counter to a most simple and cheap orgone accumulator is twice and three times as fast as it is (according to publications and a communication from the manufacturer of the instrument) to an atomic energy pile. The implications of this fact are tremendous practically. The simplicity and low cost of the basic principle of obtaining a motor force constitutes the danger.

I don't know whether any private economic interests are involved in the utilization of atomic energy. Officially, only the state has the monopoly on atomic energy. Should the latter be the case, then there would be no danger in my discovery, since the State Department should be most interested in saving money. But, on the other hand, should any private capital have been invested in the exploitation of atomic energy, then I am sure that every attempt would be made to kill my discovery, since it means loss of much money to the investors.

I would appreciate it highly if you would be kind enough to function as the adviser in this matter, with the goal to make any move impossible which would tend (as it is so often done) to keep the discovery of the motor force in the orgone energy from becoming effective socially and economically.

I would also be most grateful if you were willing to help me to contact some person in the government who would be best suited to bring this discovery to the attention of the State Department.

I have forwarded the same legalized statement to my coworkers in various countries, and I intend to publish my discovery as soon as the basic controls have been carried through. I shall also apply for a patent as soon as these basic controls will be finished.

TO   A.   E.   HAMILTON
❧ *4 September 1947*

Dear Mr. Hamilton:

I think you are not quite right doing away with the orgone as a motor force as compared with the orgone as biological energy. A motor speaks the language which the present-day world understands, whereas biological energy is a quite new and unheard-of language. Thus, most probably the mechanical orgone motor will do its part to promote the biological effects of cosmic energy, and will force its general acceptance. Seen from this angle, the discovery which I made on 8 August 1947 is of extreme importance also for your and my child.

TO L. B. SZEKELY

6 September 1947

Dear Mr. Szekely,

Your letter of 24 August again contained some interesting news. There is only point on which I disagree with you: A purely formal language, such as that of mathematics, seems to me to fulfill its function in natural science only if it

1. can also base itself on empirical observations and experiments, and if it

2. does not lose contact with the subjects of everyday speech.

I believe that only when these two conditions are met can formal logic or mathematics be used as a natural scientific tool. If these two conditions are not met, the path will inevitably lead into a "shadow world" which one can easily mistake for the real world. In the last few decades we have seen the terrible example of the effects that can be achieved by higher mathematics pursued without vision. But I do agree with you that, while clinging to what is visible and tangible, we should strive toward more general and abstract symbolic formulations of our sensations. For example, it would have been an enormous risk to the development of orgonomy if we had tried to grasp functionalism in nature before direct observation had given us the rotating orgone envelope, the light phenomena in the dark, the loss of orgone in shrinking tissues, etc.

As I have written to you, theoretical orgonomy has already achieved fundamental formulations of "functional equations," and it will probably be interesting to follow closely to what extent these equations are compatible with the logistic attempts to define functionalism in nature. But, there is no question, and it must be clear to all of us working with functionalism, that we are in the process of making the breakthrough to the functional law of nature. That is certainly not just a major but also a highly responsible task.

Since I started my research in 1920, it has always been entirely clear to me that my work was dominated by an *objective logic* which at first could not be understood, and I felt I was its executive organ. Understanding this logic and rationality in the development of observations, working hypotheses, theories, and new findings in itself forms a major part of my research work. A harmony of subject and object, of observer and observed, that was based on some kind of law, seemed to consistently permeate this logic.

Dr. Hoppe will in the meantime have informed you that in August I succeeded in discovering a motor force in atmospheric orgone; on the Geiger-Müller counter, this force already produces twice the reaction of an atomic energy pile. So my research is slowly working its way through to the quantitative determination of orgone energy.

It has already been established beyond any doubt that fundamental errors of thought have occurred in classical physics when determining the natural constants. For example, many of the natural constants discovered by me reveal not only a statistically constant number that is related to Planck's constant, but also a variable number, the variation of which seems to follow some law. In other words, I am coming across natural events in which constancy and law-based variability, strict, almost mechanical regularity, and seemingly complete freedom are all blended into one.

❖ *7 September 1947*

New facts and ideas concerning the GM reaction:

1. The "clicks" are noises similar to the crackle in radio sets before thunderstorms.

2. The whitish orgone rays are miniature lightnings, discharges of the nebulous form of orgone.

3. There are not three types of orgone rays but only three different states of one type of orgone energy.

"Fog" concentrates into bluish dots or into yellow rays. Fog is the "matrix" of energy, which discharges in whitish rays, audible as cracks.

4. Orgone and electrical tension avoid each other or hunt each other away, depending on which is stronger.

5. The 750 threshold tension is hunting the orgone rays through the system; discharges them into electromagnetic system.

6. A lightning is concentrated orgone discharge.

7. A battery electrical current is again orgonotic charge in tight space.

TO OLA RAKNES
❖ 8 September 1947

Dear Dr. Raknes:

I received your letter of 31 August on Saturday, 6 September, and I sent a telegram to you yesterday, Sunday, asking you to postpone your experiments with the Oslo nuclear physicist. The legal document which I sent to you had merely the purpose to secure my priority of the discovery. It did not deal with any details. I was afraid that you might get entangled in irrational arguments on the part of the nuclear physicist who, as we know, does not understand anything about what is going on in an orgone accumulator. The main thing was that the counter tube has to soak itself full with orgone for many weeks; most probably in the presence of a special orgone metal room, in order to give the reaction which I achieved. I know that no nuclear physicist would go to the trouble to put up a metal room, to test the orgone for months and years, and to conduct Geiger-Müller experiments *on this background*. It is not as simple as putting a counter tube into the metal box. I did not find out yet, but I shall have to, whether the same reaction will be obtained without the presence of the metal room. My report, which I am writing down now and which will be published in a few months, will contain enough details to enable any unneurotic nuclear physicist to convince himself of the existence of the motor force.

As with most of my findings, there is also the tremendous implication involved that acknowledgment of this new phenomenon would overthrow a great deal of present-day assumptions concerning atomic energy. In short, it is too much at a time to be handled by one young, most innocent nuclear physicist alone. Please, understand that I only wanted to save you troubles.

The methods of thinking on the part of the atomic physicists and on the part of orgone physics are so basically different that we must be most careful with whom we are dealing, and, first of all, we must be very strict in not delegating any authority to anyone who did not work with orgone energy for years. To me, that seems the only way to keep our balance against the present overweight of so-called nuclear physics in the public eye. The firm assertion of our authority in matters of orgone energy, *and ours alone*, seems to me a matter of further existence or nonexistence of our science.

9 September 1947

I love Orgonon. The air is clear and pure. You don't put on weight the way you do in New York.

Neill gives his lecture today.

11 September 1947

Neill goes back to England full of America.

T O   A .   E .   H A M I L T O N
❖ *15 September 1947*

Dear Mr. Hamilton:

I regret that you are hesitating to write up Neill's lecture. Your critical comments on Neill's work will be most welcome. I believe in sharp differences of opinion in important matters.

I have not only nothing against your telling about the motor force in orgone energy, to whomever you wish, but, rather, it is in the interest of the work that this major event in the fight against atomic energy should be brought home to as many people as possible.

It will interest you to know that a new counter tube gives reaction at the pointer after only about five days' soaking of orgone energy. At present, there is no doubt anymore that the orgonotic motor force exists. It is "merely" a problem of developing it.

TO ARTHUR GARFIELD HAYS
❖ 16 September 1947

Dear Mr. Hays:

I thank you for your valuable information of 8 September. It will make it easier for me to proceed.

The difficulty of my whole position consists, however, in the fact that the cosmic orgone energy has been discovered by the consequent application of the natural-scientific energy principle *in the field of human emotions* over a period of nearly thirty years. In contradistinction to this approach to natural phenomena, the school of nuclear physicists started from investigation of dead matter—i.e., chemistry and electricity. The orgone physical and the nuclear physical approach from two opposite directions met finally in the reaction of the Geiger-Müller counter. But that does not eliminate the fact that the classical nuclear physicist is completely unaware and ignorant of those processes in nature which are specifically related to living matter. "Living matter" means here a physical reality and not a mystical concept. In other words, orgone physics is an entirely new branch of natural science, unknown to physics and astronomy, relying completely on its own methods of thinking and research. A nuclear physicist who would witness the reaction of the Geiger-Müller counter to a simple arrangement of metal and organic material, either would believe that the device has gone wrong or would suspect that I had an atomic pile hidden somewhere nearby. He would be utterly baffled at the reaction. Theory, method of thinking and work, and phenomena in orgone physics are foreign and strange to the electronic physicist. I found this out in a long discussion with Dr. Einstein some seven years ago.

This difficulty is hard to overcome, when such facts should be brought to the attention of the government through institutes of atomic or nuclear physics. It is impossible to delegate any authority in orgone research to nuclear physics. Orgone is natural energy *before* matter, atomic or nuclear energy is energy *after* matter or derived from matter. Thus, orgone is not nuclear energy, but primordial, cosmic energy. According to the definition of atomic energy by the Atomic Energy Commission, orgone does not fall under their regulations.

If you add to these purely factual discrepancies the hidden animosity and lack of mutual understanding between physics and biopsychiatry from where I come, if you add furthermore the effect of the previous defamation which was intended to kill my work, including the recent publicity, you will have a fairly clear picture of the complexity of the practical problem.

Therefore, I think it would be wise to publish a preliminary report on the efficiency of the orgone and to send this printed report on the Geiger-Müller effect to the institutes you mentioned, with the request to bring it to the attention of the government, thus avoiding the danger to submit orgone research to the wrong authority.

The most beneficial advice you gave seems to me the one to get in touch with the Franklin Institute, of the existence and function of which I did not know. It would be a great thing if some powerful agency would take over the task to put the medical and technical efficiency of orgone energy to widespread use.

It may or may not be possible for you to have the full view of the extent, complexity, and legal involvements of my work at the present time. There is no doubt that, sooner or later, legal protection of this branch of natural science will be badly needed. It would, therefore, be of great value if your office would be willing to receive communications from me concerning details of our social, scientific, and legal position, in the beginning without any concrete goal except to be put in files. It may prove important and necessary sometime later that a legal office, imbued with open-mindedness and frankness, should be in the possession of the relevant facts.

25 September 1947

For years governments remain deaf and dumb when it comes to publications on new discoveries and methods of healing. But they immediately prick up their ears when a single pestilent article is published.

❖ *27 September 1947*

I am preparing my building on the hill at Orgonon.* It will, or should be, the final building, homey and representative at the same time. *I feel at home again*, coming from a farm and ending on a farm. It should represent my work, my accomplishment. I am proud of it. And I hope it is proud of me.

❖ *28 September 1947*

Is a frame-up still possible?

❖ *29 September 1947*

Hanns Eisler did not have the courage to stand up against the communists and Stalin, although he was through with them. He is in the hands of the Un-American Activities Committee now. Will be deported.

Only truth can prevail, never the evasion, but only the complete truth.

1. The communists with their ideology, practice, and terror should be outfreedomed out of this world.

2. The Un-American Activities Committee in Washington does not know what it is talking about. It is the utterly wrong agency to deal with the communists. It does not understand who it fights. When Mrs. X was once a virgin and in the course of twenty years became a prostitute, her name is still Mrs. X., but she is no virgin anymore. Now, does the committee fight Mrs. X, or the virgin, or the prostitute? Which of these three does it fight? It doesn't know because it is a dried-out law agency which does not think concretely in terms of function and change. Do they mean to fight the intended true democracy of 1917 or the fascist present setup in Russia?

3. Would they regard me as a "communist"? I was in the Communist Medical Association, in the liberal Marxistenbund, in the

---

*The Orgone Energy Observatory, now open to the public as part of the Wilhelm Reich Museum.

Social Democratic Party at the same time. They contained half the German population.

4. The communists and the socialists are the most reactionary forces in present-day society.

5. The Americans mix up profit and free enterprise system.

6. I was persecuted by socialists and communists.

30 September 1947

The relationship of electricity to orgone is full of enigmas, but it is also pregnant with the future.

❖ 10 October 1947

They brought me into the public eye in America in a shabby way. I am going to stay in the public eye in a good way. I am going to make the American, French, and Russian constitutions of democracy come true.

I shall come out of hiding. I shall give back to Henry Wallace what is Wallace's, and to Parnell Thomas from New Jersey what is his, to the Russian dictators what is theirs.

And to the simple working people what is theirs. The working people should know everything. We shall fight for the freedom of the Russian press against the dictators, but also against American reaction.

T O   A R T H U R   G A R F I E L D   H A Y S
10 October 1947

Dear Mr. Hays:

I had some reports on the investigation by inspectors of the federal Food, Drugs, and Cosmetics Department, carried through at the offices of the Orgone Institute Press and some of our physicians. These reports gave me the impression that our work is being confused with some pornographic or similar type of activities. It is too bad that inspectors in such a responsible position are not capable of distinguishing between science and pornography, that they never heard the name of Sigmund Freud, and that they feel justified in asking hidden questions as, for instance, what kind of women we are employing or what we are doing with the women, etc. The implication is clearly that of indecent, smutty, pornographic behavior on our part. They should know with whom they are dealing. They seem to be disturbed by the insinuations in Miss Brady's article that the orgone accumulator gives the patient "orgastic potency." I wish it did, but it does not. But to the average human mind, used to the smutty sex activities going on everywhere, the term "orgastic potency" has a different meaning.

In the name of the many decent workers in our field, I would like to protest against such behavior on the part of government officials. Would you be kind enough to write a letter to this effect to the proper authority under which these inspectors act. They overstepped their rights by inquiring about things which had nothing whatsoever to do with the question about the nature of the orgone accumulator. The names of two of the inspectors were given to me as Mr. John Cain and Mr. Jackman. I enclose for your information a copy of a report from one of our physicians.

13 October 1947

Raknes told me that I care too much for other people. Probably. But if I did not care or had not cared, who else would have? I am afraid my caring is not adequately developed for the tasks ahead.

TO WALTER HOPPE
13 October 1947

Dear Dr. Hoppe,

As regards the Geiger-Müller experiments: This discovery has instantly placed me in an extremely difficult situation with the American Atomic Energy Commission. A law currently exists in America which automatically forbids the publication of facts that are even remotely related to atomic energy. I assert, correctly, that orgone energy is not atomic energy within the meaning of this law, because atomic energy is defined there as an energy which is obtained from the disintegration of atomic nuclei. In contrast, orgone energy is primordial energy before all matter. Although this distinction between primordial orgone energy and secondary atomic energy (*after* matter) is absolutely correct, I have no influence on whether the Atomic Energy Commission will regard the orgone energy as atomic energy or not. The fact that the orgone functions on the same apparatus as atomic energy, and with two to three times the force, might make the American government place my research under supervision. That would naturally also affect your work. The next steps which I shall undertake are as follows: I have written a provisional report on the Geiger-Müller reaction and will send it to the government via a lawyer, *before* I publish it. If the government decides that it has nothing to do with atomic energy, I shall publish the report. If, on the other hand, the government should decide that I am working with atomic energy, then it would be automatically recognizing the existence of orgone energy. That would be very advantageous, but how I would then continue to work practically is a major unsolved problem. I am at the moment not even sure whether I can send you the provisional report without coming into conflict with the law. You will hear more on this topic in a few weeks' time.

In the meantime, the Brady article in *The New Republic* has given birth to others. The essential details of the article have been further published in Switzerland, in Scandinavia, and also in America. By separate post I am sending you a copy of *Everybody's Digest*. Thus, without wanting it, we have been brought to the attention of a very broad public. Because of this, I am now forced to set up a public relations office in order to deal with the demands. You will also be on the list of this office.

Allen and Unwin have not yet printed the *Mass Psychology*, apparently because of the shortage of paper in England. It would be very advantageous if the German edition could be published. I have it all ready for printing. Could you help?

I believe that the twentyfold accumulator can be used without any hesitation to treat cancer, because there is no risk involved. The patients would die without it anyway.

In a few days' time I will make a gramophone recording of the Geiger-Müller reactions and send you one or two gramophone records so that you get some idea how the phenomenon works.

❖ *14 October 1947*

They say I have reached the summit of my life. I say the danger is greater than ever.

Will my life have to be sacrificed in order to save children and adolescents?

I am no Christ, but I *found* what was meant by Christ.

16 October 1947

The transition from the functional realm to the mechanical realm is probably caused by the condition of the orgone. Primordial orgone is nebulous. Flashing rays are concentrated orgone.

TO WILLIAM B. WASHINGTON (TELEGRAM)
❖ *18 October 1947*

Refuse all information on unpublished orgonometric material to anybody. Nobody has a right to investigate unpublished science matters.

Also be clear in mind about the fact that the investigating public servant is *not* THE government. He is only a minor official who may or may not have his own irrational motives as we all do.

Is American society ready to absorb the orgone? If not, I shall go down. But I want to go down fighting. What I had to say should be widely known, right or wrong. I must not be transmitted to posterity as a charlatan or brothel keeper or spy or schizophrenic or adulterer, etc. In the name of our children *and* their children, understand this!

❖ *20 October 1947*

I am sleepless: This terrible responsibility. And no one can give me advice.

I could do with the world what I wanted if I were a politician, if I knew how to use power.

I shall not send the paper on Geiger-Müller to the Atomic Energy Commission. I shall only inform Lilienthal of the facts and their impact; warning against complacency, telling about my previous attempts, and refusing to take responsibility for what might develop out of my research. Whether orgone could destroy or detonate atomic bombs I do not know.

It means putting myself under the fist of the military.

It means possible seclusion. It means the wrath of the dictators. It means not making, possibly, the right decision between personal safety and the health and future of mankind.

Can it be developed from the U.S.A? Through the American government? Or through the American people? Shall I write to the American people? Would a press conference and telling the public do the job?

I should ask nobody for advice, especially not Wolfe. They are enmeshed in the question of personal security. To let a scientific "bomb" explode suddenly would be one way. To change the responsibility for the fight against Russian dictatorship from the Parnell Thomases to the true democrat would mean the victory of democracy, truth, and freedom.

I feel too small for this terrific job.

———

Yesterday I went to buy a carpet. The man who showed me around asked for my name and address. When I told him my name, he was flabbergasted: "You are not *the* Wilhelm Reich, are you, who wrote *The Function of the Orgasm?*" "I am." He took my hand and shook it. "There was never a book I studied more thoroughly than this one," he said.

TO   WALTER   HOPPE
21 October 1947

Dear Dr. Hoppe,

I am struggling with the problem of whether or not I should submit my publication on the Geiger-Müller reaction to the Atomic Energy Commission. The conflict is one between personal safety and interest in the cause, as well as in the public influence which this discovery gives me. I tend toward accepting the risk of incurring a heavy penalty and not to make my discovery known. My friends here are against that approach. I had intended to send you a manuscript on this. I myself am very concerned that the Geiger-Müller reaction could develop military consequences and perhaps fall into the hands of the Russian dictators. I have decided to send you the manuscript, but I must ask you to keep it secret for the time being and possibly only to tell Szekely about it. Please be very careful. Life-and-death decisions are involved, not only for us personally but for all mankind. Under no circumstances should the Russian dictators get their terribly bloody hands on this discovery.

Another major difficulty is the clearly unscientific attitude that has been adopted by Einstein and which is blocking the way to finding a rational solution to this question.

27 October 1947

Once again there are great decisions to be made in my life. The people around me are stagnating while I must press ahead, onward. I must adhere closely to the core of the issue. The train is not to blame that the station remains behind. Stagnation represents a great tragedy for a creative individual.

I often wonder whether the Americans really are great or whether they are petty bourgeois. Are they as great morally as they are technologically?

I sent my research papers to the Franklin Institute in Philadelphia and they have forwarded them to a biochemist.

It is always on an intellectual level that the conflicts take place.

I occasionally ask Ilse whether it is really true that people live the way they do, a dull day-to-day routine in idle talk, doing and thinking nothing, just barely existing. The words "just barely" mean a great deal in Germany today.

How correct Nietzsche is! A creative individual must not allow himself to be swept away by pity.

TO ARTHUR GARFIELD HAYS
❖ *27 October 1947*

Dear Mr. Hays:

I am sending you by separate mail a set of documents concerning data and facts of my discovery of orgone energy. Would you be kind enough to keep them on file, according to our previous agreement.

I have decided not to make any report to the government on the special Geiger-Müller reaction, but shall forward to the Atomic Energy Commission all the material published so far on the orgone energy. I would like to put the following reasons for doing so on file:

1. As you may see from the documents which I am sending you, I have tried for many years and in many places to convey the importance of the orgone energy to responsible government agencies and authorities:

The Patent Office
The National Research Council
The War Department
The Library of Congress
Dr. Albert Einstein

2. The main facts have been published for years. They are at hand for everybody who wishes to look them up, and the Geiger-Müller reaction does not bring anything especially new, except a most powerful confirmation of the *existence* of an all-pervading and most powerful cosmic force.

3. I have not encountered any military possibilities in orgone energy. Should I encounter anything of this kind, I would keep it secret and not reveal it to any government, because killing human beings is killing, whoever does it. Should anybody else discover any such military possibilities (which is utterly doubtful), then he could do so already on the basis of the facts published hitherto.

4. I do not wish to expose my discovery again to the wrong statements of scientists who are not authorities in my field.

5. Only government-supported universities and laboratories are bound to report their findings. Should I be wrong in this point, I would appreciate correction.

6. My scientific position forces me to maintain my scientific conclusion that orgone energy, being primordial, preatomic energy, is

something completely different from the "atomic energy" according to the definition of the Atomic Energy Commission. I refer to my letter of 16 September regarding this point.

I shall not publish the Geiger-Müller finding for a long time to come. I would inform you immediately should any change take place until such a publication occurs. As agreed before, I shall write letters to your office concerning certain facts, without any other intention but to have statements on file, thus counteracting any possible future frame-up from wherever it may come.

TO WALTER HOPPE
28 October 1947

Dear Dr. Hoppe,

I have long wondered whether I should involve you in the following matter and I decided that it would be advantageous if you were informed and gave your opinion:

My experience with the emotional plague over what is now almost thirty years has not left me totally unscathed internally. In the summer of 1946, after some serious soul searching, I finally described my inner situation in a "Speech to the Little Man." I had not intended to publish this speech. It was simply a way of working off my inner grief at the situation of the little man. This summer, Neill read the manuscript and he was just as enthusiastic about it as some other close friends. Whoever has read the manuscript so far, with one exception, is convinced that it should be published. I myself am emotionally too much involved in this speech to be able to reach a responsible judgment. Since Neill is currently translating it into English and its publication is a problem that faces me, I would like to get your opinion, as that of a close coworker. The following questions should be answered:

1. Does my speech tell the truth?

2. Would it be harmful or beneficial to our cause to make this truth generally known?

3. I feel that I am personally in great danger and sooner or later might, or will be, the victim of a "frame-up." Is that objectively cor-

rect? I base my feeling on my knowledge of the infinitely deep, sadistic brutality that has been inserted into the armor of a human being, between his natural decency and his external actions. This opinion would sound paranoid to many of my opponents, but it is rationally supported by the experience, persecution, and defamation suffered so far, and it is an opinion that is shared by outstanding coworkers such as my wife, Wolfe, Neill, and others.

4. Should the "Speech to the Little Man" be published without regard for any external circumstances?

5. Should it be printed and distributed only to my closest coworkers?

6. Should it be held in readiness for broad publication in the event of a catastrophe?

Over the years, it has become increasingly clear to me that the possibility of a massive frame-up must be averted. It is my intention to write a very popular book for the general public which will set straight the major misunderstandings and distortions. The "Speech" could appear as the conclusion of this book.

28 October 1947

Atomic energy is malicious, a danger to life. A clever psychological interpretation would yield the following analogy:

The primordial orgone forms matter and then finds itself imprisoned therein. It becomes brutal like any prisoner and when it breaks out of the prison it murders. However, when it can function freely in the atmosphere it has a *healing* effect.

Every psychological theory on the destructive forces in the human being has deep roots here.

TO ERNESTINE H. KETTLER *
❖ *30 October 1947*

Dear Mrs. Kettler:

I read your letter of 12 October with great interest. I can assure you that the worries which bother you are the same that bother me. I am here, and it is my function to help clarify issues the best I can. Please don't hesitate to call upon me whenever you think that I could help you. I am shutting my time only to the many nuisance requests which are coming in, but never to important discussions.

I believe that you grasped the gist of the problem: the emotional block within the mass individual which prevents him from making rational decisions. This is to my conviction the basic problem and issue of our times. Whoever helps to clarify the means to overcome this structural block in a practical way—in other words, to promote the ability of man to proceed from ideas and theories to truth and rational self-government—is a true scientific revolutionary. On the other hand, I also believe that whoever refuses to recognize this most important stumbling block in social progress, whoever he may be, a fascist who thrives on it, a red fascist who obfuscates this issue by politics, a liberal who believes in the absolute rationality of mass opinion, etc., etc., is in practical terms a foe of progress.

I would like to know more concretely about the structure and the personalities of your intellectual working group. Should it have any affiliation with or should it in any way defend the methods of the Russian dictatorship, I would have to withdraw my cooperation. This is based on the clear fact that the Russian dictatorship has as much to do with the intellectual accomplishment of Karl Marx as the present-day church has to do with the original teachings of Christ. The divergence of the true teachings of great men, and the typical divergence in its later mass interpretation and practice, is again due to the fact that the emotionally blocked mass individual is incapable of penetrating to the substance of those teachings and making them work practically. This is a tremendous problem of mass psychology

---

*A woman interested in the disintegration of the Russian Revolution and Reich's understanding of the importance of the subjective factor in the success or failure of such movements.

and social development which has existed for thousands of years and has devastated every single human endeavor to establish freedom and peace on this earth.

I do not believe that the ideas have been inadequate, but that the average human structure, blocked off from its natural rationality, as it is, is bound to distort the true ideas and is incapable of distinguishing the correct from the wrong in these ideas and, accordingly, of developing the timely and rational and eliminating the untimely and irrational.

I am glad to know that there is a group of people who fight for clarity. Every single clear thought is worth more today than ten atomic bombs.

TO   SIMEON   J.   TROPP
❖ 30 October 1947

Dear Dr. Tropp:

This letter is referring to our discussion yesterday about the problem connected with the Food and Drug Administration. To begin with, I would like to stress the responsibility involved in your task as a part of our total endeavor: Millions of human lives are depending on whether or not the Food and Drug Administration will act rationally or irrationally in this matter. What we have to avoid by all means is that some biopathic individual, be it a doctor or not, at the Administration pronounces his verdict authoritatively, without any basis in knowledge and fact. Such fake statements by wrong "authorities" have been made very often in the past. If Einstein has admitted his ignorance in our facts, then we are entitled to doubt from the beginning the competence of an average government employee in such a new and important discovery. May I, in the following, suggest ways of procedure point by point, as outlined to you yesterday:

1. We would not permit any testing of the accumulator if it would be done without the cooperation of one of our doctors.

2. We would not carry on any discussions with nonscientific employees of the Food and Drug Administration, but only with medical men and open-minded scientists.

3. Before any testing can take place, we would have to know who will be doing the testing, what will be tested, and on what kind of diseases the tests will be done.

We are not afraid of any tests. Our facts are firmly established. I was not afraid to let Einstein test the orgone accumulator. But I am afraid of possible "dead cats" in the biological sense, commissar or not commissar. Thus we would have to test the tester first. Please, be on your guard on whether you are dealing with the pest reaction according to our definition of the emotional pest, or whether you are dealing with an honest and rational attempt on the part of the representatives of the government to find out the truth about the accumulator as to its efficiency.

4. Be on guard against the possible danger of background influence of the chemical industry which is endangered by the discovery of the orgone energy as to profits.

5. Please make sure and establish this condition in a perfectly clear way that we would not enter any discussions on the orgone accumulator if the facts which have been gathered during the past four years, especially Dr. Hoppe's in Palestine, would not be taken into consideration. Please, be careful to watch the usual human attitude which will most promptly disregard the opinions of those who worked with the accumulator and only pay attention to those who know nothing about it.

6. It should be kept clearly in mind that the Food and Drug Administration did not pay any attention for many years to our clear-cut and extensive publications, but that it found interest in the accumulator instantly when a neurotic woman wrote a slanderous article about my work.

7. It would be most helpful to get statements from our doctors who worked with the orgone accumulator, especially from Dr. Hoppe, who worked with it most extensively, and to have our records on hand.

I would be only glad and would rejoice in the name of all the sick people who could benefit from the widespread use of the accumulators if the testing by the Administration would be made in a rational manner—i.e., not according to their idea of what radiation is, or to the idea of a biochemist or a nuclear physicist, but according to the facts established by orgone research, and published so far in our literature. I mean, especially and foremost, the latest, the Geiger-Müller reaction. Please, make it perfectly clear to the *proper* medical official that I would fight any irrational approach to this most burning problem of science tooth and nail. The one who in the name of the government will undertake the testing will have to prove that he believes in our honesty and that he is willing to accept our advice as to the ways and means of working with this type of energy which is completely unknown to official science.

If I may be permitted to give a last advice: Don't be impressed by the fact that it is a state administration which wants to test the device. Rely on what you know and establish your own authority. The moment we crawl, we are lost. When we maintain our facts and our dignity, we should be able to eliminate the irrational danger spots which are automatically involved with the nature of the orgone energy itself.

❖ *2 November 1947*

It is astonishing that the world of science and natural philosophy can overlook the following problem:

1. One speaks of reason as being the goal of human efforts of development.

2. One condemns nature, life, the sexual, the instinctual as *"böse,"* "animal-like," devilish.

3. Reason should conquer the base instincts. But: *Where* is this reason working, functioning? Not in the air! The answer: Reason is the uttermost expression of innermost biological laws of functioning. Nature is basically rational. There is nothing more rational than the functioning of the universe. There is nothing irrational in it, *except in man.*

We must go back to nature if we want reason.

❖ *3 November 1947*

Shall I limit myself to orgonomy or branch out into all literary directions. I feel the inner urge to write, to write in English and to tell my contemporaries how and what I feel.

7 November 1947

Have begun construction of an orgone motor.

❖ *9 November 1947*

I must study electron tubes, for they are opening up a new world for me. The orgone in the electron tube.

That is the way of great science! I found five years ago the functional identity of body orgone and secondary coil orgone. Now I could eliminate all high tension from the Geiger-Müller counter. The "wheel turns" without high tension

    a. when I touch a battery with my hands,

    b. when I let a secondary coil system be excited.

❖ *17 November 1947*

I used to stick in rotten situations for long times before extracting myself. Eva tells me she had a hard fight with her mother the end of this summer. Her mother, Annie, told her my whole idea of the orgone was a delusion, that I am paranoiac. Eva fought with her but did not convince her of her irrationality. All people, Annie said, who believed in the orgone were "hypnotized" by me, Eva included. She warned Eva not to follow me into "badness."

And with this I lived for twelve years.

I tried to convince Eva, who has my inclination for exaggerated loyalty, to watch out in her life. Not to get stuck. To have more loyalty to her own tasks and obligations, to her own talents and her own future. To imagine what would have happened if I had followed the rulings of "homo normalis" to stick to the rotten family. I would not have discovered the orgone. To imagine the damage done to man. To imagine how many people, children, youth, etc., are being broken this way by such characters. But it still hurts to hear such messages. It hurts to know of such an irrational, cowardly attitude of a woman who once loved me and, because of her warped structure, could not follow, had to be dropped. But it still hurts, not because she was my wife, but because she is a human being, and because I would like so very much to hate her, but can only despise her.

❖ *18 November 1947*

Peter is disturbed lately; cries much at home when tired. Apparently no contact with mother. Feels she does not love him really. He suffered from lack of genital play during the summer and he developed a block in breathing and a throat tic. Children cannot grow up healthy in this way. I am disturbed in my work by Peter. Peter is disturbed by our work.

❖ *19 November 1947*

Last night the U.S.A. held a common town meeting on the air with Berlin. The Germans were very excited. So was I. The thing was grand and full of the future. Imagine such international town meetings without the political background. Without political misuse of human needs!

Why is that not possible now, right now, here and there?! What a grand experience to hear two peoples communicating and listening to each other over the air. That's what radio is for!

❖ *20 November 1947*

I listened last night to the marriage of Princess Elizabeth in London. I had the feeling of a *perfectly crazy* performance, not so much on the part of the princess as on the part of the public.

This need for worshipping is, in this form, perverse. They scream for the sake of screaming. They would tomorrow scream the same way at somebody else.

There seems to be an absolute despising of women in such performances. An indignity of thinking. Even an indecency in exposing the sexual union to such an extent and degree. That so many Americans become entangled in this spectacle is really un-American.

———

The mass individual gets stuck because of his armor. Whether in the Christian belief, in some scientific opinion, in a political belief —he always gets stuck and bogged down in mechanized functioning. So the Russian way of life of today is the mechanized idea of anti-capitalism of a hundred years ago; so in America the making of money is the mechanized idea of becoming rich in a virgin country. Cultivation of land became exploitation of land.

TO   JULIAN   C.   CULVER *
❖ *20 November 1947*

Dear Mr. Culver:

I am stuck in my operations in orgone research because of uncertainty in the following matter:

It was necessary for more than fifteen years now, in order to provide the necessary money for the research work, to let a part of the money earned through my personal work go untaxed directly to the Orgone Research Fund. This money is not used for any personal purposes, but solely for construction of research facilities and current expenses for research. My policy was this: I need for personal living a certain sum per year, at present about $15,000, which money is being taxed fully. I could earn twice as much easily, if I had not to put in so much unpaid time for experiments, writing, and unpaid-for consultations. To earn this personally needed amount, I would have to put in three hours' work daily. When the need for money for research comes up, I am putting in more working hours as personal, unpaid service for the Fund. This money goes to the Fund directly as a loan in the form of services, with the intention of paying the tax due for this money when and only when the Fund will be in a position to repay these services in cash.

Another procedure is this: Physicians studying with me are gladly paying $50 to $100 per hour, because it puts them in a much better earning position in their own practice. In some cases, when the Orgone Research Fund needs money, I take for myself only, say, $30 per teaching lesson, and the other $20 goes to the Orgone Research Fund, untaxed, with the same provision as mentioned above, to be taxed when repaid to me by the Fund.

What I would like to know is whether the tax authorities would object to this. If they would object, my main counterargument would be that I do not have to work five hours a day in order to obtain my personal living expenses. The surplus time I am putting in is done for nonprofit purposes.

Would you please be kind enough to let me know whether there is any possible objection or even danger, in case of an attempted

---

*An attorney in Arthur Garfield Hays's law office.

frame-up, to this procedure, which is absolutely necessary if orgone research should be kept going.

I would like to stress the point that my discoveries would not have been possible so far if I had not provided the necessary money in the described manner. May I also stress the other point that the will that I have written proves sufficiently clearly that in the end no personal interests are involved. Do you think that any malicious frame-up could use such arrangements for an indictment for tax fraud? I have to emphasize that some aspects of my discoveries are hated deeply in some places and that the danger of a frame-up is real and great. This is corroborated by factual happenings in the course of twenty-five years.

❖ *22 November 1947*

The last galleys before printing of my cancer book came today. *The Cancer Biopathy* goes to print next week.

Good luck to it—in the name of all dying from sex starvation.

———

My lawyer's assistant said today by telephone that working for a true honest research fund—i.e., letting money you could quite legally take for yourself go to research purposes—is very dangerous if one has bitter enemies.

There are laws which fit the multitude or for protection against the cheater, but not the great task. If I had not let some money go to the Fund the cancer scourge would not have been uncovered.

All such things are "dangerous."

❖ *27 November 1947*

I wonder about the Midwest of the U.S.A. Different human beings?

Should I step into the open, into the masses?

Am I sitting like a crab on its hind legs? Should I wait for invitations to lecture or arrange them myself? West Coast wanted lectures. There is this deadly deadlock between people's wanting and not being capable of doing.

I must wait until they come to me, socially, and not only sexolog-
ically.

28 November 1947

Danger.
Karl Frank* just told me that Mildred Brady's husband is a communist, and Wertham also.
This miserable pack of political hounds should be driven out by
force.

❖ 29 November 1947

This will either make me or break me. If they give me a clean bill
of goods it means the existence of the orgone is recognized. I'll either
be denounced as a swindler or acclaimed as the greatest scientist of
the century.

T O   A R T H U R   G A R F I E L D   H A Y S
❖ 29 November 1947

Dear Mr. Hays:
I wish to stress the fact that *the slandering article by Miss Brady
was the beginning of a chain reaction set into motion, beyond any
doubt, by communist quarters.* The husband of Miss Brady is a communist.
In *Collier's* of 6 December 1947, on page 25, Henderson and Shaw
succeeded in not only taking over wrong statements from the Brady
article, but to condense twelve wrong statements, several of them
libelous, in twenty-nine lines.
I am mentioning only one of these twelve wrong statements: "The
orgone and the accumulator can lick anything from cancer to the
common cold, according to Reich." *Not only did I never say or claim
such a thing, but on the contrary, I have warned explicitly in my writings against such statements.* This statement puts me down in the

---

*A New York man who had contacted Reich regarding his interest in entering the field
of psychotherapy as a psychologist.

eyes of the readers as a faker in cancer therapy. This does not only damage my reputation, and therefore the reputation of all physicians who work with me, but it is also a criminal action in regard to the sick people who depend on our work and our help.

I think that a libel suit is necessary in order to put matters straight and to put an end to this pestilent chain reaction.

It may also interest you that two of our physicians found the galley proof of my forthcoming book *The Cancer Biopathy* in the hands of one physician who has nothing whatsoever to do with us and is not entitled to have these galley proofs. We could not find out how he got them and he refused to say.

I would like to suggest that you write a letter in my name to the editors of *Collier's*, demanding that they print, in a prominent place and not somewhere hidden, a correction of these wrong statements. Should they refuse to do so, they will be sued for libel in court.

30 November 1947

Mickey Sharaf recently remarked to Bill Washington that my case seemed like a repetition of the inquisition of the sixteenth century. This is true. A chain reaction of events has begun:

the Wertham article
the Brady article
the Food and Drug Administration investigation
Collier's magazine
and more will follow.

It was not without reason that I wrote *Listen, Little Man!* and drew up my will.

Complete victory cannot be close at hand. People are too tired, too sick for that; science is too muddled and the governments too murderous.

The fact that this situation has been caused by communists and progressives is part of the tragedy of our age.

I may be mistaken but I do not think they will be able to allow the orgone to prevail without destroying themselves.

TO ARTHUR GARFIELD HAYS
❖ 1 December 1947

Dear Mr. Hays:

My research laboratory had reports from users of the orgone accumulator and from scientific coworkers that some of the investigators of the Food and Drug Administration not only do not know what they are dealing with, but that they imply by direct and indirect questions and statements that they are making the investigation on the suspicion of some kind of *vice* activities, secret brothels, and the like.

It is quite obvious that these investigators are only used to handle swindlers in the drug manufacturing business against impotence. They cannot think in other than pornographic terms. They are, therefore, unfit to investigate such a tremendous fact as the cosmic orgone energy. We must protest most emphatically against such misuse of authority and such ignorance and damaging behavior on the part of officials who are supposed by the Constitution to be the servants of the people. We are resolved to take all necessary and possible legal steps to stop this behavior of ignorant and apparently malicious officials. The emotional pest does not halt at the door of state officials. If that were not so, we would live in a paradise and not in hell as we actually do. We refuse to cooperate further with them—as we were ready to do in the past—if they do not stop immediately this kind of procedure. It is *life-important* for the sake of the mentally and physically sick that action be taken immediately against this snowballing of defamation which was started, as we now definitely know, in communist quarters on the West Coast. It is most serious to appraise fully the fact that the long-expected attempts at a frame-up are being made by communists and Catholics in unison. The galley proof of my forthcoming cancer book in the hands of a Catholic psychiatrist in a state hospital is quite an event in this direction.

Being for prevention rather than for cure in all life situations, we feel that we should not permit any further development of this action of the emotional pest.

Would you be kind enough to reach your own opinion in this

matter on the basis of the forwarded material and to inform us through Mr. Culver about it.*

We are preparing a list of all universities, libraries, scientific personalities and organizations which have been subscribers of our literature. It might be helpful to appraise the support we enjoy in the public.

I would like to add that I am an ardent fighter for civil liberties, and, therefore, a member of the Civil Liberties Union.

2 December 1947

I return to Nietzsche over and over, to this man of wide knowledge and great suffering. His fate was to suffer for all mankind because of what he sensed, but did not understand. He even knew of the kernel of kindness buried under the block of ice.

In this matter I also return to myself again and again, to my old, sad, suffering, creative self. That is where I find my real being. At other times I live behind various masks, the "teacher," the "politician," the "leader." But in essence it is all one pulsating totality. A totality whose energy formula I found.

T O   A L L   U S E R S   O F   T H E   O R G O N E
A C C U M U L A T O R †
❖ *3 December 1947*

Dear Friend:

The Food and Drug Administration is in charge of investigating all devices which go out into the public and deal with health. This

---

*The lawyer advised Reich: "If you could sue a person for libel for what he *thinks* of you, you could do it; but the writer of this article cannot be sued for libel, she was clever enough to avoid a libel suit."

†This letter, undoubtedly written by Reich, was sent on the letterhead of the Orgone Institute Research Laboratories, Inc., and signed by Ilse Ollendorff as Administrative Assistant Director.

is, of course, a very important and necessary function of society. Unfortunately, there is so much swindling around in the realm of health measures, especially in sexual matters, that the officers of the Administration find it difficult to distinguish between our work and pornography and vice. Therefore, they began the investigation of the orgone accumulator with the suspicion of vice.

We would like to assure you that we refused to conform with the unjustified request of the investigators to give them the names of the subscribers to our literature and the users of the orgone accumulator. By some means, not our fault, they got hold of some names. We have, of course, nothing to hide, but since some of these investigators are unable to distinguish between medical attempts to establish a healthy love life and pornographic vice, we cannot cooperate with them, as we did, fully and eagerly in the beginning. We shall cooperate again to the fullest extent with this Administration, as soon as we are sure that they have stopped this type of investigation which is damaging to the reputation of this laboratory as well as to yours. An investigation under such suspicion in itself is sufficient to do damage, human structures and ways of thinking being what they are.

Would you be kind enough, in case an investigator should come to you, to cooperate with him to the utmost as far as information about your experiences with the orgone accumulator are concerned. But we would like to advise you to refuse to answer any questions concerning your private or sexual life, because this is not within the realm of their investigation.

The orgone accumulator does not, as you well know, create sexual excitement, but it solely increases the general biological energy level of the organism. It cannot provide orgastic potency as the slanderous article by Miss Brady in *The New Republic* of 28 May 1947 maliciously stated. Unfortunately, this wrong statement was taken over blindly by irresponsible writers in other publications.

We would appreciate it highly if you would cooperate with the Orgone Institute Research Laboratories, Inc., in this matter, in the interest of safeguarding the possibilities for human health by means of the orgone accumulator. We wish to assure you that we shall protect you and your moral and personal integrity to the utmost and by all legal means at our disposal as citizens of the United States.

My dear Mr. Hays:

I know very well that I am an embarrassing fact in this proper society of ours. I do not deny it. I ask too many embarrassing, simple questions and my influence is great and widespread. Previous experiences taught me that the emotional pest, in whatever form, would do *anything* to destroy my work and me. I know this sounds paranoiac. But "paranoia" means the *delusion* of persecution and not the fight against real evil. I have dared to question the rationality in the behavior of "homo normalis."

Psychoanalysts in Vienna already had accused me of letting my children watch intercourse, when I came out with the necessity of safeguarding infantile genitality. Later, rumors went around that I seduced my patients. A few years ago, a psychiatric editor fantasied in an article about me that I was held on "charges of immorality" on Ellis Island, which was not true. The editor corrected his statement publicly with regrets.

Some psychoanalysts who hated me—one of them because he was jealous without serious reason about his wife, who liked me—declared me schizophrenic. This rumor was spread throughout the world and I had to fight hard to get rid of this defamation.

Then I was held in custody by the FBI in 1941 on suspicion of being a German (or Russian) spy.

During the past few months I heard, nearly once every week from several sources, that I had died. That means there are people who wish I were dead.

I visited you some three years ago asking your advice because the head physician of the Norwegian army had told people in Europe that I was put away in a lunatic asylum in America. You advised against a libel suit at that time.

Now there are many serious indications that the attempt is being made to kill my work by the charge of vice. Now, I confess to be ticklish on such accusations because the pornography is not of my doing but somebody else's.

Let us test this assumption of mine. Only if you learn to understand the reasoning of what I termed the "emotional pest" will you be able to assist me in the oncoming flood of mud. Only then shall we be safe and shall we beat the pest.

I and a few of my students who went through it all again and again understood the danger we were in. But even I, the most experienced of all, did not dream of a vice charge until this morning when a few facts could be put together into one understandable process. We must do two things separately to meet the danger and to safeguard my work by putting an end to such sneaky attacks.

We must clearly understand the background and reasoning out of which the emotional pest acts. We must be able to identify ourselves with the emotionally sick individual to follow him in his ways of reasoning. Unfortunately, large and impressive organizations are reasoning along these lines, as for instance most sections of the church with their absolute and pernicious demands for premarital and adolescent chastity.

We must put together the facts which make sense only from the background of the emotional life and sexual ways of the emotionally sick individual.

As I have so often pointed out in my writings, the moralistic attitude and the actions of the emotional plague have their rational roots in the actually pornographic ways of sexual living of many people of the lower as well as the higher strata of society. This is what sex economy fights as "pornography" not by another morality, but by the healthy, natural, and, seen from a basic biological standpoint, self-regulating morality. The moralistic world has for thousands of years, especially since the beginning of early patriarchy, suppressed the natural genital drives; it has thus created the "secondary" or perverse and pornographic drives, and was then forced to build up a wall of moralistic, hygienically disastrous laws and rules against the same pornographic human mind which was first created by the suppression of natural sexuality. Thus, the natural and the pornographic came to find themselves in the same pot together, mixed and undistinguished from each other. *The same laws of suppression were now working against natural love and against the truly immoral, unnatural, and pornographic sex activities.*

This is quite an essential point: *Consequently, every person who advocates the natural laws of love life will be looked upon by the emotional pest as pornographic, sinful, etc., etc., according to their own way of living and thinking.* As a matter of fact, the average individual who is not sexually healthy will of necessity himself despise any genital act as smutty. I must refer to our clinical material for details.

I am advocating the natural healthy way of sexual living, as the basic element of mental hygiene, for children and adolescents, and calling a relationship "marriage" when a couple, even without a marriage license, is factually husband and wife for no other than rational and hygienic reasons. For this, I shall most probably be arrested on a charge of vice, since, in the mind of the individual or group which mixes up the perverted and the natural love life, I am logically a man who advocates and practices vice.

This point is the crux of the whole matter; everything else depends on clearly understanding this point. Every misunderstanding or suspicion which comes up in any procedure or discussion, defamation, or hate, is deriving from this point in the average human structure. To know this, to handle it rationally, means not only to fight any such charges but what is much more important: to make the world understand one of its worst dilemmas, its sorest spot. No truly honest and effective mental hygiene movement will ever come about or succeed without this essential point of view. The dangers involved in such a scientific attitude explain why nearly the whole psychiatric world does not touch upon this sorest spot, the genital love life of children and adolescents, except lately in the past couple of years, due to our efforts.

Nobody wants to get into situations as I did again and again. To conform to the present-day ways of living and thinking requires first of all defamation and neglect of genital love life, which in the unconscious and by the mystics is looked upon as criminal if lived for the sake of sexual gratification. Therefore, if the Catholic Church, or any other agency depending on the ideology which suppresses the natural love life of children, adolescents, and unmarried people, could prove that I am a kind of secret brothel keeper, they could succeed in smashing the most advanced movement in mental hygiene. As a matter of fact, a physicist, Sergei Feitelberg, who is close to hostile psychoanalysts, once called me a secret brothel keeper in a private gathering. The witness is Mrs. Elizabeth Badgeley.

Now let us put some facts together which by themselves or without this context make no sense at all:

1. Dr. Baker and Dr. Raphael* from Marlboro State Hospital found the galley proofs of my forthcoming book *The Cancer Biopathy* in the hands of a Catholic psychiatrist. Another Catholic psychiatrist, Dr. Penetaro, has in New Jersey openly declared his hostility. Dr. Mohare refused to tell how he got the galley proofs.

2. Reverend Wilkins from New Jersey reported that an examiner, Mr. Jackman, told him, when asked why the investigation is being made, that there was or is the suspicion of vice activities in the case.

3. Mr. William Washington, a mathematician at Harvard University who helps me in astrophysical calculations, was visited by the first investigator from Maine. He asked him whether he had an orgone accumulator. Washington said that he had not. Thereupon the officer told him that he most probably did not need one "since he was not married"—i.e., a married person needs the orgone accumulator to excite himself for sexual pleasure—vice.

4. In the Orgone Institute Press, the clerk was asked several times where she lived, what she did in the evening, and such questions which indicated that we were under suspicion of vice. The implication of a kind of vice activity was clear enough.

It is a matter of medical and clinical record, of great experience, that the armored individual, the one abstaining from a natural love life, is unable to tolerate the *healthy* manifestations of nature. But in the interest of human health, an end must be put to such social misconduct of ascetics who want to foist their way of life on others. As long as governments and the responsible social agencies will not make laws to that end, intolerance, frame-up actions—in short, pestilential behavior—will chronically poison our lives. I have said so in speech and writing many times for decades. I never hid my opinion on these matters of human mental hygiene. It is characteristic of the emotional structure of the emotionally sick individual that he will typically evade an open direct standpoint in these matters. I do not believe that any representative of this ideology would dare to meet me in the open forum. He would have most of the population against him. For he prevails with his damaging behavior only as long as the issues are not in the open, as long as the confusion prevails between pornography and vice on the one hand and the natural demand of

*Elsworth F. Baker, M.D., and Chester M. Raphael, M.D., students of Reich's.

the organism on the other. Therefore, it is typical of these individuals and organizations that they dodge open discussion and resort to defamation, to frame-ups for alleged vice activities, or tax evasion, or similar criminal actions. Nobody has ever done anything against, or considered as criminal the socially damaging effects of such behind-the-back smears. How many human lives have been smashed up that way, I don't have to tell you.

I chose you, Mr. Hays, as my lawyer against a possible and most probable frame-up because you seem to realize that "human nature" has something to do with such cases and criminal injustices as have been described in your book *Trial by Prejudice*. What I add to this correct attitude is a huge body of psychiatric, medical, and natural scientific knowledge to show that what is vaguely called "human nature" is a most complicated, emotionally as well as socially involved, unconscious way of reacting to *healthy*—and, typically, *not* pornographic—sexual living. The Negro is persecuted and lynched because he is believed to be closer to the bush—that is, to nature, and thus to natural genitality. The same goes for the Jew as he is perceived by the morbid human soul. The same goes for the term "anarchist," whose political attitude is identified with sexual license by rightists and communists alike. On the other hand, nobody objects to the mass of pornographic advertising, to the many really "sexy" magazines that only excite the human longing for sexual happiness without even as much as considering the disastrous lack of proper conditions for a healthy way of living, as, for instance, enough space for privacy for each individual.

This is the background out of which emanate such contemptible actions and attitudes as that of the Food and Drug Administration, or the individuals and institutions who excelled each other in defaming my name. I am most emphatically convinced that compulsory morals *are* necessary wherever the sexual pestilence and sexual crimes are at work, and their field of operation is very large; but I also believe that unless human society does finally open up and let stream in full force the sources of human natural longing for sexual happiness (not for families with twelve to twenty children), not one step will be made in solving a single basic mental hygiene problem. We shall continue to imprison adolescents in ever-increasing numbers for "juvenile delinquency"; we shall continue to imprison and to "shock" with means of the Middle Ages millions of broken human beings, the victims of the same emotional plague which derives its raison d'être and its vicious actions from the confusion in the masses of the people.

This is what I am fighting for: the prevention of emotional human misery by the establishment of a normal and natural—that is, orgastically satisfying—human life in the masses of people. As I said before, the first step in this direction is to distinguish between vice and the natural love life of children and adolescents which what is called God has implanted in biologically flourishing human bodies and souls.

It cannot be the task of this letter to show how and why the biopathic—that is, the sexually frustrated—individual is terror-stricken when he comes in touch with his own inevitably existent natural needs. He hates nothing more. He is by nothing else more provoked than by the view of a happy couple of lovers, married or unmarried, since sexual pleasure is forbidden even in marriage.

You will understand now much more easily why I had reckoned with a frame-up for two decades, why I was persecuted as a villain, a sexual psychopath, a Russian or a German spy, a brothel keeper, a schizophrenic, a medical charlatan, a wizard, even a genius, etc., etc. I wish they could make up their minds as to what I am of all these things.

I personally feel that I have reached a position in human society where slanderous public attacks cannot impair my standing. But my students, the young doctor who came out of the war and tries to establish a medical practice; the young educator who really wants to help children and has to face this pest; the gravely sick individual who needs orgone therapy desperately and hesitates to come for help to a doctor of my school and therefore dies; the secretary or clinical assistant who works in the institute and becomes afraid of a public scandal; and last, but not least, the millions of decent people who could benefit from the orgone and are kept dying or starving one way or another by such "Christian" manipulations; it is these people for whom I speak and for whom I am ready to do anything to put a stop to the public defamation of my name.

I have donated to the world a great discovery. I do not expect anything for it, no thanks, no profit, no honors. But I refuse to be smeared and to be defamed by emotionally sick individuals for the good I did or, at least, tried to do.

7 December 1947

It does not matter in the least whether I understand the harmony of the universe or not. In either case it continues to oscillate, to come into being and to die away. Understanding the harmony of the universe is merely a joy to the scientist—nothing more.

T O   J U L I A N   C .   C U L V E R
❖ *8 December 1947*

Dear Mr. Culver:

I just received your letter together with the copy of the letter from the Food and Drug Administration to you. There are several wrong assumptions in this letter:

1. I am not distributing any devices. This is done by the Orgone Institute Research Laboratories, Inc., not for commercial, but for research purposes only, without promise of any cure.

2. I do not believe that the orgone energy, a basic new energy, has factually anything to do with either foods, drugs, or cosmetics. Therefore, I personally do not believe that this agency is practically or theoretically equipped to reach a rational and proper conclusion in regard to orgone energy if it does not wish to cooperate with a physician from the corporation. Does, for instance, this government agency control the distribution of experimentation of radioactive isotopes? The orgone energy falls into a realm close to atomic energy.

3. The corporation does not "distribute the device to cancer patients." The device is distributed almost exclusively to people who are under the care of their physician. There are also patients suspected of developing cancer among them.

4. Whatever material is publishable about my orgone experiments in a responsible manner has been published. I have nothing to add to that. The forthcoming book *The Cancer Biopathy* contains all the material which I, as a medical research man, am ready to submit to the public.

5. I shall not give either names or addresses of the patients treated.

This would be against medical ethics as well as against actual laws, according to your statement.

6. Any hospital or clinic could easily repeat the experiments with the orgone accumulator and observe the results. But I doubt, the facts being as new and unusual as they are, whether a satisfactory conclusion could be reached by the Food and Drug Administration without the cooperation of a physician from our corporation. I think that Dr. Simeon Tropp would be the best person to help, since he has some experience with medical orgone therapy.

7. It is not true that "inspectors visited the Orgone Press for information and were referred to you." True is that, according to the sworn statement by Miss Wyvell,* the inspectors asked questions at the Press's office for many hours, received innumerable answers, but that finally Miss Wyvell discontinued cooperating because of the ugly insinuations which went with the interrogation. I personally advised Miss Wyvell not to give any names of readers of our literature, just because of the insinuations which indicated clearly that this administration mistook our organization for a concern of brothels or a secret vice ring. I personally refuse to cooperate further if this administration does not clearly state in writing that this suspicion of vice activities has been abandoned.

I am very busy with important research which takes all my time. I have no time for discussions on a basis as it was hitherto. I shall hold a meeting with the officers of the corporation in order to transfer all matters of the orgone accumulator to them, and I shall withdraw. I do not want my name and my mental hygiene work to stand in the way of dealings regarding the orgone accumulator. The point should be stressed, as I pointed out to you in our discussion, that the mental hygiene work should be divorced completely from the orgone accumulator, since the latter has nothing to do with orgastic potency or anything of this kind.

I am sure that our doctors and officers will be only too glad to cooperate with the government in every respect if the above-mentioned conditions of a fair investigation are fulfilled.

Unfortunately, there are many good reasons to assume that the

---

*Lois Wyvell, an employee of the Orgone Institute Press.

investigation is not being conducted on a rational basis. It is beyond my power to see what interests may be behind all that. But should such a letter not be forthcoming from the Administration, then we would have to put in an injunction against this investigation.

❧ *9 December 1947*

They, the lawyers themselves, do not believe in the existence of the orgone. They did not read the literature.

Culver said, when I gave him the letters of the physicians about the orgone: "Now I feel better"—that is, he did not believe a word before that.

It is obvious, quite obvious, that I have become unfit for dealings with average people. I am too far off in my ways of being.

❧ *13 December 1947*

I request the right to be wrong.

I refuse to do my work at the point of a gun.

I cannot give the FDA authority to investigate the orgone unless it tells me first how the Geiger-Müller counter is used on orgone.

Should I go under, my work would continue to live and save lives. But the academicians who kept quiet while I fought and suffered will have a great responsibility for their failure to act.

I am alone, desperately alone. It is true: The American newspapers take smear articles but refuse to print corrections or friendly articles.

❧ *16 December 1947*

The Food and Drug Administration retracted its vice suspicion; but now "I am sending out orgone accumulators to cancer patients"? The FDA is surely pushed by someone all out to kill the accumulator. This is a fight of Pest + State + Politics against open, honest work. The BIG GAME is on.

❧ *19 December 1947*

There are two kinds of game: BIG GAME and the coyote. There are two kinds of hunters, the Indian pathfinder and the sneaking "rat." The human race has not learned to distinguish yet between GAME and rats. It has laws against big murder; it has no laws yet against the sneaky murdering by the emotional plague. The pest only knows *that* it "wants to get me." But only I know *why* it wants to get me.

Neill wrote me that I could publish my "Speech to the Little Man" only if I were as well recognized as Einstein or Shaw. He forgets that then I would not publish this piece of truth anymore. I heard a politician in a U.S.A. film say: There is only one thing the politician cannot beat, and that is the perfect truth. The first piece of truth is that my English is not so good. And there are people who are afraid of what other people might say about my English style while the BIG GAME is on.

It is Big Game when one man fights the whole world.

It is Big Game when the state hunts a free man.

It is Big Game when the truth hunts the pest. And it is Big Game when the truth is hunted by the pest.

When the American society does not permit the Big Game to take place in a fair-play manner, when it permits underhanded methods, then—Wolfe should write a scientific biography. Hays should not defend Wilhelm Reich but attack the Food and Drug Administration for neglect of duty.

BIG GAME must be written even if everything goes all right. It is necessary to describe the anguish of hardworking people who are threatened by the pest.

Everything would be all right if only the truth could be organized as the pest is organized.

TO   ARTHUR   GARFIELD   HAYS
❖ *20 December 1947*

Dear Mr. Hays:

I received the report of Mr. Culver on his discussion with Mr. Wharton of the Food and Drug Administration. There are too many wrong statements and insinuations in Mr. Wharton's attitude to be answered one by one.

I am not a politician, and I have no economic interests involved. I have, therefore, no more time to spend on this affair. The matter will be handled by the Orgone Institute Research Laboratories, Inc., under the directorship of Dr. Willie, Dr. Tropp, and Miss Ollendorff. I am transmitting all rights to the medical use of the accumulator to the corporation, expecting no monetary compensation except the eventual return of the costs which are evident from the books. I have done my part, in discovering the orgone energy, in elaborating some of its qualities, and in constructing a device to accumulate it which, in my experience, has shown great possibilities in being useful as a medical device, though many gaps are still left open. More I cannot do. I am not ready to say more now than I have made public in my articles and books. The rest is up to the public. If the people do not want the accumulator, it is *their* responsibility and to *their* disadvantage.

If there is no way to keep public servants who behave irrationally at bay, it is the fault of the public.

If there is no legal way to make them responsible for wrong decisions which are harmful to the public, it is again the fault of the public.

If there is no legal way to find out who is working behind the scenes of it all, it is the fault of the public, which is being cheated.

I am not fighting the American government. I admire government actions like the Marshall Plan for aid to Europe or the Report of the President's Committee on Civil Rights.

I believe that the people should use their legal rights also against public servants who misuse their authority.

I do not believe that an investigator of the type of Mr. Jackman is representing the true and basic foundations of the American government. I am helping the government not to be compromised by such public servants.

I refuse to be governed by public servants who ask "what we are doing with our women." *It is none of their business.*

I am fighting for my right to have my scientific findings kept secret and to publish them whenever I deem it right to do so. To my mind, it was unlawful for the Food and Drug Administration to obtain confidential scientific documents which I had sent to a scientific institute. Scientific secrets should not be violated. I don't want any spying on my scientific activities by public servants or no public servants.

I regret very much to have to say all this, but I would like to assure you that the construction of the orgone accumulator was only a very minor affair in my total work. Therefore, I have no more time to spend on it.

I would force a lawsuit in case this or any other officer of the government would continue to "make mistakes" about my person.

❖ *26 December 1947*

It becomes dimmer every day—the object of my eagerness over thirty years—*small fry*, their loves and fears, their little silly jokes, their small cheating of themselves out of marriage bonds, their running back to security. It is all dimming out, getting smaller and farther away, as if vanishing.

Should I rejoice? I am sad: Once again man has killed a warming soul, stabbed a heart burning for him. Once again they gave power to their little sergeants.

INDEX

abiogenesis, 41, 85, 316, 317, 322
Académie des Sciences, 105
Adler, Alfred, 327
American Academy of Sciences, 400
American Civil Liberties Union, 279, 282, 432
American Medical Association (AMA), 108, 324
American Men of Science, 233, 244
American Psychiatric Association, 387
American Sociological Review, 235
Analytic Association, 86
Andrus, E. Cowles, 159
Annals of the Orgone Institute, 373, 374, 391, 393, 396, 397
arthritis, 270, 311
atom bomb, 300, 304–5, 307–10, 334, 379, 387, 399
Atomic Energy Commission, 400, 410, 413–16, 418, 419
atomic theory, 353
Avramy, Melvin, 349–50, 382

Badgeley, Elizabeth, 191, 436
Baker, Elsworth F., 437
Baldwin, Roger N., 282
Bang, Stig, 356
Barnard, Carole, 108–9, 129
"Basic Antithesis of Vegetative Life, The" (Reich), 110
Batzdorf, Dr., 178, 179
Beethoven, Ludwig van, 14, 133, 186–87, 240, 269, 316, 337, 386
Beregi, Arnim, 344–45, 352, 353, 372, 373
Bergson, Henri, 193
Biddle, Francis, 128
Bidwell, W. T., 204
bions, 8, 11, 37, 60, 73–74, 77–78, 101, 102, 104–5, 262, 286, 331,

335, 344, 395; criticisms of research on, 208; growth of clusters of, 372; Lorin, 18, 22; SAPA, 15, 21, 29, 44, 55, 198
Bornstein, Berta, 303
Brady, Mildred Edie, 387, 392, 396, 403, 413, 414, 429, 430, 433
Brentano's bookstore, 179, 259
Briehl, Walter, 6, 8
Brion, Lester, 106
Brissman, Harry, 94–96
Brupbacher, Fritz, 9
Buddha, 324

cachexia, 108
Cain, John, 413
cancer, 14, 16, 60, 75, 76, 78, 102, 106, 107, 110, 160, 211, 232, 316, 317, 322, 330, 362, 394–96, 402; animal research on, 8, 10–12, 16, 18, 26, 34, 37, 41–42, 44, 52, 72–73, 78, 97, 101, 106; emotional plague and, 112; "iron," 372; prevention of, 386; sex economy and, 284; treatment of, 83, 84, 86, 91–98, 114, 117–19, 121, 142–43, 146, 151, 158, 204, 247, 312, 347–48, 352–53, 414, 429–30 (*see also* vegetotherapy)
Cancer Biopathy, The (Reich), 14, 52n, 428, 430, 437, 440
"Cancer Shrinking Biopathy, The" (Reich), 281
capitalism, 324–25
Cardiner, Abraham, 156
Catholicism, 383, 431, 436, 437
Centre Universitaire Méditerranéen, 104, 397n
Chandler, John P., 205–6, 216–17, 229, 249–50

tion of sphere in, 146; disease processes reversed by, 270–71, 309–11, 372–73; FDA investigation of, 422–24, 431–33, 437, 440–45; fees for rental of, 374; at Hebrew Hospital and Home for the Aged, 178–79; patent applications for, 60, 121, 133, 150, 154–55, 205–6, 217, 229, 249–50, 322–23, 356–57; temperature measurement in, 58–60, 62–72, 78, 122–23, 127, 199–202, 219–20